THE
TRIUMPH
OF THE
NOVEL

By Albert J. Guerard

Novels

The Past Must Alter
The Hunted
Maquisard
Night Journey
The Bystander
The Exiles

Criticism

Robert Bridges
Joseph Conrad
Thomas Hardy
André Gide
Conrad the Novelist

THE TRIUMPH OF THE NOVEL: DICKENS, DOSTOEVSKY, FAULKNER

ALBERT J. GUERARD

NEW YORK
OXFORD UNIVERSITY PRESS
1976

For Clive and Sophia and Dhimitri

ACKNOWLEDGMENTS

This book was largely completed during a sabbatical leave from Stanford University, and with the aid of a senior fellowship from the National Endowment for the Humanities. Stanford additionally helped defray the costs of typing and indexing. Some of the work on the psychology of Dostoevsky was done during five rewarding weeks at the Bellagio, Italy, Study Center as guest of the Rockefeller Foundation.

Dickens, Dostoevsky, and Faulkner traveled widely in paperback form, and constituted a large share of the excess weight on a very small plane from Mexico City to Oaxaca. A few critics and editors, Edward Wasiolek and his *Notebooks* always, traveled with them. I am particularly indebted to Wasiolek and to George Ford for giving me the courage to enter fields where so many specialists had gone so far. I used with profit and pleasure the Library of Congress, the Harvard College Library, the Stanford University Library, the British Museum, and the Benjamin Franklin libraries of Paris, Tours, Tunis, Mazatlán, Guadalajara, Mexico City. I am particularly grateful for the unusual courtesies extended me by the librarians of Guadalajara and Mexico City.

The discussion of the composition of *The Idiot* appeared in slightly different form in a special issue of *Mosaic* (University of Manitoba, Fall 1974) devoted to a Stanford conference on "The Creative Process in Literature and the Arts." The critique of *Sanctuary* was published, also with a few changes, in the April 1976 issue of *The Southern Review*. The chapter on *Martin Chuzzlewit* was published in the July 1976 issue of *Mosaic* (University of Manitoba).

Stephanie Golden has been an expert, alert, and tolerant editor of the manuscript. My greatest debt is, as always, to the critical eye and unflagging encouragement of my wife Maclin. Only one of her many valuable suggestions is acknowledged in the footnotes.

CONTENTS

THE
TRIUMPH
OF THE
NOVEL

INTRODUCTION

A primary aim of this book is to throw some new and largely sympathetic light on three great novelists whose continuing "presence" has affected not only innumerable other writers but also our feelings about "the novel." The genre, after each of the three had passed, would never be the same. The new light should come from discerning kinships and affinities among writers from radically different cultures (but cultures in uneasy moments of transition) and even more radically different moments in the history of the novel. Kinship not influence—though Dostoevsky was conscious of his debt to Dickens and Faulkner of his major debt to both. American scholarship has not so long since freed itself from the good part of a century's obsession with influence, and I have no desire to revive the academic dead.[1] The suicide of Jonas Chuzzlewit may well have suggested the great scene of Kirillov's suicide in *The Possessed;* a young writer could learn much by studying the two, and by observing how metaphysical implications, in Dostoevsky, intensify rather than attenuate dramatic force. But the fact of influence teaches us almost nothing. That *Martin Chuzzlewit* may also have suggested (with Faulkner doubtless unaware of this) the configuration of names in *The Sound and the Fury* has a mild psychological interest, but very little literary. But the fact that Faulkner places Sairey Gamp (and Mrs. Harris) at the head of his list of favorite characters usefully reminds us that he and Dickens, and Dostoevsky too, derive fictional energy from the interpenetration of the fantastic and the substantial, altogether fleshly "real."

It would seem quixotic to hope to throw new light, where hundreds of books and thousands of articles exist. Even the pairing of Dickens and Dostoevsky (which irritates some Dickensians) goes back to the 1880's; even John Chamberlain, very early in the career, could call Faulkner a Dostoevsky of the South. Mine is, however, the first extended effort to bring the three together (though often to note differences) and to emphasize so fully creative process and the values of imaginative distortion. A single book on the three novelists, coming so late in the day, necessarily makes its selective emphases, and omits what is only too familiar. My Dickens is the inventive fantasist and comic entertainer possessed of extraordinary narrative energy and creative power, rather than Leavis's "serious thinker" and responsible social realist, or another's dark symbolist or a third's programmatic reformer. I have expressed, elsewhere, my admiration for the high intelligence and structural, stylistic mastery of *Bleak House*,[2] and I fully understand why *Great Expectations,* its orderly art and pure style, should be chosen for courses on the history of the novel. But *Hard Times* still seems to me a second-rate book. And *Dombey and Son* and *Little Dorrit,* for all their intelligent ambitiousness, do not bear comparison with the greatest realistic fictions—*The Red and the Black* or *War and Peace* or *The Ambassadors* or *The Brothers Karamazov.* My Dostoevsky in turn is the great (easily the greatest) intuitive psychologist and wayward dreamer of solitary obsessions and intense inter-personal relationships—not the religious mystic or (except in my commentary on *The Possessed*) the political ideologue. My Faulkner may seem as limited, since I give little attention to the sociologist of the South and Balzacian proprietor of a second creation. I stress instead the lover of the comic and the grotesque, the poet intoxicated by words and rhythms, the innovator carrying Conradian impressionism to extremes and going beyond this to destroy inherited forms. Only my long critiques of three representative novels are intended to be balanced and comprehensive analyses, written without too much regard for what others have said or left unsaid.

An initial assumption, which long ago brought the three together in my mind, was that unconscious creation and highly liberated fantasy played a commanding part in the work of all three. My memory of Dickens's novels (going back at least forty years for several of them) had been subtly affected by the brilliant but admittedly selective reasonings of Edmund Wilson and more recently Steven Marcus and Taylor Stoehr. What they say still seems to me largely true. But I am now less struck by the force of disturbed unconscious creation than by, first, the slightness of Dickens's mental resistance to the strange beings, events and analogies that inexplicably occur to him and, second, by the rapidity with which his imagination orders them. The neurotic component, that is, does not play a major part in the best work (though it may be partly responsible for the visions of river, labyrinth, rotting tenements, etc.) as compared with largely unresisted and nominally impersonal fantasy. The Notebooks of Dostoevsky by contrast, even more than the novels, reveal an extraordinary lack of resistance to "thoughts," a good proportion of them criminal, thrust up by a very rich unconscious and preconscious life. Dostoevsky was, compared with Dickens or almost anyone else, exceptionally unrepressed, and did not block understanding that most writers would find intolerable. Faulkner read what were, surely for him, the best books: Cervantes, Dickens, Dostoevsky, Conrad, Melville, Shakespeare, the Old Testament. But so have many other writers; the source of Faulkner's verbal power and of most of his obsessions is irrecoverable. Like Dostoevsky, Faulkner permitted criminal thoughts free rein; like Dickens, he accepted the appearance of many odd people and grotesque analogies. But even more important, especially after the mid 1930's, was his refusal to resist the extravagances of diction and rhythm that occurred to him.

A first kinship, related to this saving lack of resistance, is that all three were exceptionally fecund creators of varied and quantitatively rich worlds, with Dickens and Faulkner especially demanding a number of biographical dictionaries and treatises on London or Yoknapatawpha-Lafayette County. Dostoevsky's physical world was small and relatively bare; furniture and landscape interested him not at all. Some of his obsessives reappear, moreover, from book to book, though with changed names. But no novel of Faulkner, perhaps none of Dickens, is as rich in interesting and even moderately sane characters as *The Possessed* or *The Brothers Karamazov*.

A second kinship (sometimes forgotten of the first two) is that all three novelists were innovators, as most great writers are. Dickens came at a propitious moment, with no standard novel form yet established to follow or rebel against. His great originality thus gave less offense than it might have thirty or forty years later. It would be hard to exaggerate the delight *Pickwick Papers* gave its first readers in what seemed to them an altogether new form of entertainment, or their affection for the authorial personality already present in *Sketches by Boz*. In retrospect what is most extraordinary is Dickens's refusal to capitalize on his fantastic success, and his continuing need to experiment. Thus he produced, between 1836 and 1844, in addition to *American Notes,* six radically different novels: *Pickwick Papers, Oliver Twist, Nicholas Nickleby, The Old Curiosity Shop, Barnaby Rudge, and Martin Chuzzlewit.* They are different in narrative interest and theme, in tone and structure, often even in style. With *Dombey and Son* Dickens helped establish what would in time seem, and be in lesser writers, a standardized social realism. But *Bleak House* with its skillfully juxtaposed narrators, and *Our Mutual Friend* with its involutions and various modes of stylization, were truly experimental books, pointing the way to modern impressionism.

The obfuscations of the first part of *The Possessed* and the deliberate shadowing of Stavrogin's personality and motives carried the novel still further toward the impressionism of, for instance, *Nostromo.* Dostoevsky himself, in notes for *A Raw Youth,* began to question the wisdom of these innovative procedures. But even *Poor Folk,* which now seems a relatively slight first novel, struck Belinsky and others as altogether new in its serious unstylized treatment of poor and humble persons. The same readers at once detected, in *The Double,* Dostoevsky's radical debt to Gogol. Yet *The Double,* by transforming fantasy into psychological realism, and by brilliantly sustained ambiguity, was a more original work than even its author realized. The great comprehensive later novels—"polyphonic novels," "novel-tragedies," novels of tragic spiritual conflict—bring a new seriousness to the genre, and cast a dark shadow over it. Psychology, philosophy, religion, politics; the highest aspiration and deepest degradation; comic exposure and tragic suffering—nothing, after Dostoevsky's last novels, need be alien to the novel form. Dostoevsky, in the Noteboooks, debated motives and ideas far more than he pondered novel structure. Yet the interestingly broken structure of *The Brothers Karamazov,* with its long meditative interpolations, achieves, as does *Moby Dick,* a truly new aesthetic experience. The late novels are very modern, too, in the way a few days or weeks seem to stretch out endlessly and even transcend chronological time, with the great spiritual issues thus rendered eternal.

As Dickens came near the beginning of the standard modern novel of social realism, so Faulkner came near what may turn out to have been its virtual end. His early novels were far less original than Dickens's. Even the relatively straightforward *Sartoris* has some of the appeal of a romantic and nostalgic southern realism. *Sanctuary* was a true work of art, in spite of Faulkner's cynical declarations, but one indebted to Flaubertian method as well as to detective and gangster fiction. With *As I Lay Dying* and *The Sound and the Fury,* now seeming to write only for himself and a happy few, Faulkner initiated difficult experiments in structure and in post-Joycean renderings of consciousness and of less-than-conscious mental life. Thus, often in italics, he tried to convey (at times in language undreamt of by such a person) the essence and *quidditas* of a character: his deepest drives and unrecognized anxieties. The broken structure of *The Sound and the Fury* may have been, initially, as uncalculated as Faulkner claimed, but the form of *As I Lay Dying* (and though he wrote the book with relative ease) was generically difficult and very new. In time—in radical opposition to Hemingway and Fitzgerald and the standard novel of the 1930's and 1940's—Faulkner seemed determined to "crack forms" (as Durrell put it of his own effort) and to try out new ones, most obviously through the intercalation of seemingly unrelated narratives. A novel could be anything, and permit itself any extravagance of language, tonal discord, grotesque invention. By *Requiem for a Nun,* if not before, Faulkner had discovered the Nabokovian aesthetic joy in art as play, with the mind free to transform life and triumph over it. Faulkner (who coyly attributed his originality to cultural isolation and ignorance) is unquestionably the most important innovator in the history of American fiction.

A third obvious kinship, and one shared with many other great writers, is that Dickens, Dostoevsky and Faulkner were indisputably strange and disturbed men. One can turn to the biographies (though I will rarely do so in this book) and even to psychoanalytic configurations without being in the least reductive. One may instead admire the courage of rich creation achieved in the presence of, and to some extent "using," strong self-destructive drives. Edmund Wilson and others have demonstrated the importance of the blacking warehouse trauma and the child Dickens's sense of lost connection: an episode long kept secret from everyone, and even to a degree repressed, since Dickens could not remember how long the humiliating experience lasted. There was also, of course, the great shock of his sister-in-law Mary Hogarth's sudden death, and his subsequent fidelity to this lost love (possibly related to his love for his sister) both in "real life" and in a number of fictional fantasies.

The most obvious trait of temperament was that Dickens felt, even more strongly than Conrad, the dual attractions of chaos and control. The two could even be enjoyed almost simultaneously, as in the uninhibited acting in melodramas and the authoritarian directing of amateur or semi-professional theatricals, or in the masterful administration, through intricate plot, of *Bleak House*'s wayward and often disorderly world. The extraordinary night walks—as much as twenty-five miles at a steady four miles an hour—could serve either to summon up fictional fantasies or put them to rest. Few persons in any profession have possessed as much energy as Dickens, or shown as compulsive a need to expend it. He was altogether aware of his "restlessness": a *crise de quarante* which began in his early thirties. The story ended, psychologically speaking, with the frenzied public readings.

Dostoevsky was the most obviously disturbed of the three writers; and with sufficient reason. The murder of his father by some of his serfs; the sudden fame as a very young writer, followed by Belinsky's repudiation; the arrest for subversive activity and the harrowing experience of a mock execution (with

Dostoevsky supposing he would minutes later be dead) and sudden reprieve; the years in fetters in Siberia among generally hostile convicts; the loss of a beloved brother and beloved infant girl; the humiliations of almost incessant debt and the need to write frenziedly, but never easily, against deadlines—it is a wonder that Dostoevsky was as sane and self-disciplined as he was. The paedophilic obsession, whose origin is probably irrecoverable, was unusually conscious; the latent homosexuality was recognized at least at the level of unconscious knowledge and fictional creation. One clue to Dostoevsky's greatness was his willingness to entertain criminal fantasies, especially in the Notebooks, rather than repress them. The most obvious non-literary symptoms of disturbance were, of course, the epilepsy and the gambling mania discussed by Freud. Some of the greatest pages were written under the shadow of recurring, disabling fits. Dostoevsky clearly understood the self-destructive nature of compulsive gambling, and that the true gambler can be at peace only when he has lost everything.

We know less, psychologically speaking, about Faulkner, in spite of the immense Blotner biography. There is little evidence of childhood trauma, and no more alienation from an uncomprehending father than innumerable people experience. Faulkner's shyness, and his withdrawal (presumably into creative revery) in his late teens and in his twenties, have been duplicated in the lives of many writers. The silences and general passivity remind one of Hardy. But there is little, in Hardy, of Faulkner's persistent misogyny. The temperamental evasiveness, in many ways similar to Conrad's, was reflected in the distances, screens and involutions of impressionist method: protection from too close an approach to one's imagined world. Many novelists seem at times to confuse what has happened to them with what they have imagined; novelists are wonderfully unreliable autobiographers. But Faulkner carried the creation of a personal myth, and fidelity to it, very far: the fiction of wartime service overseas, as an aviator, and of a wound that became in time more severe. The most obvious self-destructive symptom was, of course, an alcoholism shared by many American *écrivains nerveux*. But Faulkner's disease was far worse than most, and was established long before the trauma of the brother's death in a crash for which the writer felt responsible, since he had encouraged him to fly. The wonder—with Faulkner as with Dickens and Dostoevsky, as with Conrad and Proust—is that he accomplished so much.

Personal anxieties and dilemmas can be intensified or attenuated by cultural situation, and by the rhythms of success and failure. Dickens's story from his early twenties to the end was, to the public eye, one of virtually unintermittent success; "failure" meant a sale of only 20,000 of the early installments of *Martin Chuzzlewit*. He was at twenty-four the most successful and most generally loved English author and turned thirty during the tumultuous adulation of the American tour. He had many friends among the literary and other establishments, yet remained in close touch with ordinary readers, most obviously through his editing of *Household Words*. He was, Lord Northcliffe said, the greatest editor of his or any other age; *All the Year Round* eventually reached a circulation of 300,000. Yet the restlessness was real, and the scar left by childhood; the marriage in the end was a failure, and the affair with Ellen Ternan by no means an unequivocal success. The wildly emotional and brilliant readings were carried on, at the end, by neurotic compulsion; there has seldom been a more appalling instance of a successful man's need not merely to expend energy but to destroy energy, destroy life itself, and do so in public. But, also, the readings continued the intimate connection with his public that Dickens needed, and brought in £45,000, well over a million dollars in present-day terms. It would never have occurred to him, as it would to Joyce and Faulkner, to alienate the common reader through difficulty. The Victorian novel, which he had done so much to create, remained essentially a popular genre. But Dickens was mindful of criticism, and of the emergence of rivals, and gave increasing attention to structure and style.

Dostoevsky, after his few months of early success, was dogged by failure and debt through much of his life. Dickens felt compelled to earn more and more in his early thirties, thanks to lavish establishments abroad; Dostoevsky in his early thirties was in fetters, with three years of exile to follow prison. His journalistic enterprises, coincident with *All the Year Round*'s growing success, were failures. *Time* (1861–63), edited with his brother Mikhail, was closed as revolutionary; *Epoch,* begun in March 1864, lasted only a year, consumed the 20,000 rubles the brothers had inherited from an uncle, and left 15,000 in debts. The unsuccessful first marriage led to the intermittent and tormenting affair with Apollinariya Suslova, who was as volatile as any of the novels' heroines. But the second marriage was, by and large, a success. Dostoevsky knew, moreover, some of the great literary and political figures of his day, though he scorned several of the most famous: Turgenev, Herzen, Bakunin. He achieved, of course, great literary success at last, and some of the Dickensian intimacy with a wide variety of readers through *The Diary of a Writer*. Ten years after Dickens's farewell reading, and not quite seven months before his death in 1881, Dostoevsky's Pushkin speech saw him in apotheosis, with the applause lasting for a half hour, and, as he himself described the scene in a letter to his wife: "strangers in the audience were weeping, sobbing, embracing one another, and *swearing to one another to be better, not to hate each other in future, but to love.*"

Faulkner, on the other hand, lived most of his life in a small southern college town where few, even after the Nobel Prize, knew what he was about: a failure as the university postmaster, fired for negligence of various kinds; a failure as a novelist, trying to eke out a living through pot-boiling short stories. But the Blotner biography, which omits very little (yet omits my visit and conversation in 1946, when he denied knowing even the name of Kafka), indicates that Faulkner's cultural isolation was less extreme than many supposed. He did know a number of writers, in New Orleans and later in Hollywood; he could watch a campaign for the governorship of Mississippi at very close range; ultimately he found himself in the classroom, answering the questions of students with sometimes failing memory but generally unfailing courtesy. At last he too made public appearances—for a four-and-a-half-minute high school graduation address and a long confused one at Pine Manor; and in Japan, South America, Stockholm. But long before this he had lost the public temporarily won with *Sanctuary,* and his greatest novels were financial failures. He was more esteemed in France than at home, though Malcolm Cowley's *Portable Faulkner* (1946) brought an important turn of fortune. My own reviews of *The Wild Palms* and *The Hamlet* for *The Boston Evening Transcript,* in 1939 and 1940, were somewhat defensive, and a dismayed Harvard colleague, as late as the early 1950's, was surprised that I should consider Faulkner worth teaching. But the most important historical fact may be that Faulkner's innovative structures and rhetorical elaborations ran counter to the major literary currents of his time —whether standard social realism, or the spare brutality of the best proletarians, or the journalistic collages of Dos Passos at his best, or the crisp understatement and dry irony of Hemingway. This formal isolation might seem in time to become more pronounced. It was with the anti-realists of the 1960's and 1970's, and their inventive audacity and "lexical foregrounding," that Faulkner at last seemed truly to belong. But so too at times do Dostoevsky and even much of Dickens.

A few words may be pertinent regarding the scope of this book. One of the more appalling of my youthful projects, announced in a brief 1947 monograph on Conrad, was "a book on the contemporary novel seen against the background of certain nineteenth-century intellectual and literary tendencies." At one point in my musings and multiple outlines this *Summa* was to have allotted a single chapter to Conrad, with briefer treatment for two other writers showing anti-realist impulses: Hardy and Gide. In due time I wrote full-length books on each of the three. Taken together they would, I hoped, "record the impulse away from orthodox realism, classical psychology, and conventional structure; or, the impulse toward the sombre and ironic distortions, the psychological explorations, the dislocations in form of many novelists writing in the middle of the twentieth century." But already by 1949 (in the preface to *Thomas Hardy*) I had to acknowledge that studies of Dickens, Dostoevsky, Faulkner and Kafka would also be needed, if one were to account for the novel form's great changes.

More than once, during the present enterprise, I was tempted to give in to the book's urgent demands that it be split into three. But the historic situation was now very different. Both Hardy and Conrad then needed revaluation and above all reinterpretation. Hardy had been made altogether too academic by the philosophically minded and too commonplace by those insisting on his rural realism. Even in 1958, when *Conrad the Novelist* appeared, there was still too much awareness of the anomalous master mariner, too little of the complex psychologist and intricate artist, skillfully balancing the claims of sympathy and judgment. A large library of Gide criticism had accumulated by 1950, but much of it was wildly impressionistic or angrily polemical, with little attention given to the slender but real talent of the novelist and little to the contradictions implicit in his divers longings to dissolve the self.

Dickens, Dostoevsky and Faulkner, on the other hand, are hardly undervalued, and at least Dickens and Faulkner have received both exhaustive academic analysis and some subtle criticism, whether phenomenological or psychological or linguistic or austerely "new." Of the three, Dostoevsky has been by far the most neglected by a serious criticism of fictional art; the only truly "modern" Russian critique is Mikhail Bakhtin's structural poetics, whose first edition was published in 1929.[3] The prophetic Dostoevsky—the religious mystic or conservative ideologist—still commands a disproportionate amount of attention; so too the suffering damaged soul of the biographers. Oddly enough the great pre-Freudian psychologist (to whom Freud paid the highest tribute) still awaits full analysis, perhaps because psychologists and literary critics are alike afraid to step "outside their field." But a number of American and British academic critics have written good general studies. Edward Wasiolek, editor of the indispensable Notebooks in translation, has combined historical and even psychoanalytic understanding with a close attention to structure.[4]

My intention (even as I clung desperately to the plan of a single book for the three) was to write in some sense a *rhetoric of anti-realism*. I long pondered the polemical title *The Other Great Tradition*. For I was irritated by F. R. Leavis's priggish and essentially artless view of fiction, and by the stubbornness with which many reviewers and editors (but also eminent academic critics, some of them my colleagues and friends) clung decade after decade to nineteenth-century and 1930ish assumptions concerning "the novel" and its mimetic obligations. The Leavis dismissal of Sterne and Joyce in the influential *The Great Tradition* (1948), where Dickens is seen as primarily a "great entertainer" (but with an exceptional case made for *Hard Times*), and the radically changed but even more dogmatic consecrating emphasis in *Dickens the Novelist* (1970) ("his genius as a novelist is a capacity for profound and subtle thought") seemed to demand a vindication not only of Dickens the wayward fantasist and lover of the grotesque, but also of the anti-realist tradition generally.[5] It was clearly important to insist once more that the life of great fiction, though based on an indispensable knowledge of "real life," is essentially different from it, making different demands on our sympathies and moral judgments, our sense of space and time, etc. *Great fiction is art and invention, not reduplicated reality*. The major source of F. R. Leavis's limitations as a critic is precisely his tendency to experience and talk about fictional characters as he would if they were his neighbors, and to judge accordingly the novelist's profound or immature thought concerning them. Hence his odd interest in personages who, for a serious criticism of fiction, seem relatively uninteresting and even "dead": the Axel Heyst of *Victory,* for instance, or the Arthur Clennam of *Little Dorrit.*

Another influential and infinitely richer book than either *The Great Tradition* or *Dickens the Novelist*—Ian Watt's justly classic *The Rise of the Novel*—has perhaps contributed to the confusion (of fiction and "real life") by its insistence on "formal realism" as "implicit in the novel form in general: the premise, or primary convention, that the novel is a full and authentic report of human experience" and that, whatever the truth of the report, the novel must have an "air of total authenticity." [6] Watt is, of course, too fine a critic to dismiss Sterne or Joyce. But his discriminations, so useful for a study of the eighteenth-century novel, should not be applied to the genre as a whole. The great flowering of anti-realist fiction in the 1950's and 1960's—Nabokov, Pynchon, Borges, Hawkes, Burroughs, Barth, Barthelme, García Márquez, many more—reminds us of that "other great tradition": the wayward inventors who deliberately avoid an "authentic report," and the playful stylizing fantasists from Rabelais and Cervantes to the Joyce of *Finnegans Wake* and the Nabokov of *Ada* for whom divers alienation-effects are sources of aesthetic joy: structural and parodic games, "lexical foregrounding" and "performance"; the primacy, in brief, of art over authentic rendering, of imagination over the quotidian.

In the end it seemed best to cease to worry about F. R. Leavis, and to suggest, by the simple conjunction of their names, the centrality and culminating force of the three novelists and their anti-realist love of the strange. I might well have borrowed the title of one of my own essays: "The Illuminating Distortion." [7] *Illuminating distortion,* taken in a very general sense, refers to the heightening or selective distortion of "real reality" that we find in most great fiction. The strangeness may inhere in the pictured or imagined world (chosen instead of more familiar ones) or may be due to the author's idiosyncratic way of seeing objects and events; or, often, may come from a combination of the two. Technique and style may reinforce this strangeness: oddities of rhythm and diction; compression or outlandish elaboration, and all the quickenings of consciousness induced by analogy, by symbol, by myth. Illumination may occur, paradoxically, thanks to opaque screens and verbal obfuscations. More generally, "illuminating distortion" suggests a novel's general vision of things: one that perhaps sees mysterious correspondences and hidden fatalities behind the placid surface of the everyday. The coincidences of Hardy are not always arbitrary, nor the broken connections in Dickens with one's past, nor the macabre confrontations in Faulkner, nor the torments caused by real or hallucinated doubles in Dostoevsky; nor, for that matter, the blind stumbling onto one's destiny at a dusty Greek crossroads. These are interpretations, also, of the way things (in a deeper sense of reality) really are. The strangeness in Dickens, Dostoevsky, Faulkner is frequently one of deviant impulse if not threatened sanity; characters dream and even enact what most people repress. But these impulses and obsessions may be fundamental parts of our human endowment, which it is altogether well to recognize.

Most of all great fiction, through exaggeration and surprise, through dramatizing the extreme but significant case—through absurd or macabre or radically simplified plot—throws a light (sometimes terrible, sometimes consoling) on the human capacity to endure and suffer, and on the terrible dilemmas of marginal choice. Esther Summerson discovering her mother cold and dead at the locked gate to the rat-infested burial ground; Charles Bon and Henry Sutpen at the gate to Sutpen's Hundred; Dmitri Karamazov at the window of his father's bedroom, with the brass pestle in his hand—most lifetimes possess no such crises. What is illumined by such altogether abnormal moments of conflict and stress is, simply, our human nature; what is quickened, after we have read and reread, is our capacity to feel and to attend. We learn to "care"—even about a man who sells his wife while drunk, but is determined to pay for his crime; even for a man who jumps from a seemingly sinking ship, leaving hundreds to die, but who incorrigibly hopes to recover lost honor; even for a man of higher than ordinary intelligence, but intoxicated both by theory and by a sense of social injustice (and perhaps also by unconscious identifications) who murders a helpless pawnbroker.

All this is but to say, or chiefly to say, that great fiction transcends the quotidian, and is little concerned with banal destinies.

The structure of the present book was determined by a double impulse: on the one hand to record affinities among the three writers that might enhance understanding of each, and of the novel as a genre, and on the other to explore the individual writers in terms not yet exhausted by earlier commentators. I found pleasure both in keeping the three novelists simultaneously in mind and, for long hours, in concentrating on only one of the three and even (sometimes without regard to his *oeuvre* generally) on individual books or passages that seemed to me misinterpreted or undervalued. My general approach, both in its concern with the creative process and in its inferences concerning the rhetorical control of readers, will doubtless be labeled "psychological." But my ultimate concern is with novels as works of art. The first two chapters are comparative. They emphasize the way the three writers delight in an interpretation of the fantastic and the real and create or evoke paradoxical, unexpected sympathies. The third, fourth and fifth chapters, on "forbidden games," examine the persistent presence and aesthetic significance of obsessions and fantasies which, though often mentioned by critics and biographers, are rarely analyzed systematically—Dickens's extraordinary feeling, after her death, for his sister-in-law Mary Hogarth; Dostoevsky's paedophilia; Faulkner's generalized misogyny and seeming dread (in the imagination) of normal sexual intercourse. The Dickens chapter is (except for a few pages in the later chapters on Dostoevsky) the only place where I turn to biography for help, and here only to a few facts and declarations familiar to all Dickensians. The several obsessions did not regularly lead to great writing (though "Stavrogin's Confession" is one of Dostoevsky's summits), but they did affect three interesting and generally undervalued novels here analyzed: *The Old Curiosity Shop, The Insulted and the Injured, Sanctuary.* I am not concerned with the well-known influence of the first book on the second, and I simply take for granted the justifiable exasperation that some of Dickens's pages cause. But it is time, after acknowledging its awful moments, to recover some sense of the novel's genuine, Wordsworthian spirituality, as well as its great moments of grotesque and comic creation. *The Insulted and the Injured,* in the presence of much greater novels, rarely gets the modest attention it deserves. My high valuation of *Sanctuary* as a taut work of art, in which the misogyny is for once put to good use, may well seem as perverse to some readers as Leavis's praise of *Hard Times.*

My sixth, seventh and eighth chapters offer fairly detailed studies of three major subjects that have not, in my opinion, been adequately treated: the various authorial "voices" in Dickens's work (as distinct from the voices of his characters); the interplay of conscious and unconscious psychological understanding in certain novels of Dostoevsky; the development of innovative forms and liberated style in Faulkner, with some reference to "temperament" and to congenial creative impulse. The very few words devoted to *The Sound and the Fury* are not meant to reflect a negative judgment; only that I had little to add to what others have said. But I include here an extended analysis of *The Hamlet* as a beautifully modulated work of art. Each of these three chapters could have become a long book, and the present discussions have emerged from much longer first drafts.

My book concludes with long essays on "representative" novels: *Martin Chuzzlewit, The Possessed* (a title I prefer to *The Devils*), *Absalom, Absalom!* Here I hoped to touch on most of the novels' interests and arrive at balanced assessments. I was emboldened to approach Dickens at all, in the wake of so many thousands, by George Ford's comment (in his masterful *Dickens and His Readers*) that there was still a need "to apply an awareness of the various qualities of his work to a further close reading of individual novels." *Martin Chuzzlewit* was chosen after some hesitation over *Our Mutual Friend* both as a "serious entertainment" and as exemplifying Dickens's comic gifts and love of the grotesque at their most energetic. *The Brothers Karamazov* is perhaps a greater work of art than *The Possessed,* and a more comprehensive vision of human difficulties. But *The Possessed,* certainly a great novel, is perhaps more representative of Dostoevskyan complexity and has, of course, a political interest that remains intensely alive today. (I had hoped to include a very extensive study of the Notebooks for *The Possessed,* but will reserve this for a later occasion.) I had no hesitation in selecting *Absalom, Absalom!,* which seems to me Faulkner's greatest novel, as well as his most interesting one technically.

The main premises and concerns of my critical method will be at once evident to most readers: (1) a concern with the creative process and with rhetorical effect that frankly acknowledges the fleshly existence of the writer and of readers. I cannot, after writing a number of novels, help reading in this way. There cannot be, as Jean Staborinski says, structure without a "conscience structurante", nor can there be fictional energy without an energizing mind. (2) A non-psychoanalytic but psychological approach to the interpretation of enigmatic scenes or events. (3) A high value placed on *energy* (of invention, narrative, language); on *fiction* and *play* (as opposed to documentary representation); on *tension,* especially a tension between sympathy and judgment that exists in the writer and may be consciously (as in *Lord Jim*) or unconsciously conveyed to the reader. Liberating pleasure and aesthetic joy (which may derive from these, but also from the creation and contemplation of beautiful form) thus strike me as more important in many novels, but by no means in all, than an enhanced understanding of "real reality." (4) A maintained distinction between the first reading of a novel, serial or diachronic, and a later reading, which may be both serial and spatial or synchronic, with the critical reader now more aware of aesthetic effect and of the subtle suasions that, previously, had operated on the fringes of consciousness.

I do not want to detain the general reader with a defense of these premises, some of them unfashionable in a number of quarters, and so append a Note on Method which he is free to skip. I will only add that the "we" which is used now and then in these pages is meant to denote a hypothetical ideal reader who does read a novel more than once, but not necessarily because he intends to write an article or book, and who is capable of enjoying both first and later readings, and who tries to discriminate between the two experiences.

A NOTE ON METHOD

I propose to amplify slightly my declarations concerning critical method and to acknowledge if not justify my eclecticism. It would seem to me absurd to apply precisely the same method to *The Possessed* and to *The Eternal Husband*. A knowledge of Russian *mores* and even of Russian railroads might very slightly enhance our understanding of the shorter novel and its final scene. But that knowledge might also distract us from the essential drama of *The Eternal Husband*, which is truly eternal or timeless, whether analyzed in my terms of psycho-sexual repression and recognition or René Girard's of triangular desire. But some awareness of political history, and even of Dostoevsky's acquaintance with Bakunin, Herzen, Ogarev, etc., does help us penetrate *The Possessed*'s labyrinth and assess more accurately what Shatov, for instance, is saying. So too some knowledge that Dostoevsky, "outside the book," associated lame or retarded woman and female child, may help us to recognize the association that exists within it. I would defend, in a word, a flexibility of method that makes adjustments according to a novel's *area of discourse*. (An area of discourse may correspond roughly to a novelist's conscious intentions, but can exist in spite of them. It would be difficult to write a wholly political novel without at least some slight intention of doing so. But many novels whose real subjects and areas of discourse are psycho-sexual were intended to be something else.)

My critical method in this book, except for a few wayward pages, depends very little on biography or literary history. It is essentially pragmatic criticism little dependent on literary theory as propounded in France and to some extent in the United States. Such literary theory represents a pure, ideally disinterested, intellectually challenging activity, and hence one worthy of academic sponsorship and protection. But it has very little to do with the normal, humane but often impure activities of writing and reading novels. I have to say as much of any literary criticism that pretends to the rigor, objectivity and verifiable precision of true science, or of any interpretation that lays claim to absolute validity. A fairly simple short novel such as Balzac's *Sarrasine* may surrender to the analysis of Barthes. But I have to share Kermode's view that novels resist structural analysis, and especially "a twentieth-century novel intensely aware of the generative powers of its own technology, intensely concerned to deface and transmute its structural données beyond recognition." [8] A novel, certainly a novel by Dickens or Dostoevsky or Faulkner, is infinitely more than plot, sense of space, etc. Any discoverable "deep structure" is likely to be psychological, revealing a pattern of preferences or hostilities perhaps different from those of which the author was aware. Freud was the greatest structuralist.

But to return to the specific concerns or heresies announced in my introduction and, I trust, exemplified in the book.

1) *A concern with the creative process and with rhetorical effect.* I have argued for at least thirty years against interpreting or evaluating a novel in terms of the writer's declared conscious intentions (plans). Nevertheless it is obvious that I am guilty, if these are defined with the usual breadth, of both the intentional and the affective fallacies. As a novelist fairly conscious of what I am doing, but aware of how much unintended psychological content finds its way into my work, and as a close reader of such complex writers as Conrad and Gide, I am compelled to see a novel as something that comes into being in response to creative impulses and that overcomes sometimes discernible obstacles. Incorrigibly I must infer a human writer at his desk. And I am persuaded that nearly all meaningful criticism of fiction makes unspoken and perhaps unconscious inferences about how novels get written. So too, incorrigibly, I infer a reader: someone whose feelings are to be aroused and even (as with Gide) manipulated against that reader's will, or (again obviously with Gide) whose sympathies and moral judgments can be changed. Every writer has at least one ideal or skeptical and resistant reader, who may be only himself. Obviously Dostoevsky and Faulkner, and sometimes even Dickens, may

be so "carried away" as to forget their readers or perhaps even where they are. But this occurs more rarely than most readers think. Timing especially, the pacing of a paragraph or a scene, regularly involves at least a preconscious concern with what a reader can "take in." In any event I refuse to think of a novel as something independent of living readers and their feelings, though I am as hostile as anyone to solipsistic or casually impressionistic interpretations.

It is of course important for readers—young readers especially, hoping to discover the world—to connect novels with life, even their own lives. But it is dangerous and demoralizing, especially for a mature reader or critic, to confuse fictional life with "real life" and invite characters to step out of their books; to regard them, as Leavis does, as good or bad neighbors.

2. *A non-psychoanalytic but psychological approach to the interpretation of enigmatic scenes or events.* I trust it is no longer necessary to defend applying the basic assumptions of dynamic psychology or the obvious "Freudian" categories to Dostoevsky or Dickens. The neuroses, the phenomena of condensation and secondary elaboration, of repression, etc., were not invented by Freud or his contemporaries. Most of them, presumably, have always "been there." On the other hand it seems useful to distinguish, so far as possible, between Dostoevsky's conscious and unconscious understanding (of the "unconscious," for instance), or to recognize how much more he knew than a Dickens or than the psychologists of his time.

The great fear, the "holy horror" (as René Girard puts it) is of a reductive or reductionist criticism. ("Any vigorous thought," he wisely notes, "is sooner or later bound to arrive at its own bases; it will end, then, in reduction." [9]) The kindred fear is that by going outside the work, to seek or simply admit knowledge acquired in a normal way, the critic will betray its true content. The resistance is most intense whenever technical vocabulary carries with it disagreeable lay associations. The critic's problem is how much attention to pay to these ancient fears. Thus I had to swallow twice before writing the sentence "Anal imagery, and scenes which threaten engulfment, often find a counterweight in controlled syntax if not conversational calm." For the remainder of that long paragraph had important things to say and persuasive examples to cite. Yet I knew that more than one reader, coming upon *anal imagery,* would, at the very least, skip to the next paragraph.

It is not, however, timidity that has deterred me from genuine psychoanalytic criticism, except the timidity of feeling myself insufficiently trained. Wasiolek's psychoanalytic discussion of *Crime and Punishment* does shed valuable light on it; the novel, for those who have read his essay with good will, will never be exactly the same.[10] But I am primarily concerned with what happens in an area of discourse shared, even if not entirely consciously, by the writer and a normal "ideal" reader . . . e.g., one without psychoanalytic training. Moreover, psychoanalysis is or has been as a rule more useful in accounting for the novelist than for his work. To be sure, these situations will change in time, as both writers and readers become more aware of psychoanalytic structures. I have noted that psychological content (including comic instances of Freudian displacement) in part functions as rhetoric in the fiction of John Hawkes, who has inevitably become more and more aware of his own pleasing oddities.[11]

3. *A high value placed on energy (of invention, narrative, language); and on fiction and play; and on tension, especially a tension between sympathy and judgment.* The essential problem is, of course, how the critic is to determine and demonstrate the presence of *energy,* as in the past it might have been how to determine *harmony* or *radiance.* The primary key to energy is language (the author's or a character's), but some people are more sensitive to language than others. Nearly all critics would, presumably, recognize Sairey Gamp as an energized creation and detect the energy of her own dialogue, and not a few might see, as I do, that her presence on a page confers fictional life on those around her, perhaps even on a caged bird. But by no means all critics would find Quilp's physical presence and speech as energized as I do. Some readers, by seeing him outside the book, by bringing him into their own "real" unaesthetic lives, would instead experience only disgust.

I see no theoretical way of avoiding this impasse; my judgment does indeed rely in part on subjective response. But the critic can hope to escape solipsistic response by reading a great deal, by pondering his feelings concerning what he reads, and by doing his best to subtract or discount very private factors. One would hope the critic with very bad teeth, fangs indeed, could yet contemplate with some detachment the fangs of Quilp or of Greene's *mestizo* Judas, or the decayed black stumps of old Fyodor Karamazov! Where the factors are psychosexual there can indeed be a "problem," either of too intense a sensitivity or too rigid a hostility to hidden or overt suggestion.

The problems of detecting tensions of sympathy and judgment are slightly different, and here a large body of theoretical criticism might help. Most readers tend to assume that sympathy and judgment in the normal mind go hand in hand; that one likes what one admires, and dislikes the morally reprehensible. But students, I have found, very quickly realize this is untrue. They have only to look within themselves or look at the people around them. Understanding is enhanced, moreover, by studying masterpieces where a tension or interplay of sympathy and judgment is unequivocally present: by rereading, for instance, *Lord Jim.*

4. *A distinction between first and later readings of a novel.* I find it very strange that so few critics ever make this distinction, or, if they do, fail to indicate which reading they are describing. Talk of suspense, of exciting plot, of dizzying ambiguity, of the pleasures of incessant surprise clearly refer to a hypothetical first reading. But talk of unity and a satisfying relation of the parts to the whole, of subtle reflexive reference, of foreshadowings, refers either to a subsequent reading or implies an exceptionally competent retrospective spatial contemplation of a first reading. (This would itself be a kind of second reading.) Yet critics often talk, sometimes on the same page or in the same paragraph, of the two kinds of experience as though they had been simultaneous.

It is important to recognize generic differences: to see that *Lord Jim* and *Absalom, Absalom!* and *The Brothers Karamazov,* and to a slightly lesser degree *Bleak House,* become, on rereading, different and richer books. There is a difference among the three novels we examine at length. A very large measure of *Martin Chuzzlewit's* highest pleasures come to us on a first reading: we enjoy Pecksniff, Gamp, Chollop at once. On re-reading we may simply experience those pleasures again, or with the added pleasure of recognition, though we may (especially if we are writing a book) try to analyze, for instance, the timing of Sairey's absurdities. Re-reading, we go back to old friends, as Faulkner speaks of doing with reference to his favorite novels. Our unexcited experience of young Martin's education becomes, if possible, even duller on a second reading. Some real suspense is removed from the murder of Montague Tigg and its aftermath. But the writing is occasionally so vivid that we simply re-experience the initial excitement.

A second reading of *The Possessed* is very different from a first one, especially if we read "Stavrogin's Confession" after all the rest. (If we restore it to its intended place, to come after Chapter VIII of Part II, our first reading is radically changed.) But a second reading of *The Possessed* is a different experience, even if "Stavrogin's Confession" is omitted, as it sometimes is. For we now know, more or less, who the important characters are, and what the important issues; we have begun to free ourselves from the "real life" confusion and ambiguity for which the narrator was largely responsible. By the same token— and as we encounter once again Kirillov's difficult reasonings or Shatov's very compressed declarations—we are freer to ponder the novel's philosophical issues and psychological ambiguities. And we may contemplate the structure of the whole, and the relation of the parts. This, to be sure, can have very different results. Thus Mochulsky (since he assumes a great and loved novel must be unified) finds everything in place, whereas I recognize a greatness that exists in spite of exceptional looseness and disorder.

Absalom, Absalom! is a very pure example of a novel that can be enjoyed at first and later readings, but with the later readings rendering an entirely different experience. We are no longer victims of the narrators' distortions; instead, we can take a contemplative pleasure in measuring those distortions. The balance of sympathy and judgment, as we re-experience Sutpen, Charles Bon, even Rosa, will be very different. And, presumably, we no longer struggle so fiercely with language. We have to some extent escaped the overall ambiguity and can now stand above it.

A complex novel, or a novel of psycho-moral ambiguity, then, is experienced in several ways.

First Reading. We experience, serially or diachronically, a sequence of events or rhetorical suasions; we observe character and situation develop; we wonder ''what happens next.'' We are largely victimized by distortions, even though we may develop some distrust for the narrator. Generally speaking, we are made to live through all the ambiguity that the characters experienced; and often more.

Second Reading. There may, in fact, be several ''second readings,'' whether experienced simultaneously or not:

1) We may re-experience the novel serially, continuing to care about the characters, even though we now see them differently and though we may mentally restore a chronology that was scrambled. We again move from first page to last with pleasure and even excitement.

2. But this re-experiencing may have the added pleasure of tragic or comic irony, as we see the characters blunder toward destinies of which we are now aware. We have, in addition, the contemplative pleasure of observing and measuring the narrators' distortions.

3. In addition we may contemplate (especially if we are interested in the creative process and in rhetorical manipulation)—as we move again from first page to last—the various ways in which the novelist appealed to the fringes of our consciousness on that first reading. We see what he was doing to us.

4. We can now, synchronically and spatially, see the novel as a whole, laid out before us as a complex artifact, a structure, and observe the formal relationship of the parts, and of the parts to the whole. To the degree that this spatial reading sees the novel as inert and fixed it may be regarded as less faithful than the others. For mobility and even continuing indeterminacy would seem to be the essence of great fiction.

But even if some sense of mobility is faithfully retained, a second reading would seem to be, inevitably, more contemplative than a first.

1
ANTI-MIMESIS

Our three novelists, differently obsessed and meeting across the barriers of time and changing genre, are most obviously kin in their love of the strange: the fantastic to be discovered wherever one turns. They are drawn to mysteries of personality; to the extreme psychological pressure and macabre plight; to the malice or comicality lurking in unpredictable event. Shakespeare, Dostoevsky noted on behalf of all three, did not write about the "everyday." The three are alike in their ability to discover the fantastic within the ordinary, and in their assumption that the dream-like and fantastic are "real." It was important for Dickens to have it believed that his fictions were like life. But life is very strange, and some people are simply blind: "What is exaggeration to one class of minds and perceptions, is plain truth to another." The same late preface to *Martin Chuzzlewit* can claim, presumably without tongue in cheek, that "Mrs. Sarah Gamp was, four-and-twenty years ago, a fair representation of the hired attendant on the poor in sickness."

The stern truth, Dickens claimed, was part of the purpose of *Oliver Twist*. Hence, though chastening language, he did not "abate one hole in the Dodger's coat, or one scrap of curl-paper in the girl's dishevelled hair"; of Nancy, "there is not a word exaggerated or over-wrought." So too for *Bleak House*, where "everything set forth in these pages concerning the Court of Chancery is substantially true, and within the truth." Even the spontaneous combustion of Krook is defended by scholarly references to a "prebendary of Verona" and to "one of the most renowned surgeons produced by France." Surely Dickens is closer to his actual practice when he said, "it is my infirmity to fancy or perceive relations in things which are not apparent generally." [1] The truth of the American journey in *Martin Chuzzlewit,* as against that of the reportorial *American Notes,* was admittedly selective: not the "whole truth" but the comic one. Selectivity, the art of *"omitting* those very features which in life most strongly impress us,"* Gissing (whose own fiction omits little) saw as a clue to the lifelike portrait, and Mrs. Gamp herself "a piece of the most delicate idealism. It is a sublimation of the essence of Gamp." [2] George Santayana comes close to Dickens's attitude, and to the classic defense of the anti-realist, in painting as in literature. He sees what is *really there:* "When people say Dickens exaggerates, it seems to me they can have no eyes and no ears. They probably have only *notions* of what things and people are; they accept them conventionally, at their diplomatic value." There are such people as Quilp, Squeers, Serjeant Buzfuz: "we are such people ourselves in our true moments, in our veritable impulses; but we are careful to stifle and to hide those moments from ourselves and from the world. . . ." [3]

Dickens's London, which he walked so many hours at night—the childhood haunts revisited, and the place of traumatic memory long avoided—was essential to his fantasy life. He speaks, in *American Notes,* of the stumps of trees seen in the growing dark: a stump taking on divers human shapes that "seemed to force themselves upon me, whether I would or no," these in turn seeming "counterparts of figures once familiar to me in pictures attached to childish books, forgotten long ago." This takes us very close to the process of fanciful creation. The London darkness was mysteriously peopled, as by detective Bucket's helpers suddenly appearing in the oozy labyrinth of *Bleak House,* but also, as on one of Dickens's nighttime walks, by "a man standing bolt upright to keep within the doorway's shadow, and evidently intent upon no particular service to society." The fiction is rich in menaced waterside places, tenements thrust out over the river, the lanes and byways where reorientation or discovery of one's personality (as with John Harmon) comes to seem impossible. The river and its bridges are, like Dostoevsky's Petersburg canals, the scene of ghostly nighttime encounters. The Thames freighted with bodies is a place where crimes occur, escapes are attempted, and punishment may finally be met. Dickens's London by day is a place of frenzied activity, much of it seen as by a child, magnified and grotesque. It supplies the shops and carriages of his fiction, the eccentric tradesmen, the queer faces of the casual and obsessed passersby. But it is London by night, rather—lovingly recorded at the outset of his career in *Sketches by Boz* and near its end in *The Uncommercial Traveller—* that presumably gave birth to fantastic new beings and to distortions of the old.

The essay "Night-Walks" takes Dickens past Bethlehem Hospital ("Are not the sane and the insane equal at night as the sane lie a dreaming?"), and cemeteries ("it was a solemn consideration what enormous hosts of the dead belong to one old great city, and how, if they were raised while the living slept, there would not be the space of a pin's point. . . ."), and into an empty theater (the orchestra "like a great grave dug for a time of pestilence"), and to the river with its "awful look" ("the buildings on the banks were muffled in black shrouds, and the reflected lights seemed to originate deep in the water, as if the spectres of suicides were holding them to show where they went down").

For Dostoevsky, also much given to nighttime walks, Petersburg was a magic city, the source of his "fantastic realism." For the dreamer of the *Petersburg Chronicle,* "even the most ordinary everyday trifle, the most empty routine matter, immediately assumes . . . a fantastic coloring. His glance is already attuned so as to see the fantastic in everything." [4] There is relatively little formal description in his fiction, though the few vivid details are enough to evoke unforgettably a world of dark tenements and dangerous staircases. At times Peter the Great's eighteenth-century city would seem as labyrinthine as Dickens's medieval London. The city was essential to the dreaming of Dostoevsky's underground men, as he saw in what he called, in his 1861 *Petersburg Dreams in Verse and Prose,* his "vision on the Neva." The columns of smoke rising like giants are altogether Dickensian:

> It seemed, in the end, that all this world, with all its inhabitants, both the strong and the weak, with all their habitations, whether beggars' shelters or gilded palaces, at this hour of twilight resembled a fantastic, enchanted vision, a dream which in its turn would instantly vanish and waste away as vapor into the blue heaven. Suddenly a certain strange thought began to stir inside me . . . I saw clearly, as it were, into something new, a completely new world, unfamiliar to me and known only through some obscure hearsay, through a certain mysterious sign. [5]

Dostoevsky tells of looking about and noticing "strange, extraordinary figures, completely prosaic, not Don Carloses or Posas to be sure, rather down-to-earth titular councilors and yet at the same time, as it were, sort of fantastic titular councilors." In the epilogue to *A Raw Youth,* near the end of his career, Dostoevsky could refer ironically to a Tolstoyan literature devoted to a middle aristocracy and its ordered life; he himself had discovered the reality of the fantastic Underground Man. Dostoevsky very precisely echoes Dickens in describing his own view of reality: "that which the majority call almost fantastic and exceptional, for me sometimes constitutes the very essence of the real. Commonplace phenomena and a conventional view of them is, in my opinion, no longer realism, but even the contrary." [6]

Faulkner's imagination was never at home in the city, though at a middle distance his Memphis had an energizing strangeness. His *New Orleans Sketches* are pallid compared with Dostoevsky's *Petersburg Chronicle* or *Sketches by Boz*. His fantastic reality had to be discovered in Jefferson and its environs. The first Snopeses, like Dostoevsky's first titular councilors, appeared suddenly, but in the dusty inert ambiance of Frenchman's Bend. Negroes and mules, those humblest of realities, helped free Faulkner's imagination from the sophistications of his first two novels. *Sartoris*'s mule of sacred associations ("celibate, he is unscarred, possesses neither pillar nor desert cave," etc.) provokes the first long flight of unabashed "Faulknerese." It would appear that the Snopeses, still in the background of *Sartoris,* but much of their history already well known to Faulkner, had a maieutic, liberating effect on the imagination. In the small world dominated by them, everything was permitted; no limit need be set to obsession. The presence of the Snopeses in Frenchman's Bend could turn a country schoolroom into a place of seething intensities and Homeric "probable impossibilities"—the teacher Labove's thralldom to the eleven-year-old Eula Varner's "mammalian ellipses" or the wordless love-combat, carried on over years, of Houston and his future wife, or that other teacher I. O. Snopes and his two wives, relishing the exhibition of Ike and his Junoesque cow. It seems altogether probable that the discovery of the fantastic in the everyday and seemingly peripheral—even the lesser Snopeses of Frenchmen's Bend, even Surratt-Ratliff, even negroes and mules and alcohol—helped Faulkner, in due time, imagine the extravagant plights of central tragic figures: Joe Christmas, Thomas Sutpen and his sons. Just so the first titular councilor and then Golyadkin might help in the creation of tortured consciences, in the great later novels.

The Hamlet, which ends with Flem Snopes's departure for Jefferson, is the first volume of a major triptych. In Jefferson I. O. Snopes's mules will create as much disorder as Flem's spotted horses in Frenchman's Bend, and the dissolution of Eck Snopes (with nothing of him left but a neck-brace dangling from a wire) will be even fuller than that of Krook, who left behind an oily "yellow liquor." But V. K. Suratt (later Ratliff) is already present in *Sartoris,* published eleven years before, as well as Byron Snopes and Flem. He too brings Frenchman's Bend to Jefferson, and momentarily counteracts the pallid influence of Horace Benbow. Suratt, after Bayard Sartoris has fallen from the savage stallion and been treated by Dr. Peabody, joins Bayard and "Hub" and presently even negroes in drinking from a jug of whiskey on a topsy-turvy farm; alcohol breaks through barriers of race and class. But also, in this chapter, we have much rich simile and metaphor, and a Dickensian grotesque animation of an ordinary dilapidated farm. The child David Copperfield is terrified by "a quantity of fowls that look terribly tall to me, walking about in a menacing and ferocious manner." In *Sartoris* geese drift "like small muddy clouds," parade "sedately," surge "erratically with discordant cries." their necks undulant and suave as formal gestures on a pantomime." The sun falls upon the rumps of the geese and "their suave necks, and upon the cow's gaunt, rhythmically twitching flank, ridging her visible ribs with dingy gold." As in Dickens the natural world can be grotesquely alive. There is "a junglish growth of willow and elder, against which a huge beech and a clump of saplings stood like mottled ghosts and from which a cool dankness rose like a breath."

Another area of the fantastic is to be found just off the highway in *Sanctuary*, another jug of whiskey and topsy-turvy farm. Here, as in *Oliver Twist* and *Our Mutual Friend*, or *Crime and Punishment* and *The Possessed*, the everyday world and the criminal interpenetrate, though the criminal world is generally invisible; and it is easy to step from one to the other. The Civil War, in *The Unvanquished* and impinging on memory in several books, is selectively fantastic; the most absurd exploits are the best remembered. But the early history of Yoknapatawpha County, given freest rein in *Requiem for a Nun*, is perhaps the extreme instance of reality transformed, the fantastic evoked by an immense padlock, history as extravagant metaphor; and "the pioneer, the tall man, roaring with Protestant scripture and boiled whiskey" who strutted his "roaring eupeptic hour, and was no more, leaving his ghost, pariah and proscribed, scriptureless now and armed only with the highwayman's, the murderer's, pistol, haunting the fringes of the wilderness. . . ."

Three very different works, but works essentially representative of their authors, will suggest how anti-realist impulse can work within the fabric of the familiar: *Oliver Twist, The Double, The Bear*. Dickens's mysterious world, yet a world in which community is the norm, is here largely created by plot, and this will be true even of his more ambitious novels. The mysteries of *The Double* are psychological. In later novels the divided personality, much enriched by ideological content, will be spread over several characters, or (as in *Notes from Underground*) be compressed into one. The mysterious and mythical world of *The Bear* is brooded over by a powerful and solitary authorial consciousness. The ideal is one of community, of masculine comradeship. But both Old Ben and Ike McCaslin are solitaries, as are, in very different ways, Thomas Sutpen and Joe Christmas.

The fantastic and the real are subtly interwoven in *Oliver Twist*. The fine stylized reality of the thieves and a certain amount of documentary realism, as well as the flat reality of the respectable, may be invaded at any moment by magical circumstance. Oliver can fall into the invisible criminal world simply by going out alone; he is quickly recaptured by the forces of evil, which are powerful and ubiquitous. The fairy-story embodies and evokes real and familiar childhood terrors; childhood is *like that*. It is in these terms that Angus Wilson can defend Oliver's uninteresting passivity. His disturbing standard English is, Steven Marcus suggests, a gift of grace. At one point the interpenetration of fantastic and real is truly occult: as Fagin and Monks look through the window at the dozing Oliver, but leave no trace of their passing.

The documentary aspect of *Oliver Twist* is well known. The satirical chapters concerning the consequences of the Poor Law Amendment Act of 1834, and Dickens's picture of the workhouse, even of the meager diet, are essentially true. Dickens did not and could not, in a family story of "The Parish Boy's Progress," document the highly visible sexual life of nighttime London, nor its "kennels," the gutters filled with excrement. Only a few sentences would indicate, to alert adult ears, that Nancy was a prostitute as well as thieves' assistant, and her language is thoroughly chastened. Yet that language is sufficiently vivid for the purpose of the fiction; and to make her fidelity to Sikes convincing, and her inability to break away from the criminal world. The reality of London as a filthy labyrinth is conveyed here as in other Dickens novels by the menaced worm-eaten waterside tenements thrust over the stream, and Jacob's Island and Folly Ditch. In the disused warehouse of the Monks-Bumbles interview one's very identity can be lost, the crucial evidence destroyed, dropped through a trap-door into dark turbid water and slimy piles. A real fear of engulfment and suffocation charges the writing in the scene of Sikes's death on Jacob's Island, perhaps because (even as he wrote of the crowd threatened by suffocation) Dickens was already looking several paragraphs ahead to Sikes's attempted leap into the mud of the ditch and his death by the noose dangling from the roof.

The early scene of Oliver going to his first funeral with Mr. Sowerberry evokes brilliantly a menacing filthy reality. Here too we have moldering tenements, some houses "prevented from falling into the street, by huge beams of wood reared against the walls." Dickens does not specify excrement, but his detail is as vivid as need be: "The kennel was stagnant and filthy. The very rats, which here and there lay putrefying in its rottenness, were hideous with famine." Inside, there are "some ragged children" in a corner; the corpse is "something covered with an old blanket"; the man and woman watching over the corpse are "so like the rats he had seen outside"—the man's eyes bloodshot, the old woman's bright and piercing, and her two remaining teeth protruding over her underlip. In such an environment the man's fear of putting the corpse in the ground, where " 'the worms would carry her: not eat her: she is so worn away,' " is altogether convincing. So too, as in compressed anticipation of the great Marmeladov ceremonies, that supreme macabre evocation of poverty, the old woman's "hideous merriment": " 'We should have cake and wine, too, before we go! Never mind; send some bread—only a loaf of bread and a cup of water. Shall we have some bread, dear?' she said eagerly: catching at the undertaker's coat, as he once more moved towards the door.''

There is, then, as much plausible, largely impressionistic detail as the novel's vision needs; and sometimes more. One can imagine Dickens checking on the structure of the bridge where Noah Claypole overhears Nancy give her information, as Hardy would count his paces on "Egdon Heath." Is the novel also, as Philip Collins, certainly a good authority, says, an accurate guide to Saffron Hill and metropolitan criminal life? The picture of Saffron Hill (chapter 26) has a Balzacian energy and detail. No doubt the professional cant of the thieves (" 'Crape, keys, centre-bit, darkies—nothing forgotten?' ") had a fascination for Victorian readers, as their always vivid talk, surely less "realistic," has a fascination for us. Whether Fagin and his underlings were like that, in London or anywhere else, is another matter. Presumably Fagin bears a closer resemblance to the red-headed devil of iconography than to the historic Ikey Solomons, the trainer of boy pickpockets. The Artful Dodger has a total reality, but it is a fictive reality, like that of Sairey Gamp: the man's coat reaching nearly to his heels, the knack of giving his head a sudden twitch to keep his hat in place, and a mind and tongue that move rather faster than life. His fantastic reality glides, "scuds" rather, along familiar, even pedantically named streets: "through Exmouth Street and Coppice Row; down the little court by the side of the workhouse; across the classic ground which once bore the name of Hockley-in-the-Hole; thence into Little Saffron Hill; and so into Saffron Hill the Great: along which, the Dodger scudded at a rapid pace: directing Oliver to follow close at his heels.''

The fantastic vivacity of the boy pickpockets puts them beyond the pale of moral judgment; their energy redeems. Dickens the sociologist-reporter of *Sketches by Boz* was not Dickens the novelist, as Fielding the magistrate and serious pamphleteer on crime and disorder was not the author of *Tom Jones*. Dickens's report on fourteen boy pickpockets, all under fourteen years of age, seen not so long before on a visit to Newgate, gives a different picture: "fourteen such terrible little faces we never beheld—There was not one redeeming feature among them—not a glance of honesty—not a wink expressive of anything but the gallows and the hulks, in the whole collection." The boys' disreputable pride in profession, here a "disagreeable sight," is comic in *Oliver Twist;* it becomes there a saving grace.

Oliver Twist possesses more narrative energy than a number of later and doubtless greater novels. Much of it derives from the happy interaction of characters. The Artful Dodger lends life to Charley Bates, as Nancy to Bill Sikes, who in turn is fictively inseparable from his dog. Mr. Fang the police magistrate was apparently based on one Allan Stewart Laing, who was dismissed from the bench in 1838. But his great choleric fictive reality derives from the outraged responses of Mr. Brownlow, who is in turn more alive here than anywhere else. An energizing collision of personalities has occurred.

The anti-mimetic counterforces to these realisms, both the documentary and the fictive, are obvious. The melodramatic plot (and a Dickens novel could hardly be conceived without one) is more justified than in the ambitious *Dombey and Son.* The coincidences of *Oliver Twist,* Steven Marcus writes, "are of too cosmic an order to belong in the category of the fortuitous." "For the population of *Oliver Twist* consists only of persons—the wicked and the beneficent—involved with the fate of the hero. There are, almost, no other sorts of people in it; and in a world where there is no accidental population, no encounter can be called a coincidence." [7] The plot's revelations subvert, inevitably, what appeared to be interesting psychological insight. Monks's relationship with Fagin, and his desire to corrupt Oliver, are mildly interesting so long as they seem gratuitous . . . i.e., genuinely diabolic. But his highly rhetorical diabolism is stagy and boring, like that of Rigaud-Blandois in *Little Dorrit;* his references to the devil and to hell fire, and his fits brought on by lightning and thunder, are embarrassingly insistent, like his Gothic name. The sense of occult power in Fagin is real, but has nothing to do with the traditional red hair, or even with that momentary capacity (shared with Monks) to leave no footprints. Fagin's force lies rather in the sense he gives of belonging to another order of being, slimy and reptilian yet full of diabolic energy and glee. His personality is more real than his specific evil intentions. Even his named fears in the condemned cell are less vivid than his physical presence, and "the unwashed flesh" that "crackled with the fever that burnt him up." His is an unsubduable animal existence, even as the men subdue him and disengage Oliver from his grasp. Dickens does not describe the hanging, which the reader's imagination might well refuse to believe.

The element of fairy-story and myth, on which recent criticism has rightly insisted, will continue to pervade some of Dickens's later fictions: the hero seeking his identity by passage through a labyrinth, the death and rebirth of personality after some form of immersion or imprisonment, the release of the soul from immobilizing enchantment (the princess fortuitously released in *Great Expectations* on bad editorial advice). The fairy-story, in the early *Oliver Twist* and *The Old Curiosity Shop,* has distinctly religious overtones. The myths in some of the later novels will encompass large, explicit, altogether conscious "symbols": the railroad and the sea, in the realistic *Dombey and Son,* the river and the dust-heaps in *Our Mutual Friend,* the prison of *Little Dorrit* and the fires of *Barnaby Rudge,* the houses and courts and archives of *Bleak House.* The most successful symbols may well be those which derive from substantial and exceedingly well-known realities, ones related to genuine authorial affections and anxieties: *the river,* filthy but charged with fascinating activity in Dickens's time, in which people do indeed drown, and *the waterside labyrinth,* which included the dreaded blacking warehouse, where the unwary lose their way, where connection with the past and with oneself may be lost or frighteningly recovered.

For it is here, in conveying a world of mysterious connection, in suggesting a web of hidden relationships that a wholly realist fiction would deny, that *Oliver Twist* is particularly representative of Dickens's work as a whole. Beneath the ordinary world—the relatively visible criminal world of "The Three Cripples," or the legal world of bookstores, country houses, workhouses—is an unseen world of connections: among people who have never met, but also with one's family, one's childhood, one's mysterious inheritance and self. The secret world may be malicious or providential but never, in *Oliver Twist,* neutral or inert. A current of energy flows between Monks and Fagin, his agent in evil; and chance, so diabolic it shocks even Monks, may cause Oliver to stumble against him. Chance thrusts Oliver in Nancy's arms, breaking his connection with the Brownlow household; but absent-mindedness too, which leads him to take the wrong street, and imprudence, since trouble so obviously lies in wait. A world of benevolent connection leads Oliver to the protective Maylies and Brownlows, who are connected with each other as well as with him; Rose, for whom Oliver has brotherly feelings, turns out to be his aunt. But broken connections—with one's parents, with one's very identity—may seem more real. The father of Monks and his half-brother Oliver dies leaving no will, that most formal connection with family and the past. Old Sally has robbed Oliver's mother, who has just died giving birth to him, of a clue to his identity. But she herself dies before her confession is complete. The gold locket, redeemed from the pawnbroker's by Mrs. Bumble, comes into Monks's hands, and is thrown down the trap-door into the river. This seemingly definitive annihilation is averted, the broken connection repaired, because Nancy has the courage to listen secretly to Monks and Fagin. But she in turn is overheard by Noah Claypole, commissioned by Fagin; and so loses her life.

To survey mysterious connection in Dickens's work would require, virtually, a summary of his plots. He was first encouraged in the planning of a serious novel, *Great Expectations,* by "the grotesque tragi-comic conception" of a concealed connection between Pip's rise and Magwitch. The macabre fatality of Ralph Nickleby involves both a lost connection (he has unwittingly put his own son into the Dotheboys inferno, and is virtually responsible for his death) and a connection he would like to break: the impoverished double he had ruined, an evil associate who reappears to haunt him, and provokes almost Dostoevskyan writing. The secret past returns in various macabre ways in *Barnaby Rudge.* The hangman Dennis, talking with Hugh (who will be revealed as Sir John Chester's son), discovers he executed Hugh's mother. The secret or lost connections of *Little Dorrit* are melodramatic enough, with one bearer of disgraceful secrets buried in a collapsed house. *Bleak House,* in some ways Dickens's most serious picture of contemporary England, is dependent on insidiously hidden or lost connections both for its overall vision of an undermined society and for the minute working out of individual destinies. The contagion of cholera (a very real threat) could reach from the pauper graveyard to high society in Lincolnshire, and back, the plot spinning on an illicit sexual relationship in the past, but also on two wholly unemphasized moments of recognition: Lady Dedlock chancing to look over Tulkinghorn's shoulder, to see the familiar handwriting of Captain Hawdon, and Guppy's surprise on seeing something familiar in Lady Dedlock's portrait. The novel's plot through many chapters seems hopelessly muddled, but is deliberately so; Snagsby realizes he is involved in a mystery, but has no idea what it is. Lost connection, failure of understanding and failure of language (even Guster unable to speak at a critical moment because subject to fits), are significant in a novel concerned with maladministration and the obfuscations of law. The novel has, notoriously, its network of hidden correspondences, but also some that are extremely overt, as between Krook's shop and Chancery.

Oliver Twist also foreshadows, with Fagin and Monks, the mysteries of psychological connection in later novels. Edith Dombey has her double, a complementary personality and destiny, in Alice Brown; the self-tormentor Miss Wade may be drawn to Tattycoram by a lesbian loneliness in *Little Dorrit,* but also by identification with a rejected, self-destructive personality. Jonas Chuzzlewit and Montague Tigg are closer to Dostoevskyan doubles, with Slyme also in some sense connected to them, and Nadgett too, employed by Tigg as a secret watcher. Lady Dedlock, a strongly controlled and even repressed woman, wills the crime which her double Hortense, wearing her clothes, commits. She, not Hortense, may seem the real murderer, as Stavrogin not Fedka, Ivan and Dmitri not Smerdyakov. The long-inhibited, repressed Bradley Headstone, destroying his primitive double Rogue Riderhood, also destroys himself. The secret connections of *The Mystery of Edwin Drood,* both those of personality and those of plot, remain undiscovered. But Dickens would not have been out of character had he incorporated both the ritual of Thugs and the ritual of alternating personalities.

We are still very far, in *Oliver Twist,* from the serenely quiet art of *Edwin Drood* or from the rhetorical complications of *Our Mutual Friend.* But the essential Dickens is already largely present.

The fantastic that invades ordinary reality is thus of several kinds in Dickens. The everyday world can be undermined or disrupted by a hidden world of mysterious connections that link us to each other and to the past; by secrets that return to haunt us; by unexpected interventions, which may be providential as well as malicious. To all this we may add arbitrarily imposed melodramatic coincidence. A second kind of fantastic imposition on the reality of London streets (but Dickens would repudiate the word "imposition") is that of the eccentrics of grotesque appearance or compulsive behavior or both, the Originals, with a few genial madmen to boot. The third area of fantastic creation derives, simply, from the author's temperamental love of the grotesque in presenting the visual world: his power, almost hallucinatory, to animate things.

There are hidden crimes and misalliances in Dostoevsky too (though the crucial struggles are with self, rather than with probing outsiders), and Dickensian lost connections are restored in *The Insulted and the Injured* through dramatic revelations. But the basic invasion or penetration of the everyday by the fantastic, in Dostoevsky, involves the sudden disruption of order. This sense of a world at any moment subject to radical change is not surprising, given the major traumatic events of Dostoevsky's life (the father's murder; the unexpected arrest and condemnation to death, the last-minute reprieve), given too the recurring epileptic fits and the gambling mania, with fortune to be won or lost on the turn of a wheel. The invading disorder may be individual, psychic: an eruption from the unconscious, leading to manic, gratuitous behavior. The sudden apparition of the irrational may be projected, by the author if not the character, onto a mysterious, perhaps hallucinatory outsider: a double. But the sudden disorder may be collective: a stable group literally invaded by ruffians (possibly young people corrupted by nihilist western ideas) or disrupted by the collision of several personalities, with secrets or neuroses flaring to the surface, "carnivalesque" scenes of exposure which can even lead to the mortal insult of a slap.

A social occasion may be disrupted by both individual and collective disorder, as at Nastasya's party in *The Idiot* (Part I, xiii–xvi): by neurosis, cynicism, brutality, drunkenness. She has prepared the way for exposure and confusion by the *petit-jeu* in which each guest is to recount, honestly, the most evil action of his life. Earlier we have seen a scandalized family group invaded by Rogozhin and his rowdy companions, he offering to buy Nastasya for 100,000 rubles. Now he returns, with two more disreputable associates (one of whom was said to have pawned his teeth for drink, as the late Gamp his wooden leg), bringing the money. The scene is exceedingly complex, psychologically, with Rogozhin's roll of banknotes functioning as sexual potentiality, which Nastasya can grant, withhold, transfer and, challengingly, throw into the fire. The scene is charged and controlled by neurotic responses. Rogozhin cannot take his eyes off Myshkin, foreshadowing their mysterious communication throughout the novel, while Nastasya enacts her need to degrade herself publicly, as though to relive her years of shame with Totsky. The behavior of the onlookers generally is hysterical. So too it will be at the Marmeladov funeral in *Crime and Punishment*. The calm of the monastery in *The Brothers Karamazov* is scandalously disrupted by old Fyodor's behavior. Later it will be violated even by natural disorder, as the dead Zossima gives off not an odor of sanctity but the breath of corruption.

The Double, limited though it be, is a good example of how, in Dostoevsky, the fantastic may penetrate and at last overwhelm the quotidian. The basic ambiguity of this early novel—how much of Golyadkin's experience is hallucinatory, how much real, how much simultaneously hallucinatory and real—is more equivocal than in the later books. But even there a great deal of "dreamwork" will be presented as literal reality, especially in *The Idiot*. There is comparatively little natural description or description of furniture in Dostoevsky; the Chinese vase exists so that Myshkin can compulsively smash it. Dostoevsky's realism derives rather from people and their talk. Yet Golyadkin's drab world is substantially there. His room, with its partitioned area for the servant Petrushka, is on the fourth floor, which defines in Petersburg (as it did in Balzac's Paris) a certain level of poverty. He and other "titular councilors" have a specific rank in the civil service and their definite employment (or, as with Bartleby, misemployment): to transcribe and register official documents. The story opens as, living in fantasy, Golyadkin hires a carriage and goes on a shopping spree, even ordering furniture for six rooms. But the Gostiny Dvor is a real row of shops on the Nevsky Prospect, a real street. In a moment of anxiety he visits the altogether real doctor Krestyan Ivanovich Rutenspitz, quickly reveals paranoid anxieties and experiences a minor fit. Fits regularly break through surface order in the novels, sometimes blocking awareness or, it may be, displacing forbidden sexuality. There is often the danger, after great strain, of "brain fever." And stories may terminate, like Golyadkin's and Myshkin's, in psychotic separation from reality.

The nominal object of Golyadkin's role-playing, on this first day, is to make a reputable appearance at Klara Olsufyevna's birthday party, to which he has not been invited. Turned away at the door, and after a seeming lapse of consciousness, he finds himself huddled in the midst of rubbish, partly hidden by a cupboard and an old screen, and waits there for nearly three hours, watching the party. He decides rationally to go home, and at once dashes "forward as though someone had touched a spring in him." Where action is often irrationally delayed in Faulkner, waiting for consciousness to catch up, the Dostoevskyan underground man compulsively acts against his best interests without delay. Myshkin's dread of what an unconscious self may do, as well as warnings to stay away from the Chinese vase, compel him toward it. Golyadkin, like other tormented protagonists, experiences contradictory impulses and feelings at the same time, rather than in orderly alternation. His disgrace at the party culminates in his effort to dance with Klara Olsufyevna. He has perhaps danced in fantasy; now he attempts the reality: "lurched forward, first once, then a second time, then lifted his leg, then made a scrape, then gave a sort of stamp, then stumbled. . . ." Thrown out, he runs onto the Fontanka quay, at midnight in the raging snowstorm and fog, feeling himself "killed, killed entirely, in the full sense of the word. . . ." Dostoevsky does not, as a more circumstantial realist might, remind us that this was a canal quay, and that Golyadkin is not facing the great river. What matters is "all the nameless horrors of a raging snowstorm and fog, under a Petersburg November sky," attacking him, "as though conspiring and combining with all his enemies." Golyadkin's need to "hide somewhere from himself . . . to run away from himself," and the loss of one of his galoshes, not even noticed, immediately precede the apparition of the stranger whom he will presently see as a mirror image of himself. This double—Golyadkin Jr.—has an altogether plausible appearance when the hero, rushing home, finds him sitting on his bed.

The crucial problem of hallucination and reality, with the mature reader experiencing Golyadkin Jr. as both, will be examined in my seventh chapter. Dostoevsky contemplated revising *The Double* so as to base Golyadkin Jr. on an informer betraying the Petrashevsky circle, i.e., on historical reality. This would in turn connect him with Pyotr Verkhovensky of *The Possessed*. In *The Double* as we have it Golyadkin Jr.'s first appearance is called forth by the desperate psychic need to disown part of the self. The moment of splitting is briefly and brilliantly rendered. "All at once . . . all at once he started and involuntarily jumped aside a couple of paces." Someone seemed to be standing beside him, also leaning on the railing, even saying something, "not quite intelligibly, but something very close to him, something concerning him." Golyadkin Jr.'s role changes through the novel, as the hero's need to humiliate or reassert himself changes; so too his degree of physical reality. The question of hallucination is raised with the devil-doubles of Stavrogin, Ivan Karamazov, and Ippolit in *The Idiot,* and with the mesmeric power of Rogozhin's eyes, he too in some sense a devil-double. The splitting of one character into two or more, all of them substantially real—a splitting that is sometimes conscious on the author's part, sometimes not—is perhaps the central movement of the Dostoevskyan creative process. A mysteriously appearing stranger, as the one who says "Murderer" to Raskolnikov, may seem to have risen from the ground in response to guilty need. But he turns out to be "real."

Golyadkin anticipates many later heroes in his need for self-laceration, confession, humiliation. But guilt may also erupt symbolically, as in Kafka or Freud *passim,* shattering order embarrassingly. An ink blot suddenly appears on a document he has prepared for a superior; the double offers to scratch it out with a penknife, then perfidiously fails to do so; the blotted page will be seen. Worse still is the medicine bottle dropped on the floor and smashed, and the "dark reddish, repulsive liquid" at Golyadkin's feet, as significant as the spilled brandy in *The Castle*. Even the earlier, distinctly more naturalistic *Poor Folk* has two scenes of this kind, nightmare fantasy worthy of Kafka or Kosinski. Or even Faulkner and Dickens? In the first an old man running after a hearse loses his hat in the wind and rain. Then as he runs from one side of the hearse to the other (like Golyadkin Jr. running beside the carriage taking Golyadkin Sr. to the asylum), "the skirts of his old greatcoat" flap

> "about him like a pair of wings. From every pocket of the garment protruded books, while in his arms he carried a specially large volume, which he hugged closely to his breast. . . . Every now and then a book would slip from one of his pockets, and fall into the mud; whereupon somebody, stopping him, would direct attention to his loss, and he would stop, pick up the book, and again set off in pursuit of the hearse." [8]

The second scene, very close to the embarrassments of Golyadkin, involves an interview with "His Excellency," and the sudden loss of a button. " 'A button of mine—the devil take it!—a button of mine that was hanging by a single thread suddenly broke off, and hopped and skipped and rattled and rolled until it had reached the feet of his Excellency himself. . . .' " He pursues the button: " 'Obstinacy of a sort seized upon me, and I did my best to arrest the thing, but it slipped away, and kept turning over and over, so that I could not grasp it, and made a sad spectacle of myself with my awkwardness.' " There could hardly be a more transparent sexual trauma. Amusingly enough Belinsky, who much preferred *Poor Folk* and its picture of exhausted poverty to the psychologizing *The Double,* seized upon this scene for praise. "And that torn-off button, that minute when he kisses the general's hand—why this is no longer compassion for an unfortunate man; it's horror, horror! Its horror lies in this very gratitude! *This is a tragedy.*" [9]

The Double dramatizes lapses of consciousness, and hence of time, even within the material reality of a restaurant. The fantastic, impinging on the everyday consciousness of a shop attendant, of customers, is at once comic and pathetic. On one occasion, having eaten one open-faced patty, Golyadkin is asked to pay for eleven, then sees his double in the doorway, with the last morsel of the tenth in his hand. On another he comes to himself standing in the middle of a room, amid hostile onlookers, notices "dirty plates left from somebody's dinner," and concludes that he must have used them himself. In his second disruption of a gathering at Klara Olsufyevna's, which will lead to the asylum, the focus of narration brilliantly blends distorting blur and a discerned real reality. The reader understands, as Golyadkin does not, why people are now looking at him with a "mysterious, unaccountable sympathy."

These are a few of the ways in which Dostoevsky's early short novel, which he came to speak of with distaste, is representative of his power to dramatize the fantastic impinging on the real. What we do not have there are the tense, even hysterical relationships among two or more real people, the sudden explosions of rage which may follow upon professions of affection, those of Nastasya and Aglaia in *The Idiot* or Katerina and Grushenka in *The Brothers Karamazov.* Nor do we have the crucial political vision of a society possessed: the sudden though perhaps long-planned disruption symbolized in the subversion of the governesses' benefit in *The Possessed.*

The Bear, perhaps Faulkner's greatest work of art except for *Absalom, Absalom!,* is the work of a contemplative and solitary consciousness, and what it contemplates through many pages is Ike McCaslin's experience of formative solitude. The picture is of an ideal community of hunters in the Big Woods, which even the gaunt malaria-ridden swampers at one point are free to join. The world of women and of urban anxiety has been left behind; there is whiskey and good talk. But Ike is alone through the most moving pages of the hunting story, as is Old Ben, the lonely deity of the woods: a child of ten on his stand, or following the bear's footprints, and granted his solitary vision; and moving alone through the woods at the end. He even seems alone during much of Part Four, as he ponders the ledgers chronicling his family history, and reaches the decision to relinquish his inheritance. For the highly stylized dialogue with his cousin McCaslin Edmonds, both using at times the same rich rhetoric, has the effect of interior discourse.

This sense of a solitary authorial consciousness in part derives from temperament. The young Faulkner, for all his happy childhood, was noted for his silences. A protective evasiveness was as marked as Conrad's, and is reflected in structure and style. The solitary aloof narrative consciousness brooded over a number of singularly isolated characters. The variety of isolates is extraordinarily wide: from the catatonic Joe Gilligan of *Soldiers' Pay* and the impotent Popeye, through Joe Christmas and Charles Etienne de Saint-Vélery Bon, to the old General of *The Fable,* solitary in youth on his desert outpost and, now at the height of his powers, eating by himself at his headquarters, as lonely as God or Satan. The deepest solitudes may be psychological. To be rapt, "bemused and inattentive," not quite *there* because lost in dream or neurotic obsession, or compelled to meaningless ritual acts and gestures, at times seems the norm in Faulkner's fiction, both for onlookers and protagonists.

There is rich interplay in *The Bear,* of the closely observed real and the fantastic or mysterious. The mysteriousness pertains, altogether plausibly, to a timeless natural world. The strangeness is much heightened by rhetorical pattern: metaphor, simile, allusion, and a rich panoply of myth, and by a network of correspondences and reflexive references. A symbolic connection is made between Old Ben, seen as a locomotive rushing through the woods, and the locomotive and logging train that in time replaces him (resembling "a small dingy harmless snake vanishing into weeds"), and the snake of the story's end, "the old one, the ancient and accursed about the earth." These other deities are rendered with loving precision: the shrieking little locomotive and the "lethargic deliberate clashing of slack couplings," and the old snake,

> one thick rapid contraction, one loop cast sideways as though merely for purchase from which the raised head might start slightly backward, not in fright either, not in threat quite yet, more than six feet of it, the head raised higher than his knee and less than his knee's length away, and old, the once-bright markings of its youth dulled now to a monotone concordant too with the wilderness it crawled and lurked. . . .[10]

The bear Old Ben, Lion the great blue dog, the old snake are fabulous animals, solitary and mysterious inhabitants of the woods. The great racehorse of *A Fable,* winning on three sound legs, and Flem's spotted horses in *The*

Hamlet, which give birth in the imagination to I. O. Snopes's mules in *The Town,* are exempt from ordinary laws of nature, and possess mythical power. The horse that invades Mrs. Littlejohn's establishment is metaphorically capable of flight, floats "hobgoblin" in the moon. So too is the swimming deer of "Old Man," accompanying the tall convict on the crest of the wave and suddenly vanishing upward. Of a different order of being, but still close to fantasy and myth, are the anomalies: the fox Ellen of *Sartoris* and her incompetent mongrel brood that cause the father to skulk in shame, or the less-than-six-pound fyce ready to attack the looming bear, "not humble because it was already too near the ground to genuflect." The fabulous animals have their precisely noted real reality, as did Melville's white whale. *Moby Dick* long rested on the shelf for whaling in the Harvard College library; *The Bear* was read for its details of hunting, in the *Saturday Evening Post* version, by many non-literary persons. Old Ben's crooked footprint vivifies the bear itself, but also the progress of Ike's initiation and natural knowledge. A single sentence conveys both the atmosphere of timeless myth and an intensely real present moment: "Then, standing beside Sam in the thick great gloom of ancient woods and the winter's dying afternoon, he looked quietly down at the rotted log scored and gutted with claw-marks and, in the wet earth beside it, the print of the enormous warped two-toed foot."

This real world, which Faulkner knew as well as Dickens his London streets, yet seems to exist outside historic time. It is all that is left of an innocent natural world that cannot be *owned,* a world of natural relationships and pure natural force which must kill and be killed. This force is altogether different from the greed and rapacity of the urban world trapped in time. The world of the Big Woods has an immeasurable past. Old Ben is "not even a mortal beast but an anachronism indomitable and invincible out of an old dead time. . . ." In this ancient world Sam, the half-savage guide, will mark Ike's face with blood and teach him the ritual salutation with which he greets the snake. Sam has the intuitive foreknowledge of primitive man deeply in touch with his world. He recognizes Lion as the dog needed, for the killing of the bear, but knows too that his own long life must end shortly after the bear's. "It was almost over now and he was glad." The prevailing tone of *The Bear* is one of nostalgia for this lost world. Time invades the woods by way of the logging train, and tragically enters Ike's consciousness through the ledgers' chronicle of slavery and abuse. But there is one last experience of timelessness, in the plot reserved from the sale, the "place where dissolution itself was a seething turmoil of ejaculation tumescence conception and birth, and death did not even exist," and where Ike encounters the old yet also timeless snake, and salutes him in "the old tongue": " 'Chief,' he said 'Grandfather.' "

This is, as various critics have noted, the timeless world of Myth. *The Bear* is Faulkner's *Huckleberry Finn,* but also his *Moby Dick* and *Paradise Lost.* The story is one of "inexhaustible allusiveness," as Thomas Mann remarked of "Death in Venice"; it should not, that is, be closely pinned down. Ike becomes a carpenter in not unconscious emulation of the Nazarene; his cousin McCaslin Edmonds, understanding why Ike did not shoot the bear, reads to him from the "Ode on a Grecian Urn." (Even the killing of the bear seems arrested momentarily in the familiar Faulknerian frieze: "For an instant they almost resembled a piece of statuary: the clinging dog, the bear, the man astride its back, working and probing the buried blade.") The myth of the Ideal Quest is also the myth of the Sacred Animal and Deity of the Woods. Beneath these, or encompassing them, is the "monomyth": the journey of the hero, the night journey of provisional regression or descent to the deepest sources of being, a journey that regularly depends at some point on the assistance of a primitive guide. The myth appears in very pure form in Part One, as Ike one by one relinquishes his man-made aids: the gun, the watch, the compass. It is only then, taintless, freed of direction and chronological time, lost, he can see and be seen by the bear. He is now altogether "on his own": a pure experience of recognition. But the study of the ledgers in Part Four is also a dark journey, a discovery of one's social inheritance, to which adjustment must be made.

The Bear thus embodies (in contrast to a mimetic *Bildungsroman*) both a world of actual mysterious connections and a patterning by an author conscious of mythical formulas and using deliberately the language of ritual: *novitiate, initiation, pageant-rite.* There are, in addition, a series of logical connections between the hunting story and the story of education through reading the ledgers: most obviously the need to *relinquish*—relinquish completely to the wilderness through the abandonment of artificial aids, and relinquish a material inheritance tainted by slavery. Faulkner, though given as much as other American writers of his time to anti-intellectual pronouncements, was strongly attracted by patterns and polarities, by elaborate structurings of plot, by the orderings of symbol, allegory, myth.

Dickens, Dostoevsky and Faulkner exhibit melodramatic imaginations in their most serious, most ambitious novels. The imaginations are energized by looking forward, hundreds of pages it may be, to physical catastrophes (collapsing houses, fires, murders, suicides), though these are sometimes undertreated when their time at last comes. All three notoriously enjoy concealment and delay, and that *escamotage de l'essentiel* which is also the classic response of their characters to disreputable secrets or personal guilt. Dickens's world is one of crucial family relationships kept hidden, of misalliances, of altered or lost wills and lost identities. The actual murder of old Fyodor Karamazov, and the identity of the murderer, are withheld for hundreds of pages. The very act of withholding, the complicated structural processes of retention and evasion, appear to have been energizing for Faulkner. There was, one suspects, imaginative excitement in knowing, as one's readers did not, the secret of Thomas Sutpen and Eulalia Bon.

To delay or evade revelation is one imaginative act; to avoid dramatizing the crucial event is another. Dickens did take us onto the scene of several murders, and in later years could not leave poor Nancy alone, to the astonishment of his listeners: "The murderer staggering backward to the wall, and shutting out the sight with his hand, seized a heavy club and struck her down." Dickens liked to prepare for murder through pages of portentous atmosphere, as with the murders of Tulkinghorn and Tigg. One of the most macabre configurations in Dostoevsky is muted, the murder of the mother in *Netochka Nezvanova.* But Raskolnikov's murder of the pawnbroker, including its preparation and immediate aftermath, is as dramatic as any in Dickens, though less excited in narration. Faulkner scrupulously evades the rape of Temple and the two murders of *Sanctuary,* and both delays and evades the murder of Charles Bon. But he dramatizes with harrowing intensity the aftermath of Mink Snopes's murder of Houston in *The Hamlet.*

All three novelists dramatized crimes or dark secrets in menaced houses, houses eventually gutted by fire or that collapse and suffocate. Little Nell's house, in the finally achieved place of refuge, is really a tomb, but so too is Miss Havisham's. The return of the elder Rudge to the scene of his crime after so many years, the great house gutted by fire, reminds us that we know nothing of Henry Sutpen during the forty-one years between his killing of Bon and his return to the house Clytie at last sets on fire. The house and the adjacent bathhouse of *The Brothers Karamazov* were doubtless essential to Dostoevsky's dreaming of the story, though as usual he gives relatively little detail. But Rogozhin's gloomy house in *The Idiot,* with its Skoptsy castrates on the ground floor, seems altogether appropriate for the murder of Nastasya, as her drab flat and the staircase leading to it for the murder of the pawnbroker. The Old Frenchman's Place, which reaches back to misty early legend of the region, may have had a particular value for Faulkner in his imagining of *Sanctuary.* For all three writers, imagination had visible reality to work upon: the shored-up waterside tenements of Dickens's London; the wooden houses near the hospital of Dostoevsky's childhood; the decayed great mansions of Lafayette County, some occupied by negroes.

Three major psychological novels with misalliances kept secret and dead bodies in collapsed or burning houses—*Little Dorrit, The Possessed, Light in August*—suggest striking kinships of macabre imagination as well as important divergences. A typology of names (an element often overstressed by critics) is present in all three: Tite Barnacle, Merdle and the dour Flintwinch as destructive forces in the administrative, business and private worlds; Stavrogin carrying his cross and Marya his probably virgin wife and intuitive Holy Fool; Lena Grove and Joanna Burden in antithetic worlds, and Hightower withdrawn from life. The ironic overtones of Joe Christmas's name and history, as he fulfills an inescapable destiny, is *Light in August*'s most obvious approach to symbolic pattern. The brilliantly "realistic" disrupted governesses' benefit, in *The Possessed,* is an unobtrusive microcosm of disorder and latent violence in a transitional society. Dickens's procedure is, as usual, more insistent. The Marshalsea prison is the focal center of a novel dealing with bureaucratic confusion and delay, but also with the imprisonments of inhibition, repression and fear, of neurotic self-destructiveness. Certain plot connections might suggest that Faulkner was influenced by both of the earlier novels. Mrs. Clennam feels herself divinely appointed to watch over Arthur the child of sin as Doc Hines to watch over Joe Christmas "the Lord's abomination." Marya Lebyadkin, Stavrogin's wife, is found stabbed to death in a house that failed to burn down; Joanna with her throat cut, some hours before her house has burned to the ground.

The impressive violences of the last installment of *Little Dorrit* (especially chapters XXX, XXXI) follow upon one of Dickens's most carefully written novels. And one of the most tediously theatrical, whenever the diabolic Rigaud-Blandois is on the scene. The neurotic Miss Wade, who identifies with the self-thwarting Tattycoram and her feelings of rejection, is a fine "modern" portrait of chronic self-destructiveness; but she occupies relatively few pages. By contrast the picture of the repressed, passive, prematurely aged Arthur Clennam, victim of a stunted childhood, is harrowingly monotonous. He had been brought up in "fear and trembling." So too was his father, " 'in a starved house, where rioting and gaiety were unknown' "; so too his supposed mother Mrs. Clennam, instructed in " 'the curse that is upon us' " and filled " 'with an abhorrence of evil-doers.' " She discovered, within a year of her marriage, that her husband had already been through a " 'desecrated ceremony of marriage' " with a woman of artistic temperament, a singer; and Arthur is the child of that sin. The mysterious connections that link Mrs. Clennam to Little Dorrit, and the history of a suppressed codicil to a will, are characteristically elaborate. They depend on the servant Flintwinch having a twin brother and on the fact that Mrs. Clennam has been paralyzed for years, fixed on "her black bier-like sofa, propped up by her black angular bolster that was like the headsman's block.'' The ghostly creakings (thought by Mrs. Flintwinch to be the sounds of Arthur's mother, once sheltered or hidden there) prove to be those of a house literally undermined, presumably by termites, and subject to periodic slippages. The house collapses totally, crushing the blackmailer Blandois to death. Prior to this Mrs. Clennam has preternaturally risen from the paralysis of years: her hand stirring astonishingly, then staggering to her feet, then rushing madly through the streets to the Marshalsea.

These dark happenings and occult suggestions doubtless gave Dickens much pleasure. But they are linked with one of the most energized characterizations in his work, that of the puritanic Mrs. Clennam, with her iron will and always powerful dialogue. Her physical recovery is made to seem the consequence of breaking at last through secrecy, fierce repression, rigidity: a control maintained, in the gloomy house, for over forty years. Through her narrative, screened as they might have been in Faulkner, we distantly discern the several tragedies: Arthur's father compelled into an unhappy marriage by a stern uncle; his mother forced to give up her child; the presence of Arthur " 'a daily reproach to his father' '' and his absence a " 'daily agony to his mother' ''; the boy brought up " 'in a life of practical contrition for the sins that were heavy on his head before his entrance into this condemned world.' '' None of these horrors is exploited sentimentally or at length; they are left to the reader's imagination, as he rereads, or casts back over the events.

The secret of this rather surprising restraint would seem to lie, paradoxically, in the overwhelming power of Mrs. Clennam's personality and the evangelical or Biblical rhythms of her voice. It is simply in her character to pass over with appalling swiftness the sufferings she has caused, since she thinks those sufferings deserved. In her world even a legitimate alliance with an artist—e.g., a singer taught by the dissolute Frederick Dorrit—would be depraved. She sincerely thinks herself the instrument of the Lord, aware of the curse for forty years as Doc Hines for thirty-six. Perhaps she was even sincere in withholding a codicil that seemed to reward, however indirectly, sin. The voice, in any event, is one of the most convincing of the very audacious ones in Dickens. Its power, in this like Miss Rosa's in *Absalom, Absalom!,* partly derives from the way passion is subject to the management of elaborate syntax. The outpouring of rage remains under control of the iron will, which can pause to make parenthetical asides, themselves enraged:

"When she pleaded to me her youth, and his wretched and hard life (that was her phrase for the virtuous training he had belied), and the desecrated ceremony of marriage there had secretly been between them, and the terrors of want and shame that had overwhelmed them both, when I was first appointed to be the instrument of their punishment, and the love (for she said the word to me, down at my feet) in which she had abandoned him and left him to me, was it *my* enemy that became my footstool, were they the words of *my* wrath that made her shrink and quiver! Not unto me the strength be ascribed; not unto me the wringing of the expiation!'' [11]

In a world of such intensities perhaps even the collapse of the house, if less well-prepared than the collapse of the animated mine in *Germinal,* has some of its macabre fitness.

The original misalliance in *Light in August* was also with a kind of artist: an employee of the circus, who knew Milly only long enough to leave her with ''the devil's laidby crop.'' The story of horror, more poignant and more detailed than that of Arthur's mother, is filtered effectively by three speakers: Byron Bunch summarizing coolly; Doc Hines in his evangelist babble, cackling of bitchery and abomination, and quoting a vengeful if ungrammatical God; and his wife, herself half-mad after fifty years in his company, and who has waited more than thirty for word of the child Joe. Doc Hines, with the intuition of God's instrument, had '' 'seen the womansign of God's abomination' '' already on Milly '' 'under her clothes.' '' As unerringly as McEachern pursuing Joe to the dance he takes the right shortcut, finds the Mexican seducer in the buggy, shoots him in Milly's presence, brings her home and knocks her down. Presently, instead of going for the doctor, he waits with shotgun on the front porch while Milly is giving birth to Joe. '' 'And I tried to get out the back way,' '' Mrs. Hines remembers, '' 'and he heard me and run around the house with the gun and he hit me with the barrel of it and I went back to Milly and he stood outside the hall door where he could see Milly until she died.' '' Hines, telling his wife nothing, takes the baby to the orphanage where as janitor he can watch him, and hear the other children call him Nigger. '' 'From God's own boiler room he watched them children, and the devil's walking seed unbeknownst among them, polluting the earth with the working of that word on him.' ''

For some reason Hines does not want Joe sent to the negro orphanage and whisks him away. But they are apprehended, and Joe is adopted by the sternly righteous McEachern, himself locked in compulsion, who even while whipping Joe, who is also rapt and calm, has a ''rapt, calm expression like a monk in a picture.'' Hines loses track of him for thirty years, but is on hand in Mottstown when Joe, duly waiting until the Friday after the murder of Joanna Burden, gives himself up. Cursing, ''his old frail bones and his stringlike muscles for the time inherent with the fluid and supple fury of a weasel,'' he strikes the captive. The Hineses go by train to Jefferson, where Christmas has been taken—he to incite to lynching, she to try to deter him. The old woman asks that her grandchild be allowed for just one day to live " 'like it hadn't happened yet.' " Her wish is in a sense granted when, now madly outside time, she takes Lena's baby to be Joe.

The Hines couple (it is hard to conceive of one without the other) may well be the novel's finest creations: pushed only a little beyond a rural southern reality of the time, but that little making, as with Flannery O'Connor, all the difference. The conception of Doc Hines watching Joe, as Mrs. Clennam the child of sin Arthur, was probably a major source of the novel's energy: the dirty furious little man as God's chosen instrument, preaching white supremacy to negroes who support him and believe him mad. His wife too is of her time and place and religion, though she thinks Hines, in the original episode, the agent of the devil not God. But the entire novel's world, except for Lena Grove, is one of rigidities and compulsions, as *Little Dorrit*'s of inhibition and repression. The novel's spatial form regularly presents the causative background history or trauma after the compulsion we have observed in the fictional present. The compulsions of Hightower and Joanna can be traced in part to fanatic ancestors and to childhood experience—he most implausibly controlled by an absurd Civil War exploit, she told the black race is " 'doomed and cursed to be forever and ever a part of the white race's doom and curse for its sins.' " The compulsions of Percy Grimm, moved by the Player, leave him "calm" (often a sinister word in Faulkner) and with the "serene, unearthly luminousness of angels in church windows."

The novel's vision is simply that of people bereft of free will. Compulsion may lead to a rigid compartmentalizing of life; the "sewer" of Joanna's sexuality ran only by night, as she tried to damn "herself forever to the hell of her forefathers, by living not alone in sin but in filth." The solitary compulsive Christmas, flaunting a hypothetical negro identity to provoke the punishment he craves, is one of the most grandly conceived of Faulkner's characters. He is also perhaps the most fully developed "case," presented in familiar Freudian terms.

The psychologies may seem extreme: deliberately larger than life. The macabre ironies, which Faulkner surely relished, are worthy of Hardy. Thus the betrayer Brown-Burch taken into the cabin to collect his reward, and instead finding Lena propped on the pillows. Or Joe Christmas in flight, invading the negro church, and Hightower preaching in an empty church, repudiated by his congregation, after the suicide of his wife. Hightower, interestingly conceived but as stultifying as Arthur Clennam, thinks he has found his safe refuge from disorder and mischance, his only real life a dreaming reenactment of a moment in the historic past. But his house is invaded: by Byron, and his concern for Lena; then by the Hineses and their appalling narrative; at last by Percy Grimm and the other pursuers of Joe Christmas, who will be castrated and killed there.

The scene of Joe Christmas's death is sufficiently intense for any novel's climax, though to some degree distanced by religious allusions and the continuing metaphor of the Player, and by the concluding statement that Joe, by implication like Christ, is to remain "forever and ever" a part of the collective consciousness. But Faulkner's imagination thrives on obfuscation and delay: the notorious withholding. The details of Joe's birth, with the crucial question of negro parentage still uncertain, reach us only after his arrest, and some six thousand words after Doc Hines has left unanswered his wife's question: " 'What did you do with Milly's baby?' " The other event, and the picture that surely had a controlling effect on the imagination—a woman with her throat cut, discovered in a burning house, is tantalizingly put forward, then withdrawn for more than 55,000 words. The first details given are by far the most vivid, but reach us at second hand: the head nearly cut off and smoke in the room, the countryman afraid to pick her up, lest the " 'head might come clean off,' " his carrying her in a bedcover like a sack of meal, only to discover, when the cover fell open, that " 'her head was turned clean around like she was looking behind her.' "

In the next chapter (V) the narration is inside Christmas during the thirty-six hours before the murder, but this timing is by no means apparent at a first reading. *Something is going to happen to me* is the chapter's unpunctuated ending. For the next five chapters (VI–X) we follow the moving story of Joe's growing up, and a brief rendering of his compulsive years following the Street, some 35,000 words, and in XI–XII, some 15,000, his life with Joanna until, a few moments before the murder, she asks him to light the lamp and he replies (as would Wash in *Absalom, Absalom!*) " 'It won't need any light.' " Whatever the burning house meant to Faulkner—and its smoke is seen at the very beginning—his finished novel austerely concerns itself most of all with causality and motive, and with the rigidities of compulsion, rather than with physical violence.

A lame woman and a burning house had long preoccupied Dostoevsky, and his imagination returned again and again to fires and murders in his plans for *The Idiot*. We will examine *The Possessed* in detail, in a later chapter, and Stavrogin's murder by proxy of his wife on the night of the ruined benefit for impoverished governesses. The long disorderly night ends with fires, some set as acts of social protest. But one fire, distinct from the rest, has been set to cover Fedka's murder of Marya Lebyadkin and her brother; the house fails to burn to the ground. This is also the night that Liza, fully conscious she is ruining herself, spends with Stavrogin. In the morning he confesses to her, when the news is brought of the discovered bodies: " 'I did not kill them, and I was against it, but I knew they were going to be killed and I did not stop the murder.' " Liza, rushing to the scene of the crime, is killed by members of the scandalized crowd.

The most striking thing, as we look back to Dickens or ahead to Faulkner, is the underdramatizing of this material. The plight of Stavrogin on the morning after his night with Liza, as he watches the glow of the fires, and presently hears of the murders from Pyotr, might have been as intense as Mrs. Clennam's, as she feels the past closing in. Yet the chapter begins with a quiet bitter conversation between the lovers, whose night may have been a fiasco. Only a few lines suggest that Stavrogin has something to confess. The private event of Stavrogin's crime, as we look at this section of the novel as a whole, is rigidly subordinated to the public event of social disorder. The narrator's attention is focused, at the scene of the fire, and as we approach the moment of discovery, on the comic behavior of the Governor, Lembke, unhinged by the long night of confusion and hysteria. The narrator is interested, but Dostoevsky too, in the collective "exhilarating" effect of a great fire at night, its "challenge to those destructive instincts which, alas, lie hidden in every heart, even that of the mildest and most domestic little clerk." There is a Faulknerian absurdity as Lembke rushes to help an old woman, who has returned to her burning house to save her feather bed, but cannot squeeze it through a broken window pane. A board falling from the roof hits the "unhappy governor" and knocks him unconscious. We are told, without further detail, that the governor was not killed, but that his "career was over, among us at least."

The discovered murder of Stavrogin's wife reaches us through the limited vision of the narrator, who reports briefly what he has heard: that the captain's throat had been cut, and "that his sister Marya Timofeyevna had been 'stabbed all over' with a knife and she was lying on the floor in the doorway, so that probably she had been awake and had fought and struggled with the murderer." So much for the event Dostoevsky had explored and weighed in fantasy, presumably for years. The death of Liza is also relatively undramatized. One long paragraph reports her arrival at the scene of the murder, the indignation of the crowd (for someone has identified her as "Stavrogin's woman"), and the blows that send her to the ground. A single short sentence intimates she will die. The men who struck her, the narrator quietly concludes, were "per-

haps moved by ill-feeling, yet scarcely conscious of what they were doing—
drunk and irresponsible.'' This culminating chapter's finely developed scene is
instead Liza's absurd meeting, as she rushes through the morning mist, with
Stepan Trofimovich, humiliated at the governesses' benefit, and now setting off
on foot to discover Russia.

There are, of course, more dramatic scenes of violence in Dostoevsky: above
all the intensely visualized, slow-paced murder of the pawnbroker and its aftermath in *Crime and Punishment*. But the scenes from *The Possessed* underline
important characteristics of Dostoevsky's imagination and art. His fantasy life,
as suggested by the Notebooks and skeletal outlines of the novels, was as melodramatic as Dickens's or Faulkner's, and as sadistic. He too was attracted by
macabre conjunctions of people and events, and by the extreme pressures—for
concealment and confession, murder and suicide—life may exert. But much of
the dramatic intensity remains *rhetorically unexploited,* muted, in the finished
novels. What we have instead, supremely, are theatrical confrontations in
which personalities violently collide in dialogue, with the ''extreme pressures''
not always immediately evident. So too for ''psychology.'' Nothing is more
genuinely dramatic, more deeply human, than Dostoevsky's groping, in the
Notebooks, toward an understanding of events he has imagined, such as the
murder of a lame woman. But by whom was she killed? Is there some way in
which Stavrogin, though not the actual murderer, could be morally responsible?
The final configurations are psychologically more interesting, truer, than those
of any other novelist. But there is considerably less explicit psychologizing
than in either the Faulkner of *Light in August* or the Dickens of *Little Dorrit*.

2
PARADOXICAL SYMPATHIES

This chapter is concerned not only with the novelist's paradoxical, even un-moral sympathies, but with his power to evoke these in readers. No doubt this will be shocking to the pure critic who demands attention only to the text: "a text and meaning immutable, created by no flesh-and-blood writer and without flesh-and-blood readers in mind." [1] But anxiety about the "affective fallacy" would seem altogether absurd to most serious novelists, who see their art as one of controlling the responses of readers, and not merely of creating formal structures or conveying themes and visions, or creating a new world, or redu-plicating the old one. We may sympathize with Joyce's repudiation of the crudely kinetic, and grudgingly admire the courage and ultimate privacy of *Fin-negans Wake*. And it is true that the expert pornographer and writer of spy thrillers may calculate his readers' responses with unflagging cynicism. But this is simply in another world from that of James's diaries and prefaces, of Flau-bert's letters and scenarios, of Conrad's revisions and agonizing search for the telling phrase. All three were minutely concerned with the power over readers of complex structure, of the rhythms of plot, of the timing of appeals to close reader-identification. Dickens, Dostoevsky and Faulkner are more wayward than they, and often more tolerant of what the unconscious may urge. But Dos-toevsky's Notebooks are repeatedly concerned with what readers may be made to believe, feel, see; with how much a narrator must be allowed to know or reveal, and how much motivation must be left in shadow. And even Faulkner, the difficult and private esoteric artist, often shows a paragraph-by-paragraph concern—perhaps not wholly conscious—with the reader's responses.

The concept of paradoxical sympathy by definition implies a conflict with intellectual conviction or moral judgment. I appear to have insisted earlier and more continuously than any other critic on the intensifying value, in fiction, of a conflict between sympathy and judgment. Wayne Booth's *The Rhetoric of Fiction* (1961) offers a valuable discussion of the conflict, but Booth ultimately rebels against unexpected sympathies carried so far as to seem perverse. I suggested in *Thomas Hardy* (1949) that the fiction was enriched by a conflict of which Hardy was not fully aware: a moral judgment in favor of freedom, audacity, rebellion; an imaginative sympathy with the passive, withdrawn, unfree. In *André Gide* (1951) I was concerned with a writer who was fully aware of such chess-games of the spirit. I developed the concept of sympathy and judgment in desirable conflict most fully in *Conrad the Novelist* (1958), particularly in the two chapters on *Lord Jim*. For now I was dealing with a great artist who, dramatizing the conflict in Marlow and to some extent experiencing it himself, very deliberately induced it in readers. The conflict was exquisitely controlled by technique: by Marlow's own hesitations, by the massing of witnesses and the timing of evidence, by imagery and the rhythms of sentence, paragraph, scene.

I find these complexities pleasing in their own right, and as configurations of a "fine art." But they can also mean increasing the reader's capacity for humane sympathies generally by inducing him to see *more,* and to see human impulses and difficulties in new ways. François Mauriac, exasperated at last by the extremes of Gide's iconoclasm, and by the games he played with good Catholics hoping for his conversion, speculated that his old antagonist was indeed possessed by the devil. Yet no one has put more succinctly than Mauriac the moral "task" of the serious novelist: to expose the weaknesses of the good and great of the earth, but also to "discover the hidden sources of sanctity in those who appear to have failed."

Every serious novelist is aware of the difficulty of creating, in fiction, a "positively good" man or woman . . . i.e., whose intelligence, generosity and high moral ideals do not become unreal or repugnant. Dostoevsky, desperately conceiving Myshkin, commented on the value of comedy, and pointed to two great Christian models: Don Quixote and Pickwick. In fact both Dostoevsky's feelings and his judgments regarding Myshkin remained irresolute to the end. Each of our novelists did create one (and only one) character for whom strong moral approval and intense unfeigned sympathy coincide: Pickwick, Father Zossima,

Dilsey. All three, on the other hand, developed a degree of sympathy for a number of personages we would, in real life, repudiate or find repulsive. The conditions of sympathy in fiction are, simply, not those of this "real life." Sheer brute vitality, disagreeable in the flesh, brings energy to the printed page. Jonas Chuzzlewit, Fyodor Karamazov, even Jason Compson are less repulsive to us, at our safe distance, than to the abused wives of the first two and the abused niece of the last, or to their enduring retainers Chuffey, old Grigory, Dilsey. This is true first of all of physical presence. We meet Jonas in the company of his father, whose wariness and cunning "seemed to cut him a passage through the crowded room," the son looking "a year or two the elder of the twain as they stood winking their red eyes, side by side, and whispering to each other softly." The artful composition of our first view of old Fyodor, its very insistences, creates aesthetic distance: the long fleshy bags under his eyes, the Adam's apple that "hung below his sharp chin like a great fleshy goitre," the "long rapacious mouth with full lips, between which could be seen little stumps of black decayed teeth." A final disagreeable detail—"He slobbered every time he began to speak"—is quickly neutralized by the old man's sense of humor. His goitre, he used to say, gave him "quite the countenance of an ancient Roman patrician of the decadent period."

Blunt sincerity, even if it be ruthless and sardonic, lends fictional life in a world of good manners, inhibitions, hypocrisies. The openness of Jonas's wishing for his father's death is vitalizing, in the early chapters, since it is kept at a safe distance by Dickens's humor and by his own, which is very kin to Jason Compson's: " '. . . why don't you make over your property? Buy an annuity cheap and make your life interesting to yourself and everybody else that watches the speculation.' " Jonas is as open in his desire for a little fun in the stagecoach ("Don't mind crowding me . . . I like to be crowded by gals"), and in acknowledging his penny-pinching smartness, and in cutting through Pecksniff's hypocrisies. The game he plays with the Pecksniff sisters is a cruel one, but proceeds from a fierce sense of humor: holding the presumably intended fiancée with one arm while proposing to the other. The engagement with Merry would seem to promise, at worst, a taming of the shrew battle of lively wits in an environment of the living dead. In fact Jonas revenges himself for her playfulness with a malice that has turned very somber; his sense of humor has been largely lost. Dickens's perhaps involuntary sympathy for Jonas in his rough vitality is finally overwhelmed by a reasoned disgust. Yet some of that sympathy returns in the last days of his life, as we are kept very close to his tormented consciousness.

The fictional vitality of old Fyodor is even more intense, and the conception of his character far more complex. He himself recognizes that his buffoonery has depths, even an element of self-laceration. Father Zossima, who understands everyone, urges him " 'not to be so ashamed of yourself, for that is at the root of it all.' " He can act the role of one suffering from loss of faith, playfully accusing Miusov of corrupting him, yet be genuinely disturbed by the vacancy of a world that would fail to punish him; he protests too much that this is the only life we have. But it is his incorrigible, blasphemous sense of humor that charges the monastery scene with life. He begins to babble nonsense at once, on meeting Father Zossima, and attributes his buffoonery to " 'a devil within me. But only a little one. A more serious one would have chosen another lodging.' " Admonished to be his natural self, he pretends to be brimming over with ecstasy: " 'Blessed be the womb that bore thee, and the paps that gave thee suck—the paps especially.' " He succeeds in outraging everyone, even in a moment of pretended contrition: " 'Of a truth, I am a lie, and the father of lies. Though I believe I am not the father of lies. I am getting mixed in my texts. Say, the son of lies, and that will be enough.' "

The evidence for an adverse, wholly alienating judgment is skillfully controlled. We experience the barbarousness of his behavior toward his second wife only through very brief summary, and through his own drunken acknowledgment. We see him at his worst, it may be, in his exchanges with Ivan and Alyosha, whom he sporadically respects and loves. He suggests they go together to have a look at Mokroe girls being thrashed, preaches the attractions of *vieilles filles* and young girls alike, and admits having spat on his second wife's holy image, when exasperated by her prayers. Yet he is humanized for the reader by his sottish affection for Alyosha, and even by the drunken after-dinner confabulation, with Smerdyakov and Grigory in attendance. There are times, "very subtle and complicated ones," when he has a craving for someone "faithful and devoted." He is seized in moments of drunkenness by "superstitious terror and a moral convulsion," and is glad to have Grigory near at hand.

And he is lent vitality, of course, by his frank and incorrigible sensuality. He is unequivocal in putting it, at fifty-five, at the center of his values, and intends this to be so for another twenty years. In him, excitedly, Mochulsky sees "the soul of the ancient pagan world, a cosmic force, the irresistible element of sex." "The enormous 'Karamazov' force of life has in Fyodor Pavlovich passed into lust and debauchery; but, however stifled it is by this base element, its nature remains spiritual and creative. The sensualist condemns himself and *thirsts for justice.*" [2] This is, surely, to over-intellectualize. And the openness of his lust, unsubduable to the end, would doubtless arouse less sympathy in real life, experienced at close range. But there is appalling vitality in the fiction, as Dmitri sees Fyodor for the last time, almost climbing out of the window as he peers into the darkness, waiting for Grushenka—"his pendant Adam's apple, his hooked nose, his lips that smiled in greedy expectation."

Jason Compson has no little in common with the Jonas Chuzzlewit we finally come to know: a penny-pinching meanness, a psychic cruelty that can turn to physical violence, a sardonic humor that cuts through genteel pretenses: a gross unrelenting vitality. His section in *The Sound and the Fury* is a high triumph of social realism. For this not so minor devil is also, in his public attitudes (as toward negroes and "eastern Jews"), an appallingly persuasive example of a small-town businessman of his time. The petty tyrant at home, unrelievedly vicious, is the same seething and mean creature at the store, and as he roams about Jefferson. But downtown he shares Main Street prejudices and falls into its clichés. Yet here too his sense of humor, his quick play of mind, his extreme cynicism lend him an extraordinary vitality.

The normal reader presumably experiences less grudging sympathy than a cool fascination, if only with the perfection of the portrait. We are, for one thing, exposed not to criminal impulses of the highest magnitude, but rather to petty cheating and blackmail, to mean not grand cruelties. We are, moreover, trapped within an interior monologue that uses no distancing Faulknerian language and that holds us the more closely because of its use of the present tense. How essential the outside view is, at least for any sympathy for Jason, becomes evident with the final section and Faulkner's own narration. Now we see Jason for the first time from the outside: "cold and shrewd, with close thatched brown hair curled into two stubborn hooks, one on either side of his forehead like a bartender in caricature, and hazel eyes with black-ringed irises like marbles": a moment not unworthy of the Chuzzlewit winking red eyes or old Fyodor's stumps of decayed teeth. A certain dramatic sympathy develops for him, in his absurd pursuit of the thieves to the traveling show's gaudy pullman cars, where the fierce old man goes after him with a hatchet. At last both the narrator and Mottson passersby can see a Jason rendered for the moment truly helpless, and we hear the familiar sympathetic accents of Faulknerian commentary: "Some looked at him as they passed, at the man sitting quietly behind the wheel of a small car, with his invisible life ravelled out about him like a worn-out sock."

Dickens was intellectually much less complex than Dostoevsky or even Faulkner, and though he had his rebellious side, would doubtless have been baffled or disgusted by Flaubert's and Gide's conscious efforts to demoralize: "Je veux être démoralisateur.'' So too he might have been repelled by the irresolutions of *Lord Jim* and *Absalom, Absalom!* A novel's penultimate chapter, he would argue, should make its clear discriminations between the evil and the good; when all is known, moral uncertainties cease to exist.

But Dickens was a great writer, presiding uneasily over a rich fantasy life, and so at least occasionally on the devil's side.[3] His judgment of his murderers is unequivocal, but there is no little sympathy (some of it doubtless involuntary) in the intensely imagined aftermaths of their crimes—Bill Sikes wandering in the suburbs and circling back to his death, followed by his dog; or Jonas Chuzzlewit dreading to go back to his room, then pausing on the brink of suicide; or Bradley Headstone condemned to return to the schoolroom and his factitious daytime personality, there to be badgered by Riderhood. But these sympathies do not compare with Dostoevsky's for Raskolnikov or Faulkner's for Mink Snopes. Dickens's special gift was for creating "evil" beings—extraordinarily selfish or aggressive—who seem to belong to a different order of humanity from their victims, and who are therefore exempt from ordinary moral judgments. They are great *fictive* creations: not "copied from life," whatever Dickens may claim, possessed of preternatural energy, and long impervious to the restrictions of contingency and law: Quilp and Fagin obviously, Sairey Gamp (surely "beyond good and evil"), Hannibal Chollop the American outlaw, even Riderhood and Silas Wegg. They seem generically different from the ordinary Dickens eccentric, with his one or two obsessions and tricks of speech. They are not, it must be repeated, experienced as they would be in real life. Quilp's language and comic energies divert attention from "the few discoloured fangs that were yet scattered in his mouth." Gissing remarked that "we should shrink disgusted," meeting Mrs. Gamp in the flesh, "so well does the foulness of her person correspond with the baseness of her mind," [4] and noted, we have seen, Dickens's art of omission. Yet not a great deal is really omitted: not the moist white of eye remarkably turned up, nor the black gown "rather the worse for snuff," nor the smell of spirits. But we do not experience these as directly as we experience her first real speech: " 'Ah dear! When Gamp was summoned to his long home, and I see him a-lying in Guy's Hospital with a penny-piece on each eye, and his wooden leg under his left arm, I thought I should have fainted away. But I bore up.' "

An extreme though minor case is the murderous Hannibal Chollop, whom young Martin Chuzzlewit and Mark Tapley encounter in Eden. Dickens's disgust for much less violent advocates of lynch law and slavery is recorded in *American Notes*. Chollop travels with a brace of revolvers, with sword-stick and great knife, and has shot, stabbed and gouged out eyes. Yet he seems as harmless as Stephen Crane's Scratchy Wilson. The sword-stick he calls his "Tickler," the knife "Ripper," and our first distinct impression is of his pride in his capacity to calculate the distance of his spitting. Above all he exists through the quick responses of his fierce patriotism: " 'We are the intellect and virtue of the airth, the cream Of human natur', and the flower Of moral force. Our backs is easy ris. We must be cracked-up, or they rises, and we snarls. We shows our teeth, I tell you, fierce. You'd better crack us up, you had!' "

The most remarkable instance of an anti-realist creation at least partly exempt from ordinary moral judgment is to be found in the fairy-story world of *The Old Curiosity Shop:* Daniel Quilp. His sexual puissance is real, as his wife helplessly acknowledges to her friends who urge rebellion. So too is his sexual threat for Little Nell, though hardly felt by the reader, for whom it is comically overt and undisplaced. He is, some critics have somberly insisted, a powerful image of life force and brutal undeviating *Id*. But surely he is above all a creation of grotesque comic energy and violence, the violence largely neutralized by his fierce sense of humor and his language. His cigars kept alit all night, while his wife cowers patiently nearby, are followed by the famous breakfast, as he "ate hard eggs, shell and all, devoured giant prawns with the heads and tails on, chewed tobacco and water-cresses at the same time and with extraordinary greediness, drank boiling tea without winking, bit his fork and spoon until they bent again. . . ." Small wonder such a being must have his private bachelor's place to retire to, where the minute hand of an eight-day clock has been twisted off for a toothpick.

Quilp is no more a real menace, through most of the novel, than Rumpelstiltskin. Envisioning a triumph over Swiveller he withdraws to throw himself upon the ground, "actually screamed and rolled about in uncontrollable delight." At least one of his pleasures, pinching, has a childish charm. Thus his insistence that his wife precede him. "Mr. Swiveller, who was not in on the secret, was a little surprised to hear a suppressed scream, and, looking around, to see Mrs. Quilp following him with a sudden jerk. . . ." Quilp's malice is comic as he flourishes his cudgel, urging on the wrestling boys, or as he forces a fiery Schiedam on Swiveller, boiling rum on Sampson Brass. He is marvelously in control during the cribbage game, instructing his partner with kicks yet alert to thwart his mother-in-law's efforts to taste the liquor he compels her to serve. There would seem an unsubduable *joie de vivre* and disinterested sense of fun in his terrorizing of Kit's mother from his place on the coach's roof, "hanging over the side of the coach at the risk of his life, and staring in with his great goggle eyes. . . ." Thus exempt from the laws of gravity, and his tongue lolling as no one's ever has, Quilp is a very pure example of an anti-realist creation who is yet more intensely alive, more plausibly "real," than anyone else. Did Dickens intend that we so suspend moral judgment for many pages, while we contemplate Quilp as we contemplate the giants of Rabelais? He noted his regret at having to write Quilp's last appearance "on any stage."

Faulkner is a great compassionate writer, especially in *Go Down, Moses, The Sound and the Fury* and *Light in August,* as well as a tiresomely sentimental one when Gavin Stevens becomes his spokesman, or the insufferable Chick Mallison. The direct unpatronizing evocation of negro life and mentality, with Dilsey or in such a story as "Pantaloon in Black," has a truth and dignity that Dickens rarely achieved. But also, perhaps more than any major novelist, Faulkner loved outrageous paradox, and set himself extreme rhetorical challenges—to create sympathy for the somber Joe Christmas and Thomas Sutpen at the very moment we have been exposed to their most unpleasant qualities; and, even more striking, to create intense sympathy for Mink Snopes both immediately after he kills Houston in *The Hamlet* and as, in *The Mansion,* he methodically prepares to commit this murder and (after more than forty years of obsessed waiting) the murder of Flem.

We will look, in a later chapter, at the place the murder of Houston takes in the finely balanced structure of *The Hamlet.* The murder occurs immediately following the intensely sympathetic picture of the lonely Houston, bereft of his new wife, and dying at thirty-three. Two modulative paragraphs, with Mink's already abstract view of his plight further abstracted by authorial distance, then take him "home," e.g. to the poverty and discord that are all he has to show for his life:

> It was dusk. He emerged from the bottom and looked up the slope of his meagre and sorry corn and saw it—the paintless two-room cabin with an open hallway between it and a lean-to kitchen, which was not his, on which he paid rent but not taxes, paying almost as much in rent in one year as the house had cost to build; not old, yet the roof of which already leaked and the weather-stripping had already begun to rot away from the wall planks and which was just like the one he had been born in which had not belonged to his father either, and just like the one he would die in if he died indoors. . . .[5]

The two children, seeing him, scuttle toward the house; the wife will be waiting who had watched him, eight hours before, oiling the gun. Here too, both within Mink's consciousness and without, Faulkner sympathetically evokes the extreme poverty. For he has had to oil the gun "with the bacon-drippings which was the only thing he owned that could be used for oil, which would not lubricate but in contact with the metal would congeal into a substance like soap. . . ." His wife greets him with the statement she is leaving him, but intends to be there to see him hung. He moves toward her (whose bleached hair is "darkening again at the roots since it had been a year now since there had been any money to buy more dye") and strikes her across the mouth. She and the children are soon gone, taking with them "the single pair of half-size shoes which either child wore indiscriminately in cold weather, the cracked handglass, the wooden comb, the handleless brush," a single improvised toy. But even now, in extreme paradox, the narrative's sympathy is focused on Mink, and the fact that he no longer has a cleaning rod for the gun.

> But the rod was gone now, he did not remember when nor know where, vanished along with the other accumulations of his maturity which had been dear to him too once, which he had shed somehow and somewhere along the road between the attaining of manhood and this hour when he found himself with nothing but an empty and foodless house. . . .[6]

At the end of this paragraph he hears for the first time Houston's hound, which will lead him back to the corpse, and his harrowing struggles with it, and ultimately to his arrest. The narratives of Sikes's sufferings, and Jonas Chuzzlewit's and Bradley Headstone's, seem by comparison at once over-excited and bare.

Faulkner returned to the murder of Houston fifteen years later, in *The Mansion*. Was this an effort to justify the earlier sympathy, or to meet the same appalling challenge again, or, simply, the need to circle once more in imagination one of his greatest creations? This time Faulkner makes his task the more difficult by first exposing us directly to Mink's consciousness, which is even more vulgar than Jason Compson's. To revenge himself against Houston's arrogance and vindictive legalism (to which there had been only the briefest allusion in *The Hamlet*) is also to fight back, on pride and principle, against "They": the Haves. Mink, as rigidly abstract as any Faulkner obsessive, is determined to fulfill Houston's demands to the letter before going to Jefferson to buy shells with which to shoot him.

But it is precisely on this murderous expedition that Mink again makes his intense demand on our sympathy. As the untempted tourists at the Marabar House create sympathy for Lord Jim, so here "the young men and girls in their city clothes" at the soda fountain, and those at the picture-show (which Mink momentarily glimpses through a crack in the fence), and the old people on rocking chairs in the cool dark of the yards, and the drummers in the leather chairs in front of the Holston House hotel. Mink would have liked to have seen one of Jefferson's two automobiles, but for entertainment goes to the depot, where by spending the night he can see several trains. And he does see one passenger train, "the baggage and day coaches then the dining car and the cars in which people slept while they rode." The memory is vividly with him, forty years later, this time on his way to murder Flem: "a long airtight chunk of another world dragged along the dark earth for the poor folks in overalls like him to gape at free for a moment without the train itself, let alone the folks in it, even knowing he was there." And so he waits to see a train again, not knowing there has been no passenger train through Jefferson since 1935.

The Mink who saw that earlier train, "sleepless and more or less foodless too for going on twenty-two hours now" looked "as forlorn and defenseless as a child, a boy." The Mink who emerges from the penitentiary, to commit a murder as principled as Raskolnikov's, is a bewildered old man. There is one moment of altogether Dickensian tenderness. A memory of the land "gold and crimson with hickory and gum and oak and maple" evokes the novel's single remembered moment of Mink's childhood, and the squirrel he had killed for the sick stepmother who could no longer stomach "the fatback, the coarse meal, the molasses which as far as he knew was the only food all people ate except when they could catch or kill something else. . . ." *Tout comprendre, tout pardonner.* Such is the narrative's sympathy for Mink, disoriented in an absurd Memphis where forty-four years before he went to a brothel (of which, though he does not know this, his daughter is now the madam), that the reader may be outraged to see him cheated at the pawn-shop, and sold a pistol that will probably not fire. The entire narrative, from the departure from Parchman to Mink's surrender to the enveloping earth, is one of Faulkner's most flawless blends of comedy and pathos.

The subtle balancing of sympathy and judgment, with Joe Christmas and especially Thomas Sutpen, involves overall structure. But the precise placing of the most obvious appeals for sympathy suggests, once again, a delight in doing things the hardest way. In the fourth chapter of *Light in August* we have had our one close view of Joanna Burden dead; in the fifth we are, even more intimately than in *Crime and Punishment,* inside the murderer's mind. The reader is exposed very directly—without, that is, the sympathetic commentary that controls our feelings for Mink—to a solitary life of unrelieved brutality, mental confusion, neurotic ritual action, compulsion, racial hatred, fear. We see Joe strike repeatedly the drunken Brown with his flat hand; are told that he would sometimes waken Joanna, when he desired her, "with his hard brutal hand," this before "she got too old to be any good any more." His most articulate resentment—the motive for the murder, if any one motive is to be found—is that she has begun to pray for him: one more way, we will later see, in which the soft enveloping feminine world threatens his identity. The misogyny, in this early chapter, is specifically sexual; Joe seems to watch his body "turning slow and lascivious in a whispering of gutter filth like a drowned corpse in a thick still black pool of more than water." Joe's last action of the chapter, prior to moving toward Joanna's house and the murder, is to pick a quarrel with negroes. Only once, in this somber chapter, is there a compassionate glimpse of a life Joe thinks he might have wanted: four white people sitting at a card table on a lighted veranda. " 'That's all I wanted,' he thought. 'That don't seem like a whole lot to ask.' " But the chapter ends in the murderous compulsion: *"Something is going to happen. Something is going to happen to me"*

At this point *Light in August* turns to the five-year-old Joe in the orphanage, and for some 35,000 words (chapters VI-X) evokes with intense sympathy his iron deprived childhood and the traumatic incidents that created his compulsions. The authorial consciousness and language now come more fully into play, as with Joe's earliest memory of the orphanage, "set in a grassless cinderstrewnpacked compound surrounded by smoking factory purlieus and enclosed by a ten foot steel-and-wire fence like a penitentiary or a zoo. . . ." The transition from Joe on the brink of murder to Joe as helpless innocent is accomplished with fine tact by exposing us first to another world of compulsion (Joe's uncontrollable ingestion of the toothpaste), of frenzy and fanaticism (the dietician's colloquy with Doc Hines), of gratuitous disruption of the moral world (as he finds himself rewarded with a silver dollar rather than punished for eating the toothpaste). We remain to some extent outside Joe through much of the first 5000 words, before experiencing directly his confusion as he is awakened in the dark and cold, to be taken away by a man he knows has watched him with "a profound and unflagging attention." But Hines's kidnapping is thwarted, and Joe's adoption by McEachern arranged. "Thus the promissory note which he had signed with a tube of toothpaste on that afternoon two months ago was recalled, the yet oblivious executor of it sitting wrapped in a clean horse blanket, small, shapeless, immobile, on the seat of a light buggy jolting through the December twilight up a frozen and rutted lane." The rest of the story, until Joe takes up his rigid and wracking life with Joanna Burden, is almost totally free of sentimentality. But it is, even in its darkest moments of misogynous and racial rage, intensely sympathetic.

The challenge faced with Sutpen in *Absalom, Absalom!* might seem, in bare summary, as difficult. But it is, after all, only one of that novel's infinitely complex balancings of sympathy and judgment. The central audacity is that the novel's major appeal to sympathetic understanding for Sutpen—the story of his childhood, the shock of his "innocence" confronted by Tidewater caste and class, the trauma of being told to go to the back door, the commitment to his "design"—is framed by a story of extreme inhumanity: the hunting down of the runaway French architect with dogs and wild negroes, whiskey and champagne. It is precisely at this point that he begins to tell his story to General Compson, much of it filtered through Quentin's rich contemplative language, and through General Compson's, and by Faulkner's overriding consciousness. The story is one of volitionless descent from the classless frontier mountains, into a society that could look upon his family " 'as cattle, creatures heavy and without grace, brutely evacuated into a world without hope or purpose for them, who would in turn spawn with brutish and vicious prolixity. . . .' " The child, insulted by the negro at the front door, retreats to an archetypal cave, a first step in the formation of his design. To " 'combat them you have got to have what they have that made them do what the man did. You got to have land and niggers and a fine house to combat them with.' " And so, at fourteen, he goes to the West Indies.

It is here (Sutpen sitting with General Compson on a log as he talks) that we return suddenly to the hunting of the architect, and the faulting of the dogs, who have found a sapling pole with suspenders still knotted about one. The brief episode undercuts the seriousness of Sutpen's story, but with fabulous humor and extravagance rather than any real sense of cruelty. For the architect has used his professional knowledge and moved with the ease of Tarzan: " 'had chosen that tree and hauled that pole up after him and calculated stress and distance and trajectory and had crossed a gap to the next nearest tree that a flying squirrel could not have crossed and traveled from there on from tree to tree for almost half a mile before he put foot on the ground again.' " When Sutpen's story is resumed we have a first brief glimpse of the cold abstractness of the design: that he had to put his first wife aside because she " ' "could never be, through no fault of her own, adjunctive or incremental" ' " to it. The evocation of the ambiguous Haitian experience, after another brief reference to the hunt, is enriched by Grandfather's poetic evocation of the " 'little island set in a smiling and fury-lurked and incredible indigo sea,' " its " 'soil manured with black blood from two hundred years of oppression and exploitation' ": a dark reminder of one of the novel's great themes. But Sutpen's unboasting story of an altogether mythical courage and power, in putting down a slave rebellion, and his engagement to the woman he must presently put aside, is here interrupted by the culmination of the architect hunt. The " 'little harried wild-faced man' " comes out of his cave " 'fighting like a wildcat,' " makes a long and by implication heroic speech in French, "the eyes desperate and hopeless but indomitable too, invincible too," and at last accepts the bottle of whiskey Grandfather proffers. The moment, like a number of other *beaux gestes* in Faulkner, may well belong to the "probable impossible." But it serves, in its fabulous quality, to intensify with a Shakespearean audacity the serious biographical narrative we have just left and to which we will now return.

Dostoevsky's dramatic sympathy for his created world, even for his fools and scoundrels, is the most Shakespearean of his qualities.[7] He can take us movingly through the last hours of Kirillov, a deranged saintly atheist, and the last hours of Stepan Verkhovensky, who has seen the truth and is saved, but also through those of Svidrigaïlov, in despair and irrevocably damned. No writer has entered more sympathetically into the minds of the insulted and the injured, the criminal and the outcast. The drunken Lebyadkin and Marmeladov, ruining the lives about them, can rise to spiritual eloquence; so too the murderer Fedka. For some pages (and not only when sharing his ridicule of Karmazinov-Turgenev) Dostoevsky *became* Pyotr Verkhovensky, whose comic energies had developed to the author's surprise.

In this Dostoevsky is to be distinguished from Dickens, who stayed well outside a number of his minor villains, and even from Faulkner, who at least stayed outside Flem Snopes. But Dostoevsky's special form of paradoxical sympathy consisted of imaginative fairness to an intellectual antagonist, and to ideas—dechristianized, humanist, socialist, "western"—he had himself repudiated. Dostoevsky could be stridently and unfairly wrong, notably in some of *The Diary of a Writer* editorializing. But the best fiction shows a high intellectual integrity: an ironic obligation, which we see notably in Gide and Camus, to bring out the weakness of one's own position, and the strength of the antagonist's. This is not simply a matter of presenting erroneous ideas lucidly. For personality also controls our feelings. Shatov and Kirillov, in *The Possessed,* are alike tortured by unbelief, as Dostoevsky had been. But the surly Shatov, who shares many of Dostoevsky's hard-won convictions, is less winning than the kindly Kirillov, who madly thinks to substitute himself for God.

A further high integrity, not shared by some of Dostoevsky's Christian interpreters, is to recognize that ideas do not exist in a psychological vacuum, and that a sound moral commitment may have a partly neurotic origin. Dostoevsky shares the speaker's hatred of determinism and the Crystal Palace, in *Notes from Underground,* yet also dramatizes his illusory "freedom" as a circular, involuted self-destructiveness. The greatest mistake the interpreter of Dostoevsky can make is to separate his dialectic, and final Christian and "Russian" solutions, from the flesh-and-blood personages who feel these ideas, and go through their furnaces of doubt. To say that *The Brothers Karamazov* and Dostoevsky fully achieve the position of Father Zossima, and thereby fully "dispose" of Ivan's, is to denigrate one of the greatest of imaginative creations.

The characterization of Ippolit Terentev, the seventeen-year-old dying of consumption in *The Idiot,* offers a fairly complex instance of paradoxical sympathy. He was, like Kirillov, a late importation to his novel, but Dostoevsky for a time regarded him as central. A very late entry in the Notebook dismisses him in a few words: *"the vanity of a weak character."* His personality is disagreeable, though more so to those at Myshkin's birthday party than to the reader at his protected distance. He arrives with the ragged nihilists who are stridently demanding for Burdovsky his illusory rights. He is, like James Wait of *The Nigger of the Narcissus,* a demoralizing, nerve-wracking presence, with his reminders that in a fortnight he will "certainly be underground," and that he wants to make his "farewell to men and to nature." One is reminded of old Singleton's admonition to Wait to get on with his dying; or, as a Notebook entry puts it, with reference to Ippolit's "final decision" to commit suicide, " 'You make too much of a furor about your dying. One can die more nobly.' " [8] The intended suicide, following upon the reading of the Confession, is a fiasco: Ippolit has failed to put in the firing caps. Ganya, enraged, calls him a " 'walking mass of jaundiced spite, who can't even commit suicide without making a mess of it!' "

Ippolit's Confession, *An Essential Explanation,* is nevertheless a moving protest not merely against his personal fate, but against man's condemnation to death generally. Ippolit is momentarily identified with Myshkin as a stranger, an outsider. For in Switzerland Myshkin too felt excluded from the pageant of life. Myshkin has, moreover, evoked eloquently the experience (which was Dostoevsky's own) of the condemned man who believes himself about to be executed. " 'There is the sentence, and the whole torture lies in the fact that there is certainly no escape, and there is no torture in the world more terrible.' " No subject is as important as that of the death penalty, Camus insisted, who long thought himself dying of tuberculosis. Dostoevsky's Notebook, as well as certain passages in *An Essential Explanation,* closely anticipates Kirillov's attitude toward the absurd, and by the same token Camus' reflections in *The Myth of Sisyphus.*

"Since I have only 2 weeks more, telling *the truth* or lying is absolutely the same to me."

. . .

I still have to die, for this is the one thing I can begin and end. I could also kill other men, the idea came into my head because of the false status of executioners and of society.[9]

Dostoevsky, of course, believed Ippolit's protest was "wrong," more unequivocally wrong than Ivan's less egoistic one. Ippolit's narrative is nevertheless vivid and even persuasive, not because of its true or false logic, but because the fumbling distracted *movement of mind,* and its baffled effort to achieve sincerity, is so intensely real. Ippolit breaks through pose and vanity to make a genuine final utterance on man's fate. He sees, with Camus, that it's natural for the man condemned to death " 'to believe that everyone else thinks too little of life and is apt to waste it too cheaply, and to use it too lazily, too shamelessly, that they're none, not one of them, worthy of it.' " But he also argues, as Meursault will in *The Stranger,* that the certainty of death cancels value. Before coming to Pavlosk and its trees he had stared for months at Meyer's wall: an image of the cosmic *néant.* But he does not achieve Meursault's final sense of nature's indifference as benign, nor a Pascalian pride in knowing what the universe cannot know. His revolt seems closer to underground spite than Meursault's healing rage: " 'there is a limit to ignominy in the consciousness of one's own nothingness and impotence beyond which a man cannot go, and beyond which he begins to feel immense satisfaction in his very degradation. . . .' " And why must one accept with humility? " 'Can't I simply be devoured without being expected to praise what devours me?' " His logical conclusion is that the condemned man has a moral right to suicide by way of protest, and as a last assertion of will.

The bare argument would of course be, for Dostoevsky, entirely false. But the discourse—digressive, involuted, intensely self-scrutinizing—has in fact an exceptional authenticity. Like Jean-Baptiste Clamence, Ippolit must reveal an act of mean ignominy, and the egoism latent in a genuine act of benevolence. The reader's involvement is established very early by an extremely vivid and detailed dream: of a scorpion-like reptile, seven inches long and covered with a shell, seemingly possessed of malicious intent. The family dog (who had died five years before) is brought into the room and, although terrified as by something uncanny, takes the reptile in its mouth and cracks the shell. The reptile stings the dog's tongue. " 'Whining and yelping she opened her mouth from the pain, and I saw that the creature, though bitten in two, was still wriggling in her mouth, and was emitting, from its crushed body, on to the dog's tongue, a quantity of white fluid such as comes out of a squashed black-beetle.' " At this point Ippolit woke up. The dream, which for Richard Peace carries an allusion to the scorpion of the Apocalypse,[10] may derive some of its power from its apparent reflection, in the author's unconscious, of a sexual repulsion. But its greatest force is due to the fact that it is presented, by Ippolit, without any explanation at all.

It will nevertheless be connected, in time, with a spider or tarantula seen as an image of infinite Power. A crucial experience, for Ippolit, was seeing in Rogozhin's house a painting of Christ immediately after he was taken down from the cross: the face fearfully crushed by blows, the eyes open and squinting, a body completely subject to the laws of nature. How could his followers believe the martyr would rise again? " 'Looking at such a picture, one conceives of nature in the shape of an immense, merciless, dumb beast. . . .' " At times, perhaps in delirium, Ippolit fancied he

> "saw in some strange, incredible form that infinite Power, that dull, dark, dumb force. I remember that someone seemed to lead me by the hand, holding a candle, to show me a huge and loathsome spider, and to assure me, laughing at my indignation, that this was that same dark, dumb and almighty power." [11]

This is followed by the apparition of Rogozhin, who sits near his bed and stares at him without speaking: an hallucinated devil, since the door had been locked. This culminating incident leads to the decision to commit suicide:

> "What helped to bring about that 'final decision' was not logic, not a logical conviction, but a feeling of repulsion. I could not go on living a life which was taking such strange, humiliating forms. That apparition degraded me. I am not able to submit to the gloomy power that takes the shape of a spider." [12]

It is not Ippolit's logic only that gives Dostoevsky's presentation its sympathetic force. He has instead lived in the imagination, as fully and intensely as Camus or any other convinced skeptic, the nausea of the absurd. Dostoevsky could try to answer, elsewhere, the arguments. But he could not deny Ippolit's lived experience, and the authenticity of the consciousness that moved through it.

Dostoevsky knew that even the arguments of Ivan Karamazov, a far less equivocal personage, could not be entirely answered. Thus his letter to Lyubimov regarding the first four chapters of "Pro and Contra," up to, that is, The Grand Inquisitor. "The original anarchists were, in many instances, men who were sincerely convinced. My hero takes a theme which is, in my opinion, irresistible, the senselessness of children's suffering and deduces from it the absurdity of all historical reality." [13] Dostoevsky's earlier rehearsal of such suffering, in *The Diary of a Writer,* is even more harrowing than Ivan's; the Turkish butchers and sadistic Russian parents are not straw men to be knocked down. Ivan's eighteenth-century deism—a willingness to believe in an "underlying order and meaning of life,'' and to accept at least a hypothesis of God—is expressed with humility. '' 'I have a Euclidian earthly mind, and how could I solve problems that are not of this world?' '' Yet he cannot accept God's creation, or the optimist's argument that its suffering is necessary to that underlying order and ultimate ''eternal harmony.'' His humanism very directly anticipates that of Camus:

> "With my pitiful, earthly, Euclidian understanding, all I know is that there is suffering and that there are none guilty; that cause follows effect, simply and directly; that everything flows and finds its level—but that's only Euclidian nonsense, I know that, and I can't consent to live by it! What comfort is it to me that there are none guilty and that cause follows effect simply and directly, and that I know it—I must have justice, or I will destroy myself. And not justice in some remote infinite time and space, but here on earth, and that I could see myself.'' [14]

He must therefore renounce a harmony to which the sufferings of children are necessary. '' 'From love of humanity I don't want it. I would rather be left with the unavenged suffering. I would rather remain with my unavenged suffering and unsatisfied indignation, *even if I were wrong. . . .* It's not God that I don't accept, Alyosha, only I most respectfully return his ticket.' '' Even Alyosha—pressed as to whether he would accept a scheme of ultimate happiness founded on the edifice of one baby's unavenged tears—has to say, as surely at this moment the author, that he would not.

The humanist's and skeptic's classic argument is presented with scrupulous fairness. But even more telling is the sympathy created through the attractiveness of Ivan's personality and, as with Ippolit, the intensely plausible movement of his mind. His affection for Alyosha, who has been watching him expectantly for three months, is winning; so too his desire for communication on the ''eternal questions'' before they separate. His repudiation of God's creation is not that of a soured misanthrope or solipsistic logician, but of one who thirsts for life and loves the ''sticky little leaves.'' He does not like to be in rebellion, for '' 'one can hardly live in rebellion, and I want to live.' '' As Camus would put it, in defiance of logic: *Il s'agit de vivre.*

Ivan's narrative of The Grand Inquisitor modulates brilliantly from a preface of Voltairean irony to a brief plausible evocation of the tortured suffering people in the Seville of the Inquisition, Christ's appearance among them, and the shocked response of the Grand Inquisitor. His eyes, as he witnesses the miracle of the dead child's resurrection, ''gleam with a sinister fire.'' Yet the portrait is sympathetic. '' 'He is an old man, almost ninety, tall and erect, with a withered face and sunken eyes, in which there is still a gleam of light. He is not dressed in his gorgeous cardinal's robes, as he was the day before, when he was burning the enemies of the Roman Church—at that moment he was wearing his coarse, old, monk's cassock.' '' His argument, to which Christ listens in silence, is rendered the more powerful by its accent of compassionate sincerity. To Pobedonostev, who could find no "rebuff, rejoinder, and explanation," Dostoevsky explained that the sixth book, "The Russian Monk," would provide an answer. But: "I also tremble for it in this sense—will it be a *sufficient* answer?" [15] The Grand Inquisitor suggests, as would Dostoevsky, that the Roman Church and atheistic socialism, protecting man from the burden of freedom, alike satisfy man's craving to unite " ' " all in one unanimous and harmonious ant-heap, for the craving for universal unity is the third and last anguish of men." ' " The free thought and science of socialism must end in cannibalism and will send men back to Rome and its authority at last. The Inquisitor's reasoning is based, it may be, on a contempt for the weakness of human nature. But it is a compassionate contempt. The craving for earthly bread, even at the cost of freedom, and the craving for *community* of worship, like the craving for social justice ("the harmonious ant-heap") are not in themselves ignoble, if regarded by a mundane logic. But the Grand Inquisitor's most telling argument, which led him to leave the proud and go back to the humble, " ' "for the happiness of the humble," ' " is that the " ' "great anxiety and terrible agony" ' " of freedom of choice can be enjoyed or tolerated only by the elect. Better that millions should be happy, that all should be happy except the " ' "hundred thousand sufferers who have taken upon themselves the curse of the knowledge of good and evil." ' "

Alyosha protests that Ivan's suffering Inquisitor is a mere fantasy. There is no "mystery or lofty melancholy" about the Romish army, whose simple aim is earthly sovereignty. And he guesses, correctly, that the Inquisitor does not believe in God. Yet his protests only intensify, for an unbiased or humanist reader, the narrative's sympathy. Suppose, Ivan says, there is only one such man:

"—if there's only one like my old inquisitor, who had himself eaten roots in the desert and made frenzied efforts to subdue his flesh to make himself free and perfect. But yet all his life he loved humanity, and suddenly his eyes were opened, and he saw that it is no great moral blessedness to attain perfection and freedom, if at the same time one gains the conviction that millions of God's creatures have been created as a mockery. . . ." [16]

Dostoevsky, as though in belated alarm, has Ivan acknowledge that the Inquisitor has followed the advice of the "great dread spirit" and consciously leads men to death and destruction, by lying and deception, though for their temporal happiness. Yet his sympathy for the Inquisitor, even in his unbelief, is powerful. For " 'isn't that suffering, at least for a man like that, who has wasted his whole life in the desert and yet could not shake his incurable love of humanity?' " The Grand Inquisitor stands with the great fictional heroes, and first of all Milton's Satan, who are, in their creators' imaginations if not minds, unsubduably and not ignobly wrong. Christ's only response to the Inquisitor's long discourse is to kiss him on his "bloodless aged lips." " 'The kiss,' " Ivan remarks, " 'glows in his heart, but the old man adheres to his idea.' "

In the larger scheme of *The Brothers Karamazov,* and for the Christian believer, the importance of Ivan's story is dialectical; and the argument is indeed "won" by Father Zossima. The reasonings of Ivan, for an Eliseo Vivas, lead straight to the twentieth century's carnage and oppression.[17] But Dostoevsky's great paradoxical sympathy, in Ivan's poem, is not a matter of dialectic, and its source is in the best sense fictive: in the exquisite timing of Ivan's sympathetic interruptions, in the poignant movement of the Inquisitor's mind, in the sense of a continuing moral struggle.

Such paradoxical sympathy for error, even for the nobly misguided, is rare in Dickens; we see it, but only very briefly, in his picture of the confused Lord George Gordon in *Barnaby Rudge.* But Faulkner accepted the great challenge, in *A Fable,* of writing his own "Grand Inquisitor," in the hilltop colloquy of the old General and his Christ-Corporal son. Certain of the Grand Inquisitor's arguments are suggested by the priest who has come to give the Corporal the Last Sacrament. But this priest has no personality of his own. It is instead the longer confrontation of General and Corporal, with the Corporal nearly as silent as Christ in Seville, that repeatedly evokes Ivan's "poem" as well as Milton's. The General offers his son, if only he will abandon his futile rebellion and elected martyrdom: liberty; and the privilege of exercising compassion (which could spare even the life of his Judas); and power, fame, his good name; and, most eloquently, life for its own sake.

Faulkner has intensified Dostoevsky's ambivalence toward the Grand Inquisitor (who does the devil's bidding out of compassionate concern for weak man) by making his General both Satan and God the Father, and by making his Corporal a figure of almost childlike stubbornness, glibly repetitive in his responses. But this is part of *A Fable*'s overall ambivalence, which has not been sufficiently recognized. The novel is an eloquent pacifist and anti-establishment tract, and a pessimistic one too, which suggests man can learn nothing from history. All institutions are fallible; history is a conspiracy to lead man into his endless wars. But so too, aiding institutional failure, is man's "deathless folly" and unsubduable urge to self-destruction. History, however, is also a pageant that stirs the memory and blood; it is a grand tragic spectacle. Where the Grand Inquisitor has a compassionate contempt for man's childlike weakness, the General, here giving his version of the Nobel Prize speech, has pride in man's incorrigible deathless folly. "I am ten times prouder of that immortality which he does possess than ever he of that heavenly one of his delusion." Michael Novak insists on a crucial distinction: that in Stockholm Faulkner argued that it was man's soul, his "spirit capable of compassion and sacrifice and endurance" that would prevail, whereas the General's affirmation is "curiously divergent" (in its insistence on the deathless folly and the ceaseless planning). So the two texts, he says, need to be closely compared.[18]

The implication is that Faulkner, right in Stockholm, must consider the General wrong. But Faulkner's various visions of "the last ding dong of doom" are not closely reasoned. The fact of enduring and prevailing (whether it be unrealistic idealism or mundane folly that endures, prevails) appears to be worthy of consecration. And the General's supreme valuation of life on earth, unacceptable to the Corporal, is honorable enough. They are two "articulations":

> I champion of this mundane earth which, whether I like it or not, is, and to which I did not ask to come, yet since I am here, not only must stop but intend to stop during my allotted while; you champion of an esoteric realm of man's baseless hopes and his infinite capacity—no: passion—for unfact.[19]

The General's most eloquent temptation—to accept life—comes with his parable of the condemned man and the bird. Faulkner acknowledges his indebtedness for it to James Street's *Look Away;* he might also have mentioned Ivan Karamazov's story of the murderer Richard, induced before his execution to confess his crime at last. For the General's condemned man is indubitably heroic as, hearing the bird, he seizes upon earthly life, though at the cost of the next, and repudiates his hard-won confession.

The parable of the bird is memorable, as is the vision of man on his last day, crawling " 'shivering out of his cooling burrow to crouch among the delicate stalks of his dead antennae like a fairy geometry' " to watch that final struggle of his last patriotic machines. So too is the Miltonic evocation of what the General is *not* offering his son: not Rome nor Baiae nor Cathay nor Xanadu. But *A Fable* is not *The Brothers Karamazov,* and the General-Corporal confrontation lacks both the sustained controlled intelligence of the Grand Inquisitor chapter and its remarkably compressed evocation of the disillusioned old man. In Faulkner, by contrast, there is much useless rhetorical embellishment, several hundred words of mannered writing in place of Dostoevsky's few short introductory sentences:

> "The air is 'fragrant with laurel and lemon.' In the pitch darkness the iron door of the prison is suddenly opened and the Grand Inquisitor himself comes in with a light in his hand. He is alone; the door is closed at once behind him. He stands in the doorway and for a minute or two gazes into His face. At last he goes up slowly, sets the light on the table and speaks." [20]

3
FORBIDDEN GAMES (I): DICKENS AND THE FORBIDDEN MARRIAGE

We are in the presence of three great writers who had exceptionally intense and strange fantasy lives, and who were obviously "disturbed" men of strong compulsions and conflicts. The novelist and the citizen alike experienced anxieties, but these were not necessarily the same. It is possible to connect Dostoevsky's gambling with some of his major work, as Freud has done, but difficult to do much with Dickens's violent night walks or Faulkner's violent drinking. The area of unconscious conflict (and devil's share of unconscious creation) was unusually large in all three, but so too was the amount of interesting waywardness to reach the surface. We will be concerned throughout this study with the novelist rather than the citizen; a good psychiatrist would attend rather to the latter. But the distinction is often difficult to maintain where we are dealing with "forbidden games" and psycho-sexual taboos. In this and in the next two chapters we will be concerned with largely conscious feelings and thoughts. We can be reasonably sure that these troubled Dostoevsky in life as well as in art, but not so sure with Dickens, and not at all sure with Faulkner.

It is a truism that psychological criticism cannot explain the origins of the highest creative capacities—say the comic gift that was responsible for Sairey Gamp; or Dostoevsky's unique power to split personalities and ideas meaningfully; or Faulkner's prose rhythms and baroque rhetoric . . . though with Dostoevsky and Faulkner we can speak in a general way of temperamental needs. But criticism can examine and evaluate recurrent psychological emphases and oddities, and ask whether these enrich the work. Distortion can illuminate, but it can obfuscate and sterilize too. We may say, with Thomas Moser, that Conrad's misogyny, freely indulged in his early fiction, was not there fatally debilitating, but that his later work was vitiated by conscious or unconscious insincerity, and by the attempt to look affirmatively on his heroines and on sexual love.[1] André Gide's anxieties concerning his homosexuality energized a great novel, *The Immoralist,* and were also partly responsible for his valuable generalized ethical rebellion. His writing lost much of its dynamic power once the anxieties had been appeased.

For Dickens, Dostoevsky and Faulkner, as for many people who are more than half-alive, there existed "forbidden games": tabooed acts and relationships, strong "anti-social" attractions or repugnances, threatening obsessions. An obvious consequence was that they expressed (or significantly suppressed) preoccupations that the most conventional novelists and critics would find repulsive; Dostoevsky was capable of liberating, in one day's Notebook entries, enough sado-masochistic fantasies to last most people a lifetime. These are areas of confusion and uncertainty where high clarity and precise moral evaluation, such as F. R. Leavis longed for, are out of the question. All three had much conscious knowledge of the preoccupations we will look at: Dickens's feelings toward his sister-in-law Mary Hogarth (though he may often have thought these feelings did him only honor); Dostoevsky's paedophilia; Faulkner's imaginative distaste for normal sexuality. But the degrees of dynamic and unconscious understanding varied greatly.

The essential literary question is whether these forbidden games, and the fact of their recurrence, strengthened or weakened the fiction. This will involve looking briefly at a number of books. But we will also look in more detail at three novels: *The Old Curiosity Shop, The Insulted and the Injured, Sanctuary.*

A number of anxious preoccupations stirred Dickens's imagination, and lent energy to his plots. One of the most important, emphasized by Taylor Stoehr, concerned illicit sexual relationships that crossed barriers of class.[2] These could lead to harrowing secrecies and children of lost or uncertain identity . . . who, to be sure, could turn out to be pure "children of grace." The abuse of children and neglect of their education was another. The child, faced by an infantile parent, might be forced prematurely into an adult role, in due time be tempted to rebel against all authority. There was, as Edmund Wilson, Steven Marcus and others have shown, the problematic area of one's relationship to his childhood and to a past self, and the compulsion to reenact traumatic experiences imaginatively.[3] Even to remember with precision a disgraceful phase of childhood was long "forbidden," as against the sacred injunction ("The Haunted

Man'') to keep memory green. Another dramatized dread was of dissolution of will, decay of personality. To have two personalities, one secret or unsuccessfully repressed, was an attractive forbidden game. The temptation to at least fantasied violence is very real for a number of authoritarian personalities in the novels, as certainly it was for the writer himself. The fully recorded restlessness of Dickens's middle age found some release in directing and acting in plays and in editing, in the administration of Urania Cottage (compare the ''restlessness'' of Gladstone), in the long nighttime walks, ultimately in the public readings. Dickens, as he himself was aware, could be simultaneously drawn toward chaos and control, anarchy and rigid self-discipline. The two drives are often evident in the work, as in the wayward and macabre imaginings of *Bleak House,* brought under masterful administrative control through structure and style.

A quieter anxiety involved the purity of young women, and various barriers to marriage or sexual connection. The fondest forbidden game would appear to be imagined marriage with an idealized virgin: all the more forbidden because she might be daughter or sister or sister-in-law. Is there any way, a number of plots seem to ask, to legitimize these longings?

The sexual life of Dickens, Angus Wilson remarks, is ''a shop-soiled subject.'' He offers a brilliantly succinct summary: ''he was a strongly sensual man, he had a deep social and emotional need for family life and love, he had a compensating claustrophobic dislike of the domestic scene, and he woke up to these contradictions in his sexual make-up very late.'' [4] To raise again the question of Mary Hogarth will doubtless exasperate many Dickensians. But she represented the strongest ''real-life fantasy'' in a writer unusually dependent on fantasy for his novels. Her reappearances in his work, none wholly successful, tell us something about Dickens's psychic economy and the ''mannerisms'' noted by Freud: ''these flawless girls, selfless and giving, so good they are quite colorless.'' [5]

The familiar story must be briefly recalled: that Dickens met her when she was fourteen, basked in her admiration and cheerfulness, and was pleased when (now sixteen) she moved into the small apartment on his marriage to her sister Catherine. The *ménage* in three small rooms appears to have been a happy one, but with obvious dangers. For Dickens it meant a life divided between hard work and home pleasures, the home pleasures in turn divided between the sexually available and presently pregnant wife and the virginal high-spirited young sister-in-law. With Kate pregnant, Mary assumed all innocently some of the wife's roles, accompanying Dickens in town and, with the arrival of the baby, taking charge of the household. Mary's sudden death—one evening the three going happily to the theater, the next day Mary dead—was one of the two great shocks of Dickens's life. His reaction was extreme even for a time when people were less inhibited in the expression of grief. He slipped the ring from her finger and wore it for the rest of his life, resolved to be buried with her, and was faithful to the anniversary of her death, and to her memory generally, as few romantic heroes have been. In time the fidelity may have become a deliberately cultivated daydream, like another's dream of success. But the immediate shock was such that Dickens, in the midst of appalling success, had to skip the June 1837 installments for *Pickwick Papers* and *Oliver Twist.*

Mary appears to have remained alive in a very special way, for the fantasist as for Dickens the Christian believer. She visited his dreams pleasantly every night until he made the mistake of relating this fact to his wife; then the dreams stopped. Once, years later in Genoa, he dreamed of Mary as "a spirit draped in blue like one of Raphael's Madonnas. . ." and woke in tears.[6] She remained present for the waking man as a guardian spirit: "the recollection of her," he wrote to Mrs. Hogarth, "is an essential part of my being, and is as inseparable from my existence as the beating of my heart is." [7] Writing to William Bradbury, who had lost a child, Dickens spoke of having for Mary "the fondest father's pride." [8] She could long seem, to the imagination, a watchful quasi-sister, like the Agnes of *David Copperfield.* At other times she might have been the idealized *anima,* mother of the soul or ideal feminine component of a strongly masculine personality. In time another Hogarth sister, Georgina, joined the Dickens household, she then fifteen, and presently took virtual charge of it. There were moments when the old threesome might seem to have been renewed, though Georgina was essentially the reliable self-effacing housewife, a flawless Esther Summerson. There was, even so, the image of an unattainable sister-in-law. "The perfect likeness of what she was," Dickens wrote to Mrs. Hogarth, "will never be again, but so much of her spirit shines out [in Georgina] that the old time comes back again at some seasons, and I can hardly separate it from the present." [9] Inevitably there were times when Dickens dreamed of what might have been: the old cosy *ménage-à-trois* continuing into middle age, but now an efficient *ménage-à-quatre.* In the fiction, if nowhere else, Dickens tried to imagine a still-living Mary as his wife.

Jack Lindsay proposes the further classic complication that Dickens found in the childlike Mary, the eternal sister, a substitute for his sister Fanny, the great love of his childhood.[10] Thus, Mark Spilka reasons,

> Dickens' feelings toward Mary Hogarth were incestuous; when he enshrined her in idealized heroines like Little Nell and a host of sexless saints, he was trying to disguise those feelings. If he could cast such girls in neutral, innocent roles, ap-

plaud their perfections and swathe them in sentiment, then he could veil, dilute, or repress the sexual nature of their appeal; and in an oedipal attraction, it is precisely this kind of repression which makes forbidden love seem normal and acceptable.[11]

What vitiates some of his work, Spilka argues, and accounts for the worst of its sentimentality, would appear to be both "radical distortion at the unconscious level" and, whatever its cause, an "unhealthy predilection for sexless love."[12]

The sister Fanny may indeed be the fount and origin of Dickens's unconscious anxieties. But it was the *conscious fantasy* and enduring daydream of reunion with the lost Mary that entered Dickens's fiction with little disguise; it would be impossible to say at what level the idealization of untouched virginity was "insincere." Powerful and guilt-ridden sexual impulses might well have demanded—and the more so given Dickens's domestic situation and the explicit ideals of his time—a compensatory dream of asexual, heavenly marriage. To say this does not imply a generalized sexual repugnance.

Dickens expressed some of these anxieties fairly directly. The most powerful of the novels connected with Mary Hogarth, *The Old Curiosity Shop,* is the one where the sharpest displacements and most radical distortions occur; this is a source of strength not weakness. By contrast *The Battle of Life,* a dreadful Christmas book of 1846, dramatizes very openly a version of the family romance. Steven Marcus's important discussion describes the anguish and turmoil involved in the wretched story's composition, and calls attention to several biographical connections.[13] Marion and Grace are daughters of a Dr. Jeddler (whom Dickens acknowledged to be a fictional portrait of his father); Alfred Heathfield, who shares his first name with two of Dickens's younger brothers, is a ward who has been brought up with the two girls as a brother. The daughters in turn would appear to be direct transpositions of Georgina and Mary Hogarth: Grace the "home-adorning, self-denying . . . quiet household figure" . . . a "staid little woman" and a wise housekeeper, Marion the "younger and more beautiful child," but also possessing angelic spirituality. She is Alfred's intended bride. Marion disappears at the moment of her fiancé's return from medical studies abroad: an event as unaccountable to him as Mary Hogarth's sudden death to Dickens. It is wrongly supposed that she has gone off with a dubious intruder; in fact she has simply sacrificed herself to her plainer sister, who had long before dreamed of being Alfred's wife. In time Alfred does marry Grace, who has come to resemble Marion, and they have a child named after the lost love. But six years to a day Marion returns—unmarried, unbetrothed, virginal—to explain why she had left; and to insist she had resolved never to be Alfred's wife, only his sister. She emerges from the shadow, "white garments rustling in the evening air," and "might have been a spirit visiting the earth upon some healing mission." The "glory of the setting sun" is on her brow; she has returned as from the next life. The emotional implication is that she will remain a member of the reconstituted household, though the final paragraph suggests she will ultimately marry: a concession to one's readers, but for Dickens, surely, an unthinkable event. *The Battle of Life* was written nine years after Mary's death, and though Marion's separation from the rest of the family was six years, for Alfred it was nine. At the very least *The Battle of Life* reflects Dickens's fond fulfilled wish of a Mary still with him in spirit, a better self consciously watching over his destiny. Marion and Alfred, it should be noted, have the same birthday.

Mary Hogarth's first obvious appearance, about a year after her death, is in what is now chapter 29 of *Oliver Twist,* as the angelic Rose Maylie, who is "not past seventeen," and who seems to be both of this world and of Another. She has the remembered "cheerful, happy smile . . . made for Home; for fireside peace and happiness." But the "very intelligence that shone in her deep blue eyes, and was stamped upon her noble head, seemed scarcely of her age, or of the world. . . ." Rose is stricken, suddenly and most improbably, by what appears to be a mortal illness; though no more improbably than was Mary Hogarth. But Dickens could not go ahead with his original intention, which was to allow her to die. Her pallid lover, Harry Maylie, tells her that there seemed hardly a reason to believe she would be spared, since one felt she " 'belonged to that bright sphere whither so many of the fairest and the best, have winged their early flight. . . .' " The nominal obstacle to their marriage—Rose's insistence on the stain of her illegitimate birth—is less real, to the imagination, than that she had been virtually an adopted sister. The marriage is as insubstantial as Harry himself. Closing his book, Dickens regrets he cannot go on to imagine her later years, i.e., keep her still alive.

The connection of Mary Hogarth and *The Old Curiosity Shop,* to which we will return, is a commonplace of literary history. The overt threat to Nell's purity, from Quilp and the rough bargemen, may seem less intense, for a modern psychological criticism, than the hidden menace of the grandfather. But Dickens's fully conscious mind enjoyed the fantasy of an innocent voyage to an Eden existing in a changeless past, in the company of a thirteen-year-old girl. The "healthy" *Martin Chuzzlewit* also has a gruff old man in the sexless company of a young nurse-companion, and its amusing ultimate *ménage-à-trois* of young Martin, wife Mary and the losing lover and passive spectator Tom Pinch, who finds relief in playing the organ. But the most startling forbidden game occurs in those pages where Tom Pinch and Ruth appear to live, in sen-

suous imagery as well as household tasks, as virtual man-and-wife. The idealized relationship is one in which erotic attraction exists, and all the quieter joys
of marriage, but with sexual intercourse impossible. The illustration (Tom
watching Ruth at work on a pudding) suggests father rather than brother. The
pudding, according to Arthur Washburn Brown, is highly sexualized.[14] Tom is
also to remain a member and happy spectator of the Ruth-John household, "not
the least restraint" upon husband and wife. "He could have sat and looked at
them, just as they were, for hours."

In *Dombey and Son* the fantasy of an older man living in happy sexless intimacy with an idealized seventeen-year-old girl—Captain Cuttle and
Florence—has its prurient moment. He won't dream (but Dickens after all did)
of carrying her, since this would involve touch, while she's unconscious. There
is a comparably suspect view of an unconscious girl in *Barnaby Rudge:* ". . .
what mortal eyes could have avoided wandering to the delicate bodice, the
streaming hair, the neglected dress, the perfect abandonment and uncon-
sciousness of the blooming little beauty?" There is a double barrier to be overcome in the central Walter–Florence Dombey romance. She is not yet thirteen
at the time of brother Paul's death. Later, it seems to Walter "libellous . . . to
imagine her grown a woman. . . ." He intends always to regard her as a sister, and one who, as a better self, again recalls Mary Hogarth's immutable role.
He "could do no better than preserve her image in his mind as something
precious, unattainable, unchangeable, and indefinite—indefinite in all but its
power of giving him pleasure, and restraining him like an angel's hand from
anything unworthy." These are the scruples that must be overcome before
things can end happily.

The admittedly autobiographical *David Copperfield* indulges various forbidden wishes in remarkably uncensored forms. With Dora, Dickens could enjoy
in fantasy the lost Maria Beadnell, who had not yet made her disastrous reappearance. Dora, "who was rather diminutive altogether," asks David to call
her "child-wife," an appeal that "made a strong impression"; David's mother,
as he distantly recalls her, was also a child-bride. Life with Dora is an amusing
and sad little interlude, an escape from David's undramatized hard work as a
writer. But she can be put conveniently aside, dying as gently as the dog Jip,
since Agnes waits in the wings. There is a strong identification with Steerforth,
seducer of the child-woman Emily, who enjoys her for some time as his
mistress on lazy travel abroad: identification as well as indignation and sorrow.
Identification with Dr. Strong, who seems older than sixty, and with his marriage to the twenty-year old Annie, who in the illustration looks about fifteen,
might seem remote. Annie was brought up to think of Dr. Strong as her patient

friend, teacher, and friend of her dead father; ultimately he will combine all roles, to the exclusion of the youthful Jack Maldon. Here too Dickens must have speculated on how Mary Hogarth would have responded to a change in their relationship, had she lived. For Annie it was at first " 'so great a change: so great a loss,' " when her mother presented this foster-father " 'before me, of a sudden, as a lover.' " But the marriage is quietly happy. It is, presumably, sexless.

The connection between Mary Hogarth and the bodiless angelic Agnes is much the strongest, and David's marriage to her the most serious forbidden game. She is an insubstantial dream figure through the later parts of the novel: a good angel to warn him against Steerforth, with a beautiful calm manner that makes her different from everyone. She "was always at my side go where I would; proud of what I had done, but infinitely prouder yet of what I was reserved to do." Yet David presently acknowledges that he has suppressed from his narrative "the most secret current of my mind"; Agnes is associated with a vague dissatisfaction, "the old unhappy loss or want of something never to be realized." ("Why is it," Dickens wrote Macready, "that as with poor David, a sense always comes crushing upon me now, when I fall into low spirits, of one happiness I have missed in life, and one friend and companion I have never made?" [15]) The barrier is, simply, that they have been brought up as brother and sister. David, at last aware of his true feeling, stays away from England so as not to betray that relationship. Agnes is saddened when he addresses her as Sister, and when he speaks of her as ever "pointing upward . . . ever leading me to something better; ever directing me to higher things!" Even after their marriage Agnes is a ghostly presence, as close and as distant as a heavenly light:

> O Agnes, O my soul, so may thy face be by me when I close my life indeed; so may I, when realities are melting from me, like the shadows that I now dismiss, still find thee near me, pointing upward! [16]

With *Little Dorrit* the barrier is one of quasi-paternity, but even more of age and fatigue. The obvious biographical fact is the reappearance of the lost love of more than twenty years before, Maria Beadnell, dramatized as the kindly but fat and foolish Flora Finching. Thus the unrecapturable romantic past. The apathetic defeatist Arthur Clennam might seem very remote from the successful, active, restless Dickens. But he too, scarred like Clennam by childhood, incorrigibly felt that something had been missed: "never to be at rest," as he wrote to Macready, "and never satisfied, and ever trying after something that is never reached. . . ." [17] In January 1857, almost forty-five, Dickens was acting in

The Frozen Deep (with its intense prefiguration of *A Tale of Two Cities*); the last installment of *Little Dorrit* appeared in June; in August there were the charity performances in Manchester, with Ellen Ternan in the cast; in May 1858 came the legal separation from his wife. But even before the meeting Dickens would have asked himself what likelihood there was of his still attracting a much younger woman. At a more inward level he may have once again been indulging, in *Little Dorrit,* the daydream of marriage with Mary Hogarth, but she unaged, not even Little Dorrit's twenty-two.

For this is the central and tediously drawn-out psychological problem of *Little Dorrit.* Can Clennam, who asks "the child" to think of him always "as quite an old man," overcome the barrier of paternal feeling? Can he break through repression to realize that he has a normal erotic interest in her and can marry her? Little Dorrit is distressed because he calls her "child" so often. Her angelism, though less cheerful than Mary Hogarth's, is also an obstacle. Like Mary or David Copperfield's Agnes, she is a better self guarding him and brooding over his life. The author's imagination—and not merely Clennam's—presumably remained uncertain. Clennam's boring rhetorical questions put the problem of psychic restraint explicitly: "was there no suppressed something on his own side that he had hushed as it arose?" The marriage itself seems wholly spiritualized, as they go "quietly down into the roaring streets, inseparable and blessed." Imaginatively it might have taken place in heaven, since they are unseen by the busy outside world.

In *Bleak House* Dickens offers his most complicated recasting of this family romance. The sweet competent modest Esther Summerson would appear to be a tribute to Georgina Hogarth, soon to be in full yet self-effacing control of the Dickens household, with Ada Clare, Richard's patient good angel, as Mary. Dickens himself, with growing daughters and at least one infatuation with a much younger woman (Christiana Weller) behind him, would have identified with the wise but repressed Jarndyce. Could the father-guardian of Esther become her husband? Could the marriage of Ada and Richard, virtually brother and sister, last? Woodcourt, who returns to marry Esther quietly, remains, psychologically speaking, an outsider; Esther's love for him is muted to an extreme. It would seem necessary for Richard to die, not only to illustrate the demoralizing effect of great expectations and the evils of Chancery, but so that Ada can be *an unmarried always present member of the household,* in this like Jarndyce in his "growlery." The most intense erotic relationship of the novel, that of Esther and Ada, would seem to belong to another zone of speculation, unless we surmise a momentary authorial identification with Esther. But for Esther's sake too Richard must be got out of the way. Her concern over her damaged appearance centers on Ada not Jarndyce or anyone else. The two girls talk separated by a window curtain, at last rush to their embrace and roll on the floor. Two crucial symbolic gestures—moments of illuminating distortion—are acts of secrecy. Esther takes the withered flowers of one lost love (Woodcourt) and holds them to the lips of the sleeping Ada, also a lost love. The other is her kissing the *hearse-like* panel of the door behind which Ada and Richard lie: "I put my lips to the hearse-like panel of the door as a kiss for my dear and came quietly down again, thinking that one of these days I would confess to the visit." The hearse would seem to seal Richard's fate.[18]

With Ellen Ternan on the scene a new and less angelic fictional character appears in the fiction: Estelle of *Great Expectations,* Bella of *Our Mutual Friend,* Helen Landless of *Edwin Drood.* Ellen Ternan, whom he called "Nelly," may have first appealed to him as a youthful innocent: Little Nell–Mary Hogarth in the flesh. But such an identification, when she actually became his mistress, and as she revealed certain unangelic mercenary traits, would have been imperiled. The most powerful sexual reveries of *Our Mutual Friend* involve the fiercely repressed Bradley Headstone and the trifling, by the sophisticated Eugene Wrayburn, with a girl of a lower class. But the more obvious authorial identification would seem to be with Pa, spruced up to look much younger by his daughter Bella, for their secret expedition to Greenwich. Dickens's real-life anxieties over Ellen Ternan, given their considerable difference in age, may well have been compounded by unspoken feelings for a daughter: the paternal and lover roles fused or confused. Feelings are spoken clearly enough in the novel, as Bella and John have their marriage dinner in the very room where she and Pa had dined secretly. Bella had long since imagined herself on a wedding trip with John Harmon, with "Pa established in the great cabin." The *ménage-à-trois* could hardly be more open, though a crucial gesture (what might have been a sharing of a cigarette in a twentieth-century film) recalls Esther and the withered flowers held to Ada's lips: "Bella put her finger on her own lip and then on Pa's, then on her own lip again, and then on her husband's. 'Now we are a partnership of three, dear Pa.' " [19]

It is evident, then, that reveries of Mary Hogarth went beyond the simple reiteration of a single plot. The fantasy of an ideal virginal lost love still in some sense alive, and the carefully pondered dream of a marriage that might have been—the forbidden game of marriage with sister-in-law/sister/daughter—doubtless had a share in Dickens's restlessness, his prolonged *crise de quarante.*

The restlessness was related in some way, as the autobiographical fragment shows, to a need to cope with the long-hidden blacking house episode, and the childhood crisis of separation and estrangement. But it was also, perhaps more importantly for the work, a response to repressed sensuality and violence, and the far-from-repressed need to organize and dominate one's environment. Mary Hogarth, insofar as she did represent a precious part of the self, offered a compensatory image of purity, non-sexuality, non-violence, passivity, repose. The "forbidden game" of violating that dream was not a source of great writing in Dickens, and none of the pallid quiescent avatars of Mary is particularly interesting in her own right. The Mary Hogarth fantasy was as a rule kept separate from the more disreputable energies that provoked some very sentimental fiction but also some of the most powerful and most macabre; it existed in a zone of quietness.

But there is one place where the childish purity and passivity are exposed, nearly as dangerously as in Dostoevsky, to active sensuality and other threats of violence: *The Old Curiosity Shop.* This novel, however repugnant to modern taste, and especially to the chaste tastes of the realist 1930's, has a strangeness that much greater books—*David Copperfield,* for instance—lack.

THE OLD CURIOSITY SHOP: DICKENS'S WHITE DOE

The Old Curiosity Shop is, of course, a moment in the history of the modern sensibility. The novel deeply moved readers of all social classes and intellectual levels; Nell's death saddened people on two continents, and enraged not a few. The novel's iconographic character is suggested by Dostoevsky's evocation, in *A Raw Youth,* of an "unforgettable" scene, a scene which in fact has no very close correspondence in the novel. Dickens's story, that is, lived and grew in the minds of readers. A few comments on the popularity may still be warranted:

1. The originality. There was little expectation, in 1840–41, that a novel be quietly realistic or uniformly serious, though generous sentiment and high moral feeling were welcome. A novel should entertain with variety, invention, fun. There was novelty in Dickens's stated plan: "to surround the lonely figure of the child with grotesque and wild, but not impossible, companions, and to gather about her innocent face and pure intentions, associates as strange and uncongenial as the grim objects that are about her bed when her history is first foreshadowed." The originality lay not in the threat to innocence, but in its juxtaposition with the grotesque. The principle of contrast carried over to an al-

ternating rhythm of chapters and installments: comic activity and spiritual suffering, energy and repose, the rising fortunes of the Marchioness and the declining life of Little Nell.

2. The novel, published in weekly installments (presently bound in monthly parts), was a family entertainment which could be read aloud and discussed by all. Children would discern various threats to Nell but not (one supposed) the sexual threat. The audacious fifth paragraph of the novel would evoke for many adult male readers the youthful prostitutes they themselves had seen near Covent Garden. But for children listening, the birds would be only birds:

> Poor bird! the only neighbouring thing at all akin to the other little captives, some of whom, shrinking from the hot hands of drunken purchasers, lie drooping on the path already, while others, soddened by close contact, await the time when they shall be watered and freshened up to please more sober company. . . .[20]

3. The extreme popularity of the weekly installments presumably led Dickens to take Kit more seriously, and to introduce, for his least lettered readers, the coy and cosy class-consciousness of his history as the honest loyal employee (but one who must not, finally, aspire to Nell): a change involving, in Chapters 20–22 and especially 38–40, a simpler rhetoric and a more patronizing moralism.

4. The author and his public became attached beyond all expectations to Nell, whose brief story was to have been but one of a number in *Master Humphrey's Clock*. Dickens was halfway through the novel, Forster says, when he told the author that Nell's death was inevitable; that he should lift her "out of the commonplace of ordinary happy endings, so that the gentle pure little figure and form should never change to the fancy." [21] The close conscious identification of Nell and Mary Hogarth caused the fictional death to cast "the most horrible shadow" over the author. "Dear Mary died yesterday, when I think of this sad story." [22] But as early as the death of the schoolmaster's favorite pupil (chapter 25) Dickens was posing for his readers, whose faith in immortality might be dwindling, the classic question of the death of the innocent. Nell came to seem, for the schoolmaster, a reincarnation of his lost scholar. His eloquent words define an "ideal immortality" that could give comfort even to the skeptic: "An infant, a prattling child, dying in its cradle, will live again in the better thoughts of those who loved it, and will play its part, through them, in the redeeming actions of the world, though its body be burnt to ashes or drowned in the deepest sea." Part of *The Old Curiosity Shop*'s great appeal was religious; it gave consolation in a time of high infant mortality. The narrative echoes not just *Pilgrim's Progress*. Nell's death, Malcolm Andrews

suggests, is a kind of Nativity, with those who brought little presents resembling the Bethlehem shepherds.[23] And presently the single gentleman's chief delight will be in sacred pilgrimage, to follow "in the steps" of Nell and her grandfather, "halt where they had halted."

The Old Curiosity Shop is generally regarded as the worst or almost the worst of Dickens's novels. And few things are worse than the reunion of the brothers several paragraphs before Nell's death is acknowledged, the younger brother falling on his knees to deliver his oration. The sentimentality of certain pages, the more awful because written with "sincerity" and zest, needs no documentation at this late date. But there is also much lively writing when Nell is not on the scene, and a certain amount of beautiful writing when she is.

Sentimentality was not at the origin of the novel's appeal. There is little sentimental prose prior to the seventh installment (chapter 9), and by then the novel had enthralled its public. The immediate appeal of those early chapters was instead *fictional* in a pure and traditional way, e.g. not documentary, not instructive, not poetic. They offered an unusual and mysterious situation; a plot that got quickly underway, with several threats to the child heroine; two eccentric beings who are also good talkers, Quilp and Swiveller; and much activity, both verbal and physical. The novel's real energy depends, most readers agree, on the dissolute and the wicked, and on the unconventional people met on the road. The merely good are for the most part boring if not intolerable: the Garlands, Kit and his mother, the schoolmaster, the single gentleman, the grandfather (except when he is gambling or menacing Nell), the sexton. The country performers—Mrs. Jarley, Codlin and Short—have their genial eccentricities. Mr. Grinder's company, who for convenience travel on their professional stilts, appear for only a few lines yet are memorable creations—the young gentleman twisting up his right stilt to pat Short on the shoulder, the young lady rattling her tambourine, then "the stilts frisking away in the moonlight and the bearer of the drum toiling slowly after them." So ends, almost, the seventeenth chapter. The eighteenth ends with Jerry's performing dogs, and the punished dog grinding out Old Hundredth on an organ, but accompanying the music with a short howl when "the knives and forks rattled very much, or any of his fellows got an unusually large piece of fat. . . ." There is also the moving portrait of the man who has inherited a factory furnace once tended by his father. It has provided virtually his whole imaginative life as well as his sustenance. He has a quiet reality that manages to carry the heavy allegorical weight.

The evil beings—Sampson Brass, Sally Brass, above all Quilp—have delighted even modern readers. But the issue, for the present enquiry, is Nell: so much loved in her own time, so little tolerated in ours. The fact is that through much of the novel she exists as embodied virtue (purity, innocence, courage) and embodied situation (suffering) rather than as a living child. We have to take on faith the cheerfulness she shared with Mary Hogarth, and do not ourselves hear her successful discourses as guide at Jarley's Wax Works and as guide through the old church. Her beauty creates "quite a sensation in the little country place" as she rides on a cart beside the Brigand, advertising the show, and decorated with artificial flowers; but silent after all, immobile, abstract. She is only a passive sufferer beneath the scorn of Miss Monflathers. The illustration here shows her with large white face downcast, almost disagreeably patient, while her darker grimacing tormenters, with one kindly exception, point and sneer.

But Nell was very real for her first readers. No doubt the first illustrations had a strong effect on these early readers: Nell welcomed home, escorted by the original narrator, an adolescent girl's face on a child's body; then sleeping among the objects of the shop, with grotesque masks leering. It would be interesting to know at what point and to what extent they felt her sexually threatened. Kit keeps his nightly protective vigil over the house, but is after all a *voyeur* too, "his eyes constantly on the window where Nell is accustomed to sit." The language of the original narrator, who finds Nell "more scantily attired than she might have been," has prurient overtones, and his own middle-of-the-night pacing near her house is obsessive; he cannot tear himself away. He is both aware of danger to Nell and, on the fringes of the reader's consciousness, may represent one. In due time Nell will be directly threatened by an "elderly man . . . so low in stature as to be quite a dwarf," with fangs that give him the "aspect of a panting dog"; but also, less obviously, by an even older man with a mania for gambling.

The nominal threat of the early chapters, Fred's plot to marry her off to Swiveller, shocks even him. " 'And she "nearly fourteen"!' cried Dick." Fred replies that he had meant in " 'two years' time, in three, in four.' " But the illicit potentiality has entered Swiveller's, and the novel's, imaginings. So too it enters the mind of the single gentleman, as he stumbles on a wedding, actually Mrs. Jarley's, and fears it might be Nell's. " 'I am not a going to see this fair young child falling into bad hands,' " Short says to Codlin, who in the next chapter will startle Nell by climbing to her garret, though with proper if egoistic intentions. The sexual threat is forcefully expressed by the woman at the races who bought Nell's flowers and "bade her go home and keep at home for God's sake." And there is the night with the drunken bargemen, who quarrel over "the question who had first suggested the propriety of offering Nell some beer," and whom she keeps in good humor by singing all night. By this time many readers would have regarded the already etherealized child as invulnerable to any threat so gross. At some point readers would be convinced she must and will remain innocent. The novel's strategy, as phrased less sympathetically by Mark Spilka, is that she must flee the repulsive, phallic image (Quilp) "to the chaste life of perpetual childhood—but since there is no perpetual childhood, she must die rather than risk the taint of sexual experience, as Dickens here conceives it." [24]

But what, really, of Quilp, who bluntly asks Nell how she would like to be his number two, his " 'little cherry-cheeked, red-lipped wife' "? His paedophilic, prurient language for Nell seems rather more serious than the curses he showers on his wife: "so small, so compact, so beautifully modelled, so fair, with such blue veins and such a transparent skin, and such little feet, and such winning ways. . . ." Presently, having moved into the house, he asks Nell whether she has come to sit upon his knee or to go to bed in her own little room. She will never come down any more, she says, but Quilp takes her place, throwing himself on his back upon her bed, "kicking up his legs and smoking violently." The reader may not take the threat of Quilp as seriously as he takes that of Sir Mulberry Hawk, or Steerforth, or Carker, or Headstone, or Jasper, and Spilka sees him as a psychic adolescent. But the child herself finds him a "perpetual nightmare."

The ultimate paradox is that the grandfather at times represents a greater threat; the noblest relationship of the novel is also its most suspect. Dickens sees clearly the unpleasant side of the grandfather's childishness and wearying dependence. Yet at the same time he can enjoy the fantasy of picaresque journeying with a young girl. The rhetoric, as they approach the schoolmaster's archetypal village in its "woody hollow below," is eroticized, all unconsciously no doubt: Nell "lured the old man on, with many a backward look and merry beck. . . ." It is gambling, with its startlingly rejuvenating effect, that leads to frightening violation: the loss of the gold that Nell had kept hidden from the grandfather by sewing it into her dress. The essential is that the feeble grandfather *becomes another man* when he turns to gambling: evil and obsessed, selfish when he thinks himself selfless, hanging over the money he has stolen with a "ghastly exultation." "This side of the screen is private," one of the gamblers tells the old man. But he will not be put off. The actual theft of her money (chapter 30) is the novel's most intense moment of terror, unless it be that other moment, a few paragraphs later, when she discovers who has robbed her, or when, in the opening of the next chapter, she fears he may come back to her bedroom for more: "a vague awe and horror surrounded the idea of his slinking in again with stealthy tread, and turning his face toward the empty bed, while she shrank down close at his feet to avoid his touch, which was almost insupportable." Nell's nominal task—to remove the grandfather from the possibilities of temptation, and take him into a zone of quiescence—would also seem to have been, at some level of the imagination, a neutralizing of the author's erotic fantasy. To have imagined even such remotely symbolic violation of the cherished innocent was indeed a forbidden game. (The threat is distinctly incestuous in Joyce Carol Oates's long story "My Secret Enemy," a parodic rendering of *The Old Curiosity Shop*'s voyage that brings to the surface hidden or repressed Dickensian fantasies.[25])

Nell has been physically debilitated by the journey, but would seem to have ample opportunity, at their peaceful destination, to recover her health. But she is "exhausted, though with little fatigue"—exhausted by life, and by the long effort to circumvent her grandfather's evil genius, exhausted too by the spectacle of suffering in the industrial badlands. "The strongest impulse with which the novel is charged," Marcus observes, "is the desire to disengage itself from energy, the desire for inertia." [26] The overworked author could with good reason contemplate the pleasures of rest. We may modify Marcus's statement to say that the desire for inertia plays against eager activity and the Dickensian pull toward bustling life. Thus the Marchioness is first met (chapter 34) a few pages after we have left the lonely and disturbed Nell following the sisters from a distance; she returns, her eye having been discovered at the keyhole, only a few pages after Nell has looked thoughtfully into the grave-like vault in the crypt, then at the declining sun. The drift toward death is much the stronger of the two impulses, and one authorial dream, we may hazard, was to grant Nell the *conscious death* which preoccupied Albert Camus: the gradual approach to death of which the suddenly stricken Mary Hogarth was deprived, death as a meditative spiritual experience.

The stylistic rendering of the final drift to death no doubt remains, over a number of paragraphs, indefensible. But the gradual spiritualization of Nell, for which the formula *death-wish* is inadequate, begins well before the traumatic theft of the money, and deserves to be taken seriously. The tired child falls asleep at Codlin's puppet show, but the next morning wanders in the churchyard and feels "a curious kind of pleasure in lingering among these houses of the dead. . . ." A colloquy with a Wordsworthian ancient, whose husband died fifty-five years before, suggests a *contemplative interconnection of the living and the dead*. To visit his grave had become a "solemn pleasure, and a duty she had learned to like." The approach to the paradisial village where the little scholar dies is also a descent to the grave: "the further they passed into the deep green shade, the more they felt that the tranquil mind of God was there, and shed its peace on them." Nell is almost broken-hearted by the death she witnesses. But an essential step in her education has been taken. The value of death-in-life—of immobility, quiescence, repose—is borne in on her by the contemplation of her two grandfathers: the one hanging over the money with "ghastly exultation," the other fast asleep: "No passion in the face, no avarice, no anxiety, no wild desire; all gentle, tranquil, and at peace."

A further important progress in the spiritualizing of Nell, in her disincarnation, occurs shortly after the disagreeable visit to Miss Monflathers's school, when the kindly Miss Edwards is abused. For Nell is pleased to see Miss Edwards with her visiting little sister, and regularly follows them in their walks, but at a distance. She never speaks to them:

> Their evening walk was by a river's side. *Here, every night, the child was too, unseen by them, unthought of, unregarded;* but feeling as if they were her friends, as if they had confidences and trusts together, as if her load were lightened and less hard to bear; as if they mingled their sorrows, and found mutual consolation.[27]

Nell has become, as the lines I have italicized suggest, almost a disembodied spirit who, like Wordsworth's Lucy Gray or Danish Boy, is shadowily present after death, and who can unseen watch the living, watch over them and share their feelings. That this is Nell's ultimate role—to be pure spirit not flesh and to live in myth immortally, yet maintain some contact with the time-bound earth—is at least a theoretical justification for her highly composed, unrealistic dialogue.

We return to Nell's evening walks and her following of the sisters after a lapse of five installments and nine London chapters. By now the Wordsworthian overtones are much stronger, and the associations of healing solitude, repose, death. Even the sisters are gone, and Nell is entirely alone, a "young creature" rather then "the child," and "feeling a companionship in Nature so serene and still, when noise of tongues and glare of garish lights would have been solitude indeed." A separation has gradually occurred between herself and her grandfather, and her thoughts of this change mingle, "as it were, with everything about her. . . ." A few paragraphs on she will be thrust horribly back into life, as she comes upon him with the gamblers. But meanwhile she has had a sacramental vision of the stars and their deathly peace:

> rising higher and higher in immeasurable space, eternal in their numbers as in their changeless and incorruptible existence. She bent over the calm river, and saw them

shining in the same majestic order as when the dove beheld them gleaming through the swollen waters, upon the mountaintops down far below, and dead mankind, a million fathoms deep.[28]

In the next chapter, as she leads the old man away from temptation, she is referred to, like the Emily of *The White Doe of Rylestone,* as a "superior creature." But this superiority is associated, in a first overt prediction, with death: the too bright eye, etc. The Inferno of the industrial city, and the desolation of the Midland countryside, the unemployed laborers and the starving, carry Nell beyond any "fear for herself, for she was past it now," was "very calm and unresisting." Even hunger is forgotten "in the strange tranquillity that crept over her senses." On their arrival in the long-sought village her attention is at once riveted by two small dwellings, hard by "the gravestones of dead years," and "fast hastening to decay, empty and desolate," in one of which she will die.

The house, as we return to it six chapters later, is unmistakably a tomb, an impression gloomily reinforced by the illustration. The language, as we see Nell in the evening, after the grandfather has gone to bed, suggests Paul Dombey's quiet approach to death, but also the approach to tranquility of Emily in *The White Doe of Rylestone,* that long celebration of quiescence and resignation. "A change had been gradually stealing over her, in the time of her loneliness and sorrow. With failing strength and heightening resolution, there had sprung up a purified and altered mind. . . ." The echoes of Wordsworth's poem, here very strong, are even stronger in the next chapter, as Nell enjoys peaceful solitude in the church. At times the association seems closer with the white doe picking her way among the stone effigies than with Emily. On Sundays the villagers gather round Nell on the porch of the church as Wordsworth's villagers took delight in the doe's Sabbath excursions. "Some feeling was abroad which raised the child above them all." Nell bursts into tears when a boy reveals to her that people say she will be an Angel before spring, and she looks thoughtfully into the vault shown by the sexton, calls it a "black and dreadful place!" But this is the briefest interruption of her unprotesting drift toward death.

Such then was Dickens's altogether religious vision of purity, of chastity and innocence redeeming a fallen world. The purity is sufficiently strong and ethereal to render Nell invulnerable to the normal threats of male sexuality: the night streets of London, Quilp, drunken bargemen. She is, however, robbed by the person who loves her most and who is most indebted to her: a dual personality who as a rule is gentle, childish, easily led, but who is frighteningly rejuvenated whenever he steps behind the screen to indulge in gambling. At an unconscious level, at least, the threat is sexual—the gold coin sewn in the dress, then converted to change in a purse that is robbed—and involves a terrifying invasion of her bedroom, with the bed itself deserted out of self-protection.[29] The grandfather is ultimately restored to quiescent sanity. But the process of chastening involves much suffering, and eventually costs Nell her life.

The good and innocent do not, however, really die; and Nell will always be what she has been, with her frail form not changing, unmarred by maturity. During her lifetime a close connection develops between the child and her natural surroundings, between her home and the tomb, between life and death. While still in life Nell has become a disembodied spirit, following the sisters unseen, and sharing in their joys. In this she but prefigures what her role will be after death—and what Mary Hogarth's was imagined to be—as she follows with full consciousness the fortunes of those she had loved.

4
FORBIDDEN GAMES (II): DOSTOEVSKY'S PAEDOPHILIA

Dostoevsky, far more than Dickens, allowed personal obsessions and suspect impulses free play in his imaginative work. Fantasies of violence and crime, dreams of domination and other dreams of degradation pervade the Notebooks, though the references are at times cryptic. "It was Kulishov who raped and killed her. Back to the gate." [1] The second sentence, taken alone, tells us nothing, but presumably told Dostoevsky all he needed to remember. Some censorship does occur between Notebooks and published novels, often for sound aesthetic reasons. But it is also evident that Dostoevsky worked through and got rid of some of his most violent fantasies during the Notebook stage of composition. I am referring here to dark material of which he was fully conscious. His ample but less conscious understanding, as of repressed or latent homosexuality, appears not in the Notebooks but in the finished work, notably *The Eternal Husband* and *The Idiot*.

Dostoevsky's recurrent, fully conscious, even obsessive concern with the abuse and neglect of children, and with their sexual violation, is well known and commonly referred to by biographers, though rarely explored in depth. These are truly "forbidden games," as unequivocally evil as the substitution of one's human will for God's. But their fascination for the author is unmistakable. A genuine love for children—to protect them, to educate, to redeem—is demonstrably a moral good. But how are we to know, Porfiry might have asked, which acts of love and impulses to protect are incontaminate? Raskolnikov's reaction to the dazed or drunk adolescent girl on the bench is ambiguous.

He identifies her perhaps with his menaced sister,[2] and appeals to a policeman to help protect her from a sensualist hovering nearby. But then he cynically turns on his own good deed. "Let them be! What is it to do with you? Let her go! Let him amuse himself." Later, after the murder, he feels it would be "loathsome" to pass the seat where he "had sat and pondered" after the girl was gone. Is this a sign of his new estrangement from the human community? Or a shameful sense of a Svidrigaïlov component in himself? Such issues, raised though not as a rule explicated by Dostoevsky, are far more intricate than those explored by Dickens in the Bounderby-Louisa and Clennam–Little Dorrit relationships. There are, moreover, imaginative connections not found in most writers: a strong link between sexual violation and fire, for instance. Or, in larger and even religious terms, a connection between the rape or abuse of a child and the rape or abuse of a mentally backward or crippled older woman. The child and the holy fool and those who have deeply suffered are all close to God. Of such, more than for almost any other novelist, is the Kingdom of Heaven. The gathering of children at Ilusha's grave, and Alyosha's promise of a joyful reunion in the next life, is in more than one sense the culminating Dostoevskyan statement.

It would be frivolous to pretend that Dostoevsky never shared the erotic paedophilia he dramatized repeatedly. But biographical inferences, after the lapse of a century, and with so many contradictory witnesses and commentators, are exceptionally hazardous. There is evidence he was, as a young man in Petersburg, awkward, sensitive, shy; embarrassed in the presence of women. His roommate of 1843, Dr. Riesenkampf, noted of that earlier time that he "always appeared to be indifferent to the company of women and, in fact, all but had a kind of aversion toward it." [3] There were also, perhaps not too significantly, passionate intellectual attachments and Schilleresque exchanges with Ivan Shidlovsky, a young poet and civil servant, and in 1840 with a senior classmate, Ivan Berezhetsky. Shyness in the presence of adult women, and the dread of sexual failure, often go far to explain the paedophilia of relatively young men. Years later there are good authorities—Apollinariya Suslova, Anna Korvin-Krukovskaya, his second wife Anna Snitkina—on the sensitivity, shyness and *gaucheries* of the middle-aged man. The embarrassments of the fictional underground men, as well as their proneness to self-laceration, are to some extent autobiographical. But the novels also testify, of course, to a charmed fascination with women—grown women and old women as well as young girls—scarcely rivaled by any other novelist.

Several familiar facts of family background must be recalled. One was the presence, in and around the estate where the Dostoevskys spent their summers, of a "holy fool" in tatters, a woman called Foolish Agrafyevna, who had had or claimed to have had an illegitimate child: a prefiguration of old Fyodor Karamazov's victim Stinking Lizaveta, but perhaps too of other backward or crippled victims. Another was that Dostoevsky's father began to drink heavily after the death of his wife, flogged and abused his serfs, allegedly debauched some of their daughters, and took a sixteen-year-old peasant girl to live with him. His death when the future writer was eighteen—murdered by a group of the peasants, and with the genitals twisted and crushed as in revenge—is mentioned nowhere in the correspondence, but is obliquely dramatized in the culminating novel. Dostoevsky himself did not know the details of the murder for some time. The very fact of murder was suppressed by older members of the family connection, since public knowledge would have meant sending a number of the serfs, possibly many, to Siberia, with a consequent diminution of the estate.

Dostoevsky's own affairs with women considerably younger than himself tell us nothing definitive. His catastrophic first marriage was with a lively neurotic woman in her thirties, though at the outset of this relationship Dostoevsky appears to have been the more neurotic of the two or, more exactly, of the three. (He enacted, with the rival Vergunov, no little of Pavel Pavlovich Trusotzky's role in *The Eternal Husband*.) Before this, in Siberia, Dostoevsky appears to have been charmed briefly by his pupil Marina, daughter of an exiled Pole who, when she turned seventeen, "matured, blossomed out, grew pretty, and became extremely loose." [4] He was attracted, after the separation from his wife, by several young women, but they were not adolescents. The tormenting affair with Apollinariya Suslova began when he was forty-one, she twenty-three. She was bright, erratic, egoistic, sexually teasing: the prototype of Polina of *The Gambler* and other neurotic heroines. He met Anna Korvin-Krukovskaya during an interval of the Suslova affair: he forty-two, she twenty. She found his seriousness and his jealousies wearing, and declined his proposal of marriage. Interestingly, her fourteen-year-old sister Sonya, later a famous mathematician, appears to have adored Dostoevsky. He in turn found an intelligent and attractive confidante in Apollinariya's sister (he forty-four, she twenty-two), who was expelled from the Academy of Military Surgery for radical leanings, but later became the first woman doctor in Russia. Dostoevsky was forty-five when he married Anna Snitkina, to whom he had dictated *The Gambler;* she was twenty-one. It was on the whole a highly successful marr age. The year before Dostoevsky had lived briefly with a "shopworn" but literate adventuress, Martha Brown (the name thanks to her marriage to an American sailor), whose "ties with the criminal world were so flagrant," Marc

Slonim writes, "that the police expelled her from Belgium and Holland." [5]

The compassionate interest in abused or neglected children, and in young girls driven to prostitution, is evident in *Winter Notes on Summer Impressions,* recounting Dostoevsky's first trip abroad in 1862. The Haymarket in London must have seemed even worse than the slum Hay Market of St. Petersburg, also a center of vice: a vision of a Saturday night drunken hell juxtaposed against the materialist abominations of the Crystal Palace. Dostoevsky tells of a little girl about six, rocking her head from side to side, and with a look of hopeless despair. When he gave her a coin she looked at him in astonishment and ran away as if afraid he would take the money back. Not far from here, at three in the morning, Dickens had come upon a hare-lipped youth of twenty who "rose up at my feet with a cry of loneliness and houselessness . . . the like of which I never heard." "Intending to give this ugly object money, I put out my hand to stay it—for it recoiled as it whined and snapped—and laid my hand upon its shoulder. Instantly, it twisted out of its garment, like the young man in the New Testament, and left me standing alone with its rags in my hands." [6] The late essays of *The Uncommercial Traveller,* not *Sketches by Boz* or *Oliver Twist* or *Our Mutual Friend,* evoke the barbaric reality of London. Their writing, however, is decidedly cooler and more distanced than Dostoevsky's when he reached the age of reminiscence, with *The Diary of a Writer.*

The Diary of a Writer (1873, 1876, 1877, with single issues in 1880 and 1881) gave Dostoevsky at last what Dickens had enjoyed at a much earlier age, especially with *Household Words:* informal, intimate communication with a large public that revered his advice. The extraordinary attention given to children and their abuse (32 per cent of the 1876 *Diary,* according to Rowe [7]) is not entirely obsessive. For Dostoevsky was groping toward *The Brothers Karamazov,* and had long since intended to write a novel about contemporary Russian children and their fathers. His reporting on a colony of juvenile delinquents and on foundling institutions shows a Dickensian keenness and compassion. The most vivid pages of *The Diary* describe the psychic havoc wrought by the spectacle of torture: an eight- or nine-year-old girl who had seen her father skinned alive, a Bulgarian girl about ten who had seen Turks gouge out the eyes of her brother, aged two or three, with a needle, then impale him on a stake. The long and confused report on the Kroneberg case—of a seven-year-old girl flogged by her father—blends intense compassion for the child with an obsessively detailed account of the beating and of the scars. [8] (Floggings, and the sometimes problematic survival of the victims, and the psychologies of the beaters and the beaten, occasion some of the most intense pages of *The House of the Dead.*) There is no prurient curiosity, only compassion and outrage, in the account of the Djunkovsky trial for the cruel treatment of eleven- and thirteen-year-old boys and an epileptic girl of twelve. Dostoevsky's attack on the defense lawyer in the Kroneberg case has a moving simplicity. We should approach children "with respect for their angelic countenances, for their innocence, for their irresponsibility and their touching defenselessness."

The defenselessness of young girls is a major preoccupation. *The Diary* of 1873, discussing a new play, talks of a Matryosha, herself debauched since twelve, drugging another girl so that a merchant can rape her while unconscious. Russia, Dostoevsky says, is full of such unfortunates. Later he writes of child labor, with the factories as Sodom, and hints at the debauch of ten-year-old girls. Two other 1876 articles have a touch of prurient interest and anxiety. He remarks, of a Christmas Tree party, that it is "quite cynical to dress a virtually grown-up girl in a childish frock. . . . When, at midnight, the children's ball came to an end and parents began to dance, some of these girls in short dresses and with bare legs stayed on—dancing with the grownups." The story of a twelve-year-old runaway girl, who came home unharmed, involved vivid novelistic conjecture as to what might have happened amid the dangers of the streets. The *Diary* contains two famous short fictions of ultimate degradation. The dead of "Bobok," reduced to "pure" consciousness and conversing underground, reveal their unregenerate selves: an old man has a pleasant revery of a little blonde of fifteen or so. "The Meek One" is a middle-aged underground man's narrative of his marriage to a girl who is almost sixteen but seems fourteen: a picture of psychic tyranny without comic or other relief, and without the philosophical substructure of *Notes from Underground* to divert attention from its record of pure suffering.

The most interesting case, that of Ekaterina Kornilova, is discussed for more than a year, and provides another strange link between Dickens and Dostoevsky: their defense of young women on trial for infanticide. Dickens in *The Uncommercial Traveller* is looking back some twenty-five years on his service at an inquest into the death "of a very little mite of a child." [9] Had the mother committed the minor offense of concealing the birth or the major one of killing the child? "Smitten hard by the terrible low wail from the utterly friendless orphan girl," Dickens asked some questions that gave the case a favorable turn. Dostoevsky's involvement was longer and more intense,[10] and revealed a Gidean interest in the "inexplicable crime." Is there even some unspoken implication that a "good" person may, inexplicably, commit a crime; or, again, the Gidean idea that a "gratuitous" criminal act may have no element of self-interest? Ekaterina Kornilova, aged twenty, and pregnant with another child, had thrown her six-year-old daughter from a fourth-floor window. The child was miraculously unharmed, but Kornilova turned herself in to the police. Dostoevsky, who speculated on the pathological effect of her pregnancy, interviewed her, and argued that it was better to err on the side of mercy. His intervention led to a new trial, which resulted in acquittal. In prison, he had given her paternal warnings against the dangers of Siberia. There, young and good-looking, she might easily be corrupted, her life ruined, and her child debauched in turn.

The student of Dostoevsky's work must refer to what Mochulsky calls N. N. Strakhov's "hideous calumny": [11] his famous letter to Tolstoy of November 28, 1883, first published in 1913. The allegation was that, according to a Professor Viskovatov, Dostoevsky had "boasted" of raping a little girl in a bathhouse, with the complicity of her governess. It is not even certain, Yarmolinsky notes, that Viskovatov, whom Dostoevsky disliked, had the story at first hand. "But assuming that Dostoevsky did thus unbosom himself to the man, it is still open to question whether he was confessing an act he had committed or indulging his morbid fantasy." [12]

The story has a number of versions. Anna Dostoevsky suggests the rumor goes back to a variant of "Stavrogin's Confession" in which he introduced a governess and a bathhouse, and which he read to friends. They, one of them Strakhov, advised against this version on the grounds that so to implicate a governess would make him seem hostile to the movement for women's emancipation. Another might be based on a plot, summarized for the ladies of the Korvin-Krukovskaya household in 1865, of a story planned long before: one in which a middle-aged man suddenly freed from repression recalls violating a child at the instigation of drunken companions.[13] Still another (echoing or foreshadowing a fine scene in *The Idiot*) has Dostoevsky in a discussion of shameful acts committed by decent people, and blurting out that he had seduced both a governess and her young charge. This was alleged to have occurred before his arrest.[14] A fourth version—much the most interesting psychologically, one that might have made a great short novel—has Dostoevsky following the trial of a man accused of raping a young girl and coming to identify himself with the criminal, and ultimately finding himself under compulsion to victimize the little girl in his turn.[15]

The obvious source of these stories would appear to be both the recurrence of paedophilic themes in Dostoevsky's work and the fact that "Stavrogin's Confession" went so long unpublished. Child prostitution flourished in Petersburg at least as openly as in London. Not impossibly the writer at least pondered engaging a child prostitute for an hour or a night. The basic Freudian insight—

that the dream or wish is the psychological equivalent of the act—is of primary relevance. But so too is the psychic compulsion, dramatized in *Crime and Punishment,* to confess to a crime one has not committed, out of a generalized need for punishment. The writing, in any event, shows a fascination with paedophilic impulses, and at times an imaginative sharing of them. The recurrent theme does indeed amount to an oblique confession, if only of anti-social fantasies, and an imaginative effort to rid himself of obsession.

The children's club enigmatically referred to in the Notebooks for *The Idiot* and the unwritten major novel about children might well, like the final section of *The Brothers Karamazov,* have been concerned with the development of boys, and the redemption of their aggressive energies. But this was, like *The Life of a Great Sinner,* a lost subject. The psychic or physical abuse of girl children and adolescent girls preoccupied the novelist from first to last, so much so that it is difficult to avoid catalogue. It may be useful, at the risk of abstraction, to distinguish among a few major situations.

The Psychic Abuse of Girls, Mental Distress

Several young victims of paternal abuse and family catastrophe are exposed to worse strains than Florence Dombey or Little Dorrit, and Dostoevsky's Nelly is long in greater danger than Little Nell. But Dostoevsky's more dramatic method does not allow for prolonged Dickensian *attendrissement*. Sonia Marmeladov, driven to prostitution by her father's drinking, returns with the money, then lies down with her face to the wall; in Dickens she would probably have talked on and on. The unfinished *Netochka Nezvanova,* rich in both conscious and unconscious psychological insights, is distanced by the girl's relatively calm and spare first-person narration and, in chapters 2–4, by the extreme economy with which a macabre situation is rendered. We see a very young girl made to steal money from her mother for her stepfather's drink; exposed to his crazy self-lacerations, and awakened erotically by him; compelled to witness her mother's murder. A few days later the stepfather, whom she has long thought of as her father, goes completely insane and dies. Later we see Netochka, now thirteen, in an intense erotic relationship with the volatile young princess Katia, and again at seventeen, an outsider in still another household, caught in the unspoken tensions of a failed marriage, treated harshly by the husband and supposed by the wife to have interested him sexually. The movement in so few pages from macabre extreme to quiet Jamesian or Gidean nuance is astonishing. One wonders what would have happened to this novel had Dostoevsky's arrest and imprisonment not cut it off.

As a rule we do not see the sufferings of children from within, even in this muted way. The brief, compassionate, absolutely authentic picture of the eight-year-old Liza in *The Eternal Husband* (really Velchaninov's child, brought up as Pavel Pavlovich Trusotzky's) is one of Dostoevsky's finest. We see her only from the outside, standing at the fringe of the intense Velchaninov-Trusotzky *dédoublement* and combat of wills. But not a note is out of place, from the girl's hysterical efforts to embrace Trusotzky to her quiet acceptance that she has been abandoned by him, and that there is nothing left for her but to die. The "brain fever," sometimes too opportune at moments of Dostoevskyan crisis, seems a plausible response to the strain under which she has been living. Trusotzky had brought home a "street wench," but much of the time left the child alone. In his absence she looked at the body of a man who hanged himself in the building, and is afraid that Trustozky will commit suicide. She has even seen him trying a noose. Her greatest dread, poignant in the light of so much mistreatment, is that she will not be loved; her deepest shame that Trusotzky has flung her into Velchaninov's keeping. The portrait is the more moving because of the sense it gives of being drawn from everyday Russian life. So too, Dostoevsky might have argued, were the sufferings of old Fyodor's first wife, virtually a child, or those of the fifteen-year-old bride of "The Meek One," for whom proferred love is a last straw, after so much psychic cruelty.

There are a number of other children subjected to extreme mental strain in the novels, even more in the Notebooks. The plight of the Marmeladov family after the father's accident, perhaps Dickensian in inspiration, leads to some of the greatest pages in *Crime and Punishment;* macabre humor intensifies compassion. The mute and huddled response of the children, Rowe complains, seems "strangely devoid of mental suffering." [16] But where so much catastrophe follows so swiftly, articulate response by the children would seem unlikely in life, maudlin and reductive in fiction. The great energizing voice is instead Katerina Ivanovna's, driven to distraction beyond any mother in the novels, and pouring out her wrath. The children are visibly present at the father's death, little Lida "shaking in the corner, as though she were in a fit, and staring at him with her wondering childish eyes"; the boy crossing himself and touching the floor with his forehead; the ten-year-old girl Polenka rushing in to announce the arrival of Sonia, seen there for the first time in her prostitute's gaudy clothes. We see the children clearly enough, after Katerina has rushed off with the vague intent of somewhere finding justice, "Polenka with the two

little ones in her arms crouched, terrified, on the trunk in the corner of the room.
. . .'' We learn from Lebeziatnikov that Katerina now madly intends to take
the children to beg in the streets, have them perform with a barrel-organ. His
distanced narrative prepares us for the great macabre scene where Katerina
rushes at the children and shouts at them, then rushes at the astonished crowd—
clapping her hands for Lida and Kolya to dance and Polenka to sing; exasperated by the terror of the smaller children; begging Polenka to speak to her in
French, to show that she is of a good family.

Dostoevsky dramatizes two kinds of suspect or criminal impulse which should
be kept separate, though Svidrigaïlov and old Fyodor Karamazov are guilty of
both. One is paedophilia, an erotic interest in young girls that may be largely
cerebral (whether sentimental or sadistic), but that can lead to cruel mismar-
riages, and may suggest in veiled form the further taboo of incest. The ambiguous situation that interested Dickens—an older man living in nominally sexless
intimacy with a young girl—is dramatized in several of Dostoevsky's novels,
but explored with much greater dynamic understanding. The other forbidden
game is actual sexual violation of a very young girl or of someone who is, for
the writer's imagination, in some sense a child: a backward, crippled, hand-
icapped woman. The association of helpless child and helpless idiot or cripple,
generally overlooked by Dostoevsky's commentators, is at the center of his
psychic economy.

Paedophilia

The interest in girl children, nymphets and younger adolescent girls is not entirely a question of chronological age. Dunia in *Crime and Punishment,* seen as
a charming little girl, has an erotic appeal for Zosimov, and Sonia is insistently
described, when Raskolnikov sees her for a second time, as a ''young girl, very
young, indeed almost a child,'' ''like a little child,'' ''in spite of her eighteen
years, she looked almost a little girl—almost a child.'' Ambiguity of age,
Rowe shrewdly notes, may serve the turn of certain characters (Trusotzky and
Svidrigaïlov insist their intended brides will soon be a marriageable sixteen),
but also those of the novelist wanting at times to suggest girls are younger or
older than they are.[17] Nelly, in *The Insulted and the Injured,* might have been
presented by Madame Bubnov as anything from eleven to fifteen, depending on
the tastes and depravities of her customers. Twelve and thirteen, Dostoevsky
notes in *The Diary of a Writer,* is an interesting age, since it may combine ''the
most baby-like, touching innocence and immaturity'' with a ''quick, even

greedy perceptual ability. . . . .'' Where Dickens's angelic childlike heroines combine innocence and moral gravity, Dostoevsky's most attractive adolescents have willful and fiery qualities, and may grow up to be Nastasyas or Grushenkas. Thus Nadya of *The Eternal Husband:* "a little brunette with a wild, untamed look and the boldness of a nihilist; a roguish imp with blazing eyes, a charming but often malicious smile, wonderful lips and teeth, a slender and graceful young thing, her face still childlike but flowing with incipient thought.''

Rowe's discussion of Dostoevsky's subtle stretchings and contractions of age calls attention also to a significant play of words. Thus the drunk girl Raskolnikov hopes to shield "is a 'girl' (*devushka*) when the policeman asks her where she lives, but a 'little girl' (*devochka*) when she answers thickly in exclamations that strongly suggest her victimization.'' [18] But he blurs Dostoevsky's discriminations when he says the victim of paedophilia "has almost invariably the sexual desirability of an older girl, the helplessness of a younger girl, and a near-woman's capacity for apprehending her victimization.'' [19] For a number of men, and notably the senile Prince Sokolsky of *A Raw Youth,* the sexual desirability would lie in extreme youth; "featherless chicks'' are presumably prepubescent. The earliest of Dostoevsky's paedophiles, Yulian Mastakovich, is drawn both by young girls and "near-women.'' Significantly a respectable man and important civil servant, he fondles an eleven-year-old girl in "A Christmas Tree and a Wedding''; he is also interested in her 300,000-ruble dowry. In "From the Notes of an Unknown'' he calls on a fiancée of seventeen, "who is completely innocent and utterly naive. The thought alone of this last circumstance already brought the flakiest little smile to Yulian Mastakovich's sugary lips.'' He is unaware of evil in himself, and can bask in his own good heart.

Moral considerations are beyond the calculus of old Fyodor Karamazov, the most complete of the sensualists, but he too is drawn by innocence. The "innocent appearance'' of his sixteen-year-old bride "had a peculiar attraction for a vicious profligate.'' Her " 'innocent eyes slit my soul like a razor. . . . ' '' He offers to show Alyosha a little wench, still barefoot, on whom he has had his eyes for a long time. " 'Don't be afraid of barefooted wenches—don't despise them—they're pearls.' '' Pavel Pavlovich is altogether as frank in talking of Nadya's appeal: " 'that's just what has bowled me over, that she is still going to school with the satchel on her arm full of copybooks and pens, he-he!' ''

The appeal of innocence to the sophisticated may involve a desire to corrupt and dominate; or testing one's power to commit an evil action; or, even, pleasure in contemplating one's degradation. Velchaninov seduced a girl to whom he was not even attracted, and abandoned her and her child. We do not know Valkovsky's feelings (*The Insulted and the Injured*) as he looks forward to marriage with a rich girl he discovered at fourteen, now fifteen and still in pinafores. A cynical pleasure in degrading Natasha, and not only money, may lie behind his effort to arrange a liaison with the aged Count Nainsky. Valkovsky is, quintessentially, a bored aristocrat who nearly flogs a peasant to death (the peasant dies in his hospital) so as to gain access to his wife, "a little shepherdess." Out of boredom, he says, he turned to "pretty little girls"; he is "fond of secret, hidden vice, a bit more strange and original, even a little filthy for variety. . . ." The motivations of Svidrigaïlov are still more complex, and in some ways ally him with Stavrogin, who thinks to go beyond good and evil. One side of him reveals a cerebral paedophilia that enjoys deferring sexual satisfaction; his fiancée, a month short of sixteen, is " 'still in a short frock—an unopened bud!' " Raskolnikov shrewdly comments that the " 'monstrous difference in age and development excites your sensuality' "; Svidrigaïlov responds with terrible openness that he has always been fond of children. There are " 'places where anyone who knows his way about can find a great deal.' " He has, in fact, made the acquaintance of a little girl of thirteen whom he saw dancing the cancan in a frightful den. He has offered to assist in the young girl's education. Would Raskolnikov like to meet her? In "The Uncle's Dream" the dancing of the fourteen-year-old Sonetcha and her rounded form attract the old Prince's attention.

The forbidden game of incest is at times present beneath these familiar surfaces, with stepdaughter or ward substituting for blood relation. It is always important, in dealing with obsessive material, to ask whether a gap appears to exist between the "manifest content" (which itself may be suspect enough) and the "dream-thoughts" that could have given the author a hidden satisfaction. The very openness of the incest-paedophilia fantasy in *Netochka Nezvanova*—the gross phallic exhibition of a sinister violin, the incitement to steal the mother's money, the murder and flight together—suggests both authorial unawareness and extraordinary freedom from less-than-conscious censorship. The narrator of *The Insulted and the Injured,* believing Masloboev pimped for Valkovsky in the past, has good reason to suspect he has been decoyed so as to give the Prince free access to Nelly, who turns out to be his daughter; the sexual implications, although discounted later, have been planted in the reader's mind. Velchaninov wonders about the eternal husband's attitude toward the dead Liza. His unspecified "small and nasty thought" could be that Pavel Pavlovich had paedophilic longings for the now-dead girl; or, a still more underground impulse, that he intended to throw the child in her real father's way, as once he had thrown her mother. The Idiot's rape of Mignon, in early Notebooks, derived from Dostoevsky's interest in the trial of Olga Umetskaia's parents; it was widely supposed Olga's father had raped her. In plans for *A Raw Youth* "the Predatory Type" (later Versilov) seduces his stepdaughter. This will become "by the process of displacement," Wasiolek shrewdly notes, "the seduction of Liza by the young Prince Sergei." Here (as often elsewhere) sexual complications that "appear clearly and insistently in these notes . . . are muted in the novel itself." [20]

Violation of Young Girl, Cripple or Idiot

The first attempted forceful sexual violation occurs in *The Insulted and Injured,* where the disheveled Nelly in torn and crumpled white dress escapes from the fat customer of Madame Bubnov. The culminating crimes are those of Stavrogin and Fyodor Karamazov. Stavrogin's cool rape or seduction of Matryosha, the small daughter of his landlady, occurs during the mother's absence. The child, who feels she has "killed God," commits suicide in a tiny cubicle adjacent to a privy, while Stavrogin waits in silence. His associated crime is the murder by proxy of the half-witted and crippled Marya Lebyadkin, whom he had married in a mood of ironic self-laceration. There is no evidence that sexual desire, rather than cerebral perverse compulsion, played a part in either relationship; his wife may have remained virgin. Fyodor Karamazov is altogether capable of normal sensuality; it is the very soul of his being. But allegedly he raped Stinking Lizaveta, an idiot who was virtually a ward of the community, as a stunt, at the instigation of drunken companions. She dies giving birth to the child resulting from the rape, in the bathhouse behind Fyodor's house. He, a generation later, is murdered by that child, a few yards from the scene of Lizaveta's death.

There are a number of variants on these crimes, though some never get beyond the Notebooks. Intellectual integrity as well as personal obsession demanded that all possibilities be explored. Raskolnikov, who kills a defenseless old woman, had considered marrying his landlady's ugly and invalid daughter. She was always dreaming of a nunnery; Marya Lebyadkin had lived in one. But Raskolnikov's potentiality for sexual perversion (" 'If she had been lame or hunchback, I believe I would have liked her better still' ") is largely transferred to Svidrigaïlov, and may be said to die with him. The Idiot of the Notebooks, later the Christ-like Myshkin and protector of the outcast Marie, commits a variety of crimes: rapes the abused Mignon, his foster-sister; rapes Umetskaia (*née* Mignon), who hangs herself; presently rapes the "heroine," who also hangs herself.[21] Versilov, in the published *A Raw Youth*, rapes nobody, though he has his small inadvertent share in the death of Olia, who hangs herself as a result of various sexual insults. The Versilov of the Notebooks is far more criminal as well as, at times, far more nobly ambitious. The responsibility for the death of Liza is not clear; in one note she hangs herself in a latrine, and in the next lines there are allusions to the "little beetle" of Versilov's guilt. His unequivocal Notebook crime is the seduction of a little girl who hangs herself, partly from remorse for her mother's death. It directly echoes in several ways "Stavrogin's Confession," which by now had been written but not published, and Stavrogin is once directly referred to: "Both charming and repulsive, the little red beetle, Stavrogin." [22] While waiting for Matryosha to hang herself Stavrogin watched a tiny red spider on a geranium leaf; later he wakes happily from a dream of the Golden Age, then sees a tiny dot assume the shape of a spider. Imagery of spiders is associated with evil and guilt in various novels, from the narrator's impression of Valkovsky as "some sort of reptile, some huge spider" to the raw youth's feeling, after his quasi-incestuous dream of Katerina, that he has the soul of a spider. Liza's bitter image of marriage with Stavrogin corresponds to Svidrigaïlov's of eternity: "I always fancied that you would take me to some place where there was a huge wicked spider, big as a man, and we should spend our lives looking at it and being afraid of it."

The most important criminal violation of a child, prior to Stavrogin's, is Svidrigaïlov's in *Crime and Punishment*. The Svidrigaïlov of the Notebooks as of the novel has an interesting duality. He can at the same time speak of Dunechka "with veritable fervor" and know that in no more than an hour he would be preparing to rape her. The Notebook brings into close association the death of the girl he had raped and the death of his wife in the bathhouse. Certain generous traits, preserved in the novel, are outlined in the Notebooks, but so too are cryptic ones concerning the violation of children. "Relates without any twinge of conscience that at the time of serfdom he had whipped two men to death and took advantage of innocence" and "[N.B. About the children and little beggar girls.]" and "About the rape of children, but dispassionately." [23] His cynicism, which at times approaches the *accidie* of Stavrogin, leads him to want "some kind of excess," presumably cerebral. But in a later note his impulses are more primitive. There is a "convulsive and bestial need to tear apart and to kill, coldly passionate. Animal. Tiger." [24]

The conception of a landlady's and guardian's complicity in the rape of a helpless girl, closely associated with a death in a bathhouse, is developed vividly in the finished novel. We hear rumors of the crime: Svidrigaïlov had outraged a deaf and dumb girl of fourteen or fifteen; the woman named Resslich (a relation, perhaps an aunt) had hated and beaten this girl; the girl was found hanging in a garret. The crime was hushed up. Now in Petersburg Svidrigaïlov is lodging with the same Madame Resslich, in quarters adjoining Sonia's; it appears she had arranged the meeting with his fifteen-year-old fiancée. Svidrigaïlov's dream on the last night of his life, even if suggested in part by the wild weather outside, removes any doubt concerning his guilt. He knew that girl in the coffin, in her white muslin dress: "there was no holy image, no burning candle beside the coffin; no sound of prayers: the girl had drowned herself." His wife too had drowned, dying of a stroke in her bath. Svidrigaïlov believes "in future life, in *spiders*, etc.," the Notebook tells us.[25] This will become one of the novel's most famous speeches. What if there are only spiders, or something of that sort, in a future life?

> "We always imagine eternity as something beyond our conceptions, something vast, vast! But why must it be vast? Instead of all that, what if it's one little room, like a bath-house in the country, black and grimy and spiders in every corner, and that's all eternity is? I sometimes fancy it is like that." [26]

The suicide of Svidrigaïlov, so close in time to Raskolnikov's confession and arrest, would appear to have destroyed, through the agency of the double-surrogate, a potentiality for that graver crime. Raskolnikov can now be redeemed; resurrection is possible.

The possibility of redemption for the child rapist—the very process of change, the restoration of honor, the granting of a quasi-divine grace—is revealed dynamically *in Dostoevsky's reimaginings of Versilov and especially Myshkin*. A facile objection is that the novelist, unlike God, can change a fictional personage at will, and as often as he pleases. But in fact the changes in the Idiot's character were exceedingly hard-wrought, and involved much splitting and recombining of traits. Few sinners have struggled harder to discover goodness and repentance than the author of this novel on behalf of his hero. The struggle to rehabilitate the Idiot, rapist and arsonist, has its several moments of "illuminating distortion" and equivocal rape. It is as though Dostoevsky, early in his dreaming of the novel, wanted the Idiot *to rape with impunity:* Mignon, when raped, says not a word, utters "not a single reproach," and never "even referred to it again." [27] His "brutal defilement" of the "heroine" in the fifth plan (where her identity is blurred with that of Umetskaia, formerly Mignon) is "both an overwhelming happiness to her, and death itself." [28] In the sixth plan, within a few pages, he rapes both Umetskaia and the "heroine," and both hang themselves; he "torments his wife to such a point" that she too hangs herself (the word "drowns" is crossed out).[29] Soon thereafter, no longer a rapist, he consoles the victim of the Seducer (presumably the future Nastasya of the novel) and takes the baby. His former character, as Dostoevsky himself succinctly puts it, is transferred to the son Ganechka. Ultimately aspects of it will be absorbed by Rogozhin. A reading of the turbulent Notebooks in their entirety is necessary for a full appreciation of Dostoevsky's efforts to reconceive Myshkin (though the major change when it came, the transference of traits, came swiftly). The struggle was between changing conscious intentions or ideas and half-conscious or unconscious intuitions.

"Stavrogin's Confession," as finally published, must be considered in the context of a full discussion of *The Possessed*. What we find in the Notebooks is, in effect, the reverse of that painful struggle for Myshkin's redemption. For Stavrogin emerges from the plans for *The Life of a Great Sinner,* who after much sin and suffering would achieve salvation. Dostoevsky had instead to work his way through to the painful discovery that Stavrogin could not be saved, and must end in despair and suicide. There may have been a strong subjective component in demonstrating that one as depraved as the Idiot could ultimately reveal many Christ-like qualities, though his epilepsy at last gives way to full madness. And there may well have been, in the resolution of Stavrogin's history, that condemnation of self by proxy familiar in a number of highly subjective writers, and notably André Gide. Where Dickens lightly touched and retouched the surface of a scarcely criminal daydream, Dostoevsky ruthlessly explored, again and again, the implications of a serious obsession, and would not permit himself the luxury of either conscious evasion or full repression.

There poignantly remained, to balance these visions of evil, a longing to legitimize paedophilic attraction, to overstep barriers of age, and imagine a reciprocated love. The sexless relationships of Pavel Pavlovich and Liza, of Netochka Nezvanova and her stepfather are evil, both because a repressed sexual and incestuous component may be present, and because of generalized abuse. The sentimental fantasy of *Poor Folk,* odd in such a young writer, is of a paternal older man rebuffing a young woman's invitation to visit her. He prefers a contemplative voyeuristic relationship, but enjoys knowing that he is needed and loved. Myshkin's compassion for the abject consumptive Marie, in her weakness virtually a child, involves an idealized sexless relationship, one distrusted by the community and misunderstood even by the children, though its effect on them is beneficial. Yet there is a connection with Stavrogin and Matryosha. As the distraught little girl suddenly threw her arms around Stavrogin's neck and began to kiss him violently of her own accord, so Marie would fall to kissing Myshkin's hands, and "seemed like a crazy creature in terrible excitement and delight." Matryosha's reaction is a portent of emotional collapse and suicide; Marie's is a moving moment of happiness in a lifetime of suffering. Yet it echoes the response of Svidrigaïlov's young fiancée, "too unceremoniously" taken onto his knee, and suddenly flinging herself on his neck. What, Dostoevsky asks again and again, is the emotional effect on the child of an older man's love?

The culminating effort to legitimize the forbidden game is Alyosha's relationship with Lise, who combines the victim roles of young girl and cripple, and who is in addition somewhat neurotic. Would she have married Alyosha in the continuation of *The Brothers Karamazov?* Would their relationship have remained sexless, as Lise perhaps suggests when she says he is not "fit to be a husband"? Lise, though appearing briefly, belongs near the forefront of Dostoevsky's gallery of young women: bright, witty, capricious, disturbed. We see her at the monastery, playing her alert child's game of staring Alyosha down; read her moving declaration of love that she tries to pass off as a joke; listen to her ("the little demon") as she tells him of her boredom and love of emotional disorder, her craving to destroy herself, her dreams of devils and her "frightful longing to revile God aloud." She is tormented by evil fantasies, and imagines herself eating pineapple compote while watching a child she has crucified. She movingly appeals to Alyosha to save her. The chapter ends as she asks him to carry what is presumably a love letter to Ivan, then deliberately slams a door on her finger in self-punishment. The story is inevitably incomplete. If Alyosha is to some degree unwittingly responsible for Lise's *crise de nerfs,* he also represents, Dostoevsky suggests, her only possible salvation.

There is, of course, one other novel in which he dramatized and tried to legitimize a paedophilic attraction.

THE INSULTED AND THE INJURED

This ambitious first "major" novel was, like most of Dostoevsky's work, written hurriedly and under various pressures; only about fifty pages, he said, satisfied him. There could hardly be a better example (except *A Raw Youth*) of fine material blurred through deficiencies of technique, point-of-view especially. Vanya's nominally retrospective narration is immersed in a turbulent fictional present occurring in two or more places and with two distinct plots, neither of which he wholly understands. He must rush back and forth between Natasha's rooms and his own, with periodic dutiful visits to the Ichmenyevs, and in all three places depends very heavily on reported dialogue (much of it explanatory though confused) to carry the story. He is not in a position to see, and perhaps Dostoevsky did not entirely see, the egoism behind the various self-sacrificial gestures, and his own love for Natasha is remarkably undramatized.

The novel has its moments of impressive realism: Masloboev's young wife, who longs for some social life; the Ichmenyevs, a fine picture of capricious and irritable old age; the brutal Madame Bubnov and her customers; the glimpses of tenement poverty. In a minor way, through the passive Vanya, Dostoevsky here too relives his neurotic role in the Siberian triangle: helping his rival for the sake of the apparently lost love. All three might live together, Natasha declares, and Alyosha wants to embrace him as a brother. But Vanya seems too passive to do more than run the lovers' errands; too quiet, even, to enjoy the neurotic pleasures of self-abasement. It is fascinating to watch Dostoevsky "try out" material that will inform major novels: *The Brothers Karamazov* and especially *The Idiot*. The quartets have their structural resemblance:

Vanya-Alyosha-Natasha-Katya
Ivan-Dmitri-Grushenka-Katerina
Myshkin-Rogozhin-Nastasya-Aglaia.

There are big scenes between the rival women in all three novels, and Natasha's awareness of her self-destructiveness—her frenzied consent to her ruin—is splendidly conceived. The comic confrontation of Natasha and Katya has its moments worthy of Molière, as the two vie with each other in nobility. But it lacks the passionate oscillations of *The Idiot*'s interchanges, or the dramatic twists and turns of Grushenka and Katerina. The greatest difference is that there is no dynamic relationship, in *The Insulted and the Injured,* between the men. Alyosha is nicely portrayed as a comically childish adult, without will or power to resist his own whims, wavering between the two women and really wanting both. But his hesitations and ramblings are recorded at excessive length.

Two characters, Prince Valkovsky and Nellie, almost save the book. The portrait of Valkovsky is a brilliantly incisive one of a powerful opportunist, not merely a bored aristocrat: a cynical egoist and manipulator, utterly scornful of "Schillerism" and its romantic generosities, cynical even in his moments of terrible honesty. His great moment in the novel is his long scarcely interrupted discourse to Vanya in the restaurant: the first important philosophical interpolation in Dostoevsky's work. It has some of the force which comes from a grudging sympathy with ideas and attitudes usually repudiated. Albert Camus's *The Fall* reveals a close affinity to these pages, not merely to *Notes from Underground:* the fiction of shameless exposure encouraged by a number of drinks, the insistence that "the more virtuous anything is, the more egoism there is in it," the interlarding of philosophical reasonings with concrete memories of cynicism and cruelty. The very movement of Valkovsky's mind, subtly entangling the reader, is that of Clamence; so too the terrible honesty: "I'll agree to anything so long as I'm all right, and there are legions like me, and we really are all right."

The indebtedness of Dostoevsky's Nellie to Little Nell is obvious, beyond age and name and frailty: the suffering caused by a crazed grandfather, the exposure to poverty and the need to beg in public, the sexual threat and the slow wasting away, the at last revealed mystery of parentage. Nellie is a remarkably real thirteen-year-old, with the black hair and "flashing black eyes, which somehow looked foreign," and the enigmatic gaze of a dark heroine, rather than the clear bright eye and light brown hair of the angelic Little Nell. The characterization is one of the most coherent in Dostoevsky's work. Psychologically, Nellie makes sense, "common sense," as some of Dostoevsky's splendid older young women do not. Her whims and tantrums and sudden veerings of affection or mistrust never seem gratuitous. Her silences and inhibitions are intimately part of her being and the consequence of her life. But so too are the moments when she breaks through to express anger or love.

For Dostoevsky the story represented a fuller than usual escape from repression, and the playing of the two forbidden games. On the one hand he evoked vividly a brothel where children could be procured, and a thirteen-year-old passed off as eleven if need be, and where an actual physical assault on Nellie is attempted. But also he imagined her rescue by Vanya, and the pleasing fantasy of an innocent paedophilic attraction: a young girl moving in with his hero, who buys clothes for her and is nursed by her, who is kissed by her when she thinks him asleep and who hears her declaration of love. Small wonder Vanya experiences and brilliantly describes genuine *angoisse* in the long paragraph that precedes Nellie's first appearance: a *"mysterious horror . . .* a most oppressive, agonising state of terror of something which I don't know how to define, and something passing all understanding and outside the natural order of things." The dark disturbance does not make much sense in terms of Vanya's psychic economy, but a great deal in terms of Dostoevsky's. The creative experience was one of breaking through defenses to treat openly what some of the later fictions would merely allude to. The impulse, moreover, was to legitimize the paedophilic relationship: present it as real and reciprocated love. My supposition is that the moment of bringing Nellie onto the scene, a moment of deep authorial involvement, was fraught with unformulated anxiety. The *angoisse* evoked is not unlike that preceding Myshkin's epileptic fits. These in turn, though often interpreted religiously, can also be seen as evasions of sexual encounters or substitutes for crime.

Nellie's first appearance is very moving: her perplexity as she asks Vanya about her grandfather; her silent turning away, after hearing of his death; her return to ask if the dog Azorka is also dead. Her mistrust and evasiveness and bitter pride at their second meeting are plausible, though Vanya calls her a "wild little thing." So too her silences and her long intent staring, the morning after her rescue from Madame Bubnov's, and her refusal to show the doctor her tongue. They are the silences of a "strange pride as well as wonder and wild curiosity," but also of a child who does not know what to say. The resistance to the doctor is that of one whose identity has been violently threatened. In time we learn that Nellie knew of her mother's abandonment; that she had herself begged on the streets, that she had seen her mother die. Her nervous crises are altogether plausible responses to what we know, and particularly to the effort to force her into prostitution. Thus her compulsive ripping of the muslin skirt Madame Bubnov had dressed her up in, and her sense that everyone, including herself, is wicked. Her capricious behavior with the doctor—the game of repeatedly spilling the medicine, then asking whether he will kiss her, whether he will marry her when she's grown up—has something of a normal child's need to test the limits of adult tolerance and affection; and may derive too from a desire to make Vanya jealous. But there is also, perhaps, a need to reenact the pattern, so clear in the Nastasya of *The Idiot,* of attracting and repudiating older men.

There is, moreover, a threat to identity in so much adult concern. " 'And why, why does everybody make such a fuss over me? I won't have it, I won't have it!' Nellie cried suddenly, in a sort of frenzy. 'I'll go beg in the street.' " Vanya, here less obtuse than usual, sees in her malicious resistance to the medicine a perhaps unconscious need "for some excuse to cry, to sob hysterically . . . all this to relieve her capricious and aching little heart." But there is also, as when she deliberately breaks a cup, a need to reject affection, aggravate suffering, and reenact a past misery. Thus she escapes to the street to beg, ostensibly to buy a new cup. But she is not begging from need: "Yes, my old friend was right; she had been ill-treated; her hurt could not be healed, and she seemed purposely trying to aggravate her wound by this mysterious behaviour, this mistrustfulness of us all; as though she enjoyed her own pain by this *egoism of suffering."* Even in this moment of extreme stress, when she finds herself discovered and drops and breaks the new cup, her behavior is in character. But she is as convincing in her quieter moments of uncertainty and embarrassment, blushing, or looking dreamily at the floor, or picking at the edge of the sofa. The picture of Nellie in this early novel, like that of Lise in the last one, has an intimate reality and a psychological penetration found in very few writers.

The love affair, for such it is on both sides, is dramatized with much delicacy. Vanya is attracted to Nellie from the start, but doesn't know why. An important step is taken, as with Swiveller and the Marchioness, when he wakes from his collapse to find her "compassionate and anxious little face leaning over" him; and remembers, as in a vision, her nursing attentions, and a gentle kiss on his face.[30] On another occasion he finds her asleep with her face on his pillow; the next morning her arm lies on the pillow, and he kisses it. Presently, after a brief conversation about his writing, she bursts out with her declaration of love. Her convulsive reaction has its sinister echoes, later, in Matryosha's unexpected embrace of Stavrogin, and in the little fiancée's kissing of Svidrigaïlov. But it is here legitimized, as "the need for expression and utterance grew stronger, till the inevitable outburst came, when the whole being forgot itself and gave itself up to the craving for love, to gratitude, to affection and to tears."

The warmest moments of the little romance come immediately after Nellie tells Vanya of Masloboev's disturbing visit, and openly expresses her affection, "standing before me with her eyes cast down, with one hand on my shoulder, and with the other pinching my sleeve." She has, he silently recognizes, become "sweet and precious" to him, but this creates an inhibition. "I don't know what I would have given to have kissed her at that moment." In this scene, one of the tenderest in Dostoevsky, Nellie is convincingly both child and adult: a child in her remarks on Vanya's book, and in her shyness, but adult in her awakening erotic life, conveyed in glances and gestures, and in the delicacy of her touchings.

Vanya's obtuseness—his failure to recognize her full feeling—is responsible for the behavior that subsequently puzzles him: her sullen and capricious moods, with moments of affection unwittingly revealed; at last the extreme strategy of running away, to the doctor and to the Masloboevs'. She wants, of course, to be fetched and brought back to his place. Hence the poignancy of her resistance to being moved to the Ichmenyevs', even though it be to rescue Natasha. She agrees to go, but looks at Vanya with a "strange, prolonged gaze. There was something like reproach in that gaze, and I felt it in my heart." Arrived at her new home, and tightly squeezing Vanya's hand in hers, "she kept her eyes on the ground and only from time to time stole frightened glances about her like a little wild creature in a snare." Liza, in *The Eternal Husband,* simply turns her head to the wall and elects to die; Nellie, we already know, is afflicted by a defective heart. But her illness intensifies at this point. The nervous strain is aggravated, as Vanya suggests, by her being compelled to tell her story in such detail: the grandfather's brutality and her mother's crazed suffering, the first encounter with the man who assaulted her at Madame Bubnov's. The final revelation is of another secret strain: she had known she was Valkovsky's daughter. But she did not go to him for help, and she died unforgiving. The last chapters, with their harrowing recollections and revelations, come closer than anything but the death of Ilusha in *The Brothers Karamazov* to Dickensian *attendrissement*. Nellie's bare statements of suffering ("We were walking about the streets until it was quite evening, and mother was walking about and crying all the time, and holding my hand. I was very tired. We had nothing to eat that day") lend reality to the mother's recognition of Azorka, the grandfather walking away from her, the dog's efforts to pull him back. For we have known Azorka as sullen, abject, the most repulsive dog Vanya had ever seen. But now we hear of a time of happiness when the dog performed "in the street with some actors, and knew how to do his part and used to have a monkey riding on his back, and knew how to use a gun and lots of other things." The mother was so fond of Azorka that she used to take him to bed with her.

Why, given his tendency to repeat major psychological and plot patterns, did Dostoevsky never again attempt such a paedophilic romance? The subject would have seemed, from this one partial success, very congenial. The effort to legitimize, to *normalize* paedophilia was in its way comparable to Gide's effort to present as normal and healthy, in *The Counterfeiters,* the homosexual love of a mature man and an adolescent boy; in both novels the authors were doubtless sincere. One reason may be that Dostoevsky's ambitious novel was severely criticized as a work of art, not least by himself. But another may be that the deeply felt attraction to adolescent girls, however innocent of overt sexuality, remained a forbidden game. At some level of underconsciousness, it may be, Dostoevsky held Vanya's affection—much as Nellie longed for it—to blame for her death from an overtaxed heart.

5 FORBIDDEN GAMES (III): FAULKNER'S MISOGYNY

Faulkner's misogyny presents a special problem: it is unrepressed and even undisguised, is often comically and extravagantly explicit, and offers little resistance to analysis. There is, to be sure, a distinction to be made between misogynous impulse and a healthy satirical intention. Doc Hines, self-appointed instrument of God's abomination of womanflesh, is a great portrait of fanatic puritanism. And Faulkner doubtless did see Caddy and her daughter as victims of "some concept of Compson honor" and of a myth of southern womanhood. He probably thought he admired the forthrightness of Ruby Lamar, offering her body to save Lee Goodwin, and even the mindless naturalism of Lena Grove. Yet there is much evidence that Faulkner shared, imaginatively, no little of the puritanism he satirized; and shared too the Tristan spirituality of Gavin Stevens rejecting both Eula and her daughter,[1] and the monastic integrity of the Tall Convict of *The Wild Palms,* one of his least equivocal heroes. There are other forbidden games to stir Faulkner's imagination, cross-race sexuality most obviously. But miscegenation or sexual abuse (chiefly the abuse of black women by white men) is social history not personal obsession. The more complex question is whether any intercourse with a darker partner is destructive or willfully self-destructive, as it was with Charles Etienne de Saint Velery Bon. Homosexuality, often felt as a menace, is rarely seen in overt form, and the sadistic voyeurism of Popeye is an extreme clinical case. There is also some preoccupation with incest.

It is nevertheless evident that the ultimate and repugnantly forbidden game to the Faulknerian imagination was normal intercourse with a woman of marriage-able age. We are speaking here, even more than with Dickens and Dostoevsky, of the "writer" not the "citizen," though there are tantalizing areas for specu-lation about the latter: Faulkner's extreme evasiveness and myth-making (no-toriously about his wartime experience), his shyness with women, his aloofness and passivity in his early twenties, his alcoholism. Yet in some respects we know less about Faulkner than about Dickens and Dostoevsky; the very full Blotner biography throws comparatively little light on his psycho-sexual life. Thus it seems more than usually advisable, with an enigmatic near-contem-porary, to turn directly to the work.

A first point so obvious that it is rarely made: the misogynist imagination selects, for its female victims, appalling predicaments and punishments, even extreme physical violation and pain: Temple Drake's rape or Charlotte Ritten-meyer's bungled abortion. The mindless niece who persuades the steward to leave the yacht with her, in *Mosquitoes,* for some pages seems likely to be bit-ten to death. (He in turn, obliged to carry her on his back, evokes the eroticized grass—"monstrous and separate, blade by blade"—and sinister rhythms of the misogynous early Conrad of *The Sisters* and *The Outcast of the Islands.*) We may easily forget, given the Tall Convict's outrage, that his passenger also car-ries a painful burden. The appalling flood of the Mississippi is suavely counter-pointed, in the "Wild Palms" chapters, by knives and iron cold. Faulkner's misogyny, like Conrad's, diminished noticeably with age; this led to the no-torious rehabilitations of Eula Varner and Temple Drake, and to the grosser sentimentalities of Gavin Stevens. The sufferings of the later heroines evoke a Dickensian pity: Eula Varner driven to self-sacrifice and suicide, and her daughter Linda gratuitously deafened. The twilight glow of *The Reivers* is less displeasing, and the golden heart of Corinthia Everbe Hogganbeck. For we are now frankly in the age of recollection, and the myth of lost childhood.

Faulkner, like Dostoevsky, had a rather limited feminine typology; but with the great difference that Dostoevsky found, in all of his recurring types, some-thing to love. For Faulkner, young girls before the age of puberty are not sources of anxiety; Caddy "was the beautiful one, she was my heart's darling. That's what I wrote the book about. . . ." [2] Eccentric or benignant old ladies also represented no menace; they were sexually unavailable to the imagination. Various narrators evoke eloquently a brief and precious nymphet phase. Ratliff interprets Gavin Stevens's drugstore dates with the thirteen-, fourteen- and fif-teen-year-old Linda Snopes as paternal; he wants to save her soul from "Snopesism." His image of the soul recalls—consciously? facetiously?—Faulkner's image of virginity in his Appendix to *The Sound and the Fury:* so much to be poised precariously on the nose of a seal. Linda's adult appeal, for Gavin, lies in her psycho-sexual unavailability. To her shocking four-letter word (a blank in the text) he responds, *"because we are the 2 in all the world who can love each other without having to. . . ."* Charles Mallison, shrewder here than Ratliff, notes the repetitive pattern: first the child Melisandre Backus, then Linda. But the children made the mistake of growing older: "they had to be in motion to be alive, and the only moment of motion which caught his attention, his eye, was that one at which they entered puberty, like the swirl of a skirt or flow or turn of limb when entering, passing through a door. . . ." Miss Rosa speaks of herself at fourteen, and the moment only virgins know, "when the entire delicate spirit's bent is one anonymous climaxless epicene and unravished nuptial. . . ." (Epicinity, in *Soldiers' Pay,* evokes "girls in a frieze," "lilies like nuns in a cloister," a "poplar vain as a girl darkly in an arrested passionate ecstasy.") The transitional stage is poetically described by Mr. Compson, as he speaks of Judith between childhood and womanhood, a change from shape "without substance" to womanly flesh, and "that state where, though still visible, young girls appear as though seen through glass and where even the voice cannot reach them. . . ." The glass is related, psychologically, to the urn, itself sometimes decorated by a frieze of arrested motion, so crucial throughout Faulkner's work: an urn that can be alarmingly broken.

There is, however, the moment when sexual availability occurs to the conscious mind. In *Sartoris* Frankie is no more than a tennis partner. But in *Flags in the Dust,* an earlier version of the novel, Horace Benbow's contemplation of her seventeen-year-old virginal grace is interestingly censored, with an actual blank occurring after the word *unchaste,* this followed by a question mark. In both versions Benbow observes Harry Mitchell fondle his daughter Little Belle, while the child watches Horace "with radiant and melting diffidence." Horace's love in *Sanctuary,* of the adolescent Little Belle, now his stepdaughter, is as troubled and poignant as Quentin Compson's for the menaced Caddy, and for him too an odor of honeysuckle is traumatic. He holds Little Belle's photograph, after returning from the unnerving interview at Miss Reba's, and her fatality becomes in his revery that of Temple violated above "the faint, furious uproar of the shucks." She is "bound naked on her back on a flat car moving at speed through a black tunnel. . . ." But the revery begins, sickeningly, with his sense of her sexual attraction for him, a moment reminiscent of Svidrigaïlov's dream of the little girl he had wanted to help greeting him with a prostitute's smile, or Arkady's dream, in *A Raw Youth,* of a shockingly sensual Katerina.

The niece and Jenny, the mindless flappers of *Mosquitoes,* have their small parts in that gently misogynous novel, a minor *Antic Hay*. Jenny comes to Pete in a "flowing enveloping movement"; Mr. Talieferro also feels himself enveloped as she stands beside him, "surrounded, enclosed by the sweet cloudy fire of her thighs, as young girls can." The niece's incestuous interest in her brother is amusingly overt. In an early scene they share a cigarette she has kept in the crown of her hat, now "limp, like a worm"; meanwhile he has been working on a cylinder of wood larger than a silver dollar and about three inches long; it is in two sections that fit together. In the epilogue she comes to his bed, over his protests, to engage in a sisterly version of *fellatio* that leaves him with a moistened ear:

> "Well. Be quick about it." He turned his face away and she leaned down and took his ear between her teeth, biting it just a little, making a meaningless maternal sound against his ear. "That's enough," he said presently, turning his head and his moistened ear. "Get out, now."
> She rose obediently and returned to her room.[3]

With Temple Drake, who is about the same age, we cross the line from mindless *demi-vierge* to accomplished nymphomaniac, though at the Old Frenchman's Place we see her rather as an animal in heat, fearing and wanting to be raped. Mink's future wife, at the lumber camp, was "not a nympholept but the confident lord of a harem." Summoned to her bedroom, Mink found he had entered "the fierce simple cave of a lioness—a tumescence which surrendered nothing and asked no quarter. . . ." The sexual demands of Joanna Burden are, by contrast, neurotic, the perversion cerebral. Her life is rigidly compartmentalized: "The sewer ran only by night." She likes to remind herself aloud that she is having intercourse with a negro; wants to damn "herself forever to the hell of her forefathers, by living not alone in sin but in filth," and invents furious sexual games of concealment and pursuit, fantasies of repeated rape. Joe Christmas's castration need—the striking off of the undergarment buttons as with a knife, the exhibiting himself to the "white bastards"—is in part a response to lifelong identity crisis, but also to Joanna's specific invasions of his identity. To lower the garment is to invite, all unconsciously, an alternative to terrifying normal intercourse: "the cool mouth of darkness, the soft cool tongue" and the speeding car "sucking its dust" and "sucking with it the white woman's fading cry." Conceivably repressed homosexual impulse and the castration need/fear blend in a shared misogynous vision and dread. Perhaps Joe Christmas found, at the hands of Percy Grimm, the freedom he had blunderingly sought all along.

The castrating female with *vagina dentata*, often compared to a cat, is sometimes treated comically, sometimes with unsmiling alarm. Joanna Burden waits for Joe, "panting, her eyes in the dark glowing like the eyes of cats." The powerful woman, ruthless and amoral, and somehow endowed with a sexual knowledge beyond her partner's (*"She already knows,"* Ike reflects in *The Bear, "more than I with all the man-listening in camps where there was nothing to read ever even heard of"*) threatens will, identity, moral purpose. The menace of the child Eula Varner may be engulfment by "mammalian meat," drowning; the castrating female can be more actively dangerous, since she possesses teeth and claws. "Take off your clothes," Ike's wife commands, as forthrightly as Charlotte Rittenmeyer. The hand which draws Ike down is also holding him away, suggesting sexual titillation as well as bargaining refusal. But presently it has the characteristics of a surgical instrument, "as though arm and hand were a piece of wire cable with one looped end, only the hand tightening as he pulled against it." The bed of Mink's insatiable future wife offers, in its imagery, comparable discomforts: "a bed made by hand of six-inch unplaned timbers cross-braced with light steel cables, yet which nevertheless would advance in short steady skidding jerks across the floor like a light and ill-balanced rocking chair." Charlotte Rittenmeyer's eyes, when Harry first meets her, are "yellow, like a cat's." Soon he "seemed to be drowning, volition and will, in the yellow stare. . . ." Later, in Chicago, her terrible honesty emasculates: he blunders and fumbles like a moth, in the "unwinking yellow stare" . . . "a rabbit caught in the glare of a torch; an envelopment almost like a liquid. . . ." She has "the blank feral eyes" of the predatory woman, but the tough blunt vulgarity of the male sexual athlete. In bed she would seem to be the man, "as heedless of the hard and painful elbow which jabbed him as she would have been on her own account if the positions had been reversed, as she was of the painful hand which grasped his hair and shook his head with savage impatience."

The misogynous animal imagery, like the incestuous attraction of Horace and Narcissa, is stronger in *Flags in the Dust* than in *Sartoris*. Belle Mitchell takes Horace to a quiet place while her husband is occupied on the tennis court. "Belle slid her *soft prehensile* hand into his, clutching his hand against her *softly clothed* thigh, and led him into a room beyond *folding doors*." The words I have italicized are omitted or changed in *Sartoris*, where a dusky passage, dangerous enough perhaps, leads not to engulfing doors but to a music room. The most ruthless castrating female of *Flags in the Dust*, Belle's sister Joan, simply disappears from the final version. After seeing her for the first time Horace recalls his first circus, and a tiger "watching him with yellow and lazy contemplation." The tiger was old and toothless, but Joan is not, and Horace finds himself watching her "as a timorous person is drawn with deli-

cious revulsion to gaze into a window filled with knives.'' ''Carnivorous,''
Horace reflects, on the occasion of their first conversation, a ''lady tiger in a
tea gown,'' possessed of ''feline poise.'' In due time she comes to his house.
She has her periods of ''aloof and purring repose,'' though the firelight glows
''in little red points in her unwinking eyes,'' and she is ''like a sheathed
poniard.'' The first time she spends the whole night ''she revealed another
feline trait: that of a prowling curiosity about dark rooms.''

There is also the softer menace of the fecund and the bovine. *Light in
August,* interpreted schematically, may well seem to offer in Lena Grove a celebration of the natural, against the puritanisms and the self-destructive rigidities, against Byron Bunch's mechanical ordering of his life and Hightower's
contemplative death-in-life. But she is, at her best, a serenely comic creation.
So too at times is the passenger of the Tall Convict, always associated with the
river's monstrous flood, but not comic for him, who wants to turn his back ''on
all pregnant and female life forever.'' The misogyny of Gordon in *Mosquitoes,*
which induces an early exercise in Joycean stream-of-consciousness, is serious
enough. Staring down into the water, he puts aside female temptation (''un-
muscled wallowing fecund and foul the tragic body of a woman who conceives
without pleasure bears without pain'') and expresses a Conradian anxiety over
strangling hair. But the great bovine creation—comic, mock-heroic, mythical,
ultimately romantic—is of course the child Eula Varner, the object of the
schoolmaster Labove's paedophilic obsession. He, the ''virile anchorite of old
time,'' finds himself helpless before the eleven-year-old girl who ''postulated
that ungirdled quality of the very goddesses in his Homer and Thucydides,''
and who brought a ''moist blast of spring's liquorish corruption, a pagan triumphal prostration before the supreme primal uterus.'' Her passivity is such that
even in infancy ''she already knew there was nowhere she wanted to go'' and
''might as well have been a foetus.'' She emanates, even at eight, ''an outrageous and immune perversity like a blooded and contrary filly,'' and walking to
the store gives off, her brother claims, an odor as of a dog in heat. For Labove
she may, though terrifying, have the attraction of innocence and sexuality, of
being at once child and woman. Yet she seems, with her ''kaleidoscopic con-
volution of mammalian ellipses,'' more bovine than human. She is ''tranquil
and chewing,'' like Ike's beloved cow, and like her invites classical allusions.
Eula's mythical properties, turning the schoolroom ''into a grove of Venus,''
prepare the reader for those, some fifty pages later, of the cow (evocative of
''Troy's Helen and the nymphs and the snoring mitred bishops, the saviors and
the victims and the kings''). And that ''triumphal prostration before the supreme primal uterus'' prepares us for the moment when Ike, ''lying beneath the

struggling and bellowing cow, received the violent relaxing of her fear-constricted bowels.'' The cow is of Olympian seed. Yet the highly poetic treatment may reflect an ambiguous attitude toward the natural functions. For Ike, following the violent relaxing, tries to reassure her that such a violation of ''maiden's delicacy is no shame, since such is the very iron imperishable warp of the fabric of love.'' Orgasm appears to be confused, in Ike's imagination if not the author's, with defecation.

These are some of the dangerous females. The specifically sexual menace appears to have two forms. The first, which dissolves masculine will (Eula's ''mind- and will-sapping fluid softness''), is that of engulfment or drowning envelopment. How much such imagery is meaningfully obsessive is hard to say, given Faulkner's extraordinary, often unconscious memory for his own phrases, images, analogies. The older Eula Varner Snopes, offering herself to Gavin Stevens, might leave him ''tossed and wrung and wrenched and consumed, the light last final spent husk to float slowing and weightless. . . .'' She confronts him ''with that blue envelopment like the sea'' and looks at him with a ''blue serene terrible envelopment'' before expressing her extreme feminine amorality: ''You just are, and you need, and you must, and so you do.'' On the following page Stevens can even smell ''that terrible, that drowning envelopment.'' In *Flags in the Dust* Horace is doubly threatened. His spirit drowns in his sister's serenity ''like a swimmer on a tideless summer sea''; later he thinks of the older Belle ''enveloping him like a rich and fatal drug, like a motionless and cloying sea in which he watched himself drown.'' Ike McCaslin's one recorded sexual experience, following his surrender to the terrible hand, was a kind of drowning, since ''after a no-time he returned and lay spent on the insatiate immemorial beach. . . .'' But the drowning sea may also be an engulfing morass. Thus Joe Christmas saw ''himself as from a distance, like a man being sucked down into a bottomless morass,'' submerged ''more and more by the imperious and overriding fury of those nights.'' An amusing variant sees actual quicksand in terms of female sexual organs, rather than the other way around, as old Gowrie helps extract the body of his son, in *Intruder in the Dust*,

> the body coming out now feet first, gallowsed up and out of the inscrutable suck to the heave of the crude tackle then free of the sand with a faint smacking plop like the sound of lips perhaps in sleep and in the bland surface nothing: a faint wimple wrinkle already fading then gone like the end of a faint secret fading smile. . . .[4]

Small wonder the Tall Convict prefers the ''consolingly hard ground that can break your bones'' to water, which accepts you ''substanceless and enveloping and suffocating, down and down and down.''

Some of the Faulknerian envelopments have the familiar ring of the *auflösung* of romantic literature, and of the impulse (both dreaded and longed for) to lose consciousness in a form of maternal sea. The second sexual menace, most harrowingly experienced by Joe Christmas, involves a horror of menstruation. Christmas, the most clinical "case" in Faulkner's fiction, combines the two fears. His childhood trauma as he ingests the cool invisible worm of toothpaste—hidden among the soft womansmelling garments, as the dietician and the interne make love—is echoed in his first sexual experience, as he takes his turn with the negro girl. "There was something in him trying to get out, like when he used to think of toothpaste." In the dark, "enclosed by the womanshenegro and the haste," leaning, "he seemed to look down into a black well and at the bottom saw two glints like reflections of dead stars." Presently he is sickened to hear that women are "doomed to be at stated and inescapable intervals victims of periodical filth"; his measured response, in attempting to cope with this horror, is to shoot a sheep and immerse his hands in its blood. Quentin Compson recalls his father's comment on women's mysteries:

> Delicate equilibrium of periodical filth between two moons balanced. Moons he said full and yellow as harvest moons her hips thighs. Outside outside of them always but. Yellow. Feetsoles with walking like. Then know that some man that all those mysterious and imperious concealed. With all that inside of them shapes an outward suavity waiting for a touch to. Liquid putrefaction like drowned things floating like pale rubber flabbily filled getting the odour of honeysuckle all mixed up.[5]

The horror of lost virginity—of "the swine untethered in pairs rushing coupled into the sea"—is suggested in the instances of blocked phrasing here, as well as by the image of floating contraceptives.

Michael Millgate has commented on the significance of the recurring urn imagery in Faulkner's work, his preoccupation with motion in stasis. But it is surely evident that the urn is also a primary sexual symbol which may or may not be broken: *la cruche cassée* of Greuze as well as Freud. Appalled on his first date with Bobbie Allen, as she informs him it's the wrong time of the month, Joe Christmas leaves her and presently vomits: "In the notseeing and the hardknowing as though in a cave he seemed to see a diminishing row of suavely shaped urns in moonlight, blanched. And not one was perfect. Each one was cracked and from each crack there issued something liquid, deathcolored, and foul." A related horror is suggested by Horace's dream of black matter running from Belle's mouth on galley 22 of the unrevised *Sanctuary*,[6] displaced menstrual flow it may be, though in the final text there is explicit reference to the "black stuff that ran out of Bovary's mouth and down upon her bridal veil.'' By contrast is the "almost perfect vase of clear amber" created by Horace in *Sartoris:* "larger, more richly and chastely serene, which he kept always on his night table and called by his sister's name in the intervals of apostrophizing both of them impartially in his moments of rhapsody over the realization of the meaning of peace and the unblemished attainment of it, as 'Thou still unravished bride of quietness.' '' The word in *Flags in the Dust* is *quietude*. And in *Flags in the Dust* a conversation with Narcissa (removed from *Sartoris* entirely) both makes his incestuous wishes explicit and connects them with virginity. It's "all sort of messy: living and seething corruption glossed over for a while by smoothly colored flesh; all foul, until the clean and naked bone.''

The preoccupation with incest is connected both with a veneration of virginity and, less demonstrably, with a dread of normal intercourse. But Horace's love of the chastely serene Narcissa does not preclude physical attraction. About to inform her that he intends to marry Belle, Horace restlessly touches objects on her bedside table, sits on the edge of the bed, lays his hand on her knee, apologizes for leaving her alone at night. "For a while he sat brooding on the wild repose of his hand lying on her covered knee.'' Presently, after more restless touching of objects, he strokes her knee again. Later, they meet as in a lover's embrace, as he comes in out of the rain, "whipping his sodden hat against his leg. . . .'' The presumably unconscious sexual image is worthy of the early Conrad. In *Flags in the Dust* there follows a scene in which Horace conjectures that there are "any number of virgins who love children walking the world today, some of whom look a little like you,'' whom he might conceivably marry, and this is in turn followed by the compact account of his affair with the feline Joan. But in *Sartoris* we move directly to the car accident and old Bayard's death. The incestuous attraction, reduced with the revision of *Flags in the Dust,* remains very overt in the typescript of the original *Sanctuary.* And Belle has recognized the incestuous drive. "You're in love with your sister. What do the books call it? What sort of complex?'' [7]

The most eloquent and most succinct critical statements on Quentin Compson's incest fantasies are, of course, those of Faulkner himself in the Appendix to *The Sound and the Fury:*

Who loved not his sister's body but some concept of Compson honor precariously and (he knew well) only temporarily supported by the minute fragile membrane of her maidenhead as a miniature replica of all the whole vast globy earth may be poised on the nose of a trained seal. Who loved not the idea of the incest which he would not commit, but some presbyterian concept of its eternal punishment. . . .[8]

Does the novel itself support so much emphasis on Compson honor? The most moving recollections would suggest more intimate and more primitive feelings: the knife at her throat which has overtones of dreaded sexual penetration, during their talk of suicide, with the knife presently dropped; or the brief memories of physical contact in childhood, in themselves innocent enough. His deepest concern would seem to be her loss of virginity *per se* rather than the loss of family honor. A leaf in the water in which Quentin will drown carries echoes of the maidenhead that obsesses him; in death there is purity, no touching, no giving or taking in marriage. We have reached an important moment in Quentin's last day, as he hides the flat irons under the end of the bridge:

> Where the shadow of the bridge fell I could see down for a long way, but not as far as the bottom. When you leave a leaf in water a long time after awhile the tissue will be gone and the delicate fibers waving slow as the motion of sleep. They don't touch one another, no matter how knotted up they once were, no matter how close they lay once to the bones.[9]

The incestuous impulses and relationships in *Absalom, Absalom!* are complex and intense, but like so much else in the novel are distanced by the rhetoric of the narrators and by the novel's choreographic formality. No commentator could hope to improve on Mr. Compson's own analyses. His reasoning, for Henry, begins with an elaboration on Faulkner's in the Appendix to *The Sound and the Fury*. His "fierce provincial's pride in his sister's virginity was a false quantity"; it "must depend upon its loss, absence, to have existed at all." Through the brother-in-law he may, by identification, enjoy the sister. But also, identifying with the sister, he may experience a homoerotic connection. That it would be doubly incestuous is, however, not known to Mr. Compson:

> In fact, perhaps this is the pure and perfect incest: the brother realizing that the sister's virginity must be destroyed in order to have existed at all, taking that virginity in the person of the brother-in-law, the man whom he would be if he could become, metamorphose into, the lover, the husband; by whom he would be despoiled, choose for despoiler, if he could become, metamorphose into the sister, the mistress, the bride. Perhaps that is what went on, not in Henry's mind but in his soul.[10]

Mr. Compson's version of Charles Bon's love is, in turn, a perfect example of René Girard's mediation and triangular desire.[11]

> It was because Bon loved not only Judith after his fashion but he loved Henry too and I believe in a deeper sense than after his fashion. Perhaps in his fatalism he loved Henry the better of the two, seeing perhaps in the sister merely the shadow, the woman vessel with which to consummate the love whose actual object was the youth—this cerebral Don Juan who, reversing the order, had learned to love what

he had injured; perhaps it was even more than Judith or Henry either: perhaps the life, the existence, which they represented.[12]

One further misogynous creation, virtually contemporary with *Absalom, Absalom!*, is of genuine and sometimes frightening interest: Laverne of *Pylon,* shared by her husband Shumann and the "parachute guy" Jack, and loved hopelessly by the blundering unnamed reporter (who is at once Christ-figure and a skeletal harbinger of death, an appalled Miss Lonelyhearts and fatally interfering Myshkin). Near the novel's end, and prior to a scene as desolate, direct and stark as any in Hemingway's short stories (as her child is turned over to the dead Shumann's father), three compassionate pages tell of Laverne's victimization, at fourteen and fifteen, by her sister's husband. The adult Laverne is as tough and masculine as Charlotte Rittenmeyer ("pale strong rough ragged hair" . . . "tanned heavy-jawed face"), and her amorality is more forthright. The two men, on the birth of her child of uncertain parentage, and with her approval, at once roll dice to determine which she will marry. The reporter is fascinated by the seemingly disinterested freedom of the threesome, and the fraternity of barnstorming flyers generally. But his voyeurism evokes, at one point, familiar misogynous rhetoric: " 'I could hear all the long soft waiting sound of all womanmeat in bed beyond the curtain.' "

Laverne's response to crisis is fiercely sexual. Angered by Shumann's willingness to risk his life in a dangerous plane (and with both Jack and the mechanic Jiggs in the room) her hard hand strikes his cheek:

> clutching and scrabbling about his jaw and throat and shoulder until he caught it and held it, wrenching and jerking.
> "You bastard rotten, you rotten—" she panted.
> "All right," he said. "Steady, now." She ceased, breathing hard and fast. But he still held the wrist, wary and without gentleness too. "All right, now . . . You want to take your pants off?"
> "They're already off." [13]

From here we move to one of the novel's rare flashbacks, and Laverne's terror on the occasion of her first parachute jump, as she climbs not back into the front seat she had left but into the pilot's, "astride his legs and facing him." The scene, in its comic misogyny and cool treatment of terror, dread both of sexuality and of death, has an audacity belonging more to the 1970's than to the 1930's. The imagery of mutilation is truly Faulknerian, however: a safetywire, a belt that catches him across the legs:

> In the same instant of realising (as with one hand she ripped her skirt hem free of the safetywire with which they had fastened it bloomerfashion between her legs) that she was clawing blindly and furiously not at the belt across his thighs but at the fly of his trousers, he realised that she had on no undergarment, pants.[14]

He soon finds, even as he tries to keep the plane in position, that he is fighting off both Laverne and ("the perennially undefeated, the victorious") his erection. Coming out of a "long swoon" he remembers to roll the plane in the right direction and so rids himself of one burden. The next thing he remembered "was the belt catching him across the legs as, looking out he saw the parachute floating between him and the ground, and looking down he saw the bereaved, the upthrust, the stalk: the annealed rapacious heartshaped crimson bud." She is carried to jail by the outraged village officers on the field, one of whom frenziedly covets her, having seen "the ultimate shape of his jaded desires fall upon him out of the sky, not merely naked but clothed in the very traditional symbology—the ruined dress with which she was trying wildly to cover her loins, and the parachute harness—of female bondage."

Such are some of the terms of Faulkner's misogyny, which would appear to be more intense and more complex than Hemingway's or Conrad's, and more conscious as well. The limitations of this attitude are obvious. Yet it contributed an important share to a small masterpiece, *Sanctuary*.

SANCTUARY

Sanctuary is much underrated, partly because of Faulkner's grossly misleading comment that it was a pot-boiler written in a few weeks, but also because it is so unlike the "greatest" Faulkners; seems to lack the manifest seriousness of *Light in August, The Sound and the Fury, Absalom, Absalom!* and *The Bear*, as well as their difficulty. *Sanctuary* belongs more than most of Faulkner's novels to a recognizable mode of American writing: the tough tight compassionate grotesque picture of suffering, depravity, defeat. There is no redemption in *Sanctuary* other than the redemption of art. The vision is at best one of stoic defeatism, but concludes in despair and a recognition of the void: Horace returning to the horror of life with Belle; Popeye refusing to appeal his absurd sentence; Temple yawning in the Luxembourg gardens, in the season of rain and death. (The Temple of *Requiem for a Nun* is an altogether different person in an implausible "new life.") The relatively short sentences and objective narration and laconic dialogue may remind us of Hemingway. But the truer affinity is with Flaubert, distancing vulgarity through poetic detail and serenely composed syntax. *Sanctuary* is what Dostoevsky would have called, I think, a *poem*. Meanness and evil and depravity, *seen as such* and with precision, but seen also with compassion, constitute a work of beauty, precisely as does

Toulouse-Lautrec's painting of an ugly middle-aged prostitute wearily raising her shift.

Far more than with Dickens and Dostoevsky, the obsession was put to artistic use. Faulkner's misogyny, that is, gave form, solidity, energy to a general vision of contemporary depravity and timeless evil. But *Sanctuary* is a picture, not merely a "vision," of the contemporary depravity, specifically of north Mississippi, more generally of prohibition America. A real lynching occurred at the Oxford courthouse, several years after the publication of *Sanctuary,* and Memphis with its gang conflicts was known as Murder Capital of the U.S.A. The real life contrast for Faulkner was not merely between his somnolent college town and Memphis (where he enjoyed exploring the fringe world of entertainment and corruption) but between the daily tedium of Lafayette/Yoknapatawpha county and its sporadic outbreaks of violence. The "jazz age" students and the resentful townies, Gowan Stevens and his pride in his drinking, the delegation of women protesting Ruby Lamar's stay at the hotel—these are not figures of fantasy, though this might be said of the millionaire lawyer, weighing 280 pounds, who has installed his special bed in Miss Reba's establishment, or the police commissioner discovered there, naked and dancing the Highland Fling. At a fine line between documentary realism and soaring fictional vision stands Senator Clarence Snopes, whose twin brothers Vardaman and Bilbo were named after well-known Mississippi politicians. The soiled hat and greasy velvet collar and "majestic sweep of flesh on either side of a small blunt nose" would have been at home in Dickens's London. He is *non persona grata* at Miss Reba's for feeling the girls' behinds while spending nothing: " 'Look here, mister, folks what uses this waiting-room has got to get on the train now and then.' " The Memphis depravities (except for Temple's) reach us refracted by the grotesque, or by Miss Reba's comic vision, but also by Clarence Snopes's cupidity and cynical humor. Thus the *bas-fonds* misery and exploitation of the negro whorehouse he leads the young innocents to, lest they spend three dollars again:

> "Them's niggers," Virgil said.
> " 'Course they're niggers," Clarence said. "But see this?" he waved a banknote in his cousin's face. "This stuff is color-blind."

Miss Reba's establishment, except for Temple's room, seems a place of good-humored innocence. Virgil's and Fonzo's classic mistake, and their own innocence sustained for so long, adds to a familiar iconography that tempted even Gide in *Lafcadio's Adventures*. Red's funeral, only a slight parodic extension of gangster ceremonies of the twenties, is also kept at a comic distance.

This is but to say that Memphis, the legendary Babylon for north Mississippians, is appropriately stylized. But the "normal" depravities and deprivations of the Old Frenchman's Place, running to ruin and jungle, are intensely real: the slaving Ruby with her sickly child in the box, fiercely cursing; the blind and deaf old man edging his chair into the sun; the mattress of shucks and that other bed of corncobs and cottonseed hulls and the barn loft with its rat. The four men move in somnambulistic, mechanical lust in the room where Temple stands terrified in the corner and the bloody Gowan lies on the mattress. Later the room is in a darkness where Tommy's pale eyes glow faintly, like a cat's, and Popeye's presence is known from the odor of brilliantine. The scenes are taut, spare, intensely real: great dramatic writing.

Interwoven with the general depravity, the picture of the time and place, is Faulkner's deeper vision of evil embodied in the impotent Popeye and the amoral Temple in her nervous animal lust. Theirs is a more than ordinary, "normal" corruption. Popeye reaches us in part through traditional symbolism: evil as blackness, as hollowness, as mechanism. Faulkner like Melville knew the power of blackness, Benito Cereno's sense of "the negro" as a spiritual coloring, though in the 1970's he might have used a different language. Popeye is in fact white, of a "queer, bloodless color"; Temple's early reference to him as that "black man" is a response to the incongruous black suit, which becomes a kind of mask, the accouterment of his gangster role and an assertion of identity. Popeye is simply, as Benbow talks to Narcissa and Miss Jenny, "that little black man." But in a later passage the blackness is generalized: a "black presence lying upon the house like the shadow of something no larger than a match falling monstrous and portentous upon something else otherwise familiar and twenty times its size. . . ."

Popeye is, even more than Conrad's Kurtz or James Wait, a hollow man, bereft of any inner humanity to help him confront the void. He *is* his black suit, his slanting straw hat, his cigarette, his gun; he is his role, perhaps learned from movies as well as life, of a gangster people are afraid of. He is also the mechanical man, composed of inanimate parts, with doll-like hands and eyes "two knobs of soft black rubber," "the face of a wax doll set too near a hot fire," bloodless, and with "the vicious depthless quality of stamped tin." The first compelling image is of inexplicable evil and gratuitous terrorism, as for two hours the squatting Popeye watches Horace across the spring. Through much of the Frenchman's Place section his malice remains shadowy, enigmatic: a pleasureless need to control, humiliate, scorn. The murder of Tommy, coldly casual, disposes of a minor irritant and is punishment for minor disobedience; the murder of Red follows upon a passionless presentation, to Temple, of alternatives. But the evil becomes more meaningful as it is traced to Popeye's impotence. For the relationship of spiritual impotence to individual and collective violence is sociological and psychological reality. Popeye cannot even drink. His only pleasures are smoking and wearing the black suits of his terrorist's role; and the sadistic voyeurism. The voyeurism, the cerebration of sexuality and conversion of thwarted impulse into gesture and sound, is at once an emblem of inhumanity and sad psychological fact. Minutes before the corn cob rape, watching Temple, Popeye "began to thrust his chin out in a series of jerks"; the shooting of Tommy on so little provocation, moments later, may be a first substitute for sexual act. Later, at the brothel, Miss Minnie will see Temple and Red naked as two snakes with Popeye above them making a whinnying sound. But we have already seen, unforgettably, the nervous displacement on his first visit to Temple in the brothel, Popeye crouched "beside the bed, his face wrung above his absent chin, his bluish lips protruding as though he were blowing upon hot soup, making a high whinnying sound like a horse."

The final chapter attempts, with some success, the turnabout of sympathy so effective with Joe Christmas, Thomas Sutpen, Mink Snopes: the revelation of childhood and later deprivation and trauma as cause. There has been some criticism of Popeye's acceptance of the death sentence "for killing a man in one town and at an hour when he was in another town killing somebody else," his refusal to appeal. But these pages are very moving, and Popeye in his cell is one of the loneliest of the many solitaries in American fiction—the "man who made money and had nothing he could do with it, spend it for," and whose last demands are for cigarettes and hair-lotion. The pages have some resemblance to the final ones of *The Stranger*. But unlike Meursault Popeye can take no comfort from the void, and the benign indifference of things; he experiences the void without recognizing that it exists. He merely smokes while the minister prays, where Meursault has his healing burst of rage.

My assumption is sufficiently unusual as to bear repetition: that Faulkner's misogyny, a tendentious attitude consciously indulged in *Sanctuary,* acted as a controlling, selective influence, very much as did the determination to write a spare, objective, nominally impersonal narrative, one relatively free of comment on the thoughts and feelings of the characters. In this his dual strategy had real affinity with Flaubert's in *Madame Bovary* and even more with that of Conrad in *The Secret Agent,* who restricted himself to a bleak vision of London as a slimy aquarium, with its anarchists and policemen essentially kin, and restricted himself too to a coldly ironic, deglamorized style. This is not to say that Faulkner's denigrative view of women was "insincere" in *Sanctuary,* only that it was more than usually unrelieved. The misogyny was not diffuse and compulsive, as often in the early Conrad, but recognized and accepted. Thus the letter to his editor Hal Smith, in which he tells of his "book about a girl who gets raped with a corn cob" and of "how all this evil flowed off her like water off a duck's back." Or, still more succinctly: "Women are completely impervious to evil." [15]

The misogyny can take different forms, as we see if we compare the Narcissa of *Sanctuary* with her portrait in *Sartoris,* where she is, for Horace, the urnlike and unravished bride of quietness. Now, instead, she has the "serene and stupid impregnability of heroic statuary. . . ." She is stupid enough to tolerate Gowan Stevens, but highly efficient in her betrayal of her brother's secret to the District Attorney. She may be a plausible rendering of a southern woman of good family of her time: "I cannot have my brother mixed up with a woman people are talking about. . . ." But convention is carried very far when she says she can't see what difference it makes who committed the murder. "The question is, are you going to stay mixed up with it?" We know that Temple is willing to see an innocent man die. But so too is Narcissa, if only by selective inattention.

The changes in Little Belle, from *Sartoris,* are perhaps the normal ones brought by years. For the child whose "eyes were like stars, more soft and melting than any deer's," has changed for Horace, who now hears "the delicate and urgent mammalian whisper of that curious small flesh which he had not begot and in which appeared to be vatted delicately some seething sympathy with the blossoming grape." He stares "with a kind of quiet horror and despair, at a face suddenly older in sin than he would ever be, a face more blurred than sweet, at eyes more secret than soft." Little Belle, who picks up a man on a train, would seem to owe something both to the daughter Quentin and, as the incestuous fantasy associated with honeysuckle suggests, to Caddy. But no traumatic memory or fantasy of Caddy's brother is as terrible as Horace's, as Little Belle blends into Temple, while the "shucks set up a terrific uproar beneath her thighs." After hearing Temple's story, and as he approaches the house, where he will look at Little Belle's photograph, Horace has a vivid apprehension of the void, Conrad's cooling, dying world: "a world left stark and dying above the tide-edge of the fluid in which it lived and breathed. The moon stood overhead, but without light; the earth lay beneath, without darkness."

The vulgarity of the college girls is unrelieved, as they trade secrets of sexual attraction and prepare for the dance, the air "steamy with recent baths, and perhaps powder in the light like chaff in barn-lofts"; the barn connects them with Temple. The fierce vulgarity of Ruby Lamar is another matter, and the novel's view of her ambivalent. She is loyal, courageous, indestructible, but with some of Charlotte Rittenmeyer's frightening forthrightness. The narrating consciousness would seem to share Horace Benbow's horror over her blunt offer of herself in payment, this in turn not unlike Gavin Stevens's dismay with Eula and later Linda Snopes.

Miss Reba, however, exists in a sphere above and beyond questions of misogyny or moral judgment, and in this is like Sairey Gamp, to whom she may well be indebted. Her memories of life with Mr. Binford, the "two doves" now symbolized by two angry and worm-like dogs, have some of the quality of Sairey's fantasies, though Mr. Binford will, in *The Reivers,* have a material reality. The Miss Reba of *Sanctuary*—ample, commanding, humorous, loquacious—is intimately connected with the dogs, as they moil at her feet, snapping, or are kicked away. They share her asthmatic life, "climbing and sprawling onto the bed and into Miss Reba's lap with wheezy, flatulent sounds, billowing into the rich pneumasis of her breast and tonguing along the metal tankard which she waved in one ringed hand as she talked." She has her fine fictions, as does Sairey, of what is due her profession: "Me trying to run a respectable house, that's been running a shooting-gallery for thirty years, and him trying to turn it into a peep-show." She has her practical realism, assures Temple her maiden blood will be worth a thousand dollars to her, and drinks to the devirgination. The prose, with a macabre precision worthy of Flaubert, comments ironically on the event by describing the drawn shades:

> She lifted the tankard, the flowers on her hat rigidly moribund, nodding in macabre waes hail. "Us poor girls," she said. The drawn shades, cracked into a myriad pattern like old skin, blew faintly on the bright air, breathing into the room on waning surges the sound of Sabbath traffic, festive, steady, evanescent.[16]

Miss Reba is, like Sairey, an indestructible natural force.

Temple Drake is one of Faulkner's finest brief creations. A casual reader might see her as a run-of-the-mill "flapper" of her time, driven swiftly to nymphomania by the traumatic incident of unnatural rape. (In fact, she is unaware until later of what happened: "You couldn't fool me but once, could you?") Instead she is, as Flaubert saw Emma Bovary, "naturally corrupt," and like Emma comes to take the initiative with her lover and issues her sexual commands. Gowan Stevens, the Frenchman's Place, Memphis simply help her realize her potentialities, which are already indicated by her name on the lavatory wall. She is the good petter, the *demi-vierge* and teaser known for saying, presumably at the moment of truth, "My father's a judge." Two of her protective fantasies before the rape suggest the sexual content of past reveries: she hopes to turn into a boy and to have a chastity belt. The third, to be a veiled bride in a coffin, all in white, may call Svidrigaïlov's victim as well as Emma's nostalgic reveries of past innocence. But Temple differs radically from Emma, whose provocations were certainly more severe (the two villages and the dull husband), and whose sensuality had its poetry of delicate appearance and romantically dissolving will. Flaubert was, notoriously, ambivalent, and even shared the reveries he scorned. But the portrait of Temple in the taut *Sanctuary* is unequivocal and unredeemed.

The insistent denigrative imagery is remarkably effective. Temple is a mechanical being at the trial, dressed in the role of the gangster's moll. But in other major scenes she is an alert and savage animal, generally a cat: mindlessly springing (into cars and off a train, onto and off the porch, out of the crib and back in), running in animal fear, crouching and writhing, pausing, returning in animal heat. At Miss Reba's she turns restlessly in a littered cage. In the barn loft she is both a girl frightened of rats and herself a cornered rat. But eventually it is the real rat, who has just leaped at her head, that is terrified by the larger animal presence. Its squeaking functions, after a first reading, as brilliant anticipation of Popeye's helpless animal sounds:

> The rat was in that corner now, on the floor. Again their faces were not twelve inches apart, the rat's eyes glowing and fading as though worked by lungs. Then it stood erect, its back to the corner, its forepaws curled against its chest, and began to squeak at her in tiny plaintive gasps.[17]

The female animal that runs from the house and back wants to be caught. The pattern is set as she gives Tommy one of her slippers to hold ("Durn ef I could git ere two of my fingers into one of them things . . . Kin I look at em?") but jerks her skirt down and springs up when she finds him looking at her lifted thigh. She has been told by Ruby to get away before dark, and is terrified of Popeye, yet is drawn two ways by feline nerves: "Temple met Popeye halfway to the house. Without ceasing to run she appeared to pause. Even her flapping coat did not overtake her, yet for an appreciable instant she faced Popeye with a grimace of taut, toothed coquetry." As real danger looms Temple wedges a chair against the door, but suddenly springs to her feet and takes off her dress, "crouching a little, match-thin in her scant undergarments." The divergent animal impulses to flee and to be caught turn to submission at Miss Reba's. She has played her game with the doctor, holding the covers to her throat. After he has left she springs from the bed and bolts the door. But presently, with fantasies of waiting for a date at home, she gets up and looks at herself in the mirror, at first seeing nothing, then "her breast rising out of a dissolving pall beneath which her toes peeped in pale, fleet intervals as she walked.'' She unbolts the door through which the two terrified dogs will presently come, to cower under the bed, and later in the evening Popeye.

The dissolving pall might have been imagined by Flaubert; elsewhere too, in this scene, delicate imagery comments in his manner on the sexuality which has become Temple's whole life. We return, several pages after the cracked shade associated with Miss Reba's toast to her maiden blood, to that shade, with everything else now eroticized:

> In the window the cracked shade, yawning now and then with a faint rasp against the frame, let twilight into the room in fainting surges. From beneath the shade the smoke-colored twilight emerged in slow puffs like signal smoke from a blanket, thickening in the room. The china figures which supported the clock gleamed in hushed smooth flexions: knee, elbow, flank, arm and breast in attitudes of voluptuous lassitude. The glass face, become mirror-like, appeared to hold all reluctant light, holding in its tranquil depths a quiet gesture of moribund time, one-armed like a veteran from the wars.[18]

The passage both conveys Temple's consciousness, her drowsing movement toward acceptance (in the next paragraph she will unbolt the door) and, with the last clause, comments ironically on it and on Popeye's impotence as well. Later in the chapter a passage justly admired by Cleanth Brooks, who sees it as relentlessly exposing ''the pretentious sleasiness of the room,'' is also effective for its specifically sexual imagery. A paragraph that begins with imagery of enveloped sexual penetration ends with a slop jar, also enveloped:

> The light hung from the center of the ceiling, beneath a fluted shade of rose-colored paper browned where the bulb bulged it. . . . In the corner, upon a faded scarred strip of oilcloth tacked over the carpet, sat a washstand bearing a flowered bowl and pitcher and a row of towels; in the corner behind it sat a slop jar dressed also in fluted rose-colored paper.[19]

Temple's imaginative anticipation of the rape, as she evokes it for Horace, is a triumph of artistic tact. There is expert modulation from her first simple sentences to efficient narration and imagery of great precision. She conveys her intense ambivalence, dreading and wanting the rape, and suggests persuasively, though indirectly, appalling physical detail. The picture of the completed nymphomania, as we see it at the Grotto and in the room she has commandeered, on the night of Red's death, is conveyed through imagery suggesting a death of her own. Once again there are affinities with Emma Bovary: ''shuddering waves of physical desire,'' the eyeballs drawn ''back into her skull in a shuddering swoon'':

> Her eyes began to grow darker and darker, lifting into her skull above a half moon of white, without focus, with the blank rigidity of a statue's eyes. She began to say

Ah-ah-ah-ah in an expiring voice, her body arching slowly backward as though faced by an exquisite torture. When he touched her she sprang like a bow, hurling herself upon him, her mouth gaped and ugly like that of a dying fish as she writhed her loins against him.[20]

The passage is echoed briefly as she leaves the trial, moving toward the four young men, bodyguards presumably employed by Popeye: "She began to cringe back, her body arching slowly, her arm tautening in the old man's grasp."

The measure of willed evil, as opposed to ordinary depravity and sexual neurosis, is taken twice, as she condemns first Red, then Lee Goodwin to death. She may for a time be under the illusion that Red has some chance for survival, when she telephones to make the assignation, but Popeye sees it as a free choice: " 'I'm giving him his chance,' he said, in his cold soft voice. 'Come on. Make up your mind.' " The risk seems to her worth taking. (*Requiem for a Nun*'s reimagining of this incident radically reduces her guilt.) Her perjury at the trial is unexcited, and like that of a drugged person. The imagery of fish returns: "Above the ranked intent faces white and pallid as the floating bellies of dead fish, she sat in an attitude at once detached and cringing, her gaze fixed on something at the back of the room." Her gazing recurs three times in the short scene. She is perhaps terrified by the bodyguards who, whether hired by Popeye or Eustace Graham, would remind her of the real murderer. But in a larger sense she seems to be gazing past the once familiar world, with its pretenses of order and legality, the world of the baseball game she had wanted to see, into the discovered world of evil; and beyond it into a void.

As Flaubert took commonplace and boring "material" and of it made a thing of beauty, so Faulkner with the sordid and mean; the violent, corrupt, depraved. Corresponding to *Sanctuary*'s ironic, pessimistic, insistently misogynous vision was a willed tautness of narrative method and style. The compression, by no means as natural to Faulkner as to Hemingway or Flaubert, was a source of energizing intensity; the author felt, as the reader feels, the presence of what is left out. The narrative compression is in places extraordinary. Goodwin's trial has only one short chapter and a few paragraphs more; the aftermath of the trial and the lynching even less. (The lynching is merely alluded to in an earlier version.) The poignant evocation of Popeye's background and diseased, neurotic childhood has a few pages only; his trial and the verdict three sentences, less than a hundred words. His jury, like Goodwin's, is out eight minutes. The spare narrative of Popeye awaiting death, quietly and as though indifferently, is as moving as that of Wilbourne in *The Wild Palms,* whose reflections reach us in a rich rhetoric—the one marking his days with cigarette stubs, the other pinching the cyanide tablet in a folded cigarette paper into powder and emptying it on the floor, since between grief and nothing he has elected grief, and fifty years in the penitentiary.

The plot may have been "horrific," in Faulkner's scornful word, but the most violent events are treated very briefly, or merely suggested, or omitted altogether. The death of Tommy comes with a sound "no louder than the striking of a match: a short, minor sound shutting down upon the scene, the instant, with a profound finality, completely isolating it. . . ." And the rape in the next paragraph is distanced for us by Temple's act of self-displacement, which has her tossing and thrashing not in the crib but on the rough, sunny boards outside, beneath the blind and deaf old man. Her harrowing account to Benbow does not reach the rape. She hints at some instrument, in raging at Popeye, but the corn cob is revealed, and then most briefly, only at the trial. The traumatic doctor's examination, at Miss Reba's, occurs between paragraphs; Red's murder between chapters. The movement of the narrative is so swift that little room is left the reader for prurient imaginings.

The compression also obviated the interiority that Faulkner found so tempting, and that does threaten *Sanctuary* when Benbow is on the scene. The account of Temple and Gowan at the Old Frenchman's Place (V–XIV) is a triumph of spare, objective, nominally impersonal narration, as free of characters' thoughts and named feelings as any novel of Hemingway. We have a few laconic mutterings of Tommy, and a few short sentences on the reflections of the disgraced Gowan. Of Temple's interior torment almost nothing is "told." "Now I can stand anything, she thought quietly, with a kind of dull, spent astonishment; I can stand just anything." Four paragraphs later, perhaps deceptively suggesting a rape has already occurred, she feels "her insides move in small, tickling clots, like loose shot." Other than that there is only the oblique moment of the rape: "Something is going to happen to me," then the scream "Something is happening to me!" and the fantasy of being outside at the old man's feet. That is all. Elsewhere instead of reflections we see Temple running, springing, crouching; see her moving distractedly in the room; hear her talk; see what she sees.

The narrative is lean, but that is hardly the word for the language. Stylistically there may be some debt to Hemingway as well as to detective fiction, but the greater affinity is with Flaubert. The strategy on the one hand is to juxtapose scenes of natural beauty with the sordid, the mean, the violent, by way of ironic commentary, and to maintain aethetic distance. The corresponding strategy is to make precision and beauty of language, as it copes with meanness and depravity, function in the same way. Ideally the two strategies go hand in hand. They do in the humble event of Temple relieving herself outdoors. She moves through a lovely Mississippi landscape, but it is not lovely to her, who is almost as alien there as Popeye: the weeds *slash* at her. And the words *scar* and *sunshot,* for all their denotative precision, suggest a world full of menace. The turn of the next to last sentence is Flaubertian, with its denigrative *"kind of despair";* so too the sentence before that, with its placing of *clung* and its swift dying fall. We are, as often with Emma Bovary, both inside and out; see both Temple and the world she sees, as she stoops and twists "through a fence of sagging rusty wire and ran downhill among trees":

> At the bottom of the hill a narrow scar of sand divided the two slopes of a small valley, winding in a series of dazzling splotches where the sun found it. Temple stood in the sand, listening to the birds among the sunshot leaves, listening, looking about. She followed the dry runlet to where a jutting shoulder formed a nook matted with briers. Among the new green last year's dead leaves from the branches overhead clung, not yet fallen to earth. She stood here for a while, folding and folding the sheets in her fingers, in a kind of despair. When she rose she saw, upon the glittering mass of leaves along the crest of the ditch, the squatting outline of a man.[21]

Two brief descriptions of Ruby's child combine Flaubert's coldness of clinical detail and composed "written" style with the distancing device of abrupt allusion to something very remote, here Paris street beggars. The two passages come some 20,000 words apart:

> Upon the lumpy wad of bedding it could be distinguished only by a series of pale shadows in soft small curves, and she went and stood over the box and looked down at its putty-colored face and bluish eyelids. A thin whisper of shadow cupped its head and lay moist upon its brow; one arm, upflung, lay curl-palmed beside its cheek.[22]

> It lay in a sort of drugged immobility, like the children which beggars on Paris streets carry, its pinched face slick with faint moisture, its hair a damp whisper of shadow across its gaunt, veined skull, a thin crescent of white showing beneath its lead-colored eyelids.[23]

The last sentence suggests, as Temple remarks after the earlier one, that this child is going to die. Flaubert too, recording the chatter of the shucks inside the mattress where Temple lay, might have seen "her hands crossed on her breast and her legs straight and close and decorous, like an effigy on an ancient tomb."

These remarks are not intended to suggest pastiche, but only to note affinities with the most conscious and controlled of stylists. It is pleasing to see a sentence begin with a Flaubertian notation of the Saturday countrymen in town, tranquil as sheep, move to an altogether Flaubertian yoking of cattle and gods, but end with Faulknerian sinuous rhythm and glamor:

> Slow as sheep they moved, tranquil, impassable, filling the passages, contemplating the fretful hurrying of those in urban shirts and collars with the large, mild inscrutability of cattle or of gods, functioning outside of time, having left time lying upon the slow and imponderable land green with corn and cotton in the yellow afternoon.[24]

This is the crowd that, again leaving the land, will be back on Monday to visit the undertaker's parlor where Tommy lies dead.

A novel totally free from "Faulknerese" is inconceivable, and *Sanctuary* has its amusing instances. Temple's limited view of fading light in Memphis gives way, through a clock face, to "a disc suspended in nothingness" and ultimately to no less than "the ordered chaos of the intricate and shadowy world upon whose scarred flanks the old wounds whirl onward at dizzy speed into a darkness lurking with new disasters." He would be a purist indeed who begrudged such momentary extravagances. More regrettable is the highly literary consciousness and decadent rhetoric of Horace Benbow, some of which goes as far back as *Soldiers' Pay:* the view, for instance, of the college girls as "pagan and evanescent and serene, thinly evocative of all lost days and outpaced delights. . . ." Horace's preoccupations are inherited from an earlier version, where he played a more important part. His confrontation with Popeye at the spring is excellent, and his sardonic talk there persuasive. But his drunken monologue in the second chapter reads as though memorized from something he had published in a college literary magazine of the early twenties. "So each spring I could watch the reaffirmation of the old ferment hiding the hammock; the green-snared promise of unease. What blossoms grapes have, this is. It's not much: a wild and waxlike bleeding less of bloom than leaf, hiding and hiding the hammock. . . ." Such writing, and the implausibly remembered dialogue with Little Belle, initiate the misogynous vision. But its prettiness threatens to destroy the reality of the Old Frenchman's Place. The decadent rhetoric has close affinities with Faulkner's early poems. Generally speaking, the educated consciousness in Faulkner is at a disadvantage—whether Benbow's, or Gavin Stevens's in other novels—as against the earthy or laconic talk of the blacks and Ratliff, and as against the raw reality of those who physically suffer and die, the criminals and their victims and the very poor.

Horace Benbow is in some ways useful to plot. The confrontation at the spring gives the novel a great start, and there are advantages to seeing the sinister Frenchman's Place environment before Temple and Gowan get there. The novel depends on two coincidences—that Horace should leave the road for a drink at this particular spring, on his walk from Kinston, and that he should meet Clarence Snopes on the train. But these are meaningful enough in a fiction where the ordinary safe world and the hidden criminal society are seen to be so close. Clarence Snopes brilliantly exemplifies the knowing corrupt politician who moves at ease in both. Horace has his one effective moment of quick intelligence as a lawyer, when he resumes the conversation with Snopes. But Snopes's mind moves quicker still. Horace's education in evil, which has been stressed by some critics, is hardly essential to the novel, though his final surrender is a moving act of despair. He does not, like Temple and her father, go to Europe as he had dreamed of doing; his return to Belle, to the horror, is that of a man whose will has been broken. It is an important moment in the overall misogynous vision. Horace is not necessary, however, as an outside moral intelligence. For that moral intelligence, a very firm one, is supplied by controlling technique and controlled vision, and most obviously by evaluative style.

The essential fact of structure is the willed compression we have noted. The overall movement of the novel is remarkably firm, astonishingly so when we consider how much revision consisted of reshuffling chapters, with much pasting of galleys and rewriting. The introduction of Clarence Snopes, a fine comic rather than sinister portrait, brings new energy when it is needed. But even more important are the justly famous but rarely discussed chapters of Virgil and Fonzo at Miss Reba's (XXI) and of Red's funeral and its aftermath (XXV). Michael Millgate interestingly calls attention to similarities between *Sanctuary* and *Measure for Measure;* we might add that the Virgil/Fonzo episode is altogether Shakespearean, both in its sustained comedy and in the rhetorical effect of its coming at this juncture. In the simplest terms it may be said to bring comic relief and a necessary relief from tension. From the start and through chapter XIV and the report of a death at the Old Frenchman's Place, over thirty thousand words, the taut narrative has commanded exceptional fixity of attention. There are no vacant places or instances of slack, neutral language to invite reader revery. Chapers XV–XVII, largely seen through Horace's eyes, return us to a more ordinary but depressing world. The long chapter XVIII, relieved only by Miss Reba and the snapping dogs, carries the still-bleeding Temple from the Old Frenchman's Place to the bed on which she lies thrashing, with Popeye beside her bed making his high whinnying sound. In Chapters XIX and XX, with Horace again, we contemplate his steadily darkening world, into which the fat obscene reality of Senator Clarence Snopes twice briefly intrudes. Chapter XX ends with Snopes announcing he (who "if it's there" knows "where it is") is going to Memphis.

Instead, with Chapter XXI, it is Virgil Snopes we see arriving in Memphis, with Fonzo: the one pretending to know where things are, the other on his first trip and eager for adventure. The great chapter is so memorable that it is shocking to discover how short it is, some three thousand words: the search for a hotel, and Fonzo's growing awareness of his guide's ignorance, the hesitation before a house with two fluffy white dogs in the yard, the discovery that Miss Reba has daughters, the speculation that she must be a dressmaker (since they have found a woman's undergarment under the washstand), their visit to a brothel which must be kept secret from their "landlady," and the appearance of cousin Clarence, who berates them for their folly in spending three dollars on pleasure, when cheaper negro establishments are available. The chapter, while physically within the novel's world of depravity, has in fact freed us from it into a purely aesthetic world of unalloyed joy, with disbelief suspended. There is no lapse in the bright innocence and gullibility of the two hicks, whose inferences are always wrong. The exchanges are kept very brief, giving the reader no time to protest. No fools outside Shakespeare are more innocent than the two returning from the brothel, worried that Miss Reba will evict them. With Clarence's appearance, and his sardonic comment at the negro whorehouse, we return to a world in which evil and suffering are real. But for these few pages, two-thirds through a dark experience, we have been entirely freed from it, as we are in various Shakespearean interludes.

The relationship of real world and world of aesthetic play is, with Red's funeral party, somewhat more complex. The chapter complements and complicates the novel's darker intensities, rather than freeing us from them entirely. The preceding chapter (XXIV) begins with Temple restless in her cage, demanding more to drink, making what will prove a fatal telephone call. We see her in the car with Popeye, with whom she is now on familiar terms: can call him "daddy" yet pour out her scorn of his impotence, and be silenced by his ringed hand, the ring "like a dentist's instrument." The scene at the Grotto is intensely cinematographic: laconic dialogue, the music and the dancers and the four sinister men; Red standing in the door; the crap-table and Temple's drunken gambling; her demand for a room; the intense dialogue with Red, while her hips grind against him. The brief paragraph of her writhing nymphomania is in a normal novelistic mode. But the rest of the chapter keeps to the cinematographic manner, and creates a world in which gangsters' thugs may force one across a dance floor, and a man condemned to death, perhaps knowing himself doomed, can raise his hand in "a short, cheery salute." By the end of the chapter we are altogether in the world of the movies, a stylized world with its different kind of "reality."

The movement of chapter XXIV, both in timing and in detail, is thus from fairly conventional novelistic realism to the stylization of the gangster film, where death is not quite real. This movement prepares us for chapter XXV's "atmosphere of macabre paradox," and the grotesque and parodic black humor of the funeral party. The initial shock (Red throwing dice, then on the next page in a coffin) is perhaps essential, by way of preparation for the fun, with the mourners as far from the real reality of death as Virgil and Fonzo from the reality of Miss Reba's. Our attention is recurringly fixed on the huge bowl of punch on the table draped in black, which will be a fulcrum for the steadily increasing disorder: "They surged and clamored about the diminishing bowl." But attention is also called to the bouncer, the "bullet-headed man who appeared to be on the point of bursting out of his dinner-jacket through the rear, like a cocoon." For it is he, the professional queller of disorder, who will ultimately bring on the catastrophe, and the corpse tumbling to the floor, the wreath coming too, "attached to him by a hidden end of a wire driven into his cheek." The outbreak of violence matches that of *The Day of the Locust.* But in this moment of chaos Faulkner's imagination anticipates the movement of Flem's spotted horses:

> The bouncer whirled again and met the rush of the four men. They mingled; a second man flew out and skittered along the floor on his back; the bouncer sprang free. Then he whirled and rushed them and in a whirling plunge they bore down upon the bier and crashed into it. The orchestra had ceased and were now climbing onto their chairs, with their instruments. The floral offerings flew; the coffin teetered. "Catch it!" a voice shouted. They sprang forward, but the coffin crashed heavily to the floor, coming open. The corpse tumbled slowly and sedately out and came to rest with its face in the center of a wreath.[25]

As the novel has modulated through the stylization of cinema to this wild anti-realist fun, so now it modulates back toward novelistic realism, and the darkness of Goodwin on trial. It must return from a parodic view of an outside world of anonymous strangers, the gangsters at the funeral party, to the very small world of Horace, Goodwin, Ruby, ultimately Popeye and Temple. The modulation is accomplished brilliantly through a *reprise* of Miss Reba back at home after the party (the two snapping dogs flung back "against the wall in muted thuds"), drinking with Miss Myrtle and Miss Lorraine. At first the talk is playful, and death is still unreal; Red as a corpse "looked sweet." But gradually, as the women go on drinking, and as Miss Reba thinks of herself and Mr. Binford, two doves not two dogs, the talk turns professional, and to Red's folly in taking a chance with Popeye's girl. There is another joking exchange, but with an underlying seriousness: the respectable shooting gallery Miss Reba had run for thirty years, which Popeye tried to turn into a peep-show. The narrative becomes more serious, until Miss Reba at last evokes, for the first time very explicitly, the sexual triad: "Yes, sir, Minnie said the two of them would be nekkid as two snakes, and Popeye hanging over the foot of the bed without even his hat off, making a kind of whinnying sound."

These chapters, and *Sanctuary* generally, reveal much technical expertness and aesthetic tact in what should finally be regarded, like *The Secret Agent,* as a serious and even tragic *entertainment,* one based on a deliberately selective view of reality and an unashamedly misogynous vision. But to say this is not in the least to say that it is not a high work of art. And it is art—as we look back on the kindred challenges of personal obsession: on Dickens's revery in its sentimental extremes, on the great insight but also the disorder of Dostoevsky's— that makes the difference.

6 THE DICKENSIAN VOICES

The concept is of a "personal voice" discoverable in the work of every truly original writer: a voice that is the intimate and often unconscious expression of his temperament and unborrowed personality, a voice that in its structures and rhythms reflects the way his mind moves, and reflects too the particular needs and resistances of his spirit.

1. A writer's personal voice is often to be distinguished from his *style*, which may involve his particular modifications of the linguistic conventions of his time, or, simply, his fairly direct imitation of another writer's mannerisms. Thus within the formal structure of Miltonic blank verse (a style) we may detect, in *The Excursion,* a grave Wordsworthian voice expressing a temperament far more negative and fearful than Milton's. The voice and temperament are responsible for much evasive abstraction, but also for those double negatives which so often seem doubly negative in effect. Now and then, in Faulkner's highly imitative early poems, or in the decadent sinuosities of *Soldiers' Pay,* we may detect a voice that is unmistakably Faulknerian.

2. The personal voice discoverable in the prose usually has some relationship to the writer's speaking voices, in conversation or in public discourse. But this relationship may be distant and elusive. Conrad's speaking voice was totally unable to express the lovely and highly personal rhythms of his novels.

3. Many characters in Faulkner's novels, and very notably in *Absalom, Absalom!* and *A Fable,* speak "Faulknerese." But a writer's own underlying voice is generally to be distinguished from the most original voices we hear in

the characters' dialogue. Only Dickens could have written Sairey Gamp's dialogue, and her unconscious humor has, of course, some relationship to Dickens's sense of the ridiculous, in his life as in his writings. Yet the movement of her mind, shared briefly by Mrs. Piper of *Bleak House,* is *sui generis* and expressive of a temperament that is certainly not the author's. Dickens was a great ventriloquist both as writer and as public performer, practiced the many voices for his readings, and successfully became radically different personages. Granted that the very greatest Dickensian writing is to be found in dialogue, we must look elsewhere for a voice (or for voices) that, discernible in the first work as in the last, is expressive of his temperament and his alone.

4. It is important to distinguish this personal voice or voices from those that, though deeply felt, are clearly "borrowed." Dickens loved stage melodrama, certainly took it more seriously than anyone can today, and may well have been sincerely "carried away" when, in scenes of reconciliation or noble self-sacrifice, he fell into its logical formulas and balanced periods. " I owe it to myself, that I, a friendless, portionless girl with a blight upon my name, should not give your friends reason to suspect that I had sordidly yielded to your first passion, and fastened myself, a clog, on all your hopes and projects.' " Dickens was as aware as we are of his fondness, at other moments of moralizing excitement, for a prose that came close to blank verse; and asked to be admonished accordingly. "The tíes that bínd the weálthy and the próud to hóme may be fórged on eárth, but thóse which línk the póor mán to his húmble heárth are óf the trúer métal and béar the stámp of Héaven."

A full rhetorical study of Dickens would need to take a census of such impulses, in all their sometimes dreadful sincerity, as well as of the *vox clamantis* in its various powerful accents, often coldly passionate, moralizing on the Condition of England. "This is the Court of Chancery; which has its decaying houses and its blighted lands in every shire; which has its worn-out lunatic in every madhouse, and its dead in every churchyard . . . ," etc. The roles taken by the moralizing Dickens markedly affect style. Thus Dickens appears to speak in his unmediated journalistic persona when he writes, in *Pickwick Papers,* of those imprisoned for debt. "This is no fiction," he goes on to say. The voice commenting on solitary confinement in the Philadelphia prison (*American Notes,* chapter 7) is non-fictional. But so too is that of David Copperfield contrasting the "plentiful repasts of choice quality" given prisoners, compared with the fare of soldiers, sailors, laborers.

In the present chapter we will take these several Dickens manners, familiar to his readers for well over a century, for granted: the melodramatic, the sentimental, the angrily or dispassionately moralizing. Their strengths and eccentricities have been long admired, discounted or deplored. We may also put aside at once all neutral or uncharacteristic prose. The first six chapters of *Nicholas Nickleby,* for instance (the section prior to the arrival at Dotheboys Hall), are uniquely artless, inchoate, slovenly to an extreme; it is not surprising to learn that Dickens needed to add material at the last moment to complete the second monthly part. But the efficient simplicity and impersonal directness of many "filler" paragraphs of *Pickwick Papers*—passages intervening between the moments of authorial high spirits and buoyant dialogue or absurd invention— are also uncharacteristic. They suggest the true writer's instinct for economy, but that is all. They could have been written by someone else.

5. The distinction between prose with a strong personal voice and prose that seems essentially *written,* even written as by a machine, is elusive, and transcends such rougher distinctions as formal and informal or colloquial and "Mandarin." Faulkner's most elaborate baroque prose, that of *Absalom, Absalom!,* has an unmistakable voice. The distinction may be clarified by reference to an intelligent "major" novel that often lacks a personal voice: *Little Dorrit.* The novel was written and revised with care; Dickens may have wanted, in the presence of Thackeray and other new competitors, to achieve a more conventional "literary" success. The manuscript, John Holloway notes, "is a maze of corrections, insertions, deletions on every one of its near thousand pages." [1] The reader is more than usually aware of the poised pen, and of the long sentence's skeletal outline also poised, its structure predetermined. "During many hours of the short winter days, however, when it was dusk there early in the afternoon, changing distortions of herself in her wheeled chair, of Mr. Flintwinch with his wry neck, of Mistress Affery coming and going, would be thrown upon the house wall that was over the gateway, and would hover there like shadows from a great magic lantern." The sentence is polished and composed, not displeasing in its varied rhythm, complex in syntax; but static, impersonal, lacking momentum. The static impersonality is still more evident in the many passages of analytic commentary, especially those that are bound to Arthur Clennam's quiescent view of things, his negativism and passivity. "The shadow of a supposed act of injustice, which had hung over him since his father's death, was so vague and formless that it might be the result of a reality widely remote from his idea of it." Elsewhere, to an unusual degree, Dickens adopts the stultifying submersion in a character's calm consciousness, with a pretended elimination of author or narrator, that would become standard in the first third of the twentieth century.

Technique or fictional method may be energizing or stultifying, may release or suppress personal voice. But so too for the novelist's "material," the fictional world he observes or creates. *Little Dorrit* is divided between the defeated, the passive, the imprisoned—and the passionate, including the passionately self-destructive or fiercely repressed. Thus Flintwich, Miss Wade, Tattycoram, occasionally Merdle, above all Mrs. Clennam, are energizing, whereas Arthur, the Father of the Marshalsea and Henry Gowan are debilitating in their several ways. The various pictures of failure—the failed marriages of Pet Meagles and Fanny, the rebuffs of the Circumlocution Office, the lost fortunes, the senile babbling—are intrinsically depressing. Yet Dostoevsky reminds us again and again that gloom and failure can lead to energized writing. The author's own attitude toward his fiction is also of first importance (and there is no little evidence that Dickens was often bored by *Little Dorrit*); so too his choice, which can be unconscious but often is not, as to whether his will be an oral or a written narrative.

6. Yet the distinction between prose with a personal voice and highly composed written prose is not necessarily a distinction between good and bad, as our reading of *Sanctuary* should show. Nor is it necessarily a distinction between the plain and the consciously rhetorical. *Our Mutual Friend* is the richest of the Dickens novels in artifice, rhetorical device and experiments in stylization, in startling shifts in narrative consciousness, even in Joycean word-play. Henry James detected with good reason a sense of authorial strain. Yet through most of the novel we hear a personal voice, often highly energized, and feel a personal consciousness that commands and overrides all.

But now to enumerate several Dickensian voices, still begging the question as to whether these are but variants of a single personal voice.

THE GRAVE INTERIOR VOICE

The voice is calm, bemused, contemplative; intimate yet detached; a muted prose, much given to pause. It is, to speak roughly, the voice of *David Copperfield,* but is discernible at times in all the novels, and very noticeably in the early chapters of *Great Expectations* and in *Edwin Drood*. It can be heard at moments in *Sketches by Boz* (see "Scotland Yard," "The First of May," "Brokers' and Marine-Store Shops") and regularly in the lovely retrospective personal essays of *The Uncommercial Traveller,* very late work. It can be called an autobiographical voice, but, more accurately, a voice proceeding from a deep unchanging core of self. (The most explicitly autobiographical paragraph of *David Copperfield,* the first paragraph of chapter 42, on the rationale of success, does not proceed from this deep core of self but rather from an

acquired public personality and self-image.) The memoir written for John Forster may serve as a touchstone for intimacy and sincerity, with its measured
disposing of, closing off of the trauma of the blacking warehouse and attendant
parental neglect. The pauses and qualifications, the balanced rhythms of a calm
speaking voice, the placing of the climatic *stricken dumb* and *my own wife not
excepted,* the vehement punctuating *thank God*—these lines, bringing memory
under control, are at once very natural and very composed, a quintessentially
personal voice within very orderly writing:

> From that hour until this at which I write, no word of that part of my childhood
> which I have now gladly brought to a close, has passed my lips to any human
> being. I have no idea how long it lasted; whether for a year, or much more, or less.
> From that hour, until this, my father and mother have been stricken dumb upon it. I
> have never heard the least allusion to it, however far off and remote, from either of
> them. I have never, until I now impart it to this paper, in any burst of confidence
> with anyone, my own wife not excepted, raised the curtain I then dropped, thank
> God.[2]

The passage is directly echoed in chapter 14 of *David Copperfield:* ". . . a
curtain had for ever fallen on my life at Murdstone and Grinby's. No one has
ever raised that curtain since. I have lifted it for a moment in this narrative,
with a reluctant hand, and dropped it gladly." The image of the curtain has
been altered, in *Great Expectations,* since it there falls on life's "interest and
romance." But it has been evoked by Pip's future as a blacksmith, nearly as
hopeless as the young Dickens's in the blacking warehouse, and the tone of
quiet authenticity is much the same: "Never has that curtain dropped so heavy
and blank, as when my way in life lay stretched out straight before me through
the newly-entered road of apprenticeship to Joe."

The *David Copperfield* prose, characterized by great "sobriety" (Sylvère
Monod), is at once conversational and formal. It follows the natural movement
of a mind experiencing, chronologically, moments and impressions that presently become meaningful "spots of time." Martha Endell is seen following
Emily and Ham in a fictional present that foreshadows Emily's pursuit by
Steerforth, and that perhaps recalls the vexed garments of a Wordsworthian
girl: "She was lightly dressed, looked bold, and haggard, and flaunting, and
poor; but seemed, for the time, to have given all that to the wind which was
blowing, and to have nothing in her mind but going after them." A notational
prose thus turns meditative. The flow of mind that both records experience and
composes it is more at ease, of course, in a prose of recollection and nostalgia,
as when David returns to the Wickfield house near the very end. He recalls
himself as a child, watching across the ancient street on wet afternoons, "while

women went *clicking* along the pavement in pattens, and the full rain fell in slanting lines, and poured out of the water-spout *yonder,* and flowed into the road.'' The words I have italicized evoke a sound from the past and a place in the present: vivid particulars. The passage continues with the return of a specific lost time, the memory of tramps on the road at dusk, the feeling "fraught, as then, with the smell of damp earth, and wet leaves and briar, and the sensation of the very airs that blew upon me in my own toilsome journey.''

The return to Canterbury evokes a deeper, more tragic sense of vanished time: personal losses, remembered in quiet conversational tones, modulate to a general sense of all loss, through historical allusion and metaphor. Sound dissolves in air, as life in the deep of Time, as circles do in water. The combination of naturalness and composed syntactical formality is altogether characteristic of this grave interior voice:

> The rooks were sailing about the cathedral towers; and the towers themselves, overlooking many a long unaltered mile of the rich country and its pleasant streams, were cutting the bright morning air, as if there were no such thing as change on earth. Yet the bells, when they sounded, told me sorrowfully of change in everything; told me of their own age, and my pretty Dora's youth; and of the many, never old, who had lived and loved and died, while the reverberations of the bells had hummed through the rusty armour of the Black Prince hanging up within, and, motes upon the deep of Time, had lost themselves in air, as circles do in water.[3]

This personal autobiographical prose, or prose of pretended autobiography (as with Edith Summerson and Pip) invites the pleasing rhythms of a calm speaking voice. Calm: for it also tends to limit eccentricities, melodramatic excesses of rhetoric or sentiment. First-person narration, for which an identifiable mind is nominally responsible, creates certain inhibitions. So too does narration in the present tense, if there is a personalized watching narrator anchored in the present, unable to control the events he observes, and without time to pause for tender ruminations. In Dickens, as in many other writers, the first person is generically friendly to a plain style, but a plain style that may lend itself to much variety and occasional striking embellishment. The plain style of *Great Expectations* has much distinction; the plain style of *Hard Times* almost none. The beautiful fifth chapter of *Great Expectations,* with the capture of the convicts, is written in a pure unobtrusive prose that "take us there," the more so because it is not limited to a child's language but only to his vision. "Our lights warmed the air about us with their pitchy blaze, and the two prisoners seemed rather to like that, as they limped along in the midst of the muskets. We could not go fast, because of their lameness; and they were so spent, that two or three times we had to halt while they rested.'' The consciousness of Pip, by no means as close to the author as David Copperfield's, is generally more restrained. We may even discern an ideal of fidelity not unlike Hemingway's in certain passages: to record things precisely as they happened in the order of their happening, with accumulating clauses separated by *and,* where Hemingway would have used short sentences beginning with *He* or perhaps *The.* Thus the rowers on the river, in their effort to save Magwitch:

> And soon the tide began to slacken, and the craft lying at anchor to swing, and presently they had all swung round, and the ships that were taking advantage of the new tide to get up to the Pool, began to crowd upon us in a fleet, and we kept under the shore, as much out of the strength of the tide now as we could, standing carefully off from low shallows and mud-banks.[4]

These lines are wholly free of the childhood terrors, animistic visions and grotesque distortions that enrich so much of Dickens's work. But the pure interior voice, the voice of *David Copperfield* and *Great Expectations,* can accommodate these too, as it can accommodate the dislimning drifting world of the dying Paul Dombey, and the deep solitudes of his sister Florence. Thus Pip on Joe's back, as they venture into the dim wilderness where the escaped convicts may be hiding: imagining the cattle as humanly angry, and feeling very particularly what he could not then have phrased: "the shudder of the dying day":

> The sheep stopped in their eating and looked timidly at us; and the cattle, their heads turned from the wind and sleet, stared angrily as if they held us responsible for both annoyances; but except these things, and the shudder of the dying day in every blade of grass, there was no break in the bleak stillness of the marshes.[5]

Dickens's success in conveying a child's menaced vision of things, needs no demonstration, nor his power to keep that vision alive in an adult consciousness, whether a fictional character's or his own. The elms on a windy evening, for the infant David, are "like giants who were whispering secrets." The aging Dickens of *The Uncommercial Traveller,* going abroad, reaches Dover, where "the sea was tumbling in, with deep sounds, after dark, and the revolving French light on Cape Grinez was seen regularly bursting out and becoming obscured, as if the head of a giant light-keeper in an anxious state of mind were interposed every half-minute, to look how it was burning." The precise and evocative *tumbling* sea and light *bursting out,* the Wordsworthian *deep sounds,* the giant light-keeper grotesque yet humanly anxious, his head *interposed* (a cool distancing word), and the colloquial afterthought that truly animates the giant: *to look how it was burning*—the passage is altogether characteristic in its play of inventive and ironic consciousness, of child's and adult's, of intimacy and detachment. Florence Dombey, no longer a child, experiences some of the child's vision in a narrative that metaphorically equates death and the sea:

> The weathercocks on spires and housetops were mysterious with hints of stormy wind, and pointed, like so many ghostly fingers, out to dangerous seas, where fragments of great wrecks were drifting, perhaps, and helpless men were rocked upon them into a sleep as deep as the unfathomable waters.[6]

The child's vision similarly animates the adult David Copperfield's narrative, as he and Peggotty follow Martha Endell, the prostitute friend of Emily, to the waterside desolation: a "melancholy waste of road near the great blank Prison." (The drawings present David even in his twenties as frail and small.) There are menaces here to which Dickens's imagination always responded, out of a fear of engulfment or drowning or other imprisonment: a sluggish muddy ditch, marshy land, the carcases of rotting houses, and iron detritus of various sorts, things with sharp edges or evocative of the undersea, "and I know not what strange objects" sunk into the soil. Green hair emerges from a darkness of anal imageries, as it might well for a child. By artful snytax not only the paper with rewards for drowned men but the drowned men themselves *flutter* above a high-water mark, in a sentence which concludes with an actual descent into the ooze:

> Slimy gaps and causeways, winding among old wooden piles, with a sickly substance clinging to the latter, like green hair, and the rags of last year's handbills offering rewards for drowned men fluttering above high-water mark, led down through the ooze and slush to the ebb-tide. There was a story that one of the pits dug for the dead in the time of the Great Plague was hereabout; and a blighting influence seemed to have proceeded from it over the whole place.[7]

Anal imagery, and scenes which threaten engulfment, often find a counterweight in controlled syntax if not conversational calm. The grave interior voice prevails moments before discovery of the pit into which Stephen Blackpool has fallen. "Mounds where the grass was rank and high, and where brambles, dock-weed, and such like vegetation, were confusedly heaped together, they always avoided; for dismal stories were told in that country of the old pits hidden beneath such indications." The meeting-place of Sim Tappertit's conspirators, in *Barnaby Rudge,* is reached by way of a dark blind court, "an ill-favoured pit," and by steep and slippery stairs: "any rashness or departure from the beaten track must have ended in a yawning water-butt"; the vault has a "close and stifling atmosphere." The detail is vivid—"little trees of fungus sprang from every mouldering corner"—but the prose rhythms are circumspect and controlled. This is true for the rather more threatening Folly

Ditch of *Oliver Twist,* where syntax suggests an effort to keep the slimy vision at a distance: "wooden chambers thrusting themselves out above the mud, and threatening to fall into it—as some have done; dirt-besmeared walls and decaying foundations; every repulsive lineament of poverty, every loathsome indication of filth, rot, and garbage;—all these ornament the banks of Folly Ditch." The specifically anal suggestion of a filthy Paris staircase, in *A Tale of Two Cities,* is doubtless social history, and certainly less violent than Smollett's earlier vision of a similar Paris scene. Dickens's prose is almost Augustan: "The uncontrollable and hopeless mass of decomposition so engendered, would have polluted the air, even if poverty and deprivation had not loaded it with their intangible impurities. . . ." Vivid detail of burial, of engulfment, rather than excited rhythms, animate Quilp's Wharf—"a little wooden counting-house burrowing all awry in the dust as if it had fallen from the clouds and ploughed into the ground." Two of the most intense evocations of oozy entanglement are non-fictional: the Faulknerian rendering of the Mississippi, in *American Notes,* and the ooze and wet of a drydock beneath a ship still building in Chatham Dockyard, in *The Uncommercial Traveller:*

> Then, to go over the side again and down among the ooze and wet to the bottom of the dock, in the depths of the subterranean forest of dog-shores and stays that hold her up, and to see the immense mass bulging out against the upper light, and tapering down towards me, is, with great pains and much clambering, to arrive at an impossibility of realising that this is a ship at all. . . .[8]

The beauty of Dickens's double vision in *David Copperfield*—the child's or youth's world in its vivid integrity, the past as it was, yet seen wistfully through a screen of time, with key words to suggest both the past self and the backward-looking man—is most pronounced in the five retrospective chapters narrated in the present tense (2, 18, 43, 53, 64). Sylvère Monod notes that these chapters both accelerate the narrative, since each covers a tract of time, and slow it, thanks to the contemplative tones. Scenes succeed each other in "a kind of theater of memory." [9] The second of these chapters refers to the "silent gliding on of my existence"—*gliding,* a significantly recurring word in Dickens, with its suggestion of phantom movement not determined by human energy or will, of a perhaps fatal drifting too, and a silent life of the spirit that goes on amid whatever bustling activity:

> A moment, and I occupy my place in the Cathedral, where we all went together, every Sunday morning, assembling first at school for that purpose. The earthy smell, the sunless air, the sensation of the world being shut out, the resounding of the organ through the black and white arched galleries and aisles, are wings that

take me back, and hold me hovering above those days, in a half-sleeping and half-waking dream.[10]

As in "During Wind and Rain" and many other Hardy poems, the older man watches nostalgically, but also helplessly, actions not in his power to correct, and which seem to be happening again in a timeless Proustian present/past. One of the earliest and most poignant of these recapturings of the past distinctly anticipates Marcel's double vision of Combray, blissful yet permeated by the knowledge that the earthly paradise was lost, and, for David, that the pretty young mother, here out of breath, soon died:

> Now I am in the garden at the back, beyond the yard where the empty pigeon-house and dog-kennel are—*a very preserve of butterflies, as I remember it,* with a high fence, and a gate and padlock; where the fruit clusters on the trees, *riper and richer than fruit has ever been since, in any other garden,* and where my mother gathers some in a basket, while I stand by, bolting furtive gooseberries, *and trying to look unmoved.* A great wind rises, and *the summer is gone in a moment.*[11]

The words I have italicized convey the nostalgic later consciousness.

The logical extension of such a double vision is Conradian impressionism, with its freedom to sweep over a long stretch of the past, which it can pause to vivify by digression. The long fourth paragraph of *David Copperfield* offers a very pure example of the impressionism Ford theorized, and he and Conrad practiced. David can remember with amused equanimity that he was born with a caul (a membrane that had enclosed the foetus, sometimes found on a baby's head); in retrospect we see this talisman to protect from drowning may subtly prepare for Steerforth's death and David's charmed life. That such an intimate "part of myself" should be put up for sale, and be won years later at a raffle in the child's presence, may indeed prefigure the violation of natural right by money, like the sale of Marty South's hair in *The Woodlanders.* But the movement of the paragraph—good-humored, urbane, even jocular, an ingratiating early encounter with the reader—serves especially to establish authority, both intimacy and detached control, a sense that both the remote past and the present are well in hand. A writer who knows so well the old lady who won the caul many years before can be counted on to know whatever he chooses to reveal. As in Conrad, a digression within a digression on the old lady leads the speaker back to his story.

I have commented thus fully on the "grave interior voice" because it seems to me the most personal of Dickens's manners, and one on which other tonalities and stylistic strategies will draw. Dickens was rather less conscious of his readers than usual, I suspect, when he wrote this prose; was writing, so to speak, for himself, and as an artist who loved rhythms and words.

THE DETACHED CONTEMPLATIVE VOICE

It is dignified, even stately, suave, magisterial; non-autobiographical; meditative, and tending to abstraction. This voice can be cold, disdainful, ironic; and (in *Edwin Drood*) the voice of an older man without illusions, the voice of a completed wisdom.

This voice obviously shares with the preceding one a sobriety for which Dickens is rarely given credit, or which is passed over by his more sentimental admirers. It can reach us in long stately sentences and masterfully controlled paragraphs, as in the present-tense chapters of *Bleak House,* whose speaker may be called a "roving conductor" and who should not be confused with Dickens himself. But this voice can also convey a long view of things very briefly. Succinctness, by abridging life, by ignoring its saving density and texture, establishes distance. It can coolly survey, in a sentence or two, the passing of years. "The little plaintiff or defendant, who was promised a new rocking-horse when Jarndyce and Jarndyce should be settled, has grown up, possessed himself of a real horse, and trotted away into the other world" (*Bleak House*). "The chopped-up murdered man had not been lowered with a rope over the parapet when those nights were; he was alive, and slept then quietly enough most likely, and undisturbed by any dream of where he was to come" (*The Uncommercial Traveller*). "Among the vanquished was the master chimney-sweeper, whilom incredulous at Staggs's Gardens, who now lived in a stuccoed house three stories high, and gave himself out, with golden flourishes upon a varnished board, as contractor for the cleansing of railway chimneys by machinery" (*Dombey and Son*). Such brevity and authorial distance, by its nature ironic, may turn easily to full scorn: "They must have powerful motives for a secret residence, or be reduced to a destitute condition indeed, who seek a refuge in Jacob's Island" (*Oliver Twist*). Dickens's contempt for the idle, the "inhabitants unwilling to get out of bed" (the demi-monde of gamblers and swindlers of the Leicester Square area) extends to the criminally violent of temperament, such as the maid Hortense of *Bleak House.* At an extreme the scorn is satisfied with mere itemizing, as in the stage-directions of the Nighttown section of *Ulysses:* "Mr. Snagsby appears: greasy, warm, herbaceous, and chewing" (*Bleak House*). Oddly enough the compulsively active Quilp is once disposed of in precisely the chill tones used by Conrad for the indolent Verloc in *The Secret Agent* (as in the phrases I have italicized), with Quilp and Sampson and Sally Brass ironically reduced, like Ossipon and others, to role:

> *The bland and open-hearted proprietor* of Bachelor's Hall slept on amidst the *congenial accompaniments* of rain, mud, dirt, damp, fog, and rats, until late in the day; when, summoning his valet Tom Scott to assist him to rise, and to prepare

breakfast, he *quitted his couch,* and *made his toilet.* This *duty performed,* and his *repast* ended, he again *betook himself* to Bevis Marks.

This visit was not intended for Mr. Swiveller, but for *his friend and employer,* Mr. Sampson Brass. Both gentlemen, however, were from home, nor was *the life and light of law,* Miss Sally, at her post either.[12]

The "roving conductor" of *Bleak House* (who conducts the reader not the action, and musingly watches the actors in an unrolling present place and time) offers perhaps the best example of this cool contemplative voice. He could also be called, no doubt, the fictive *auteur,* the "alleged author" who differs in subtle ways from the flesh-and-blood author of *Bleak House.* He is uninvolved and for the most part unmoved, is "above the strife," and in even literal, spatial terms seems located slightly above the characters, who are of course unaware of him. For the voice is truly disembodied, ghostly. To be above the strife is to take a clearly aristocratic stance. In this the roving conductor's voice differs from Esther's humble and measured one, but also from Dickens's "interior" voice, which is both sadder and more intimate. The voice is aristocratic not least in its scorn of idle aristocrats, Voluminia and the rest, as the comparable voice in *Our Mutual Friend* is scornful of the *nouveau-riche* Veneerings and their entourage. The roving conductor of *Bleak House* has a finely classifying consciousness, a temperament that organizes and that maintains its aloofness through a variety of rhetorical devices and techniques, through superior intelligence and cool, evenly-paced irony. The irony is obvious when Lady Dedlock is introduced, watched from a distance, as by the "fashionable intelligence." It operates with great subtlety when, near the end and with exposure imminent, it gives a stylized rendering of her consciousness. The wordiness and elaboration of syntax convey this ironic view, and Lady Dedlock's reluctance to look at her plight squarely, her continuing need to think evasively. The passage is close to Marlow's narration by conjecture in *Chance,* and like his becomes, even in its intellectuality, dramatic:

> For as her murderous perspective, before the doing of the deed, however subtle the precautions for its commission, would have been closed up by a gigantic dilatation of the hateful figure, preventing her from seeing any consequences beyond it; and as those consequences would have rushed in, in an unimagined flood, the moment the figure was laid low—which always happens when a murder is done; so now she sees that when he used to be on the watch before her, and she used to think, "if some mortal stroke would but fall on this old man and take him from my way!" it was but wishing that all he held against her in his hand might be flung to the winds, and chance-sown in many places.[13]

Dombey and Son, the most carefully written and most consciously literary of the novels before *Bleak House,* sometimes uses this contemplative cool voice, sometimes a more ponderous "written" language. There is more explicit psychological analysis, with its usual invitation to authorial abstraction, than in the earlier novels. A fictive *auteur* now and then speaks in the present tense, commenting with detachment:

> Changes have come again upon the great house in the long dull street, once the scene of Florence's childhood and loneliness. It is a great house still, proof against wind and weather, without breaches in the roof, or shattered windows, or delapidated walls; but it is a ruin none the less, and the rats fly from it.[14]

A cool brooding consciousness is responsible even for the overtones of fairy tale that Kathleen Tillotson has discerned, and can lead to a contemplative prose: "The spell upon it was more wasting than the spell that used to set enchanted houses sleeping once upon a time, but left their waking freshness unimpaired." The distinction between cool contemplative *auteur* and the tender-hearted Dickens *in propria persona* is strikingly illustrated by their commentaries on Florence in her solitude:

> Florence lived alone in the great dreary house, and day succeeded day, and still she lived alone; and the blank walls looked down upon her with a vacant stare, as if they had a Gorgon-like mind to stare her youth and beauty into stone. . . .

> And did that breast of Florence—Florence, so ingenuous and true—so worthy of the love that he had borne her, and had whispered in his last faint words—whose guileless heart was mirrored in the beauty of her face, and breathed in every accent of her gentle voice—did that young breast hold any other secret? Yes. One more.[15]

The difference between the two passages suggests how valuable, as a corrective to lax *attendrissement,* a fictive authorial identity could be. It was but one of a number of the ways in which technique saved. The pages recounting the gradual drift toward death of the child Paul Dombey are saved by masterful control of a limited point of view. Dickens keeps us very close to the consciousness of the child who, thinking he is about to leave school for a period of convalescence, is in fact quietly leaving life. Dickens manages this while using richly suggestive language, at times, to convey the child's "crowds of thoughts": "Where those wild birds lived, that were always hovering out at sea in troubled weather; where the clouds rose and first began; whence the wind issued on its rushing flight, and where it stopped. . . ." But meanwhile we see enough of the observed world to understand it more fully, and the reason for his new freedom from the school's discipline.

A detached, contemplative voice must achieve its distance in one way or another, if only by assuming a fictive narrative stance. But time, and the distance lent by history, can serve. Of Dickens's two historical novels, both dealing with revolutionary violence, *Barnaby Rudge* is much the more distinguished as well as the more controlled. The narrative is leisurely and calm through most of its first half (up, that is, to the onset of the Gordon riots), often with the generalizing quality of the historians Dickens had read, and an even pace not unlike Hawthorne's. Critics generally speak only of the riots, and comment on Dickens's growing sympathy with the rioters. But *Barnaby Rudge* is one of his best straight narratives, and one of his most conventionally realistic in detail. Even the intense pages on the riot are relatively controlled, both by long periodic sentences and by precise detail:

> although the glass fell from the window-sashes, and the lead and iron on the roofs blistered the incautious hand that touched them, and the sparrows in the eaves took wing, and rendered giddy by the smoke, fell fluttering down upon the blazing pile; still the fire was tended unceasingly by busy hands, and round it, men were going always.[16]

There are powerful energies at play in *Barnaby Rudge,* not least that of the sexually puissant Hugh, who shares Quilp's aggressiveness but not his malice or his grotesque charm. But I suspect its very moderation, rather than any specious violence, has discouraged casual readers of *Barnaby Rudge* and led to undeserved neglect.

THE DICKENSIAN JOG-TROT AND "DIVINE PRATTLE"

> The first ray of light which illumines the gloom, and converts into a dazzling brilliance that obscurity in which the earlier history of the public career of the immortal Pickwick would appear to be involved, is derived from the perusal of the following entry in the Transactions of the Pickwick club. . . .[*The Pickwick Papers,* opening sentence.]

> The Reverend Septimus Crisparkle (Septimus, because six little brother Crisparkles before him went out, one by one, as they were born, like six weak little rushlights, as they were lighted), having broken the thin morning ice near Cloisterham Weir with his amiable head, much to the invigoration of his frame, was now assisting his circulation by boxing at a looking-glass with great science and prowess. [*The Mystery of Edwin Drood,* ch. 6, opening sentence.]

The jog-trot is as exasperatingly familiar as any manner in English literature, and demands little commentary here: facetious and much given to polysyllabic humor; high-spirited or pretending to be; cosy and congenial; deliberately ingratiating; to all appearance effortless. It can be relied on to open monthly parts or chapters, or to accomplish transitions, or to fill space when invention has momentarily flagged, and its facility can be, as with the later blank verse of Wordsworth, fatal. It often seems to have served as a warming-up exercise at the beginning of a chapter or part, before energized writing could begin. A shift of scene, in the twelfth chapter of *Oliver Twist,* is representative of this manner, which for some readers no doubt has its charm:

> when the Dodger, and his accomplished friend Master Bates, joined in the hue-and-cry which was raised at Oliver's heels, in consequence of their executing an illegal conveyance of Mr. Brownlow's personal property, as has been already described, they were actuated by a very laudable and becoming regard for themselves,

and so on for another hundred and fifty woolly words.[17]

The jog-trot was a means of initial ingratiation, or of resuming an easy relationship with the reader after the lapse of a month. The opening paragraph of *The Chimes* both illustrates the process and comments on it: "There are not many people—and as it is desirable that a story-teller and a story-reader should establish a mutual understanding as soon as possible, I beg it to be noticed that I confine this observation neither to young people nor to little people, but extend it to all conditions of people," etc. It would perhaps be accurate, for the Christmas stories, to speak rather of *artful prattle* than of *casual jog-trot,* since the rhetorical task could be delicate: a congenial reassuring playful voice must compensate for and override the pathos of the stories, must induce tears yet keep suffering at a distance, and remind us that all will finally be made right in the end. Dickens had made his contract with his readers—broken in *The Old Curiosity Shop,* after all, but kept in the revised ending of *Great Expectations* and of course in *A Christmas Carol.* "Scrooge was better than his word. He did it all, and infinitely more; and to Tiny Tim, who did NOT die, he was a second father."

The quotation from *Edwin Drood* suggests that the jog-trot, as natural to Dickens as breathing (or night walking) is to be found from beginning to end. But there are in fact very few instances of this jocularity in *Edwin Drood,* and even this one has its dark side, quite apart from the six little brothers. For Crisparkle's activity is singularly solitary here, as is his piano-playing, in a sad novel of lonely turmoil and broken human connection. A fully relaxed playfulness or unimaginative high spirits, the effortless running on-and-on, is rare in the major novels of the middle period, from *Dombey and Son* through *Great Expectations,* and is also fairly rare in *Barnaby Rudge, Hard Times* and *A Tale of Two Cities,* but startlingly frequent in *Our Mutual Friend.* The manner, whether relaxed or energized, is perhaps as natural for Dickens as the "grave interior voice," his high spirits as natural as his recurring insecurity and gloom.

The lover of picnics and excursions and good dinners, as well as the lover of verbal play, is evident in the catalog of fruiterers' shops in *A Christmas Carol,* as luscious as Joyce's Dublin market, or the Covent Garden market of *Martin Chuzzlewit,* even to its "lusty snails and fine young curly leeches," or the richly laden "closet of closets" in *Edwin Drood.* The playfulness of many kinds, which lent itself so well to innocent family reading aloud, largely constituted "the Inimitable." No amount of twentieth-century criticism can wish it away.

The playfulness can be a corrective to suffering, or protection from it. But it can also screen the reader from a too realistic contemplation of villainy. One of Dickens's finer strategies is to endow such repulsive beings as Riderhood and Venus and Wegg with their own brands of forensic nonsense; all three enjoy playing with language and logic. Perhaps the best example of rhetorical neutralizing of violence and horror and evil by humor is seen in Squeers in *Nicholas Nickleby.* The evil dissolves in absurdity when he says that to pay for medical treatment for his own wounds, he exposed five of the little boys to scarlet fever. His own bill could then be spread out among theirs and thus be paid by the parents. This extravagance leads, with a Snopes pride, to his stratagem for boys who get weak and ill: to let them graze in a neighbor's turnip field. "There an't better land in the county than this perwerse lad grazed on, and yet he goes and catches cold and indigestion and what not, and then his friends bring a lawsuit against *me!"*

THE VOICES OF RHETORICAL EXERCISE

There are stylistic experiments and self-conscious rhetorical flights in all of the novels. This was inevitable in a highly original writer of great verbal facility, coming in an age of transition for both the novel form and the literary language. The prose was "revolutionary," as George Ford remarks, and was therefore seen to be barbarous by many contemporaries. Not least revolutionary was the unpretentious grave interior voice, which departed so far from the balanced periods of even third-rate Augustans. The impulse to "make it new"— which resulted in six different novel forms in so few years, from *Pickwick* to *Martin Chuzzlewit*—also existed, though less obviously, for language. Even *Nicholas Nickleby* and *Barnaby Rudge* have their consciously experimental marathon sentences. *Martin Chuzzlewit,* we will see, has far more "literary" flights—some exhibiting sheer high spirits; some, presumably, a desire to counteract the book's somber, long-sustained pessimism.

Dombey and Son followed upon a period of relative rest (though such rest as would exhaust most writers), and is one of the most carefully wrought of the novels, one of the most "realistic" too in its pacing and its accumulation of detail. Here for the first time, Steven Marcus surprisingly remarks, "is a voice that seems to be listening to or overhearing itself; its tone reverberates inwardly, and though the prose is direct, it is not simple nor without subtlety." [18] My own view is that *Dombey and Son* constantly calls attention to its *written* quality: less personal utterance than authorial wit and contrivance, a sophisticated polish. The great dreary Dombey house as an enchanted place under a wasting spell, with a poor lonely princess within, is splendidly conceived, yet evokes wordy abstraction and a bewildering shower of similies and metaphors:

> The passive desolation of disuse was everywhere silently manifest about it. Within doors, curtains, drooping heavily, lost their old folds and shapes, and hung like cumbrous palls. Hecatombs of furniture, still piled and covered up, shrunk like imprisoned and forgotten men, and changed insensibly. Mirrors were dim as with the breath of years. Patterns of carpets faded and became perplexed and faint, like the memory of those years' trifling incidents. [19]

The symbolism of sea and train (one a natural and pleasing correlative of death, the other a man-made agent of destruction) is carefully executed; so too the underlined metaphorical connection of Carker and cat. Conscious literary experiment is evident in the sustained effort to reflect Carker's dazed consciousness through a flow of passing scenes (chapter 55) and in an amusing effort to reflect what was after all a relatively new sensation, the sound of train wheels: "Through the hollow, on the height, by the heath, by the orchard, by the park, by the garden, over the canal," etc.

In other passages Dickens anticipates (perhaps more than anywhere else in his work) the dreary realism of the 1930's: both home decorator descriptions and psychological analyses awkwardly combining the character's view of things with the author's in a pretense of objectivity. "Rich colours, excellently blended, meet the eye at every turn; in the furniture—its proportions admirably devised to suit the shapes and sizes of the small rooms. . . ." And, "New accusation of himself, fresh inward lamentings over his own unworthiness, and the ruin in which it was at once his consolation and his self-reproach that he did not stand alone, were the sole kind of reflections to which the discovery gave rise in him." Which of the two modern manners is the deadlier? Even the "originals" of this intelligent novel are contrived and extraordinarily repetitive: Captain Cuttle and Major Bagstock and Mr. Toots. The novel's theme is important and intelligent: the accumulation of capital as self-destructive, with

Dombey's design as inhuman as Sutpen's, and his great house a failure: money corrupting individuals while the new railroads cut through and destroy the land. Yet the enduring fictive life of the book lies in Paul and Florence as children, and, to a less degree, in the Dostoevskyan portrait of Edith Dombey, as proud and violent as Nastasya in *The Idiot,* fleeing with Carker not only to humiliate her husband but also, for a time, to degrade and humiliate herself.

David Copperfield and *Great Expectations,* with their quiet first-person narration, and the more comprehensive novels of the middle period (*Bleak House* and even *Little Dorrit*) are all written with distinction. Each has its rhetorical experiments—in *Little Dorrit*'s early chapters, for instance, an attempt to come closer to characters' consciousness through clusters of incomplete sentences. But *Our Mutual Friend* is by far the most rhetorical and most innovative of the novels, technically, with more conscious artistry than is commonly supposed. Dickens's is by no means an art that conceals art. But the novel's richness and diversity of theme, and its occasional surprising modernity, and its varied array of grotesques, also its several grand scenes of death and resurrection—these have led critics to take technique for granted, and turn attention elsewhere.

It is nevertheless evident that rhetorical elaboration and stylized distancing of the material were necessary to the author. Dickens was less confident than usual of his invention, and seemed conscious of diminished powers; wit and rhetorical surprise could be a means of beating material into life. Cool ironic distance, achieved through various rhetorical games, was appropriate enough for social satire. But rhetorical play could also mediate between the reader and the various grotesques; and, at times, between the author and scenes he found embarrassing. There was also the commendable impulse to renew himself, and an impatience with the measured straightforward movement of *Great Expectations*. The novels from *Dombey and Son* through *Great Expectations* were more orderly, more intelligent, saner than those from *The Pickwick Papers* through *Martin Chuzzlewit;* critics are of course right in discerning increased control. But vivacity and strangeness had been lost.

Our Mutual Friend, though so rich in conscious rhetorical device, and though reaching us through a number of perspectives, rarely loses the sense of a watching personal consciousness and voice. A glance at the first four chapters, one of the most ostentatious monthly parts in Dickens's work, will suggest how conscious rhetoric and personal voice interact. This first installment introduces with great ease several social worlds, and establishes mysterious connections among them. There is the brutal world of body-snatchers and waterside poverty, "where accumulated scum of humanity seemed to be washed from higher grounds"; and the sophisticated, bored or cynical Veneering world of aristocrats, *nouveaux-riches,* idle lawyers; and the Wilfer world of lower-middle-class family life. There are the corruptible in all three worlds, or people already corrupted by money. A dead man's money, accumulated through mounds of dust, garbage, waste, can whimsically try to effect, years in advance, a marriage between two people who have never met. The Veneering world is one of polished or cynical pretense, but capable of casual brutality and insolence to the poor. In this real Victorian world Lizzie Hexam, secretly helping her brother to an education, would be natural prey for a young lawyer with time on his hands. The novel swiftly moves from one world to the next, and before the end of the monthly installment the slightly suspect John Rokesmith has moved into the Wilfer house as a lodger.

The brief, strangely calm opening chapter, with Gaffer and Lizzie Hexam on the river and a body towed behind, is told as by a ghostly witness. Style confirms the watcher's comment: this is business-like and plain, these are things of usage. The conversational voice carries easily a certain amount of authentic river detail, moves naturally to the brief brilliant dialogue of Gaffer and the still unidentified Rogue Riderhood. There is a moral distinction, at this very bottom of the economic world, between robbing a dead body and a live sailor. Gaffer establishes thus early the right of the poorest outcasts and eccentrics to engage in forensic and verbal play: "Has a dead man any use for money? Is it possible for a dead man to have money? What world does a dead man belong to? T'other world. What world does money belong to? This world. How can money be a corpse's? Can a corpse own it, want it, spend it, claim it, miss it?" These few pages constitute one of the novel's several scenes that live on in the imagination after dead chapters are forgotten.

The first monthly part remains brilliant, sometimes exasperatingly so, after repeated readings. The second chapter, "The Man from Somewhere," is a pyrotechnic display of skill. A controlling consciousness and scornful voice persists through many changes of narrative focus. The chapter must evoke boredom and triviality, the tedious unreality of the Veneering dinner party, but do so without becoming boring. And it must convey evasiveness through stylized and evasive techniques. In this world of the new rich reality is kept at a distance, in conversation, through irony, witty allusion, anecdote. And all is pretense: the guests do not even know their host. The narrative brilliantly maintains a double vision. It has access to the minds of various guests, and can simultaneously convey their thoughts and comment on these thoughts. Thus the extended metaphor of Twemlow as a dining-table, to whom leaves can be added for a larger party. He is the Veneerings' one genuine aristocrat, to be used, treated by them as an object.

Both the Veneerings' cynicism, collecting their guests, and the author's overall view, are conveyed through the reduction of people to professional role: "an Engineer, a Payer-off of the National Debt, a Poem on Shakespeare," etc. The reporting of scene and dialogue is selective and stylized: artifice recording a highly artificial social game. We may have a shorthand summary of dialogue interrupted by an actual exchange of words. The words of the four Buffers are connected by a bracket covering four printed lines, as three rhyming lines are linked in an eighteenth-century poem: an open acknowledgment of artifice. The watching consciousness, now in the guise of the great looking glass above the sideboard, comments on those at the table. "Reflects Veneering; forty, wavy-haired, dark, tending to corpulence, sly, mysterious, filmy—a kind of sufficiently well-looking veiled-prophet, not prophesying." "Reflects Mrs. Podsnap; fine woman for Professor Owen, quantity of bone, neck and nostrils like a rocking-horse, hard features, majestic headdress in which Podsnap has hung golden offerings."

The watching consciousness, with aristocratic disdain for these pretenders and their scorn for each other, can keep its distance by reducing action to metaphorical fun and, tiresomely, by polysyllabic humor. Lady Tippins, with the ices at the end of the dinner, is a "hardy old cruiser" who "has last touched at the North Pole. . . ." Into all this artificiality the hint of a story, of real life, intrudes. Mortimer at first can tell it only through clever evasive allusion, but presently drops his pose of indolence. The subject "must have been a boy of spirit and resource, to get here on a stopped allowance of five sous a week; but he did it somehow, and he burst in on his father, and pleaded his sister's cause." The father dies, leaving a will stipulating that the boy, to inherit, must marry in time a girl, then four or five years old, he has never seen. Years later, now in fact, the "man from Somewhere" is on his way home to "succeed to a very large fortune, and to take a wife." Mortimer has scarcely finished his story when a message arrives for him. Reality has indeed intruded on artifice; life on an interesting dinner-table story. The message is that the man from Somewhere has drowned.

The third chapter takes Mortimer and Lightwood to Hexam's place and thence to the police station for a look at the body, which occurs between sentences. They continue their light persiflage in a chapter that reaches us largely through dialogue. Eugene is arrogant toward Charley Hexam, frightens Lizzie with one hard look, and arouses Gaffer's anger. There is a gulf between these non-practicing young lawyers and the reality of the police station, seen in extended metaphor as a monastery, the Night-Inspector as a cool recluse, a professional who keeps his head. He is properly suspicious of the stranger Julius

Handford, who asks to see the body and is dazed by the sight. Efficiently the chapter moves to the inquest, after a tender scene between Lizzie and Charley Hexam. The chapter has brought a first confrontation of several major characters; it has suggested the major themes of artifice and reality; indolence and energy; impersonation and befuddlement; class-conflict. With the fourth chapter, after this solid groundwork of mystery—the materials alike for social satire and a "police tale"—we experience an entirely different world: the plausible and with one exception likeable Wilfers at home, on what begins as a quite ordinary evening. The rhetorical stylizing is less obvious in this fourth chapter. But it is there. For the narrative consciousness can interrupt dialogue for brief incisive description or, as with the first impression of the new lodger (and future husband) for shorthand notation: "A dark gentleman. Thirty at the utmost. An expressive, one might say handsome, face. A very bad manner. In the last degree constrained, reserved, diffident, troubled." This narrative consciousness, now with a recognizable Dickensian playfulness—sprightly, cosy, affectionate—completes the first monthly part on a friendly note, after the earlier satire and gloom. Yet the last lines are ominous, suspenseful. Bella might have been even more reluctant to take lodgers "had she known that if Mr. Julius Handford had a twin brother upon earth, Mr. John Rokesmith was the man."

The paradox, generally, is that *Our Mutual Friend,* richer in artifice than any of the other novels, regularly reaches us through a personal voice, the author's or another's. To say this is not necessarily to make a value judgment. The artifice may be insufferably tricky, the voice embarrassingly coy. But both are present. There is a constant interplay of distance maintained by stylizing rhetoric and intimacy achieved through personal commentary and colloquial turns of phrase. A few more examples of stylization must stand for many.

Authorial metaphor to convey intense introspection, inner turmoil.

> And John Rokesmith, what did he?
> He went down to his room, and buried John Harmon many additional fathoms deep. He took his hat, and walked out, and, as he went to Holloway or anywhere else—not at all minding where—heaped mounds upon mounds of earth over John Harmon's grave.[20]

For over three thousand words Harmon, in a device highly unusual for Dickens, has summarized through nominal interior monologue the crucial incident of his near-drowning. Drugged, he had experienced a kind of night journey in which he lost the sense of his own identity. His inward debate serves, simply, as an authorial omniscient harking-back to make up what is missing of the past. There follows a scene in which Bella forcefully repudiates "John Rokesmith."

Hurt, Harmon determines in the long night walk to keep his real identity hidden. Dickens thus disposes of this long inward debate in a few sentences.

Stream of consciousness. The wedding of Alfred Lammle and Sophronia Akersham elicits, as the Veneering world generally does, a variety of stylizing devices. Lady Tippins's surview, which might be "realism" to a post-Joycean reader, must have seemed to Victorian readers an extreme stylized departure from normal narrative:

> "Twemlow; blessed release for the dear man if she really was his daughter, nervous even under the pretence that she is, well he may be. Mrs. Veneering; never saw such velvet, say two thousand pounds as she stands, absolute jeweller's window, father must have been a pawnbroker, or how could these people do it?" [21]

The next sentence is an authorial summary of stream-of-consciousness rather than the actual flow: "Attendant unknowns; pokey." And this sentence is followed, with a new paragraph, by what might be an observing society journalist's mental notes: "Ceremony performed, register signed, Lady Tippins escorted out of sacred edifice by Veneering, carriages rolling back to Stucconia, servants with favours and flowers, Veneering's house reached, drawing rooms most magnificent." The overall impression is of authorial effort to get over this ground rapidly, yet animate it through artifice.

Stylized summary of unrecorded dialogue. The scene is a lively Molièresque one, with Mr. and Mrs. Lammle carrying on a conversation on behalf of Georgiana Podsnap and Fascination Fledgeby, who are too shy and stupid to speak for themselves. The dialogue is interrupted by stylized summary, in which an overhearing consciousness reflects the unrecorded real voice: "Fascination wished to know if the colour were not called rose-colour. Fascination took rose-colour to mean the colour of roses," etc.

Stylization of unrecorded dialogue, and "cosy" situation, coy to the extreme of having a baby talk. " 'I won't,' said the inexhaustible baby, '—allow—you—to make—game—of—my—venerable—Ma.' " In the following chapter the narrative voice, upon the removal of "the Inexhaustible," adopts Bella's version of baby talk, which for some readers may be even less tolerable: "whereupon Bella withdrew herself from the presence and knowledge of gemplemorums, and the screaming ceased. . . ."

The reasons for stylization, the aesthetic aims or temperamental necessities, will vary from book to book, and chapter to chapter. The playfulness can be a means of ingratiating the family reader, and of forcibly bringing energy to scenes that lack vitality. It is possible too that Dickens, more aware than before of criticism, and after several more realistic novels, was self-conscious over a

return to some of the manners and methods of earlier novels—the grand macabre scenes and the heart-warming ones (including the heart-warming death of
Johnny), the revelations of identities, the melodramatic confrontations, the
large symbols of river and dust heaps, the appearance of such grotesques as
Wegg and Venus. Extreme artifice may also indicate an evasion of psychologically intractable material, or embarrassment in its presence. Polysyllabic
humor is very frequently an indication that the imagination is ill at ease. The
treatment of Bella's wedding at Greenwich (Bk.IV, ch.2), in the presence of
Cherubic Pa, carries evasiveness to an extreme, with half-a-dozen major stylizing devices in as many paragraphs, and not a few minor ones; and all of these
enlisting variants of a single coy, generally exasperating voice.[22]

It would be misleading to conclude this brief commentary on such a note of irritation. *Our Mutual Friend* is in many ways a remarkably intelligent, audacious, inventive, modern book, and it exhibits more novelistic skill and stylistic
ingenuity than any of Dickens's contemporaries possessed. It is the work of,
certainly, the most original stylist among the novelists of his time. But it only
occasionally sustains for any length the quiet, chaste, varied, often lovely prose
to be found in the "grave interior voice" and at times in the "detached
contemplative" one.

There was, however, one more novel, though Dickens did not live to complete it. A pleasing contemplative voice is heard in *The Mystery of Edwin
Drood* from beginning to end, but more distinctly in the chapters written in the
present tense. Almost the same calm prose records Neville's feelings after he
had left Edwin and Jasper in a rage, and stood "in the midst of a blood-red
whirl" and, a few lines later, Crisparkle's quiet piano-playing. The fictive *auteur* (much less regardful of the reader than *Bleak House*'s roving conductor)
watches bemused the trials of these puppets, his own passions all subdued:
"Some wildly passionate ideas of the river dissolve under the spell of the
moonlight on the Cathedral and the graves. . . ."

All of *Edwin Drood* that was published in Dickens's lifetime (through
chapter 16) is written with great distinction, though George Bernard Shaw dismissed the novel as a failure of fatigue and age. "The murmur of the tide is
heard beyond; but no wave passes the archway, over which his lamp burns red
behind his curtain, as if the building were a Lighthouse." In rhythm as in diction and composed syntax this modest sentence is very pure Dickens. Even one
of the speaker's most audacious moments (as he enters for a few moments
Durdles's dreaming mind, and drops what would presumably have been one of
the plot's major hints) has a bemused quietness: "He dreams that the footsteps

die away into distance of time and space, and that something touches him, and that something falls from his hand.'' For this ambiguous story of murder and secrecy is bathed in a circumambient as if moonlit calm. Dickens had selected a cathedral town as his setting for the first time, and Cloisterham is the Rochester of his childhood. The present-tense contemplations are comparable in many ways to the nostalgic moments of *The Uncommercial Traveller* and its quiet prose of recollection. Thus a lovely paragraph, the opening of chapter 14, evokes the faces of Cloisterham children, returned ''from the outer world at long intervals to find the city wonderfully shrunken in size. . . .'' The vision that magnified trees into giants now sees the world as very small. To these returned children

> it has happened in their dying hours afar off, that they have imagined their chamber floor to be strewn with the autumnal leaves fallen from the elm-trees in the Close: so have the rustling sounds and fresh scents of their earliest impressions revived when the circle of their lives was very nearly traced, and the beginning and the end were drawing close together.[23]

7
THE PSYCHOLOGY OF DOSTOEVSKY: CONSCIOUS AND UNCONSCIOUS UNDERSTANDING

The title and even sub-title of this chapter could be justified only by a very long book, one that certainly demands to be written. Many have paid tribute, sometimes uneasy tribute, to Dostoevsky's pre-Freudian insights; Freud himself found *The Brothers Karamazov* "the most magnificent novel ever written" [1] and declared, on his seventieth birthday, that everything he had discovered was already present in Dostoevsky's work. [2] But the very magnitude of the challenge, as well as the dread of going outside one's discipline, has deterred the best psychiatric and best literary minds. Dostoevsky's later novels were written at a time when there was much interest, both professional and amateur, in the "unconscious," though psychoanalytic insights remained to be codified. His work shows a conscious understanding of unconscious processes beyond that of most professionals, whether his contemporaries or ours, and gives a more intimate picture of neurotic experience. His work reveals, moreover, an access to his own unconscious greater than that of any other major novelist. Insistence on so much psychological insight dismays critics bent on stressing only the religious mystic, or only the political or social ideologist, or only the literary man working in a Gogolian or other literary tradition. Two of the most useful commentators on Dostoevsky, Konstantin Mochulsky and Mikhail Bakhtin, show no understanding of dynamic psychology, and interpret the most obvious psycho-sexual situations in religious, intellectualist or (Bakhtin only) formalist structures. Their work is not, of course, recent, though Bakhtin's is in some ways remarkably modern. For a few, even today, the specter of anachronism rises. A usually courteous Slavic scholar felt compelled to interrupt a lecture, in which I had remarked that Dostoevsky was the greatest of the Freudian novelists, to comment that Freud was still a student when Dostoevsky died. I could reply that he was also, in his insights, the greatest of the "post-Freudians." For the complexes, neuroses, psychoses, all existed before Freud or Dostoevsky was born, for great intuitive minds to discern; and even some of the strategies by which courageous spirits coped with them.

The purist anxieties of the New Criticism, bent on protecting literature from extrinsic life, are by now largely history. But there remain Dostoevsky scholars (never much concerned with *those* purities) who still feel that the novelist's historically recognizable ideological concerns and commitments are menaced by psychological explanations—this though no writer concerned himself more with the personal, sometimes neurotic, bases of commitment. There remain also a number of scholars, literary and psychological alike, who object to an eclectic psycho-literary approach, and ask one to choose between some particular psychoanalytic approach . . . and nothing. This demand ignores both the extraordinary variety of Dostoevsky's insights and the degree to which the best professionals today are themselves highly eclectic.

The present chapter can do no more than suggest some of the interests and methodological problems that a major study would have to take up. One of these is certainly the relationship of classical psychological understanding (say Molière's or Stendhal's) to common-sense eclectic psychiatric understanding and to formal psychoanalytic interpretation. The focus will here be narrowed (!) to the general question of the novelist's conscious and unconscious understanding of psychic process and unusual behavior. The literary intentionalist, with his historical training and general rationalist bias, would normally have a greater respect for conscious understanding. And of course a psychoanalyst writing a textbook would aspire to a fully conscious awareness of what he's describing. But such full awareness (or the illusion of it) could be crippling to a novelist in two ways. It could lead him to abstraction and excess exposition, and tempt him to impose a system on living reality. This was the great danger for the Freudian novelists of the 1930's. A striving for full, even academic understanding could also inhibit or block access to the unconscious, and the "knowledge" it has to offer. The greater dynamic and dramatic interest of Dostoevsky, Simon Lesser argued, lay in the fact that whereas Flaubert refused even unconscious knowledge of latent homosexuality (specifically in *Madame Bovary*), Dostoevsky did not.[3] Dostoevsky's creative power was such that he could, more than any other novelist, profit from both conscious and unconscious intuitions. I would like to add, as a final preliminary, that a great novelist's psychological knowledge may have genuine validity as science, even though that may not be its purpose. No treatise on the neurotic gambler's compulsion to lose is "truer" than Dostoevsky's *The Gambler,* no study of alcoholism "truer" than *Under the Volcano,* no analysis of repressed homosexuality and the dangers of repression "truer" than *The Immoralist.* These novels can be read for an altogether non-literary "profit," even though the three writers were long unable to profit by their own insights.

The psychological interests of *The Possessed* will be deferred to a later chapter.

The Double (1846), we have seen, is highly representative of Dostoevsky in its vivid interpenetration of the fantastic and the everyday. He came to look on the short novel with distaste, perhaps because it was severely attacked by Belinsky and others so soon after the success of *Poor Folk.* He never had a more genuinely serious idea, he wrote in *The Diary of a Writer* in 1877. "But the form of the story was an utter failure". Soon after publication he was willing to agree that the short novel was intolerably drawnout and therefore boring. There is, in fact, an extreme lapse of literary tact very early in the narrative: the burlesque description of the birthday party that opens Chapter IV, with an authorial voice replacing the narrator's cool and sprightly one. Without question the novel is overlong and repetitious, with tedious stretches in Chapters IX and X. It is possible to account for the tedium fairly precisely, and the loss of fictional energy. Certain components of the narrative—the confusion of the letters (IX), the lengthy dream and the long paragraphs of interior monologue (X), even the seemingly realistic dialogue between the two Golyadkins (XI)—shatter the delicate balance of ambiguity of the best chapters: is Golyadkin Jr., the double, real or hallucinated or simultaneously (for the reader) both? In these weakly specific pages we lose the exceedingly effective triple vision of the most dramatic parts. The triple vision is that of Golyadkin's hallucinations or distortions, of the narrator's watchful and distant irony, and of objective reality as indicated by the laughter or consternation and, ultimately, the compassion of observers in the background, watching the sick man, as indicated too by the words and stares of his immediate interlocutors.

The double would seem largely hallucinatory on his first appearance, but also on his last, as he skips from side to side of the carriage carrying Golyadkin Sr. to the asylum. But what of his changing appearance and behavior at the office? Is someone actually there, a new employee with at least a distant resemblance to the sick hero? Is the story Gogolian or Kafkaesque symbolism, in which wholly impossible fictions—a nose getting into a carriage, an enormous dung-beetle trying to get out of bed—movingly reflect deep and common human anxieties? Or is it serious psychopathology of autoscopic hallucination? Only ruthless logic demands a commitment that will hold for every chapter and page. A sensitive reader can experience *The Turn of the Screw* both as ghost story and as a study of neurotic hallucination: either way we see Quint on the tower or the tragic figure of Miss Jessel on the stairs. And so for *The Double,* though it is highly possible the reader will see Golyadkin Jr. "doubly double"—see both a flesh-and-blood clerk in rather clear outline and a figure blurred as by badly corrected eyeglasses or by the onset of madness.

Such tolerance of ambiguity may distress literary logicians, and psychoanalytic critics even more. Does the story, however amusingly ambiguous, or however true or false clinically, lead to a rich credible insight into important human conflicts? Lawrence Kohlberg finds such a question unacceptable. The psychoanalyst, he writes, "brings to literature the habits of the clinic which require that a decision or diagnosis be made, and the habits of a scientist which require that a hypothesis be judged, not as inspiring, but as true or false." [4] (Oddly enough Kohlberg, one of the best psychoanalytic critics of Dostoevsky, is guilty of serious misreading. To say that the double "accompanies" Golyadkin Sr. home is to destroy both the psychological and the dramatic impact of Golyadkin Sr.,[5] terrified, following the stranger through the streets, presently to find him "sitting before him on his bed.") The particular danger of psychological or psychoanalytic criticism is that of losing, through an attempt to pin neurosis down and name it, a large and obvious meaning. A single wise sentence of Edward Wasiolek would protect from many pitfalls: "Case histories in literature are not case histories in psychology, but they are also not entirely different." [6] The difficulty has come, with *The Double,* from trying to achieve a clinical precision. For Otto Rank, *The Double* is a classic portrayal of a paranoid state.[7] Kohlberg acknowledges that there are indeed resemblances with phenomena of paranoid states: disowning projection, paranoid "delusions or hallucinations of persecutory figures" that "emerge from feelings of shame and pathologically low self-esteem." [8] The "experience of a hallucinatory duplicate of the self is not," however,

> explained by, or consistent with, a paranoid psychosis. The typical paranoid concept is one of a spotless self being unjustly blamed and tortured by evil others. In contrast, Dostoevsky's hallucinatory or semi-hallucinatory Doubles persecute their creators by asserting their identity with them, and usually their creators are aware that the Double is their "other self." [9]

Such self-awareness is "quite alien to the paranoid state. If the paranoid persecutors were to be experienced as duplicates of the self, the defensive function of the hallucinations would break down, since they would no longer protect the self against the awareness that it is the possessor of shameful impulses.'' [10]

Is a genuine psychoanalytic interpretation of *The Double* possible, we may parenthetically ask, where we know so little of Golyadkin's life prior to the opening of the story, and nothing of his childhood? But the major difficulty would seem to lie in Kohlberg's need to answer Rank and to assume that the story deals with a specific and unchanging psychic complaint. I am pleased by his more general comment that Dostoevsky's ''consciously 'split' characters do present classical symptoms of the obsessive-compulsive character'' [11] or Stanley Coleman's that ''Dostoevsky depicted what he himself subjectively experienced, the simultaneous presentation of conflicting feelings and impulses.'' [12] But literary and psychoanalytic critics have alike failed to take into account the changes that occur in Golyadkin Jr. in response to Golyadkin Sr.'s psychic needs. These changes are, simply, the heart of the story. They also correspond to the real-life experience of identification and projection, neurotic and even unneurotic, as the ''other'' takes on different roles.

We could, if we wished, see in Golyadkin Jr.'s changing roles obvious instances of the Freudian triad, and of the ego-ideal to boot. But to enclose the double even within this large quartet would falsify. Here, very briefly summarized (and so losing some of the story's nuances) is what the double, for the sick hero, appears to represent. It adds up, in terms of Dostoevsky's largely conscious understanding, to a picture of an isolated, insecure and guilt-ridden man suffering from delusions of persecution, anxious with good reason about his sanity, and moving toward a total separation from reality.

1. *Golyadkin Jr. as a humiliated person seeking indulgence and patronage.* Dostoevsky wisely tells us nothing of the hours that follow the first encounter; there is no evidence that the double spent the night in Golyadkin Sr.'s room. But the hero's presentiments that he will find something amiss at the office are realized, since Golyadkin Jr. appears there and is seated opposite him, a timid new employee. After work, though the hero wants to go his separate way, the intruder pleads for magnanimity and an indulgent hearing. He is downtrodden in appearance, crushed, scared. Invited to Golyadkin Sr.'s rooms, he speaks flatteringly of the hero's ''innate goodness and excellence of heart,'' and tells of his own failures, and of persecution by his enemies. He would seem to meet the hero's need to encounter and protect someone even more humble than himself. They drink together and Golyadkin Sr. gets drunk. For a brief time he sits on the edge of his guest's bed.

2. *Golyadkin Jr. as interloper and image of success.* At the office, the next morning, the double is too busy to give the hero more than a scant greeting, is

already bustlingly successful, and assumes the role of intermediary with his superior. He calls attention to a huge ink blot, offers to eradicate the blot and, in the ensuing confusion, seizes the papers and takes them in to the Director's office. He has both called attention to shameful (and suggestive) error and offered the hero's good work as his own. But when the enraged Golyadkin Sr. challenges him, the double refers insinuatingly to the preceding night, and suggests homosexual advances were made.

3. *Golyadkin Jr. as a shameful disorderly self, to be disowned if possible.* The hero's desire to protect a separate identity is intense; he would give a finger of his right hand, if that would eliminate the double. A symbolic castration, like John Jay Chapman's loss of his hand, might protect and appease. Golyadkin Sr. is afraid his double will misbehave and disgrace the name they share; in fact he is soon embarrassed by an instance of apparent manic activity. The hero has ordered and eaten one open-faced patty in a tavern, but is asked to pay for eleven. In the doorway he sees the double, finishing a tenth patty. The dream that opens chapter X, though threatening credibility, presents the hero's guilt in relatively direct form: "some well-known, trifling, or fairly sizeable piece of nastiness which he had seen, heard, or even himself committed. . . ." When the two Golyadkins next meet, it is the hero who has sinned, the double who accuses him of nastiness.

4. *Golyadkin Jr. as moral accuser.* The double, a model of successful, extrovert activity, shakes the hero's hand in the friendliest way, even "with a kind of tearful emotion." But the reconciliation is illusory; the double appears to make further suggestions of homosexuality, or perhaps masturbation, and wipes the fingers that have touched the guilty one's hand. The double accuses him of corrupting and deceiving his German landlady. The enraged Golyadkin Sr. pursues the double's cab, manages to climb in, then falls off "like a sack of flour." In a restaurant, where he is uncertain whether he has eaten the dinner of which he sees the remains on a table, another trauma of sexual guilt occurs: his medicine bottle, with its dark reddish, repulsive liquid, smashes on the floor.

5. *The movement toward the asylum, with Golyadkin Jr. assisting.* The hero has waited for two hours in Olsufy Ivanovich's yard, outside the scene of his initial disgrace at the party; Golyadkin Jr. invites him inside. Here, after their hands have been joined in seeming friendliness, Golyadkin Jr. gives the hero a "Judas kiss," and now a terrible "stranger" appears (but not really a stranger), the doctor Krestyan Ivanovich. The double, who no longer conceals a "malicious, indecent joy," leads the way to the carriage, and even appears to follow it for a time, skipping from side to side, as it sets out for the asylum.

In psychological terms *The Double* thus transcends the clinical question of "autoscopic hallucination" (which in real life is very rare) [13] or that of a "normal" paranoid psychosis. An unchanging duplicate of the self might well not provide "the defensive functions of the hallucination." But the most important feature of Golyadkin Jr. as double is precisely his capacity to change in purpose and even in manner. This is the story's structure and the structure of the hero's illness. Beyond this *The Double* conveys, perhaps not altogether conjecturally, what illusions of persecution (based on real persecution from within) and the experience of encroaching madness may be like, as reality gradually recedes, returns in flashes of authentic observation, at last is almost totally lost.

The interpretive problem with *Notes from Underground* (1864) is not wholly dissimilar. Where the psychoanalytic critic, in trying to assess Golyadkin's "case" clinically, may ignore the obvious psychological movement of the story, so here the literary historian (bemused by stated original intention and historical context) may minimize such psychological movement or even deny its existence. The further problem, a recurring one with Dostoevsky, lies in the close relationship of ideology and neurosis. To separate them, in the hope of keeping "ideas" pristine, is to lose a central insight.

Notes from Underground is the most intense and most authentic rendering in Dostoevsky, perhaps in all novelistic literature, of neurotic suffering seen from within. But it is also a document of major philosophical interest. We know that Dostoevsky intended a critical essay on Chernyshevsky's *What's To Be Done,* with its Fourierist phalanstery and Crystal Palace insuring eternal spring and summer. Instead he wrote, at the bedside of his dying wife, *Notes from Underground.* The narrator's diatribe against the central assumptions of scientific determinism has, like those of Nietzsche and Baudelaire, a nineteenth-century ring, and it is natural to think in terms of the French positivists, of crude profit and loss calculus, and of the argument, in *What's To Be Done,* that self-interest or "advantage" is the solid base of human action. But the philosophical issue has been a major one for some two hundred years, and among thinkers of the last hundred for whom Chernyshevsky may be only a name. Stressing the specific satirical intent has led a number of critics, though perhaps not the majority, to miss *Notes from Underground*'s timeless psychological and moral interest. Other critics (noting that the underground man presents his argument against determinism in the 1860's, then tells of his romantic dreams and his humiliations as a young man in the 1840's), have devoted attention to generational change in Russia, though an unbiased reader would see full continuity between the theoretical self-lacerations of the first part and the dramatized self-humiliations of the second. Concern with historical context has led Andrew

MacAndrew to miss even the philosophical meaning of the story. The narrator, as he sees it, "has switched from romanticism and Utopianism to determinism and utilitarianism (i.e. the position of Chernyshevsky and his nihilist followers)," and, though hating it, "is forced to accept determinism." [14] But the narrator not merely revolts against determinism. He refutes it, he believes successfully, and does so by the concrete instances of his own self-punitive behavior as a young man of twenty-four. He shows, with the most passionate reality, a man motivated not by "advantage" but by a craving for suffering and humiliation. Dostoevsky's understanding of self-destructive impulses, and their relation to guilt, would seem conscious and virtually complete, though not necessarily planned. "Sometimes I fancy that it will be rubbish," he wrote to his brother, "but still I write with passion; I don't know what will emerge." [15]

What did emerge is a great fictional portrait and confession, no more tied to its time than Camus's *The Plague* (which was full, for early French readers, of allegorical references to the Occupation and the Resistance) is now tied to the second world war. A great literary work is likely, almost by definition, to transcend a satiric or parodic intent and origin. Rousseau, identifying with the paranoid Alceste, rejected the satirical intent of *Le Misanthrope*. A latent sympathy had indeed been "put there", however unconsciously, by Molière, who had his share of real enemies. A far richer duality lies behind *Notes from Underground*. Given his hatred of the predicament of determinism, MacAndrew says, Dostoevsky "cannot possibly be trying to present the underground man's revolt as that of a neurotic, psychotic, or sado-masochistic freak, as has been so often maintained." [16] But in fact Dostoevsky is saying that this revolt of the irrational against logic is that of a very sick man, which is by no means the same as saying it is unworthy. Dostoevsky might well have understood R. D. Laing's view of schizophrenic retreat as at times a legitimate and necessary response to intolerable conditions. But there was of course, for Dostoevsky, another, better way out of the impasse of freedom as viciously circular suffering: Christ. The crucial tenth chapter of the first part, with its repudiation of socialist comforts, was seriously cut by censors. Fearful at seeing allusions to faith and Christ amid such fevered and dark rantings, they simply cut them out. "Those swine of censors—where I mocked at everything and sometimes *blasphemed for form's sake*—that's let pass, but where from all this I deduced the *need of faith and Christ*—that is suppressed." [17]

It may be useful, since there has been so much debate, to outline in the simplest terms my own understanding of the relationship of the two parts.

The narrator of forty, who begins "I am a sick man," is obsessed with sincerity, but his swarm of contradictory feelings makes accurate confession difficult. He sees himself as a "man of acute consciousness" (which regularly leads to inertia) as distinct from *l'homme de la nature et de la vérité* and normal man of action; he is, moreover, "divorced from the soil and the national elements." Now retired, he lives in isolation, as withdrawn as a mouse under the floorboards. "There in its nasty, stinking underground home our insulted, crushed, and ridiculed mouse promptly becomes absorbed in cold, malignant, and above all, everlasting spite." The narrator's extreme narcissism and low self-esteem lead inevitably to hostility and aggression, much of it turned against himself. He is disturbed because his finest feelings, the "good and the beautiful," accompany or coexist with his most degraded impulses and actions. Yet he can take a kind of pleasure in incongruity and in his own degradation, an aesthetic contemplation of the ruined self.

There are a few crucial asides—that he commits loathsome actions in the "disgusting Petersburg night"; that as "though of design I used to get into trouble in cases when I was not to blame in any way." These hints will be developed in the second part. But here the argument gradually shifts. The deepest hostility is to the "stone wall"—the laws of nature, of natural science and mathematics, that allegedly rob man of his freedom of will. And now the narrator's hostility against himself can be turned to good account. For the keystone of the positivist-utilitarian arch (and prison) is that man can act only out of self-interest, seeking his own advantage, according to a calculus of pleasure and pain. But the underground man argues, with Baudelaire and Nietzsche, and fifty-six years before *Beyond the Pleasure Principle,* that men can and do act against their apparent advantage and interest, even court "peril and danger." For

> man everywhere and at all times, whoever he may be, has preferred to act as he chose and not in the least as his reason and advantage dictated. And one may choose what is contrary to one's own interests, and sometimes one *positively ought* (that is my idea). One's own free unfettered choice, one's own caprice, however wild it may be, one's own fancy worked up at times to frenzy—is that very "most advantageous advantage" which we have overlooked. . . .[18]

Dostoevsky no more than Gide with the *gratuitous act* could break the circle of logic, though Gide slightly sophisticated the argument by saying that a *disinterested* act was not necessarily good. For Gide as for Dostoevsky the free act is, really, the irrational act, even an eruption of the unconscious. The more serious difficulty lies in the identification of caprice and "free unfettered choice." Dostoevsky may have shared the underground man's logical fallacy. But he also felt such secular freedom was not enough.

The great compelling point of the first part is that the pleasure principle does not always apply, and may even be seen as degrading. The second part, recording three instances of self-destructive behavior, would seem to prove this theory of freedom in the flesh and along the bone: the continuously humiliating effort to meet an officer on an equal social footing; the reenactment of schooltime humiliations by inviting himself to a private dinner of hostile former schoolmates; the sado-masochistic treatment of the prostitute Liza, and the rejection of her love. In all three episodes the underground man recognizes that he is acting compulsively. But he cannot help himself.

Such would seem to be the structure of *Notes from Underground,* and the relation of its two parts. The novel, however suspect its proof of free will, joins major works of Schopenhauer, Nietzsche and Melville, and crucial statements of Baudelaire, in denigrating a mechanistic psychology and ethics, and in asserting the claims of the irrational. Seldom have ideas been *felt* as intensely. The psychological configurations of Part II are unusually clear, and convey a vivid picture of still-adolescent narcissism (though the hero was then twenty-four) and low self-esteem expressing itself in aggression. The sense that he is unlike anyone else is particularly disturbing. He longs for "a vista of suitable activity," but, especially in periods of remorse following dissipation, takes refuge in dreams. His isolation is extreme. He has little communication with his disapproving servant, and to "plunge into society" means a visit to his superior at the office. In his isolation, and spending most of his time at home reading, he tries "to stifle all that was continually seething within me":

> One longed for movement in spite of everything, and I plunged all at once into dark, underground, loathsome vice of the pettiest kind. My wretched passions were acute, smarting, from my continual, sickly irritability. I had hysterical impulses, with tears and convulsions.
>   And so, furtively, timidly, in solitude, at night, I indulged in filthy vice, with a feeling of shame which never deserted me.[19]

The passage may suggest masturbation, but the paragraph concludes: "I was fearfully afraid of being seen, of being met, of being recognized. I visited various obscure haunts." And later we learn that he had already visited the brothel of the final confession. That the vice is left uncharacterized is psychologically effective, and dramatically too. *Only let the reader think evil,* as James commented of *The Turn of the Screw.*

The ramblings and digressions of the second part are in fact exquisitely controlled. It is highly significant that the sudden confession of "dark, underground, loathsome vice" is immediately followed by the incident of the tavern, where he sees someone thrown out of a window. The unexplained linking in memory is of precisely the kind to catch a psychoanalyst's attention: the first confession of underground vice leads to the first instance of self-destructive, presently compulsive behavior. The hero goes into the billiard room of the tavern. " 'Perhaps,' I thought, 'I'll have a fight too, and they'll throw me out the window.' " But the officer whose way he blocks simply treats him as an inanimate object, moving him aside. His spite against the dehumanizing officer is maintained for several years. His ultimate plan for revenge is to confront him on the Nevsky Prospect (where he himself wriggles along "in a most unseemly fashion, like an eel") and compel him to step aside. Such recognition of his humanity would have been "revenge" and rehabilitation. Unfortunately it is always the underground man who gives way. At last the two collide, the hero having closed his eyes when three paces from the enemy. The officer pretends not to notice. However, "I had kept up my dignity, I had not yielded a step, and had put myself publicly on an equal social footing with him."

The obsessive affair would seem to represent both an effort to establish identity and a chronic need to be humiliated. But there is also the suggestion that the hated and powerful officer is (like Golyadkin Jr.) a potential object of love. Once he composes a "charming" letter to the officer, luckily not sent, imploring him to apologize and hinting at the alternative of a duel. The real hope was for friendship. "How we should have got on together!"

The second self-punitive incident follows some talk of his escape into romantic dreams, where his heroism would be recognized, and a further enigmatic reference to vice. In his loneliness he visits an old schoolmate, Simonov, with whom he "had at one time spent some rather soulful moments," though in fact he had changed jobs to "cut off all connection with my hateful childhood. Curses on that school and all those terrible years of penal servitude!" The narrator knows Simonov dislikes him, realizes the visit is a mistake. He gets more humiliation than he bargained for. At Simonov's is a "very bitter enemy of mine from our days in the lower forms" and another schoolmate; they are discussing a farewell dinner for Zwerkov, an officer possessing all the confidence and masculine power the underground man lacks. He, to the manifest annoyance of the three friends, insists on inviting himself to the dinner.

The dinner is, of course, a catastrophe. The underground man must reenact in full measure the humiliations of his school days, and childishly exasperate his companions, as though to test the point beyond which forgiveness is impossible. These were the "filthiest, most ludicrous, and most awful moments of my life. No one could have gone out of his way to degrade himself more shamelessly, and I fully realized it, fully, and yet I went on pacing up and down from the table to the stove." Between the call on Simonov and the humiliating dinner are crucial recollections of childhood, and of the terrible rejections that must be lived through again.

The final humiliating episode is the most poignant. The underground man follows his companions to the brothel; is with the young prostitute Liza for two hours without saying a word to her; wakes to find her staring at him. There follows a long conversation in which he rends the girl's heart. The humiliated mouse has found someone to humiliate in turn. He tells her that she has given up everything, will be turned out and descend to meaner brothels, will die young. The girl is deeply moved and, to his consternation, comes to the underground man's flat; she is determined to leave the brothel. But his compassion at once vanishes. He says that he had only wanted to humiliate her with his sentimental harangues. "Power, power was what I wanted then, sport was what I wanted, I wanted to wring out your tears, your humiliation, your hysteria. . . ." But suddenly he begins to speak with a terrible honesty of his abjectness. Liza, like Sonia a potential savior, recognizes his unhappiness, holds her hands out to him, throws her arms around him. He is reduced to a blubbering child in a mother's arms. "They won't let me . . . I can't be good!" But soon his need for mastery returns. He embraces her, drawn to her and hating her at the same time, and, in an ultimate humiliation, thrusts money in her hand, driving her away. The underground man is incapable of love.

Notes from Underground, which in so many ways influenced Camus's *The Fall,* ends with the underground man showing a rhetorical strategy comparable to that of Clamence. The "I" suddenly gives way to "we," as though to draw the reader or listener into the circle and distribute guilt: "we are all cripples, every one of us." Does Dostoevsky reach Camus's insight that to claim identification and distribute guilt thus is an act of reprehensible egoism? Camus, uneasy to be honored as a secular saint in early middle-age, without doubt made through Clamence an oblique confession of unworthiness. The confession of Dostoevsky, intensely conscious of his disorders and his love-hate ambivalences, is scarcely oblique. And yet he may also have intended, as Mochulsky claims, no less than a picture of universal fallen Man.

Chernyshevsky, in any event, is left very far behind in this great masterpiece of psychological literature.

At this point it may be useful, before turning to a fuller commentary on several major works, to compare a novel showing extensive conscious understanding of a neurosis (*The Gambler*) with two oddly related scenes, from the early *Ne-*

tochka Nezvanova and the late *The Idiot,* in which Dostoevsky dramatized, powerfully, situations he was far from understanding consciously.

The Gambler (1866), dictated in just under a month, is a small masterpiece even in terms of social realism: a Balzacian picture of pride, cynicism, greed, and of seedy Russians abroad. The vignettes are brilliantly incisive: Polina (drawing upon Dostoevsky's almost contemporary agonies with the volatile Apollinariya Suslova), Mlle Blanche the avaricious French *demi-mondaine,* the stolid insufferable Germans and the frenzied little Poles at the Grandmother's elbows as she plays, above all the imperious and wildly impertinent Grandmother herself, who suddenly appears among her expectant heirs and loses much of the fortune they are counting on. But *The Gambler* is also, or first of all, an exceptionally fine and controlled model of the psychological *récit* in which a self-analytic narrator both relives neurotic torment and throws, however grudgingly, a fairly clear light on it—the insight, most obviously, that the true gambler's compulsion is not to win but to lose, for whatever peace loss will bring. The Grandmother, lucky at her first try, returns to the tables with a real hope of winning, but the narrator Aleksei's need is to exhaust himself, lose everything, *spend*. Gambling, Dostoevsky wrote to Strakhov in 1863, involves the whole personality. ''But the chief thing about it is that all his vital juices, forces, impetuosity, daring have gone into *roulette.*'' [20] The novel was saved from a debilitating explicitness—the chill that sometimes comes from such full conscious understanding—by the fact that the compulsions remained unimpaired for Dostoevsky himself, who rushed back to the gambling tables shortly after finishing his book. He continued, like Malcolm Lowry, to live the neurosis he had so brilliantly clarified. The novel is saved too by technique; by the fact that Dostoevsky does not allow his narrator a continuous coherent understanding. The author's awareness is, that is, carefully separated at times from Aleksei's. But even the narrator knows he cannot be at peace until the sensations of risk have been exhausted, all his money is gone, and humiliation is again inevitable.

Dostoevsky clearly sees (and momentarily Aleksei too) that gambling is in conflict with his love for Polina and thrusts it into the background. Aleksei does not say in so many words that gambling is a form of eroticism, but his imagery (presumably discovered by Dostoevsky's *unconscious* understanding) reflects the Freudian connection between gambling and masturbation, in the essay ''Dostoevsky and Parricide.'' He is fascinated by the piles of gold ''that glow like embers'' and by the ''huge rolls of silver, over two feet long that lie around the wheel.'' The loved one is simply excluded in moments of gambling frenzy. The movement of the hands is compulsive, both during roulette and after.

> There were moments when I completely forgot about Polina. At one moment I was sorting my bundles, folding them up together, at the next I was arranging all the gold in a single pile; then I left it all and began to pace up and down the room with rapid steps, suddenly lost in thought; then, a moment later, I was back at the table, counting the money again. Suddenly, as though coming to, I rushed to the door and hurriedly locked it, turning the key twice.[21]

The gambler's ultimate experience, exhausted by the satisfaction of loss, is one of narcissistic solitude.

The two scenes showing considerably less conscious understanding, and with remarkable structural resemblances, come from what would have been Dostoevsky's first full-length novel, interrupted by his arrest in 1849 and never finished, and from one of the masterpieces of world literature. The scene in *The Idiot* (to which we will return) is of course the one in which Rogozhin leads Myshkin to the bed where Natasha lies so strangely still, her deathbed in fact. Myshkin, identifying with the criminal, seems to accept the crime at once, and Rogozhin, as to seal some kind of bond, insists they sleep side by side at her feet. The woman both men have loved is now out of the way. A lasting union cannot be tolerated, it may be, even on an unconscious level, and the two are separated—Rogozhin to Siberia, Myshkin into madness. It seems evident that Dostoevsky was capable of understanding (as Simon Lesser argues), if only at an unconscious level, the homosexuality latent in his narrative.[22] We must immediately add that the scene can simultaneously entertain other meanings, even a religious one. The great harrowing predicaments, in literature as in life, cannot be pinned down by a formula or phrase.

Netochka Nezvanova is the first-person narration of three traumatic episodes in the life of a sensitive girl, four years old at the time of her earliest memories and seventeen when the novel abruptly breaks off. The second narrative is an unhurried restrained evocation of passionate attachment between two preadolescent girls, with much touching and kissing, an attachment which even in their own eyes comes to seem illicit. The third (with Netochka, now seventeen, caught up in the obscure tensions of a household, and between a husband's cruelty and a wife's anxiety) has the measured calm of a Gidian *récit* such as *Isabelle;* the subject might have attracted Henry James. But the earlier narrative (chapters II-IV) of the child Netochka and her stepfather Yefimov is another matter, and draws on deep dynamic energies and powerful displacements. Yefimov's is a story of deterioration, like *Poor Folk* and *The Double,* but this time the underground man is an artist—a violinist who has either squandered his talent or never had any. Living in extreme poverty, he openly wishes for the death of his wife, since he regards her as a barrier to rehabilitation and success. Such at least is his conscious reason for wanting her out of the way. The child Netochka is devoted to Yefimov, *whom she long believes to be her real father,* in time with intense erotic feelings:

> And thus I was growing up in our garret room, and gradually my love—no, I might better say my passion, though I do not know a word strong enough fully to convey the unbridled, tormenting feelings I had for my stepfather—reached a kind of morbid perversity. . . . I was practically delirious with joy whenever he happened to caress me even casually.[23]

Yefimov has presumably created the "morbid perversity," if only by inducing her to steal from the mother money he will use for drink. In the culminating episode he returns from a great violinist's concert (one that convinces him of his own nullity) and, as the terrified child secretly listens and watches, plays his own violin wildly, after entirely covering the sleeping mother with a blanket and other things. The mother's body, the child observes, remains oddly still; she is appalled, like Myshkin gazing at the unmoving Natasha under the sheet. The stepfather says they must leave, now that "it is all over," and the child agrees that it is time for them to go. But first he leads her to the bed and shows her the mother's body, already cold and blue. His disclaimer of guilt is an incoherent aside. He is "apprehended in a fit of raving lunacy" and dies two days later.

At a superficial level the story can be attached to the romantic tradition of the mad musician and disordered genius, who has been presented with a diabolic gift. But the story's real intensities are of a different order. There are major displacements at work, beginning with the substitution of stepfather for father, or for some unrelated adult male. (In an early plan for *A Raw Youth,* Versilov seduces and makes pregnant his stepdaughter Lisa.) We have, in effect, a strong erotic relationship of a grown man and a young child, but with the erotic feelings flowing in both directions, and seen (this unusual for Dostoevsky) from the child's point of view. The relationship is so intense that the intervening mother must die. The strongest substitution, which occurs before the murder, is that of violin-playing, or the exhibition of the violin, for sexual play. (In *The Idiot,* following revelation of the murder, Myshkin wants to hold the cards with which Rogozhin and Natasha used to play; the movement of hands is again important.)

The crucial passage hardly requires commentary. In it we see unconscious energies at work, liberating "thoughts" few writers would acknowledge:

Soon Mother went out, and then he could not restrain himself. He began kissing me till I was in a state of almost hysterical ecstasy, laughing and crying at the same time. Finally he said that because I was such a good, clever little girl he was going to show me something very beautiful, something I would be delighted to see. Whereupon he unbuttoned his waistcoat and took out a key that hung from his neck on a black cord. Looking mysteriously into my eyes as if wanting to see in them all the pleasure which, in his opinion, I ought to feel, he opened the trunk and carefully took from it a curiously shaped black case which till that moment I never knew he had. He lifted the case with a kind of veneration, and seemed to be completely transformed; there was no longer a trace of mockery in his face, which all at once had assumed a rather solemn expression. He opened the mysterious case with the key and took from it an object I had never seen before. Carefully and reverently holding it in his hands, he told me that it was a violin—his instrument. . . . At last he kissed the violin and gave it to me to kiss. Seeing that I wanted to examine it more closely, he led me to Mother's bed and placed the violin in my hands, but I noticed that he was trembling all over for fear that I might break it. I held the violin in my hands and touched the strings, which gave out a faint sound.[24]

The "father" promises Netochka he will show her his violin every time she is a good, clever, obedient girl.

There could hardly be a clearer case of sexuality, *fully recognized in the unconscious,* transformed into a series of obvious symbolic objects and acts. The two murder scenes, major instances of "illuminating distortion," structurally similar even to the strange complicity of Myshkin and Netochka, would appear to satisfy, through unconscious creation and understanding, the author's two strongest psycho-sexual drives—the homosexual and the paedophilic.

Crime and Punishment (1866) is Dostoevsky's masterpiece of sustained and coherent dramatic narrative, and a uniquely authentic picture of personality in deep conflict—struggling toward the commission of a crime, then struggling toward confession and, less consciously, toward repentance. Psychological issues are interwoven with the ideological and the moral, with a religious solution in the offing as the alternative to suicide and despair. *Crime and Punishment,* like *Lord Jim* and *The Mayor of Casterbridge,* is one of those great narratives in which the unawakened man enters the moral universe through his crime, as an early Notebook entry observes: "N.B. His moral development begins from the crime itself; the possibility of such questions arises which would not have existed previously." [25] The novel is no more than Conrad's and Hardy's an exercise in abnormal psychology, though the severity of Raskolnikov's anxieties and repressions results in much compulsive behavior and even periods of amnesia. It is a supreme novelistic record of stress, and of the struggle to subdue as well as appease guilt.

The straightforward narrative coherence is the more remarkable because it emerged from so much confusion, both in the conscious planning stages outlined in the Notebooks and in the half-conscious or unconscious dreamings only dimly shadowed there, and recently given plausible psychoanalytic interpretation by Edward Wasiolek.[26] Much of the coherence (as compared with the disorder of *The Possessed* and *The Idiot*) may be due to the novel's concentration on one man, with every major event and major character importantly related to him.

A potential source of confusion lay in Dostoevsky's very close identification with his protagonist. He had experienced the European ideological nightmare that preoccupied great ambivalent writers from Balzac and Stendhal to Nietzsche and Gide—the attraction and menace of the individualist determined to realize himself through *free* action: action that has freed itself from conventional moral law and even from everyday motives of self-interest. Yet he could also sympathize with the idea of the *homme supérieur* escaping the rut, and bringing progress through a "new word." There is also much conceptual confusion concerning the motives for the particular crime: the motives and theories repeatedly reassessed in the Notebooks, and in the novel as well. One of Raskolnikov's motives is humanitarian: to provide, by killing the moneylender, money needed by his mother and sister, and that he himself would need for the pursuit of a socially useful career. The extraordinary man exempted from the quotidian moral law will eventually do more good than harm, according to any reasonable calculus of pleasure and pain. The competing and presumably more genuine motive, which connects Raskolnikov with Julien Sorel and Stavrogin alike, rather than Napoleon, is to test the limits of his individualist strength and assert an absolute freedom of self-will. Mochulsky and others find the motives contradictory, as indeed they are. But many "normal" lives are full of such contradictions. There are contradictions even within the lives of Raskolnikov's hypothetical extraordinary men. The *libido dominandi* may be exerted not only in magnifying self but in seeking "the destruction of the present for the sake of the better." It may also, here closer to Nietzsche, involve solitary conquest of a "natural" self. Raskolnikov recognizes with disgust that he is not strong enough to live with his crime. This is precisely the question raised with Gide's Lafcadio, and even suggested with Julien Sorel. All in all, *Crime and Punishment* may be the better for these conceptual hesitancies. For uncertainty is at the core of Raskolnikov's agony.

The novel had to survive a much more serious conflict than this one, and still on a largely conscious level, for the author as for his character: was Raskolnikov's tormented response to the achieved crime one of guilt over the transgression of taking a life, or merely remorse, regret that he had committed a "blunder"? Was cowardice rather than inner moral strength and a genuine need for punishment behind his compulsion to confess? Was confession morally insignificant, since what was needed was the capacity to repent that comes to Raskolnikov, like a gift of grace, in the Siberian epilogue? For the modern secular reader the answers should be clear. Whatever his conceptual hesitations, Dostoevsky's dynamic understanding presents not mere regret for a mistake, and not only a sense of estrangement from the human family, but a sense of guilt revealing itself in altogether characteristic risk-taking that will lead to necessary, craved punishment. And this meaning is clear even in Dostoevsky's famous letter to M. N. Katkov, the first outline of the plot for other eyes than his own. The uncertainty of the motives is there, but also the underlying psychic and moral orientation. Here, as in the novel repeatedly, we see foreshadowings of Conrad's *Under Western Eyes:*

> There are no suspicions of him nor can there be. Then the psychological process of the crime unfolds. Unresolved questions arise before the murderer, unsuspected and unexpected feelings torment his heart. The truth of God and the law of nature take their own, and he finally feels forced to give himself up . . . in order to be once again part of humankind, even if it means perishing in prison.[27]

"In both novel and notes," as Wasiolek summarizes matters, "Raskolnikov does not understand why he must confess, for he insists in both versions on his right to kill a useless louse." [28] *But Dostoevsky knew, both dynamically in the imagination and at times consciously, why.* The punishment is that demanded by repressed guilt. This is evident not only in Raskolnikov's dangerously irrational behavior and speech, but in the periods of fitful apathy, inertia and depression. Dostoevsky makes clear in several places, as he does in *The Eternal Husband,* the relationship of depression to repressed conflict and impulse. In the opening of Part VI, which follows upon Raskolnikov's discovery that Svidrigaïlov had overheard his confession to Sonia, "it was as though a fog had fallen upon him and wrapped him in a dreary solitude." There were long periods of complete apathy. "He seemed to be trying in that latter stage to escape from a full and clear understanding of his position." The false confession of Nikolay, by offering impunity and so making his own confession more remote, also results in lethargy.

The feelings of guilt, remorse, regret come and go, and the guilt is much of the time repressed. But the movement toward confession is a steady one; the deepest drives are risk-taking and self-destructive; the price must be paid. Mochulsky's long discussion evokes movingly the novel's atmosphere, but wholly misreads the central psychic conflict. Misled by the Epilogue (and perhaps also by a Christian feeling of his own that non-religious self-punishment "doesn't count"), Mochulsky sees a new strong personality emerge after the period of illness. "The new *strong individual* is endowed with 'animal-like cunning,' unheard-of boldness, a will to live, and diabolical pride." [29] Mochulsky sees the wildy reckless talk with Zametov in the tavern as a sign of insolent strength; so too the return to the old woman's apartment and his giving the porter his name and address. But these are obviously the acts of a man perhaps anxiously testing the limits of his danger but, above all, needing to relive his crime and needing to be caught and punished. In Mochulsky's version the moral and psychological force of the confession is virtually lost. Raskolnikov's surrender to the authorities "is not a sign of penitence but of pusillanimity: for him punishment is an 'unnecessary shame' and 'senseless suffering.' " [30] In Mochulsky's reading, presumably, the *punishment* of the novel's title is external: eight years of penal servitude.

Mochulsky's error doubtless stems from his inability to grasp what Dostoevsky so brilliantly intuited in this and other novels: that both guilt and the effort to subdue it may operate beneath full consciousness, and often in contradiction to surface argument. But it also doubtless stems from Dostoevsky's notorious Epilogue, as well as from Raskolnikov's expressions of angry pride in the hours preceding his surrender. For the Epilogue (of which there is no mention in the Notebook plans) is meant to show that moral self-condemnation and the acceptance of legal punishment are not enough. The heart must be changed by God's grace, which suddenly flings him at Sonia's feet in tears. Thus and appallingly, after the great last page of the novel proper, we are given the picture of a Raskolnikov still unregenerate, and who finds "no particular terrible fault in his past, except a simple *blunder* that might happen to anyone." For religious conversion and Christian repentance to come after, even long after, a secular moral crisis and public confession of guilt is altogether possible. The weakness of the Epilogue (apart from the suddenness and brevity with which the conversion is reported) lies rather in its devaluation of that earlier moral crisis. The most Dostoevsky will now concede is that Raskolnikov had perhaps been, at the brink of confession, "dimly conscious of the fundamental falsity in himself and his convictions."

Never did a novel's coda and explicit moral more violently contradict its essential meaning. The Epilogue does indeed belong to "another story," and should not control our interpretation of the novel proper.

At a wavering line between conscious and unconscious understanding we see, as often in Dostoevsky and very obviously in *The Double,* actual persons and outward happenings interiorized and thus become *psychic events*. I mean by this something stranger than conceptual splitting of characters, or the projection of traits and impulses, as in Dostoevsky's final Notebook entry: "Svidrigaylov is despair, the most cynical./Sonia is hope, the most unrealizable." There is, for instance, the stranger who says "Murderer" and who appears just after Raskolnikov has felt in the hole under the wallpaper where the stolen articles had been. The stranger might have "sprung out of the earth." Later, in the course of Porfiry's interrogation, Raskolnikov tries to reassure himself that the man "had no real existence," and so could not give evidence. He returns to his apartment, and is there confronted by the mysterious stranger, more than ever hallucinatory in appearance. He turns out to be a real person, who had been in the next room during Nikolay's confession, and had overheard it. He has come to ask forgiveness for his evil thoughts. In a lesser novelist all this might seem disappointingly contrived. But in Dostoevsky's world overhearing can itself be a psychic event, as we see with Svidrigaïlov too. He is listening in the next room, as Raskolnikov confesses to Sonia. His coming may seem as occult as that of Protos in *Lafcadio's Adventures,* and like Protos he takes a diabolic intellectual interest in the murderer. He even brings a chair, so that in the future he can listen in comfort. He has begun to occupy a place, as Hawthorne put it, in "the interior of a heart." An intimacy is very quickly established, and a "hidden power" that Raskolnikov recognizes. He will listen, strangely unprotesting, to Svidrigaïlov's account of his attempt to seduce his sister. With Razumihin, at a critical moment, there can be wordless communication of the dark truth.

Various critics have seen Svidrigaïlov as the despairing cynic and nihilist Raskolnikov might have become, truly beyond good and evil; his death, coming so close to the confession, would appear to free Raskolnikov from these potentialities. But there are other potentialities. Wasiolek, in his 1974 article, "Raskolnikov's Motives: Love and Murder," remarks that "erotic motives loom large" among the symbolic equivalents of the two men. He comments on Raskolnikov's suppressed erotic relationship with his sister and sees Svidrigaïlov's "sexual aggressiveness as in some way an externalization of what is hidden in Raskolnikov's unconscious." [31] One of the potentialities (if I am correct in seeing a close connection in Dostoevsky's imagination between crippled or retarded girl and girl child) is a perverse paedophilia. Svidrigaïlov had allegedly outraged a deaf and dumb girl of fourteen or fifteen, possibly with the connivance of his present landlady. Raskolnikov had been engaged to his landlady's mentally backward daughter, ugly and an invalid: "If she had been lame or hunchback, I believe I should have liked her better still." He himself raises with Porfiry the question of a man of forty violating a child of ten. Is it to be attributed to environment? We may refer again to Raskolnikov's enigmatic reactions to the young drunken girl on K— Boulevard, "quite a child," a moment of possibly illuninating distortion. He addresses the fat sensualist hovering nearby as "Svidrigaïlov." His initial impulse to protect the girl is followed by the cynical suggestion that the dandy be allowed to have his way. After the murder he experiences a "loathsome feeling" as he passes the bench where the girl had been. The Svidrigaïlov "component" here first shunned, then shamefully indulged, could combine paedophilic and incestuous wishes. In Dostoevsky's imagination the link of sister and the young drunk girl was clear, as a notebook entry indicates: "He sells his sister to a dandy from K— Boulevard." [32]

The area of central conflict and largely unconscious understanding in *Crime and Punishment* has been fascinatingly explored in Wasiolek's article. Building on W. D. Snodgrass's 1960 perception that the landlady and the pawnbroker are displaced representations of Raskolnikov's mother (so that in striking at the pawnbroker he could strike symbolically at her),[33] Wasiolek offers a rich and coherent psychoanalytic interpretation of Raskolnikov's motives. His real enemy is not society but his loved ones, the mother and the sister, ultimately himself. The competing humanitarian and superman motives for the murder are rationalizations. The hostility to the sister and especially to the mother goes much deeper than is accounted for by their attempts to encroach on his freedom and impose a "dutiful son" identity. He must "protect himself against a conscious admission of erotic affection for his sister." [34] For the mother, a more radical threat, there was "the original love, which he had to bear and struggle against without the aid of the interdicting father. The deep grudge would be then against the repugnant and hateful thing that he had fantasized, and which he had to suffer alone." [35] It is "the meaning of the hateful mother within him"—the mother of sensual love—he must kill.

Sonia, embodying "clean-dirtiness" in Raskolnikov's eyes, now has a much more interesting role than in the classic interpretation. Raskolnikov

> must come to love and forgive the hateful and repugnant mother within him, and consequently that part of himself; and he does this by way of Sonia, who is not only the religious redemptrice, but also the psychological redemptrice. . . . By loving Sonia, the prostitute, he accepts the dirtiness of love, because it is not actually dirt, no more than it was with his mother, though the phantasies of childhood made it so. Sonia is the living embodiment of "clean" dirtiness, of corruption that is redemptive.[36]

A brief summary cannot do justice to Wasiolek's carefully reasoned article: its striking analysis, for instance, of the dream of beating the mare, which is now seen to embody the novel's central meaning. In it Raskolnikov is "killing his mother, the pawnbroker, and the landlady, and in turn being tormented and killed by them. Most of all, it shows us a Raskolnikov who is killing himself, who is tormenter and tormented, victimizer and victimized, killer and being killed." [37] It might be argued that Wasiolek's schema (which sees the pawnbroker's sister as a distant disguise for Dunia, with sexuality now out in the open) fails to account for the fact that the death of Lizaveta has scarcely any reality for Raskolnikov. It is as though only the moneylender, in his inner world, has been murdered. The classic explanation would be, of course, that only the pawnbroker's murder was "intended" or "wished." A psychoanalytic rendering might argue that the mother-component was so strong and hateful, at the critical moment, that the sister-component scarcely seemed to exist. The sister-component might also, on the other hand, be attached firmly to Sonia's redemptive role, and attached (by the same token) to Dostoevsky's fond dream of sexless intimacy with a young girl. For Raskolnikov had seen Sonia, on their second meeting, as "almost a child," and the relationship with the Little Mother in Siberia is sexless.

This is but one of a number of places where conscious and unconscious meanings, sometimes logically contradictory, can coexist fictionally, and where nothing is gained by trying to cancel out. Raskolnikov's conscious sufferings and anxieties and debates, his frenzies and his apathies, the suspenseful record of a mind on the rack, will no doubt remain the heart of the fictional drama, however his motives be explained. But the novel possesses strangenesses and energies that could not have existed without the author's dynamic, often unconscious, understanding of deeper, repressed conflicts.

The Eternal Husband (1869) also shows a remarkable combination of conscious and unconscious understanding, but with the forbidden materials closer to the surface. In such a work of genius, René Girard writes, "il n'y a plus d'écart entre les intentions subjectives et la signification objective." [38] This seems to me true for certain pages that indicate, more concisely and more explicitly than usual, Dostoevsky's conscious awareness of the "unconscious" and its devious ways: of repression, and the anxieties that accompany the escape of painful memories from repression, and of the degree to which painful "accidents" may be purposefully self-punitive and ultimately satisfying. This is particularly true of the chapter "Analysis" (XVI), which might have appeared, with some rephrasing, in Menninger's *Man Against Himself*. But there are large areas of uncertainty, and Girard's sense of the "signification objective" (which minimizes a latent homosexual component) is very different from mine. [39] There is even, in this complex double story and story of identity crisis, a continuing and not displeasing uncertainty as to who is double for whom. Which of the two men enacts the other's disowned wishes? Which is the persecuting judge? Very early in the story, reflecting on Pavel Pavlovich's reappearances, Velchaninov says: "It's I, I, who am pestering him, not he me."

The Eternal Husband, as Dostoevsky looked back on it, seemed "disgusting and vile." He had himself played something of the eternal husband role in his unhappy first marriage, showing extraordinary indulgence and affection both for Maria Dmitrevna's first husband and for a present rival. There were flarings of intense hostility too, suggesting what Freud calls normal jealousy experienced bisexually: "that is to say, in a man, besides the suffering in regard to the loved woman and the hatred against the male rival, grief in regard to the unconsciously loved man and hatred of the woman as a rival. . . ." [40] *The Eternal Husband* thus meant a distant reliving of early moments in a painful, ruined marriage and, in addition, an oblique revelation of repressed homosexuality. The bisexual disposition, Freud wrote,

> must certainly be assumed in Dostoevsky, and it shows itself in a viable form (as latent homosexuality) in the important part played by male friendships in his life, in his strangely tender attitude toward rivals in love and in his remarkable understanding of situations which are explicable only by repressed homosexuality, as many examples from his novels show. [41]

The original idea for the novel involved other menacing material: the belated escape from repression of a forgotten crime: the drunken violation of a ten-year-old girl.

The eternal husband triangle is a classic instance of "forbidden game" in which the cuckolded husband is, more than once, an accomplice in his own betrayal. There may be an unnatural, even total blindness to what is going on. Charles Bovary of the bandaged eyes, capable of relishing Rodolphe's cigar, stares with equal innocence at Léon and Rodolphe, and is not even aware that his house is being sold from under him. Dowell in *The Good Soldier,* blindest of accomplices, admires the courage and virility of Edward Ashburnham, his wife's lover and subsequent lover of Nancy Rufford, and comically stumbles on imagery that reveals the real situation: "He seems to me like a larger elder brother who took me out on several excursions and did many dashing things whilst I just watched him robbing the orchards, from a distance." Geoffrey Firmin in *Under the Volcano* has thrown his wife Yvonne together with his brother Hugh and with Laruelle in the past. In the novel's present he slips a long-delayed postcard from Yvonne under Laruelle's pillow: a moment of Dostoevskyan spite and intense sexual jealousy, perhaps, but also a drunken recognition that the shared Yvonne had provided the ground for the renewal of friendship and connection between the two men. In Dostoevsky's novel Pavel Pavlovich performs the cuckold's crazy dance with Velchaninov, with Bagautov, with Velchaninov again, with Golubchikov at the very end. Such a husband "can no more escape wearing horns than the sun can keep from shining; he is not only unaware of the fact, but is bound by the very laws of his nature to be unaware of it." Pavel, it turns out, is not wholly unaware. The cuckold admires his manly betrayer, enjoys being in his company, may identify strongly with him. "What high opinion he had of my powers of seduction!" Velchaninov reflects. "Perhaps it was just my powers of seduction that made the most impression on him."

At the outset we see Velchaninov, a man of thirty-eight or thirty-nine, troubled by vague anxieties and depression, with the convictions of a lifetime likely to be "transformed under the melancholy influences of night and insomnia": suffering from the *crise de quarante*. The surprising changes in thoughts and convictions, the hypochondria and restlessness, the new taste for solitude, the disturbing emergence of repressed memories from a shameful and ridiculous past—these are familiar components of the crisis of early middle age. Such is Velchaninov's state when he begins to encounter, with an uncanny sense of familiarity (and with a "peculiar, undefined animosity") a man with mourning crepe on his hat. Pavel Pavlovich appears and reappears as mysteriously as any Dostoevskyan double, "as though he had sprung out of the ground." The confrontation that occurs at last follows a disturbing dream, with accusations of a concealed crime, at three o'clock in the morning; significantly, like the captain of *The Secret Sharer* who had negligently left the rope-ladder overside, Velchaninov had closed but not locked his door. The sense of dynamic projection is so strong that an uncanny atmosphere remains, even after the intruder is recognized and begins to speak. He is the husband of the Natalya Vassilyevna with whom Velchaninov had had an affair nine years before, and who has recently died. Does the husband know they were lovers? Has he come to avenge the past, or out of some underground self-tormenting impulse? Pavel Pavlovich, no hallucination, is living with an eight-year-old girl, Liza, whom Velchaninov quickly suspects must be not Pavel's daughter but his own. Pavel speaks of his late wife as the "priceless bond of friendship" between them, and very soon seems bent on reenacting his cuckold's role. He insists on taking Velchaninov to see the fifteen-year-old Nadya, whom he hopes to marry. The young girl is disgusted by Pavel, at once attracted by the more assured Velchaninov.

Pavel Pavlovich would thus seem to be an authentic though fleshly double and emissary from a disgraceful past. He must be disowned: a disreputable drunk who has rapidly gone to seed in the last months, who neglects Liza and exposes her to the shameful presence of a prostitute, who hints slyly of the "sacred" bond between them, who is a paedophile, who presently makes homosexual advances. All these potentialities of self must be repressed, evaded or confronted; and repudiated in the end. The crisis is forced by Pavel, whose spite and even hatred for Velchaninov is accompanied by an intense attraction. He insists they drink together, seizes and kisses Velchaninov's hand, demands that Velchaninov kiss him. The response is puzzling: "For some minutes Velchaninov was silent, as though hit by a cudgel on the head. But suddenly he bent down to Pavel Pavlovich, who was shorter by a head than he, and kissed him on the lips, which smelled strongly of liquor. *He was not perfectly certain that he had kissed him, though!*"

The sentence I have italicized suggests a crucial area of anxiety, which becomes more conscious after the two have visited Nadya. "Velchaninov was suddenly panic-stricken; he was not at all anxious that anything should happen, or that a certain line should be overstepped, especially as he had provoked it." Shortly thereafter, much against Velchaninov's will, Pavel spends a night in his rooms. Has Pavel come to embrace him or to murder him? During the night Pavel comes to his bed, holding a razor; Velchaninov, clutching it to protect himself, is wounded in the hand. Thereafter the two men struggle for several minutes in the dark.

Psychologically, the incident is critical for both men. With Pavel's departure in the morning, Velchaninov's awful depression vanishes; he feels an "immense, extraordinary joy." For the first time in weeks he has scarcely thought of Liza, who had recently died, "as though that blood from his cut fingers could 'settle his account' even with that misery." He is even "convinced that the illness had been over completely at the moment when, after falling asleep so exhausted, he had, an hour and a half later, sprung out of bed and thrown his assailant on the floor with such strength." But Pavel Pavlovich too, he suspects, had craved punishment. "Yes! That 'eternal husband' had to, was obliged at last to punish himself for everything, once and for all, and to punish himself he snatched up the razor—by accident, it is true, still he did snatch it up!" The uncertainty of identities could hardly be more pronounced. A crucial confrontation with homosexual impulse would appear closely allied with a need to pay for nagging and diffuse guilts. (The murderous embrace, followed by the need to tie Pavel's hands behind his back, suggests that *homosexual* is more appropriate than *homoerotic,* with physical connection desired and feared. The Victorian author of *My Secret Life,* whose homosexual urge was long repressed, took pleasure not only in sharing a woman but in entering her immediately after the man engaged for that purpose.)

What are we to conclude then, of the several moments of illuminating distortion—Velchaninov's uncertainty as to whether he has kissed Pavel on the lips, or the fact that both men derive some psychic satisfaction from the incident of the razor, or the prolonged wrestling in the dark room which seems responsible for the dispelling of Velchaninov's depression; or, more generally, that each at times functions as a double for the other, though Velchaninov's consciousness is the central one, with Pavel more frequently satisfying the other's psychic needs? It is Pavel who occupies the stronger latent homosexual role and who initiates the intimacies. He is the more guilty of the two. It is Pavel Pavlovich not Velchaninov who wants to marry the fifteen-year-old Nadya, though Velchaninov is attracted to her. And there is one more innocent tragically violated. Velchaninov, observing the child Liza is unhappy and neglected, takes her to live with the Pogoreltzev family. But she, shame-ridden and despairing, wants to stay with Pavel. She soon falls ill and dies. Dostoevsky, to summarize, in *The Eternal Husband* confronted several familiar demons. He faced, powerfully and fairly consciously, threatening homosexual tendencies, and also, more obliquely, dramatized both the old erotic attraction for an adolescent girl and the old traumatic fantasy of an abused, in some sense violated, younger child. The three demons or areas of guilt are largely displaced, after much struggle and uncertainty, from Velchaninov onto Pavel Pavlovich. But to make the transference complete would have been morally unacceptable.

It is evident that *The Eternal Husband,* for all its moments of Molièresque comedy, touches on the darkest preoccupations of the great long novels. Is this the reason Dostoevsky himself thought of the story as "vile"? [42]

To limit discussion of *The Brothers Karamazov* in any way is distressing: to have to omit its energized suspenseful narrative and grand structure; its cross-section of Russian life, with everyone drawn into the family drama; its vision of human community and traditional bonds, and of dialogue as the essential human act; its unequivocal presentation, at last, of the author's religious convictions, with values for once realized in positive action rather than through their betrayal and violation. It is, certainly, one of the greatest of novels of inter-personal relations. I intend to return, on some other occasion, to these grand concerns. In terms of our present subject, *The Brothers Karamazov* offers an exceptional opportunity to distinguish between kinds of psychological understanding, between the classical and the modern or dynamic, and within the dynamic between the fully conscious and the gropingly intuitive or even unconscious.

1. *The Brothers Karamazov* is the richest of Dostoevsky's novels in classical, common-sense observation of life and rational *connaissance du cœur humain:* the great humane "psychology" of Molière or Fielding or Stendhal (who also had, to be sure, occasional Freudian insights). The novel is incomparably rich in a wisdom based on experience, and it is also rich in characters who reason articulately on human behavior: Father Zossima, Ivan and his devil and the Grand Inquisitor, both the prosecutor Ippolit and the defender Fetyukovitch in spite of their mistaken assumptions. Dialogue, and particularly dialogue involving Ivan, is more coherent and more penetrating than in most of Dostoevsky's fiction. Many of the novel's central interests, moreover, are those of classical human comedy: pride and jealousy (whether felt by monks or humiliated women or the poor); old Fyodor's "normal" sensuality and greed, and the Karamazov lust for life generally; love-hate ambivalence (of which the seventeenth-century dramatists knew a great deal); the progress toward sainthood of Father Zossima and the hesitations and grief and loyalty of Alyosha. We may see by comparing the central "quartets" of *The Idiot* and *The Brothers Karamazov* (Myshkin-Rogozhin-Nastasya-Aglaia/Ivan-Dmitri-Katerina-Grushenka) how much more rational or classical the later novel's configuration is. No psycho-sexual or other hidden attraction exists behind the mutual jealousy and hatred of Katerina and Grushenka. Katerina may suffice, where the point I am making—the presence of a classical psychology—is so obvious. Her great inexpungeable trauma was having put herself up, in a sense, for sale. She had "come to" Dmitri for the 4500 rubles needed for her father, and had been allowed to go off scot-free, a further humiliation. Her innocence, chastity, etc. have to be taken on faith; we scarcely ever see her in a moment of calm. But her love-hate ambivalence are normal enough in a Dostoevskyan world, as in a Stendhalian for that matter; she might be descended from Mathilde de la Mole, and might also have cut her hair out of self-lacerating pride. The two women are competing for the prisoner, as the two in *The Red and the Black,* and Katerina humiliates herself twice at the trial: once to save Mitya and once, when she sees Ivan dragged off screaming, to destroy him. She is driven by pride and the need to dominate, such pride as leaves in some doubt whom she loves-hates the most. She might, with a slight chastening of the nerves, have been conceived by Shakespeare.

2. Conscious use of contemporary psychology or of intimate personal experience. Dostoevsky's accounts of epileptic seizure are persuasive, authoritative, even to the insight (no doubt less than conscious) in *The Idiot* that an attack

may obviate or replace an unacceptable sexual impulse. But Ivan's "brain fever," like much brain fever in the novels, would seem to have dramatic or symbolic rather than scientific interest. Even the hallucinated doubles seem closer to a medical reality ("autoscopic hallucination") than those periods of brain fever and their vague etiology.

3. No novel is richer in coherent and conscious pre-Freudian understanding of basic human conflicts, drives, strategies: most obviously the Oedipus complex and the recognition that the wish is psychologically equivalent to the act, and must be punished accordingly. At the gray margin between classical and modern psychology stands the picture of Dmitri's restlessness and irrational flarings and self-destructive impulses, and his aristocratic "thirst for suffering," all dimly reminiscent of Stavrogin. He himself offers the novel's best explanation of his hysteria and incoherence in the past: unconscious or half-conscious conflict, and the effort to suppress the awakening "new man": " 'It was perhaps just because ideas I did not understand were surging up in me, that I used to drink and fight and rage.' " It ought to be possible, at this late date, to dispose of the Oedipus complex in *The Brothers Karamazov* (or at least the fact of its coherent presence there) in a footnote or subordinate clause: a casual reference to Dmitri's wishes, and to the importance of Grushenka in the pattern of parricide. But Mochulsky's influential and often admirable book sees the drama in different, simplistic terms: "The calculations regarding money are only a pretext, the rivalry for Grushenka is only the exterior reason for their struggle: two sensualists have clashed; the 'earthly Karamazov force' has risen up against its own self." [43] In response we can only point to a few central impulses and incidents: that Dmitri claims his father wants to put him in prison out of jealousy over Grushenka, and believes sexual relationship with the father would make his own marriage with her impossible. "And if she goes to the old man, can I marry her after that?" Simple defilement or incest taboo? So Arkady in *A Raw Youth:* "How could I think of marrying her if I thought he loved her? After all, we *are* father and son, and it would be too disgusting for words." The essential for Dmitri is to be *on the watch,* and prevent the cherished one from going to the father's room. Dmitri's child's dream, "watching and spying in agony," is to "seize her and bear her away at once to the ends of the earth." He has found a room *from which he can watch,* and he openly threatens murder (talking to Alyosha) in the event he can't prevent their meeting. Significantly it would be by using Grushenka's signal code that he could gain murderous access to the father's room, where an essential part of old Fyodor's sexuality, the money in its envelope, lies hidden, he thinks, in the bed.

The strongest evidence for an authentic Oedipal triangle lies in the fact that Dmitri is not jealous of the two men with whom Grushenka has slept in the past: her protector Kuzma Samsonov ("which is psychologically interesting," the prosecutor Ippolit remarks) or the Polish lover to whom she seems about to return. Even on the way to Mokroe, in the turmoil of contemplated suicide, Dmitri can imagine "effacing" himself. Anything, he has earlier implied to Alyosha, would be tolerable except his father's sexuality. "I'll be her husband if she deigns to have me, and when lovers come, I'll go into the next room. I'll clean her friends' galoshes, blow up their samovars, run their errands." Richard Peace asks rhetorically of this passage, "Is this a jealous man?" [44] We must respond, "Beyond doubt, yes"—though Dostoevsky may have been unaware of this and of his two sexual metaphors. An accompaniment of the Oedipal trauma can be the jealous, self-lacerating need to see reenacted—not acted—the mother's violation, even to the point of imagining her a prostitute, and survive the renewed anguish. More pertinently Peace remarks that Fyodor is "the one rival who could turn Grushenka into a second mother for him." [45] In the final exchanges the mad passion is still Katerina's, and Dmitri's for her. Grushenka will be the "good" lifelong companion.

The reader is long made to think of Dmitri as the murderer and may continue to feel him guilty (since his behavior is so guilt-ridden and self-destructive) even after the truth has been revealed. He has knocked his father down, threatened to kill him, certainly wished him dead. The Oedipal threat of punishment by castration is evident rather in Smerdyakov, the actual murderer, and in Ivan's relationship to him. Ivan, cooler and more intellectual than Dmitri, comes to think of himself as the murderer by proxy. He has corrupted Smerdyakov by persuading him that "everything was lawful" and has dazed him with rationalist subtleties. Smerdyakov is highly intuitive. He has detected that Ivan as well as Dmitri wishes the father's death. *"You* murdered him; you are the real murderer, I was only your instrument, your faithful servant, and it was following your words I did it." When Smerdyakov urges Ivan to go to Chermashnya, and thus leave the father unprotected, he is in effect asking him to become a passive accomplice in a murder now certain to occur. His role, as true psychological "double" for Ivan, is to extract his secret wishes and enact them, and insist on complicity.

Central to the novel's meaning is its "Freudian" assumption that a criminal wish, especially a parricidal one, is a guilty act for which punishment must be suffered. In fact the crime, without Ivan, would not have occurred. Smerdyakov's answers, when he is pressed for a motive, seem half-hearted. He would have been in a position to blackmail Ivan for the rest of his life; he could have gone to Moscow or Paris. None of this is convincing, and he gives Ivan the money of his free will. There is no explicit evidence at all for Peace's argument that the murder was an act of religious fanaticism. Smerdyakov would indeed seem to have been the mere instrument of outside forces: whether (psychologically) to fulfill the brothers' wishes or (psycho-mythically, with the punishment castration) to avenge the original crime against his mother. His suicide conveniently puts him out of the way, leaving the trial with its ambiguities. But, also, his role has been fulfilled. That role is not least interesting when, though not present, he functions as an interior voice and self that must be suppressed. At a critical moment Ivan feels an intense desire to go to the lodge and beat Smerdyakov. Instead he listens to the sounds of his father moving below. He will think of this eavesdropping as "the basest action" of his life. What precisely is stirring in the unconscious is not revealed. But he wakes the next morning feeling extraordinarily vigorous, and is now ready to leave his father unprotected. The incident of the peasant with whom Ivan collides shows the same pre-Freudian understanding of symbolic action. The collision is in a sense the peasant's fault; Ivan does not *actively* "kill him" (he returns to help him in time), but leaves him unconscious to freeze to death. This could be a reenactment of his complicity, still not fully acknowledged, in his father's death; *he had let him die.* But also he could, enacting his murderous wish toward Smerdyakov, appear to show that he was really, literally, capable of murder. (The scene will be brilliantly reimagined in *Under Western Eyes.*)

4. There are several important instances of less conscious psychological understanding, but coherent understanding nevertheless. There is an important connection between money and sexuality: not only the money old Fyodor withholds from Dmitri, but (even more interestingly) the money Dmitri withholds, the half kept sewn in a little bag after the first Mokroe orgy, and his consequent shame. Granted his reasoning that he is thus not yet fully a thief, since something of the money entrusted to him by Katerina remains, other forces would seem in play: the erotic shame of the gambler who does not risk his last coin, and the shame of withholding part of one's sexuality. Dmitri's journey into the forest, where he hopes to get money from Lyagavy by ceding his rights to his copse at Chermashnya, would appear to be a classic intuitive dreaming of the mythical night journey, as even the chapter heading in the original suggests: "The Journey of a Soul Through Hell." The rights to the woods, of which Fyodor was depriving him, came to him from his mother. The night of crisis was the more significant for Dostoevsky's imagination because Chermashnya was the name of the village near which his father was murdered. Structurally, the very brief episode has several components of the classic night

journey: the difficult passage to a primitive place, where profound "dejection clung about his soul like a heavy mist," the discovery of a sleeper who cannot be awakened, the near death from suffocation and, next morning, the disorientation on finding himself surrounded by forest and not knowing which way to turn. The very short episode has the character of *something that had to be gone through,* by the author if not Dmitri. Two other epidoses have essential components of the night journey: confinement and spiritual change. The fenced garden of old Fyodor's is a dark place where the entire history of misrule began; the few pages as Dmitri sits astride the fence, then approaches the window, knocks, pulls the pestle from his pocket, seem much longer in retrospect, especially when we learn of his change of heart. Confinement in prison is also for Dmitri, as for Julien Sorel and Meursault, an opportunity for spiritual change.

5. Unconscious psychological understanding and "illuminating distortion." Much in the interviews of Ivan and Smerdyakov, and in Ivan's dialogue with the devil, justifies Mikhail Bakhtin's intellectualist formula: each interlocutor is closely connected with, and speaking to or for, the concealed thoughts and "interior" or hidden voice of the other. The formula is adequate where we are dealing with clearly definable thoughts, wishes, intentions. But it helps us not at all when we are faced by the occult coincidence of Ivan's dream of the devil and Smerdyakov's suicide, or with psychic forces that exist on a non-verbal level. A very pure example of illuminating distortion, a strangeness that may ultimately and dazzlingly clarify, involves Ivan's shock, on his first and last interview with Smerdyakov, on seeing the sick man's white stocking, from which the money will be taken. It should be recalled that Smerdyakov has been described as effeminate, even emasculate:

> He was wearing long white stockings and slippers. Slowly he took off his garter and fumbled to the bottom of his stocking. Ivan gazed at him, and suddenly shuddered in a paroxysm of terror.
> "He's mad!" he cried, and rapidly jumping up, he drew back, so that he knocked his head against the wall and stood up against it, stiff and straight. He looked with insane terror at Smerdyakov, who, entirely unaffected by his terror, continued fumbling in his stocking, as though he were making an effort to get hold of something with his fingers and pull it out. At last he got hold of it and began pulling it out, Ivan saw it was a piece of paper, or perhaps a roll of papers.[46]

The roll of money is like a "loathsome reptile" for Ivan. Conceivably he knows what Smerdyakov is about, and is terrified by the thought that he is about to see the money for which, nominally, Fyodor was killed. But the emphasis is on the stocking: " 'You frightened me . . . with your stocking,' he said, with a strange grin.' " The white stocking, Richard Peace valuably argues, connects Smerdyakov with the sect of Castrates, "who referred to themselves as 'The White Doves,' dressed in white, and called the process of castration itself 'whitening' (*ubeleniye*)." [47] But Peace's conclusion—that the murder, and taking the 3000 rubles, was motivated by religious fanaticism—seems highly implausible, and violates major meanings. *Surely the motive for the murder is that Ivan wished Smerdyakov to commit it.* The response to the white stocking, and to the slow removal of the garter, is primitive and unexplained: a horror, it may be, at the physical sign of castration in his half-brother and double, in a sense in himself. Impotence may be the symbolic as well as physiological consequence of a debased inheritance. But with it Smerdyakov (now Smerdyakov-Ivan) is brought meaningfully into the story of Oedipal crime. For fear of castration is archetypally a motive for rebelling against the father and actual castration is rebellion's punishment. But here, as with the culminating scene of *The Idiot*, it would seem unwise to insist on a single explanation.

The father-son conflict in *The Brothers Karamazov* is far more interesting for a number of reasons, not least the greater vitality of old Karamazov and the higher intelligence of the sons. But *A Raw Youth* (1875) offers a fascinatingly coherent displacement of the Oedipal triangle: a socially acceptable story of family conflict is doubled by an intense version of the illicit family romance. In the first story Arkady, the illegitimate son of Versilov and Sofia, who is the wife of the absent serf Makar, a much older man, has intensely ambivalent feelings toward his intelligent, powerful and wayward father, and compassionate love for his angelic, i.e. asexual mother. The son, longing to keep the "family" together in spite of tension and bickering, will do what he can to see that the father remains faithful to Sofia. He probes the mystery of apparent hostility between Versilov and the beautiful widow Katerina Akhmakov, whom he himself finds fascinating. He learns that Versilov has loved her in the past, still loves her, even proposes marriage. But the father's almost insane desire is thwarted, partly thanks to Arkady, and we learn in the Epilogue that the father, "only half the former Versilov," will never leave the mother again. The family has been saved. The son has resolved many of his confused feelings toward the father, and blames much of Versilov's worst behavior on a sickness, specifically on his "double," and on the split between his feelings and his will.

But this is not the "real story." The major dramatic conflict, and one that entirely dwarfs the theme of intellectual generations, is of father and son for the love of Katerina. This transfer of the Oedipal rivalry from one triangle to another (with the father's potential mistress as symbolic mother) can be found in reports of clinical practice today. The Oedipal relationship of Arkady and Katerina is brilliantly developed. (Once, in the notes, the "Youth" says to the "Princess": "You are like a mother to me." [48]) She is older than he, much older in terms of *savoir-faire*. Arkady overhears her repudiation of himself as oafishly immature. He is, almost throughout, in the position of a child speculating on his parents' (one a surrogate mother's) sexuality: probing, eavesdropping, even peering from a hiding place. His conscious love for Katerina is idealizing. And presently the archetypal wish is fulfilled: he overhears Katerina tell Versilov that she no longer loves him. Any close connection is a thing of the past. Yet at this moment Arkady feels a need to see Katerina degraded (with Versilov also a witness): see her give herself to the blackmailer Lambert in exchange for a compromising document.

But the fact is that this compromising document, which gives Arkady his only power over Katerina, has long been in his own possession, *sewn in the lining of his coat*. And we learn he had repressed the thought of using that document to win her sexually. The recognition comes thanks to a dream. In it Katerina's lips are inviting; the mother-substitute is sexualized, as is, presumably, that document sewn in the lining. The imagination, reenacting the primal violation, must prostitute the surrogate mother. Dostoevsky is here very attentive to degrees of repression and consciousness:

> All this must have been hatched long before and been stored in my perverted heart; it was all part of my *desire,* although my heart was still ashamed of it during my waking hours and my brain still did not dare to formulate consciously anything of the sort. But, in my sleep, my soul had shown and explained exactly what was hidden inside me; it had given a complete, absolutely accurate picture and, what is more, in a prophetic form.[49]

Prophetic in a sense, though Katerina spits in Lambert's face in the novel's last real scene, while Versilov and (unknown to Versilov) Arkady watch.

This climax, one of the most melodramatic in Dostoevsky, is psychologically coherent, relentlessly so. When the enraged Lambert pulls out his gun both Arkady and Versilov leap from their separate hiding places; Versilov seizes the gun and strikes Lambert with it. Katerina faints; Versilov carries her back and forth in his arms. The position of Arkady, once again a child, is humiliating: "I was trotting behind him, for I was afraid of the gun he was still clutching in his right hand." He pleads with Versilov to put Katerina down on the bed, and is surprised when the father does so, and kisses her pale lips. But suddenly the gun flashes through the air; he has swung at Katerina with it. Arkady seizes his hand and shouts for help. And in fact the son at least partly triumphs. Versilov turns the diverted gun onto himself. But Arkady, pushing his hand upward,

causes the bullet to hit him in the shoulder not the heart. He has saved his father's life yet also had his share in a token wound. Above all, Katerina has
been saved from that highly erotic gun. In the Epilogue Versilov—no gun now,
surely impotent in terms of the fantasy, "only half of the former Versilov"—is
in the position of the child, with Mother sitting by his bed.

It is interesting, given this late configuration, to look back on a very early,
dream-like and singularly transparent short novel of Oedipal conflict, *The
Landlady* (1847). Mochulsky, after plausibly arguing its autobiographical character (Ordynov as withdrawn and fantasizing artist), sees it as a romantic story
of demonic possession—old Murin living with the bewitched wife-daughter Katerina—and as developing the "theme" of the faint heart. But the story is an
almost undisguised rendering of the Freudian family romance, so undisguised
as to suggest a total freedom from repression. Ordynov, in spite of Murin's
hostility, is welcomed as a lodger by the angelic young Katerina, and at once
falls ill. In his revery Katerina evokes memories of a mother's embrace, while
Murin is confused with the "mysterious old man" who persecuted him as a
child. The three live in very close quarters. Ordynov, lifting himself by a nail
in the wall, looks in on the old man in bed, Katerina stretched on a bench beside him, resting her head against his shoulder. Ordynov bursts into the room;
Katerina springs up with a start. Murin seizes a revolver, shoots and misses,
and has an epileptic fit. In a later, and culminating, crisis Ordynov seizes a
dagger to attack Murin, but is paralyzed by his smile; his dagger falls to the
ground, and is kicked aside. And Katerina is definitively lost. The story has
many interesting complications. Perhaps the most important, given Dostoevsky's enduring obsessions, is that the angelic but corrupted mother-figure is
also childlike, and (according to Murin) is not quite sane.

The Notebooks for *"The Idiot,"* taken together with the novel, bring us very
close to turbulent and dynamic creative process: to an intense struggle among
competing conscious intentions; to conflict between conscious and unconscious
understanding; to the courageous admission of materials almost any other novelist would have repressed or turned away from in dismay. These Notebooks,
compared with those of *Crime and Punishment* and *The Brothers Karamazov,*
reflect preliminary dreamings and gropings for character and theme, rather than
the structural manipulation of material already conceived. To discern the ultimate creative choices we must look to the completed novel. Somewhere between the two kinds of evidence one may look "outside," as to the famous
January 1868 letter to the niece S. A. Ivanovna, where Dostoevsky declares his
intention to depict "a *positively beautiful individual"* and, with allusions to

Don Quixote and Pickwick, "beautiful simply because at the same time he is also comic." [50] But this intention was discovered very late indeed.

One obvious difficulty was that Dostoevsky long failed to see who his characters were or which were the main ones. Even in very late notes Ippolit (who like Kirillov came late in the planning, and whose moving testament is as detachable as Father Zossima's or The Grand Inquisitor) was briefly seen as "the main axis of the whole novel." Edward Wasiolek's illuminating, often brilliant summaries of the various plans emphasize how "names and qualities live in these notes in a fluid relationship," [51] with traits repeatedly redistributed as characters come to the forefront and recede. Wasiolek describes succinctly the great oddity: that only in the Seventh Plan did the Idiot become "humble, forgiving, sincere, Christian . . . in short, the Myshkin of the final version." [52] "The pure, noble Christ-like traits that had existed from the very beginning and had been given at different times to the uncle's son, to Ganechka, and to the Idiot's wife, are now centered in the Idiot himself." [53] Much earlier in the Notebooks Myshkin was *double* in the way that Stavrogin would be double, with the potentialities for salvation of a Great Sinner. But less than two months before Dostoevsky was to submit the first part of his novel, Wasiolek notes, the Idiot "has a wife, rapes Umetskaia, burns his finger, sets fire to a house, loves the heroine and torments his wife." [54]

The Idiot's redemption, after long authorial resistance, occurs within the Notebooks not the novel, where he is noble from the start, and is accomplished by the simple (simple!) splitting of self into two (with a few traits distributed elsewhere)—the coarse, brutal, sensual, proud, self-willed traits being transferred to Rogozhin, while the Christian humility and compassion are retained. Dostoevsky was fully aware of this transference of traits, but did not perhaps see clearly that one human being had become two or that the two must ultimately be united. Granted his dislike of explanations in his novels, much in the hold that Rogozhin had over Myshkin probably remained mysterious to Dostoevsky himself. Their reunion at Nastasya's deathbed, Rogozhin's insistence that they sleep side by side at her feet, Myshkin's instant seeming acceptance of the crime and total identification—all this may indeed suggest that Dostoevsky was capable of understanding, at whatever level of consciousness, the homosexuality latent in his narrative. For Mochulsky, who stresses a religious myth-plot of perdition and redemption, deathly seducer and potential liberator have alike failed Nastasya and are therefore accomplices who have killed her by their "love." [55] At the very least we can say that at Nastasya's deathbed two beings were reunited, two sides of a single self, that had been rather violently torn asunder.

Such, briefly, are a few bare essentials of the evolution of Myshkin in the Notebooks. But if we turn to the novel (looking only incidentally to the Notebooks for help) we see the creative problem in larger terms.

The Conflict of Common-sense and Dynamic Psychologies

We may discern, even more than in Dickens, fictional worlds within worlds, and the gradual narrowing of a pictured Russian world, the world of "social realism," to the intense interpersonal relations of six or seven persons, then four, then three, then two who are ultimately one. In the background, barely noticed, is ordinary Russian life: the drunken poor in Petersburg, the vacationers in the park at Pavlovsk, the bystanders in the hotel where Myshkin has his fit, the virtually anonymous community shocked at the prospect of the marriage to Nastasya, and as hostile as those at Lucetta's wedding in Casterbridge or Sutpen's in Jefferson. Nearer to the reader is the novel's accepted social circle of ordinary named persons—not so ordinary, after all, since they are Russians and Dostoevskyan Russians. Some are virtually Dickensian eccentrics (Ivolgin, Rogozhin's rowdies and the radicals who protest Myshkin's inheritance). But there are also the relatively well-balanced aristocrats and nobodies at the betrothal party, and the wonderfully vivacious women of the Epanchin household. Dostoevsky's scenic, uninterpreted, unflaggingly inventive presentation of Myshkin's first day in Petersburg, more than a fourth of the novel in length, makes of Part One one of literature's great triumphs of realistic narrative.

There is a conspicuous narrowing of the lens, and of the fictional world, as we become aware of the central quartet as such: Myshkin, Rogozhin, Nastasya, Aglaia. On the one hand Dostoevsky saw their desires and anxieties and neuroses in common-sense terms, and their ballet of shifting relationships, and reasoned about them in the Notebooks. Who is to marry whom? Who is to murder whom? Even Aglaia is seen capable of murder, and the Idiot himself from very early in the plans. A more coherent common-sense psychology is apparent as we turn to the novel, and most critics never go beyond it. Myshkin's Christ-like humility and compassion for the "fallen" yet pure Nastasya, living in her hell of suffering and madness, and a normal fascination with her beauty, may account for much of his eccentric behavior. Christian forgiveness of the "brother" Rogozhin he had hoped to save, and with whom he had exchanged crosses, might lead to that reconciliation at Nastasya's deathbed. In such naturalistic terms his several fits may be attributed to reasonable anxiety and his final madness to extreme strain and grief. There is a hint, for the alert eye, that impotence may be one reason for his behavior. Yevgeny Pavlovitch at one point, "with great psychological insight," contributes just such an analysis as a cautious modern critic might come up with: the interest in the woman's question, the curiosity concerning Russia, the heart-rendering story of Nastasya heard on the first day, her beauty . . . "Add to that your nerves, your epilepsy, add to that our Petersburg thaw which shatters the nerves, add all that day, in an unknown and to you almost fantastic town, a day of scenes and meetings."

In such common-sense terms Rogozhin's behavior, if reduced to summary, may also seem explicable: a proud man intoxicated by his new riches, eager to revenge himself for past humiliations, infatuated by Nastasya, at times respectful of Myshkin and at times deeply jealous, driven at last to murder by the loved one's exasperating oscillations and withdrawals. Aglaia is simply and plausibly a vivacious, fun-loving, teasing young woman, as proud as any of the others and so vulnerable to humiliation; and jealous of Nastasya. The portrait of the hysterical self-lacerating Nastasya is entirely convincing. Really discovered by her guardian Totsky at twelve, his mistress at sixteen, her life now seems devoted to humiliating him and humiliating herself. With others she seems compelled to provoke then repudiate sexual desires, as though in reenactment of her years with Totsky. She is a poignant victim of manic and depressed moods, of the *folie circulaire*. Her noblest impulse is to save Myshkin from herself; her strongest one is to reenact her degradation. To save Myshkin she tries to marry him off to Aglaia, which only adds to the latter's rage. Myshkin regards Nastasya as literally mad, and therefore needing his care: what some see as his fatal generosity and compassion.[56] It would appear she went to Rogozhin at the end with full knowledge that she was going to her death.

Such are the intense personages in an explicit drama of inter-personal relations, with three neurotics tearing at each other and at themselves. The relatively sane and almost child-like Aglaia is drawn into the furnace of this interior drama helplessly, as such people are in "real life," while Ganya and other suitors remain outside and watch aghast. At times Myshkin not merely desires both Nastasya and Aglaia—the dark depraved beauty and the child-like one—but seems almost to believe he can have them both: an illusion which might be attributed, simply, to his estranged "innocence." It is evident that on one level of consciousness Dostoevsky thought about his story in these more or less clear terms. He might, that is, have conceived a novel by Flaubert or James.

But this summary scarcely touches on the deeper intensities of *The Idiot*. Once we look at the strangest scenes of the book, its moments of illuminating distortion, we are concerned with darker matters, and poor Aglaia simply drops out of the picture. At another, still conscious level, Dostoevsky saw his triad of lovers, but Myshkin and Rogozhin especially, in terms of mysterious connections. A more intuitive psychology, that is, was operating parallel to and sometimes in conflict with the one formulated by Jamesian common-sense, and outward happenings often seem to be psychic events. The shifting of partners within the triangle, for one thing, sometimes involves the complicity of all three. The first meetings of Rogozhin and Myshkin and Nastasya, are "uncanny," as though someone known long before had been recognized, someone (Freud would say) who had sprung from within. (The first meeting of Myshkin and Nastasya, for Mochulsky, is a mystical one of two exiles from paradise, who "remember their heavenly homeland . . . as 'in a dream.' " [57]) Rogozhin sets a recurring pattern at the start when he proposes—although he doesn't know why he is so drawn to Myshkin—that they visit Nastasya together. Much later Myshkin assures Rogozhin that he will not stand in their way, though he believes marriage with Nastasya would be perdition for them both. "And how could he have left her when she ran away from him to Rogozhin?" "Why, he himself had wanted to take Rogozhin by the hand and go *there* with him." Later still, when Nastasya has sent Rogozhin to bring Myshkin to her, the Prince urges the messenger to come too. The drama of complicity, of a deep willingness to share the loved one, could hardly be more explicit.

Nastasya's pattern, in turn, is to move to the brink of marriage with one, then rush feverishly to the other, as though something essential were missing. It is much as though the three were drawn somnambulistically into meetings they do not understand, and through sudden repudiations and reconciliations. In the novel's last pages the three are indeed united, as it were against the outside world, the *whole world of outside appearance and external events,* not merely the world threatening punishment in Siberia, madness in Switzerland. The trivialities of rational dialogue, of everyday activities, of "social realism" are behind them. But by now there are really only two, since Nastasya Filipovna lies dead. On the way to the dark funereal house Rogozhin insists that they walk on opposite sides of the street, as though to preserve a psychic separateness. But separation is overcome in the most extreme way, as Myshkin not only accepts Rogozhin's crime but wonders whether the knife that threatened him in the hotel was the one that killed Nastasya. He asks to see and hold the cards with which Rogozhin and Nastasya used to play. But even this symbolic sharing gives no satisfaction. "A new feeling of hopeless sadness weighed on his heart; he realised suddenly that at that moment and a long time past he had been saying not what he wanted to say and had been doing the wrong thing, and that the cards that he was holding in his hands and was so pleased to see were no help, no help now.'' Shortly thereafter Rogozhin shows the first signs of hysteria, and Myshkin begins to stroke his head, his hair, his cheeks. ''Quite a new sensation gnawed at his heart with infinite anguish.'' By morning, when people come, they find the murderer raving, and Myshkin unable to understand questions or recognize people around him. Before the immensity of such a scene any single explanation—be it latent homosexuality or ultimate spiritual brotherhood or reunion of components of the self—would seem oversimple and reductive. But the spiritual drama has indeed now narrowed to Hawthorne's ''interior of a heart.'' The two are one, and the aftermath of separation—Rogozhin to Siberia, Myshkin to Switzerland—seems scarcely more plausible than the epilogue to *Crime and Punishment*.

By what process of invention could Dostoevsky render such deeply inward workings, more inward than *The Secret Sharer*'s, without sacrificing the dramatic interest of two persons struggling for and sharing a third? One answer lies in the use of the occult: the more than mesmeric power of Rogozhin's eyes—more, because Myshkin is aware of those watchful, glittering eyes even when there is no possibility of his really seeing them. His awareness of the eyes is associated, moreover, with his epileptic fits. To be sure Myshkin is not alone in succumbing to their power. Nastasya says that two terrible eyes are always gazing at her, and she knows their secret: Rogozhin keeps a razor wrapped in silk as did a murderer in Moscow. And when she catches Rogozhin's eyes in the crowd collected for her wedding, she rushes to him as to a devil or robber bridegroom, and is whisked away as by a fairy-tale coach.

We hear of Rogozhin's fiery eyes on the first page. But the first instance of their occult power comes at the railway station on Myshkin's return from Moscow: a ''vision of strange glowing eyes fixed upon him in the crowd that met the train.'' Later that day Myshkin feels himself held by Rogozhin's gaze, and, for the first time, has warning signs of the fits he had five years before. They discuss Rogozhin's possible marriage. Myshkin, who says he is very fond of Rogozhin, will not stand in their way. But will it not be as though Nastasya, marrying, were deliberately asking to be drowned or murdered? Near the end of the chapter Myshkin twice picks up a knife from a table and Rogozhin twice takes it from his hands. It would seem related, psychologically, to the knife of Stavrogin's thoughts, of his will to see Marya Lebyadkin dead . . . which at once becomes a real knife in his agent Fedka's hand. In the next chapter, as though to combat Rogozhin's growing intention, Myshkin tells the story of a man who asks for God's forgiveness in the very act of cutting his friend's throat for a watch. And Rogozhin in turn proposes that they exchange crosses and be spiritual brothers. But Rogozhin's eyes glow at their parting. Is he driven against his will, as perhaps Coleridge's Geraldine with her snake's small eye? In the pages to follow the threat of a fit darkens, and Myshkin once again feels the way he had that morning, with the eyes fixed on him. An "insuperable inner loathing" gives way to remembrance of the moments of ecstasy that precede a seizure: harmonious joy, a sense that *there shall be no more time.* Now, as the mental darkness deepens, he has his vision of union with Nastasya and with a Rogozhin who would feel compassion for her. For "him, Myshkin, to love her with passion was almost unthinkable, would have been almost cruelty, inhumanity." He longs to take Rogozhin by the hand and go with him to Nastasya's house. But instead on the staircase of the hotel, a man is waiting in a hollow niche, and the *same two eyes* meet his own. It is Rogozhin with the knife. Myshkin's long-anticipated epileptic fit now ensues, and presumably saves him from death. It may also be seen, in Freudian terms, as a protection against an unacceptable impulse.

Myshkin's forgiveness is total, and totally unexplained: Christian forgiveness or indulgence for the secret sharer? "We were feeling just the same. If you had not made that attack (which God averted), what should I have been then? I did suspect you of it, our sin was the same in fact." In the novel's next to last chapter Myshkin recalls the eyes as they had looked at him in the darkness. Was Rogozhin even in Petersburg? "He could not have explained if he had probed his own thought why he should be suddenly so necessary to Rogozhin, and why it was so impossible that they should not meet." And now it seems as though Rogozhin will appear if only Myshkin mentally summons him. "What if he suddenly comes out of that corner and stops me at the stairs?" Minutes later, Rogozhin does appear: "follow me, brother, I want you." He takes Myshkin to the house where the crime has already in some sense been committed by them both. "Rogozhin's face was pale as usual; his glittering eyes watched Myshkin intently with a fixed stare."

The premonitions of fits and the fits themselves, the depression and inner loathing succeeded by a vision of ecstatic harmony outside time, the illusion of watchful *eyes* even when Myshkin is alone, the need to go to Rogozhin and be united with him (if only through the shared Nastasya, even through the dead Nastasya), the knife intuited and the knife in Rogozhin's hands, the remorse for having unjustly (!) thought Rogozhin capable of murder—so much intimately associated, *connected* material conveys a deeply inward psychological or spiritual experience, one that defies common sense. Even the broad elastic concept of the double seems to beg the question. *The important fact, again, is that Dostoevsky did not permit his formulated common-sense reasonings to interfere with his rich intuitive imaginings.* The Notebooks touch on this dynamic material only briefly, and a single entry may combine the carefully reasoned and the intuitive. The scene at Nastasya's deathbed, one of the greatest in novelistic literature, is once summarized in three lines, followed by two words of authorial self-approval:

> Goes to Rogozhin in despair.
> (He murders.) Summons the Prince.
> Rogozhin and the Prince beside the corpse. Finale.
> *Not Bad.*[58]

Significant Undertreatment or Omission

One other strategy, partly unconscious, protected the dynamic and mysterious inward drama: the omission or undertreatment of certain crucial events and even periods of Myshkin's life. We are given only the briefest allusions to Myshkin's month in the provinces with Nastasya, when he saw her almost every day, though it "had had a fearful effect upon him, so much so that he sometimes tried to drive away all recollection of it." Earlier still, according to the shadowy rumors that open Part II, there had been an awful orgy at the Ekaterinhof Vauxhall, in which Nastasya had taken part, presumably with Rogozhin and his followers, and (this more than rumor) Myshkin had spent that night at Ekaterinhof, returning at six in the morning. This is the night following Nastasya's blatant "sale" of herself to Rogozhin for 100,000 rubles and her rejection of Myshkin's offer to marry her without dowry. Dostoevsky gives no details at all, leaves entirely in shadow what would have been, for Myshkin, an intensely traumatic, psychologically determinative experience. Even more significant may be the undertreatment (tantamount to repression?) of Myshkin's six months in Moscow, a period perhaps as crucial as Stavrogin's shadowed time in Petersburg. For during three of those months there had been long hours spent with Rogozhin, and "meetings, moments of which had left a lasting memory in their hearts." But of these meetings we learn next to nothing. Significantly, Myshkin's recollection of the Moscow days immediately follows the breaking of the Chinese vase at the betrothal party and immediately precedes a fit. Association with Rogozhin thus shatters a primary sexual symbol and, because of the fit, makes marriage with Aglaia seem out of the question. The undertreatments are altogether extreme, and are perhaps related to the radical confusions of identity, or linkings of personality, that precede the confrontation in the hotel stairwell.

Such in brief, and in far simpler form than it is experienced in the novel's dense reality, is one essential drama of creative process in the writing of *The*

Idiot. Some of the novel's ambiguity and uncertainty of movement is merely distracting. There are many pages that remain confused rather than dynamically ambiguous. But the greatest scenes, those we cannot forget, also resist facile or exclusive explanation.

A Burned Finger "Displaced"

Even this general description of the creative situation may seem excessively orderly, as we lose ourselves in *The Idiot's* first half-dozen plans. We may take, for instance, the burned finger that runs through the Notebooks, usually without explanation—the Idiot's finger until fairly late in the plans, ultimately Ganya's. A recent *fait divers,* one that fed the long preoccupation with abused or violated young girls, is referred to in the first plans: the trial of the fifteen-year old Olga Umetskaia in September 1867 for setting fires to buildings on her father's estate, and of the parents for neglecting her upbringing and for beating her savagely. The daughter may have been raped or seduced by the father; a finger had been broken by the mother. In one of Dostoevsky earliest fantasies the Idiot, teased by "Mignon"/Umetskaia, rapes her, sets fire to the house and on her command burns his finger; in a later plan he sets a house on fire with her. The fourth plan momentarily anticipates a major configuration of *The Possessed:* a raped young woman, a house set on fire, a loss of desire for "the heroine," "a sudden total apathy," suicide . . . and once again the unexplained burned finger. (In some places the burning appears to be a test of love.) The burned finger sometimes occurs before the rape, as though itself a glowing sexual object; sometimes after, as in token of self-punishment. And once it is associated with a greater crime: Ganya strangling Aglaia. Little remains in the completed novel of a single burned finger. Aglaia tells Myshkin that Ganya burnt his hand before her eyes to show he loved her more than his life, and kept his finger in the fire for half an hour. But she has then to acknowledge this was a lie. An event referred to almost obsessively in the Notebooks would thus seem to come virtually to nothing.

But not really nothing. A much more powerful association of money, sexuality and fire (with the violation of the young Nastasya in the background) occurs with the great scene that ends Part One. Rogozhin has met Nastasya's fierce challenge and arrives with the hundred thousand rubles she had set as her price. He lays the money on the table, a phallic roll six inches thick and eight inches long, wrapped in a copy of the *Financial News.* In her frenzy of rebellion and self-degradation Nastasya asks who will take her for nothing, and Myshkin offers to marry her. But this is only a diversion in the real movement and meaning of the scene. She says she cannot allow herself to ruin such a child; the ruin of children is more in Totsky's line. "I've been Totsky's concubine. . . ."

Her challenge is rather to Ganya, who had planned to marry her for a dowry supplied by Totsky. She will throw the money in the fire; it will be Ganya's to keep if he is willing to snatch it out. "As soon as the fire has got it all alight, put your hands into the fire, only without gloves, with your bare hands and turn back your sleeves, and pull the bundle out of the fire. If you can pull it out, it's yours, the whole hundred thousand. You'll only burn your fingers a little. . . ." All stare at the smoldering roll of notes. Ganya, his vanity stronger than his greed, resists saving the money; but faints. Thereupon Nastasya herself pulls out the notes; the inside of the roll was untouched. *She lays the roll of notes beside Ganya, while Myshkin and the others watch*. The common-sense interpretation—that she honors ironically Ganya's self-control and shows her scorn for the others—hardly touches the power of the scene. Rather this: she alone, who has withheld herself from Totsky for five years, after the years of adolescent concubinage, now controls sexual energies and will transfer them as she pleases. Ganya is impotent because unconscious, however; the watching Myshkin is also impotent, if only because a child. The money has been taken from the baffled Rogozhin, though he will moments later seem successful. Is there some hint that he too is impotent? On the ground floor of his gloomy house is a moneychanger's shop owned by one of the Skoptsy sect of castrates. And his Christian name Parfen, Richard Peace notes, is the Greek *parthenos*, meaning virgin.[59]

All this is but to say that Dostoevsky erected a powerful cluster of associations—burning finger/burning roll of money/sexual crime against a young girl/impotence/confusion of sexual partner and sexual role—without ever clearly explicating his meanings. Once again the unconscious, and half-conscious envisionings too, wrought better than he knew; or, for that matter, better than most of his critics. This doubtless accounts in part for the immense power and reality of a scene that, in bare summary, might seem implausible and even ridiculous.

The Idiot, like many great novels, had its share of lost subjects that preoccupied its author. Dostoevsky long clung to the changing Ganya as a central character, and to the Umetskaia story with which he had begun. There were multiple efforts, as Wasiolek remarks, to "use the theme of the maltreated child, the cruel and ugly environment of childhood and its effect upon the soul of the adult, the horrifying prospect of a father's betrayal of his God-like trust. . . ."[60] Another great imminent novel intrudes now and then in the Notebooks to play its part in delaying a final discovery of theme: *The Possessed.* There are a number of parallels between the Idiot and Stavrogin, who also returned from Switzerland: the Idiot filled with "morbid pride to such a degree that he cannot help considering himself a god, and yet *at the same time* he has so little esteem for himself (he analyzes himself with great clarity) that he cannot help despising himself intensely, infinitely, and unjustifiably." [61] The Idiot like Stavrogin has made a secret and absurd marriage with an abused innocent, one who like Marya Lebyadkin has qualities of the Madonna. This abused innocent is presumably Marie of the novel, seduced by a commercial traveler and sheltered by Myshkin in Switzerland. Stavrogin's linked crimes of *The Possessed* (the murder of his wife, the violation of the child Matryosha and the passive attendance upon her suicide by hanging) are even more closely juxtaposed in the Notebooks for *The Idiot.* For there we see Myshkin's wife, in one plan, hanging herself, the repeatedly raped Mignon hanging herself too and even, for good measure, the "heroine," who also had been raped.

It is perhaps well to recall that the incidence of violence in the Notebooks is greater than in the finished *The Idiot.* As Dostoevsky rid himself of many political speculations in the Notebooks for *The Possessed,* so here he worked his way through no small number of imagined crimes. The most remarkable fact, given so much confusion and turbulence, so many violently contradictory ideas (and so much contemporary distress in his personal life) is that *The Idiot* got written at all. It should be consoling for aspiring novelists to know that Dostoevsky, when he had completed the 75,000 words of his very great Part One, had no real idea what was to happen next. This novel, like more than one of Conrad's, was saved by financial necessity: by the need, in spite of everything, to struggle on. [62]

8
FAULKNER: PROBLEMS OF TECHNIQUE

A prevailing tendency of Faulkner criticism has been to shrug off or minimize his playful eccentricities of form and style, and emphasize instead more familiar interests: sociological, ethical, psychological—a tendency, that is, to "normalize" and intellectualize the wayward, render it orderly and safe. The normalizing, to open at random the vast library of Faulkner criticism, may be exemplified by Olga Vickery:

> The two worlds of economic and sexual activity explored in *The Hamlet* receive broader definition in *The Town* in as much as Flem Snopes and Eula Varner transcend their relatively restricted roles in the earlier book to represent two constant, warring elements in man and his society—the conscious and the subconscious, the civilized form and the primitive urge, the drive to conform and the desire to rebel. The one realizes itself in social power and order, the other in the potency of the individual.[1]

The statement has its fragments of truth, but is really irrelevant. It has nothing to do with the extravagances of conception and artful shiftings of tone that redeem this mediocre novel's later chapters. Olga Vickery writes, as do many others, as though she were dealing with a standard social realist.

There has been, in brief, a general failure to talk about Faulkner's innovations and audacities unless (like the Benjy section) they represent puzzles to be solved, or to recognize a *playfulness* grounded both in complex evasive temperament and in a dissatisfaction with conventional novel form. Conrad Aiken's 1939 essay on Faulkner's style remains one of the best, with its emphasis on luxuriance and exuberance of sound. I recall my own delight a year or two before that, opening a ten- or fifteen-cent first edition of *Mosquitoes,* to come upon "Twilight ran in like a quiet violet dog. . . ." It was a delight, despite my education in the chastities of Hemingway, in audacity, playfulness, outrage. The rest of the paragraph, I now see, has a closer affinity with the fin-de-siècle prettiness of *Soldiers' Pay* than with any later style: the "three spires of the cathedral graduated by perspective, pure and slumbrous beneath the decadent languor of August and evening." But there is already the sense of language as play (not merely language as communication) which we associate with Joyce and Nabokov, with the Dickens of *Our Mutual Friend,* or for that matter with Milton and Shakespeare.

The analogies with Conrad, if we look at Faulkner's more difficult experiments, are as always instructive: the complex impressionistic structures and brooding styles as the expressions of aloof, meditative temperaments, and of minds much given to irresolution and conflict. Faulkner is at times capable of genial warmth and an intimate connection with his imagined world; Conrad almost never. But *distance,* achieved by indirection, by point-of-view and elevation of language, is congenial to both. In neither do we find Dickens's easy intimacy with his reader or Dostoevsky's intense theatrical closeness to his imagined world. Walter Slatoff's important study of Faulkner's style and vision, *A Quest for Failure,* insists on tension and conflict at every level, on blocked feeling, on the balancing of polarities, and on an unwillingness to close in on things. Slatoff concludes, almost reluctantly, that these must be in part matters of temperament. What he fails to emphasize is that tensions ultimately *are* released, both for author and reader: in part through playful extravagance, but most obviously through prose rhythm: running rhythms that override and subdue the conflicts. It is useful to distinguish, in looking at Faulkner's longer sentences, between a Jamesian movement (perversely parenthetical, irresolute, locked in the play of logic and nuance) and a rapid movement I call Miltonic (onrushing, driven even by syntax to a high-pitched monotone, and maintaining a certain elevation through dazzling analogical surprise). Both movements are playful, as Borges and Nabokov are playful, and to that extent liberating: sources of pure aesthetic joy. But it is the more rapid movement, the running rhythm impatient of punctuated or other pause, that relieves tension and, it must be acknowledged, sometimes submerges meaning under a rush of sound.

A number of books could be written on Faulkner's rhetoric. The present chapter will confine itself to a few of its major forms: the counterpointing of essentially separate narratives in a single book; the arts of modulation evident in the conclusions of several novels; the complex mixture of modes or tones in

The Hamlet, with its pleasure in incongruity; the rich language and liberated rhythms of the Faulknerian voice.

Nothing is more evident than Faulkner's growing dissatisfaction with inherited novel forms. *Soldiers' Pay, Mosquitoes* and *Sartoris* were relatively straightforward, rectilinear, traditional narratives, though even in them (as in the earliest Conrad) we may detect an effort to break free of realist inhibitions. In *Mosquitoes* a notable freeing of language occurs as Faulkner uses for approximately a thousand words (in the Semitic man's story of Mrs. Maurier's marriage) the technique of *narration by conjecture* which proves so congenial in some of the later novels. And there is of course the crucial moment of liberation in *Sartoris,* the apostrophe to the mule, as Faulkner realizes *anything is permitted* to a "Homer of the cotton fields," even analogy with St. Anthony: a free flight of rhythm and fantasy of some five hundred words. The first two major experiments in counterpointed narrative, *The Sound and the Fury* and *As I Lay Dying,* do not juxtapose really separate stories or separate worlds, and are too familiar to demand analysis here. It is essential, surely, to discount Faulkner's version of *The Sound and the Fury*'s composition and structure: that the story, not yet satisfactorily rendered, had to be retold and retold. Its appeal lies rather in the deep ironies of shifting time and shifting perspective and in the beauty of the individual parts. One real originality of *As I Lay Dying* is its juxtaposition, startling for 1929, of the tragic or pathetic and the farcical. But its great technical problem was to render communal, ritual, largely physical movement through counterpointed solitary consciousnesses. This compounded the initial difficulty of conveying an ongoing present through very brief interior monologues rather than long or retrospective ones.

Light in August has its counterpointed worlds that rarely touch: Lena's bucolic acceptance and natural flow, Joe Christmas's compulsive self-destructiveness and the neurotic or puritanic rigidities surrounding him. But the most striking experiments involve the counterpointing or interlocking of separate stories that have seemingly discrete "subjects," and occupy different points of space and time: *The Bear, The Wild Palms, Requiem for a Nun, A Fable.* It is overwhelmingly evident that Faulkner felt the novel form needed renewal and wanted, as Durrell put it of his own effort, to "crack forms." But it would be interesting to know whether these extreme experiments had their origin in the double plots of Shakespeare and Dickens, or even in such radical breaks of narrative movement as Ippolit's story in *The Idiot* or "The Russian Monk" and Grand Inquisitor interruptions of *The Brothers Karamazov.*

The question of how Faulkner wrote *The Wild Palms,* to which he himself gave different answers, is irrelevant to a consideration of its effect. There are thematic connections between the interlocked "Wild Palms" and "Old Man" chapters: the lovers' frenzied flight from security, the convict's desperate effort to recover it; their defeat by nature and blocked flow, his triumph over it, and over primordial turbulence; the botched abortion, the successful birth as on an earthen ark out of Genesis; and, perhaps not least, the aghast masculine heroes threatened by two forms of female sexuality. But these logical connections appear in a retrospective analysis of the novel, rather than in its vital experiencing. More important: the interlocked narratives provide "relief" by shifts back and forth from one kind of extreme intensity to another, and from the largely realistic and spare story of Wilbourne and Charlotte Rittenmeyer to the richly rhetorical, mythical narrative of the heroic convict. The language of "Old Man" expresses the river's turmoil, a primordial chaos, yet also keeps the reader at a necessary distance from the convict's "real" inner life. In "Wild Palms," on the other hand, distance is at times reduced almost to zero. We could hardly be closer to Wilbourne's painful experience, as, already a prisoner, he waits for Charlotte to die.

The logical connections in *The Bear,* between Ike's education through hunting and his education through reading the ledgers, are too familiar to be rehearsed again. The connections, once discovered, have a certain appeal to the order-loving structuralist mentality, but are less moving than the sense of mystery created by symbolic overtone and reflexive reference. The radical shift of mode at the end of Part Three, from clear dramatic narrative (" 'Leave him alone,' he cried, 'Goddamn it! Leave him alone!' ") to deep obfuscation and involuted legal reasoning, makes startling demands on the reader. The complex and often sardonic windings of family history take us far from the deaths of Sam Fathers and the bear. But the very difficulty of this long section makes the hunting story, both as we return to it in Part Five, and as we reread the whole, a darker, more meditative experience. The hunt, moreover, had reached its great climax in Part Three, and a long interruption was perhaps necessary before the poignant story of the last hunt. The extreme difficulty of Part Four, like the extreme difficulty of *Finnegans Wake* or even parts of *Ulysses* (or the substantial difficulty of *Absalom, Absalom!*) has another value: it provides a guarantee against casual reading.

Requiem for a Nun, a much greater oddity, extends still further the formal limits of the novel, which can now be a three-act poetic play, each act preceded by a dithyrambic and whimsical historical essay. Once again Faulkner would seem ready to judge himself as he judged his contemporaries: by the audacity of the attempt, if necessary by the magnitude of the failure. The formal rebellion is all the greater because the play, which audaciously endows Temple Drake with a spiritual life, is recasting the materials of one of Faulkner's most realistic, least intellectual novels. The most obvious connection between the historical essays and the religious drama lies in the meditative impulse embodied in rich authorial language. But there is a logical connection too. One is created by his heritage, which is all that Mississippi and the South have been. "Listen, stranger; this was myself, this was I''; and it took Thomas Sutpen to make all of us. But our older heritage is that love of evil which Temple Drake, breaking through the protective persona of Mrs. Gowan Stevens, acknowledges in herself.

Here too aesthetic play, the pleasure in cracking forms, may be more significant than the logical connections. The element of rhetorical relief is again present. There is the counterpoint of dark closet drama, the claustrophobic atmospheres of Temple's story and her entrapment by guilt, against the historical open spaces, the Frenchman and the Spaniard and the "Anglo-Saxon, the pioneer, roaring with Protestant scripture and boiled whiskey," the wild sweep of time and change. The narrative escapes from private trauma to free authorial fantasy. But there are also times when the verbal waywardness of the Miltonic and Shakespearean flights, in the historical essays, makes a narrowing of the lens to Temple and her bleak modernity momentarily welcome.

The single intrusion of "Notes on a Horsethief," slightly less than a tenth of *A Fable,* hardly constitutes counterpoint, though Faulkner's need to break conventional novel form is again manifest. Logical connections exist, but they are far more obvious in analytic summary than in a normal reading. "Notes on a Horsethief" is a story of secular love and its golden legend, juxtaposed against war's "grimed and bloodstained" chronicle (also eternal, though often imaged in terms of ecclesiastical history) and the story of Christ returned to earth to lead a mutiny. In both stories there is a highly emotional drama of public, collective complicity with idealistic individual actions—the theft of the fabulous race-horse (so that he can continue to race, though on three legs, rather than be retired to stud); the Christ-corporal's organizing of the mutiny. In both there is a sense, deeply pessimistic in the war story, of people moving without volition or even awareness of what they are about. All institutions and all hierarchies are doomed to fail; history is a futile spawning of event. But also, consolingly, we see individual human beings struggle in vain against the heroism and idealism thrust upon them. The foul-mouthed groom, obscenely repudiating the lawyer's allegations of idealism, is for a brief time a docile, naturalized farmer, eventually the heroic sentry resisting in vain his high destiny: not Mister Harry, but 'Mistairy,' e.g. *mystère.* The American interlude comes as a real relief from the dark gloom of wartime France and the army bureaucracy; it contains, moreover, a number of pleasing echoes from earlier novels. "Notes on a Horsethief" is, in purely logical terms, an "affirmative" moment in what is, with *Sanctuary,* the most pessimistic of the novels. But a major difficulty remains: Faulkner would appear to have little faith in the truth of his own creation. It is only a wishful dream of what humanity might be, with destructive volitionless movement and failure the realities.

These instances of split structure and ironic counterpoint are moments in the history of the novel. But Faulkner also showed traditional expertise in the manipulation of the reader's feelings, notably at the close of several very emotional novels. Careful modulations serve to undercut moments of intense but vulnerable feeling, and permit the reader to disengage himself gently from the novel, even, in some instances, with a sense of recovered warmth and life. In *Light in August,* following the death and castration of Joe Christmas, the narrative modulates carefully, though certainly at too great length, to the comic ending of Lena enjoying her travels, with the faithful Byron in attendance and eventually to be rewarded: "My, my. A body does get around. Here we aint been coming from Alabama but two months, and now it's already Tennessee." Between the timeless meditation on Joe Christmas's crucifixion, which is to become part of the collective consciousness, and the furniture dealer's amused view of Byron and Lena, Faulkner presents the long history of that other self-destructive, Hightower, and his obsessive connection with the past. We are thus disengaged from the terrible intensities of Christmas's last moments through the sad, slow, pallid story (but with its own moments of grotesque absurdity) of Hightower's withdrawal. To end the book with him might have been not untrue to the novel's overall vision. But it would have left the reader intolerably imprisoned in its world. Lena, taking us over the Tennessee border, provides a necessary, satisfying escape: "life goes on."

The ending of *The Wild Palms* (which in this as in other ways recalls *The Nigger of the Narcissus*) is deeply ironic; the heroic adventure, with the archetypal setting and ultimate challenge of the elements left behind, concludes with a return to ordinary, vulnerable, even mean humanity. Faulkner's reduction of his hero is ferocious. The next to last chapter of "Old Man" had concluded, after a lovely image of Mississippi in June, with the tall convict's heroic return bringing the woman and the boat, wearing his clean suit of penitentiary clothing. This is followed by the last chapter of "Wild Palms," which ends with Wilbourne's one heroic moment, his choice not to die. *"Yes,* he thought, *between grief and nothing I will take grief."* The brief final chapter of "Old

Man'' returns us to ordinary humanity: the talk of the warden, the deputy, and the governor's young man, and the legal absurdity that adds ten years to the tall convict's sentence for ''attempted escape.'' The convict's subsequent narrative includes, improbably, trouble with a ''fellow's wife,'' which in turn leads to the unspoken memory of his hour—seduction? rape?—''with a nameless and not young negress, a casual, a straggler whom he had caught more or less by chance on one of the fifth-Sunday visiting days, the man—husband or sweetheart—whom she had come to see having been shot by a trusty a week or so previous and she had not heard about it. . . .'' But sympathy is restored as we return again to his heroic arrival with the boat, and the narrative's (not his) evocation of his one sweetheart and her one visit to the prison, where she was soon ''in animated conversation with one of the guards.'' As the last paragraph of *The Nigger of the Narcissus* ends on an accent of restored comradeship, so our last view of the convict is of a quasi-monastic reserve and renewed repudiation of the female world.

The final chapter of *The Town* offers a superb example of artful modulation toward disengagement. The novel moves back and forth between Gavin Stevens's romantic love for Eula Varner and her daughter Linda and a rich anthology of ''Snopeslore.'' Seventeen years have passed since the publication of *The Hamlet:* hence the retelling of Flem's spotted horses and of the murder of Houston. But there are fine new stories as Flem rids Jefferson of I. O. Snopes and Montgomery Ward Snopes of the pornographic ''Atelier Monty,'' and there is the superb black humor of the generous Eck Snopes's demise. The story of I. O. Snopes's mules in the widowed Mrs. Hait's yard, and of one mule tangling with her white-leghorns, renews the ''Spotted Horses'' pleasures: ''the mule that came out of the fog to begin with like a hant or a goblin, now kind of soaring back into the fog again borne on a cloud of little winged ones.'' The episode brings welcome relief from the sentimental delicacies of Gavin and Linda. But Flem's mastery of the town, and determination to have Linda's share of the Will Varner inheritance, leads to Eula's suicide. And Linda will not be free to leave Jefferson, and escape Snopesism, until Eula's monument with its marble medallion and virtuous epitaph (Flem's crowning hypocrisy) has been completed.

The first pages of the final chapter are sentimental in a particularly Faulknerian way, as Gavin suppresses his grief with evasive talk, and even refuses whiskey Ratliff obtains for him, then gives way both to grief and a kind of rage, and at last begins to cry. The novel, had it ended here, would have lost its intended balancing of idealistic love story and comic Snopeslore. The challenge to the writer was to free the reader from Gavin's emotional crisis without simply repudiating it ironically; and also to free us from the cynicism of Flem's triumph, Snopesism that had ceased to be comic. Faulkner's brilliant solution was to introduce, abruptly, the most outrageous Snopeses of all, but outrageous to the point of affectionate parody: Byron Snopes's four half-Indian children, each with his wired shipping tag addressed to Flem, the littlest one dressed in what might have been a nightshirt "or maybe a scrap of an old tent." They didn't look like people, children: "They looked like snakes." Their first exploit is to invade the Coca-Cola bottling plant for syrup. The child with the six-inch switchblade knife pulls it on the policeman who urges them to go home. Their next is to cook and presumably eat a Pekinese worth five hundred dollars. Sent by Flem to Dewitt Binford's in Frenchman's Bend, they dismantle their bed, are unaffected by knock-out opium pills; their host, venturing to approach them, receives "two thin quick streaks of fire, one down either cheek of his face. . . ." Clarence Snopes, who plans to train them to hunt in a pack, is almost burned at the stake. So the time has come to send them back to El Paso. But there have also been hints, through these pages, that the wild Indians are also, after all, children. There was the Coca-Cola syrup, and the candy bars and pop (sometimes only mud inside the candy bar papers) with which Clarence tried to train them. The scene at the station, with a considerable crowd, swiftly and affectionately restores their humanity, as Charles Mallison ventures to approach with the goodies Ratliff has provided, the eight eyes not looking at the proffered orange or at anything until the girl,

> the tallest one, said something, something quick and brittle that sounded quite strange in the treble of a child; whereupon the first hand came out and took the orange, then the next and the next, orderly, not furtive: just quick, while Ratliff and I dealt out the fruit and bars and paper bags, the empty hand already extended again, the objects vanishing somewhere faster than we could follow, except the little one in the nightshirt which apparently had no pockets: until the girl herself leaned and relieved the overflow.[2]

The final view, as they "mount and vanish one by one" into the train, is altogether affectionate. But the critical reader's experience of disengagement is more complex than this. It consists also in an amused awareness of how much the writer has "done" in less than four thousand words.

The Mansion, we have seen, audaciously creates sympathy for Mink Snopes in the days and hours preceding the murder of Flem. The stylistic modulations after the murder are quite as audacious, as Gavin Stevens and Ratliff find Mink where they had expected, in the cellar of his gutted house, "blinking up at them like a child interrupted at its bedside prayers." The first deepening of tone through style occurs as they move away from him in the dark: "Overhead, celestial and hierarchate, the constellations wheeled through the zodiacal pastures: Scorpion and Bear and Scales; beyond cold Orion and the Sisters the fallen and homeless angels choired, lamenting.'' The passage prepares us to enter Mink's primitive consciousness, and his superstitious fear of sleeping on the ground. ''So he would walk west now, since that was the direction people always went: west.'' The novel's longish last two paragraphs subtly blend Mink's consciousness and the authorial voice. Tired, his mission of over forty years accomplished, Mink decides he can now lie down, and he feels the ''first faint gentle tug'' of the ground. The final paragraph modulates through his sense of his identity beginning to creep, seep, flow into the ground, and that all will be ''mixed and jumbled up comfortable and easy there,'' to authorial eloquence, and, in full disengagement from the novel's record of suffering and absurdity, a reminder that in the dust we are equal made:

> himself among them, equal to any, good as any, brave as any, being inextricable from, anonymous with all of them: the beautiful, the splendid, the proud and the brave, right on up to the very top itself among the shining phantoms and dreams which are the milestones of the long human recording—Helen and the bishops, the kings and the unhomed angels, the scornful and graceless seraphim.[3]

The language recalls—an unconscious irony?—Ike's vision of the dawn in *The Hamlet,* as he moves toward his beloved cow, and the moment—''Helen and the bishops, the kings and the graceless seraphim''—when they are about to lie down together.[4]

The Hamlet (1940) provides a good opportunity to assess Faulkner's mastery of these arts of modulation in a whole novel, and his success in a composition blending disparate modes, tones, feelings. *The Hamlet* is not as a rule looked at in these terms.[5] It is, after all, our first full introduction to the unsubduable depraved reality of the Snopeses. It is less eccentric and less innovative in structure than *The Sound and the Fury, As I Lay Dying* and *Absalom, Absalom!*. Hence there has been a predictable emphasis on its sociological interests, and on its thematic juxtaposition of love and commerce. By the novel's end Flem, impotent but married to the book's goddess, has taken over entirely Frenchman's Bend and is ready to move on Jefferson. The importance to Faulkner of the ''real reality'' of Frenchman's Bend–Beat Four came home to me when, in 1946, he told me, as a local fact that might interest me, of federal officers vanishing in that corner of the county, but with some of their clothing presently seen on the natives—a story that appears, of course, on the second page of this novel I had reviewed for the *Boston Evening Transcript* six years before. Much of Faulkner's fiction was based on observed reality. But also his imagined Snopes world became extremely real for him, as it does for us.

The critical emphasis on a rural realism, especially when tempered with some recognition of humor, is understandable. It is nevertheless more accurate to see *The Hamlet,* even more than *As I Lay Dying,* as an artful, essentially poetic or musical composition that deliberately mixes modes: naturalism and myth, comedy and pathos, the macabre and the good-humored, violence and natural beauty; the cruel and the sordid distanced and evaluated by language. We may insist on the fact of *composition,* and on the delicate relationships among the novel's parts, even though we know that much rearrangement of earlier writing occurred. For what we have is the published book, and it is, especially after the first two chapters, an exquisitely balanced creation manipulating with assurance a variety of reader responses. The challenge to the critic, which few have undertaken, is to move through the novel from first chapter to last, noting its divers suasions and pleasures within an overall complex harmony.

Book One ("Flem"), some forty thousand words, is more episodic than the rest: a *comic history* of the arrival of the Snopeses in Frenchman's Bend, watched (as in Hardy) by a peasant chorus as well as by the shrewd itinerant Ratliff. Book Two ("Eula"), about thirty thousand words, is a playful *mock-heroic myth:* the obsessed anchorite teacher Labove and his bovine pupil Eula, the grown goddess Eula and her suitors, her marriage to the froglike Flem, and his besting of the Prince of Darkness in legal argument. Book Three ("The Long Summer") comprises the *pastoral idyll* of the idiot Ike's love for a cow, also a goddess, twelve thousand words, and the *tragic narrative* of Houston, his murder by Mink Snopes, the aftermath and Mink's arrest, some twenty-seven thousand words—both chapters conveying the intimate experience of limited minds through elaborate authorial language. Book Four ("The Peasants") brings the story—*comic, pathetic, poetic, bemused*—of the spotted horses auction and the ensuing disorder, twenty-eight thousand words, and the *sardonic coda* of the lot seeded with coins, thirteen thousand words. This time Flem has bested even Ratliff, who is momentarily corrupted by the prevalent greed.

This, in the largest terms of tonality and genre or mode, is *The Hamlet*'s movement, one that defines it as a "serious entertainment." But the overall effect and final achievement depend even more on the shifts of tone within the individual sections. It will be possible to comment on only a few.

Book One. The novel opens with an assured, formal, historian's overview of Frenchman's Bend. But the controlling intelligence, at once genial and ironic, is that of Ratliff, who was perhaps suggested by Hardy's itinerant reddleman. There is an essentially comic treatment of ruthlessness, chicanery, greed. Ab Snopes the barn burner, with the bitter *ressentiment* of the always-defeated, is the means by which Flem establishes himself in the community. But Ab is bested by the fabulous horse trader Pat Stamper. The long third chapter of this episodic book records the arrival of more Snopeses in fairly straight prose. Authorial distancing is rare.

Book Two. The shift, with the introduction of the child Eula—"too much of leg, too much of breast, too much of buttock; too much of mammalian female meat"—is to controlled, highly playful extravagance, with much abstract language. The authorial elaboration is juxtaposed ironically against scraps of country dialogue and vivid particulars of community life. The heat of the stove in the village store seems to have "an actual smell, masculine, almost monastic—a winter's concentration of unwomaned and deliberate tobacco-spittle annealing into the iron flanks." The poetic distance is built on intimate country knowledge, as of a night buggy ride:

> —the long return through night-time roads across the mooned or unmooned sleeping land, the mare's feet like slow silk in the dust as a horse moves when the reins are wrapped about the upright whip in its dashboard socket, the fords into which the unguided mare would step gingerly down and stop unchidden and drink, nuzzling and blowing among the broken reflections of stars, raising its dripping muzzle and maybe drinking again or maybe just blowing into the water as a thirst-quenched horse will.[6]

The great energizing impulse was to see both Eula and the obsessed schoolteacher Labove in terms of poetic, mock-heroic myth—he the "virile anchorite of old time"; she, now eleven, postulating "that ungirdled quality of the very goddesses in his Homer and Thucydides: of being at once corrupt and immaculate, at once virgins and the mothers of warriors and of grown men." Eula soon becomes, even for the shrewd and wary Ratliff, a true goddess, "one blind seed of the spendthrift Olympian ejaculation. . . ." But Faulkner too was obviously moved by his own myth-making, and the prose turns momentarily sentimental in its celebration of "dream and hope." His disengagement from the story, itself romantic, is a brilliant act of ironic and poetic imagination: to evoke a relic and its subsequent mundane history, one of the actual buggies that had played a part in the Olympian story. The passage is reminiscent of Dickens's nostalgic evocation of abandoned coaches in *The Uncommercial Traveller*. The disengagement from romantic myth is completed with the sudden shift to the fantasy of Flem in hell, successfully arguing with Satan, and repudiating even the offer of the gratifications, since, "for a man that only chews, any spittoon will do."

Book Three: The Long Summer. The story of Ike's love for the cow (which, it must be remembered, was sexually fulfilled) is Faulkner's most audacious experiment in aesthetic distancing. Yet elaborate rhetoric may well be a better vehicle for conveying an idiot's unspoken, in a sense unspeakable romantic love than the broken notations of Benjy's monologue:

> the bright thin horns of morning, of sun, would blow the mist away and reveal her, planted, blond, dew-pearled, standing in the parted water of the ford, blowing into the water the thick, warm, heavy, milk-laden breath; and lying in the drenched grasses, his eyes now blind with sun, he would wallow faintly from thigh to thigh, making a faint, thick, hoarse moaning sound.[7]

More pretentious passages go beyond this to suggest that Ike's love partakes not only of the quality of classical myth but of a primordial response to nature. The rhythms are at times uncomfortably close to blank verse.

The rhetoric keeps at a considerable distance acts which, lovingly romantic for the idiot, would be disgusting to a normal consciousness—Ratliff's for instance. Thus for Ike, receiving "the violent relaxing" of the cow's "fear-constricted bowels," who speaks to the cow, "trying to tell her how this violent violation of her maiden's delicacy is no shame, since such is the very "iron imperishable warp of the fabric of love." His effort to push the terrified cow up the slope of shifting sand, during the fire, is presumably a metaphorical, comic evocation of a sexual act. "Again, his shoulder to her hams, they rushed at the precipice and up it for a yard or more before the treacherous footing completely failed. He spoke to her, exhortative; they made a supreme effort," etc. A literalist will argue that there would hardly be time for sex while escaping from a fire. But this is to minimize Faulkner's humor and playfulness.[8] While describing the "real" effort to escape the fire he is also conveying the nature of Ike's sexual experience to the fringes of the reader's consciousness: an experience that may in fact occur only at the end of the section, as they "lie down together." Cleanth Brooks is probably on solid ground in repudiating the argument of T. Y. Greet, with its suggestions of the Grail legend. "It may be that the fall of rain is described only once in the novel, but water is coming from somewhere: Frenchman's Bend is no desert." [9] Yet the rain that Ike receives through his hair and shirt and against his face, while real gauzy rain, is also a metaphorical suggestion of an act of love, one that leaves them soaking wet. "His overalls are heavy and dank and cold upon him—the sorry refuse, the scornful lees of glory—a lifeless chill which is no kin to the vivid wet of the living water which has carried into and still retains within the very mud, the boundless freedom of the golden air. . . .''

The anti-romantic aftermath of the long poetic episode modulates in cool, still formal language—through a somber picture of the lonely enraged Houston, who owned the cow, and of the poor farmer whose feed Ike was stealing—to Ratliff's insistence that all dalliance with the cow, and not merely Lump Snopes's commercial exhibition of it, must stop. He agrees to the macabre cure: Ike must eat of the flesh of the loved one. ''There is evidently no doubt in Ratliff's own mind what has to be done,'' Cleanth Brooks writes, ''just as I take it there was no doubt in Faulkner's mind. The doubt, I suspect, will come only from readers who have become so habituated to the modern world of the lunatic irrational that the only crime is the inhibiting of one's own or someone else's self-expression. . . .'' [10] The question of Faulkner's moral judgment on actual bestiality strikes me as beside the point. Any such judgment was suspended for the duration of his pastoral idyll, which had been presented with full sympathy: we have been transported, through these elaborate pages, outside the ''sane moral world.'' What we do have, as often in Faulkner, is a need to provide an ironic *coda* and mock his own creation. The dying close (with I. O. and Eck bargaining madly as to how much each must pay for the cow) also serves as a transition to the second chapter: the story of Houston's marriage, his murder by Mink, the beginning of Mink's long punishment.

This long chapter is without question one of the summits of Faulkner's art: intense dramatic action as well as intense sympathy are kept under full control and at a necessary distance by a precise, rich, at times stately style. The chapter begins with what promises to be another Faulknerian story of improbable obsession: the fourteen-year-old Houston four and five and six years behind— ''bulging in Lilliput,'' ''a giant knee-deep in midgets''—repudiating the efforts of a demure girl, his future wife, to help him get through school. He flees in panic at sixteen and is away twelve years, seven of them living with a woman he had taken out of a Galveston brothel, then goes home as in volitionless return to what he had to do all along. He is happily married for a few months, a period covered in just under a page. The cold irony of such brevity is followed by one of those startling short sentence surprises by which Faulkner likes to open paragraphs: ''Then the stallion killed her.'' Three poignant paragraphs evoke Houston's solitude and grief; they are followed by another shock: ''He was still alive when he left the saddle.'' The moments of his dying, after Mink's shot, are covered in some four hundred words that brilliantly oscillate between intense monosyllabic interior monologue and abstract authorial commentary.

The transition to the deeply sympathetic picture of the murderer is also accomplished through authorial abstraction: "It was as though the very capacity of space and echo for reproducing noise were leagued against him too in the vindication of his rights and the liquidation of his injuries. . . ." This almost Johnsonian prose establishes a distance that intensifies rather than attenuates sympathy and dramatic vividness. The stylistic strategy, through much of the long section, is to maintain a calm, measured pace, with considerable formality of diction, in the presence of confusion, horror, dread—the howling of Houston's dog; the difficult stuffing of the body in the rotten hollow of a tree and its necessary extrication, with an arm now shockingly missing; the hound's attack and his return after Mink had thought him dead; the buzzards; the growing likelihood of detection. The abstract language is nearly always precise. The generalities are reinforced throughout by vivid particulars: a possum's "choked infant-like cry, scrabbling among the sticks" or the "rasping off with his knuckles" of the tree's rotten fibre, "so that a faint, constant, dry powder of decay filled his nostrils like snuff."

We are alone with Mink (or with him, and the corpse, and the hound) for over seven thousand words (226–36, 253–59). Intensity is thus sustained at extraordinary length, and through largely expository prose. The long interruption in the narrative, surely longer than was necessary, is unevenly successful. There is sardonic rightness in Lump Snopes's moral outrage because Mink had failed to take the money from Houston's body, and in his insistence that they return together to recover it. Mink's strategy in stalling him off—to propose a game of checkers, a game described in some detail—is a reductive intrusion of authorial playfulness; there is no place in Mink's barren life for games. But the evocation of Mink's leaving home at twenty-three is very moving. He was seeking the sea. "Perhaps he was seeking only the proffer of this illimitable space and irremediable forgetting along the edge of which the contemptible teeming of his own earth-kind timidly seethed and recoiled. . . ." He finds employment at a logging camp, and there meets his future wife: "he saw not a nympholept but the confident lord of a harem." In time he too has his chance to enter her bed, that "fierce simple cave of a lioness." The sudden shift from authorial aloofness and amused abstraction occurs with their abrupt marriage, after the failure of the logging enterprise. It is another instance of dramatic transition to the vivid particular, and to another artful blend of the pathetic and the comic.

> They returned to his native country, where he rented a small farm on shares. They had a second-hand stove, a shuck mattress on the floor, the razor with which he still kept her hair cut short, and little else. At that time they needed little else. She

said: "I've had a hundred men, but I never had a wasp before. That stuff comes out of you is rank poison. It's too hot. It burns itself and my seed both up. It'll never make a kid." But three years afterward it did. Five years later it had made two; and he would watch them as they approached across whatever sorry field or patch, fetching his cold meagre dinner or the jug of fresh water. . . .[11]

The chapter concludes with the fall and exceptionally cold winter, as Mink waits in jail for Flem to return from Texas and save him, and with a glimpse— in bitter disengagement from so many pages of dramatic and sympathetic intensity—of Ike playing with a battered wooden effigy of a cow.

Book Four. The story of Flem's horses, no doubt best-known as the separately published "Spotted Horses," has a rather different impact when read as part of *The Hamlet.* "Spotted Horses," ending with the appalled judge's adjournment of the court, is wonderfully self-enclosed. There is no past or future, and the outside world scarcely exists. But the pathos of Mrs. Armstid is intensified in the novel, which ends with Henry digging madly for coins on the Frenchman's Place, Flem watching him. The structural effect of the spotted horses narrative, in the novel, is to provide needed relief, a change in tone and perspective, after the long immersion in two impoverished, tragic, certainly abnormal lives.

The narrative, whether read as a separate long story or as part of a novel, is a masterpiece of timing. The escape and flight of the horses has been prepared from the first page, where we see them "gaudy motionless and alert, wild as deer, deadly as rattlesnakes, quiet as doves." Faulkner's comic imagination was energized by "outrage": rational expectation confronted by the unexpected, the madly inappropriate, stillness suddenly translated into violent motion. The ponies, who have never seen corn, are quietly ranged along the feeding-trough, but greet the dry rattling of the corn-pellets with "a single snort of amazed horror," then a cracked plank and the hallway dissolving "in loud fury." The converse is delayed, as though unbelieving, response, as in some animated cartoons. The ponies turn the barn door into matchwood, but the boy Eck still keeps his eye to the vanished knot-hole. The horse in Mrs. Littlejohn's house, having just crashed into the melodeon (which "produced a single note, almost a chord, in bass, resonant and grave, of deep and sober astonishment") is outraged, on entering a bedroom, to discover Ratliff in his underclothes and with a sock in his hand. But Ratliff is outraged too. "For an instant he and the horse glared at one another. Then he sprang through the window as the horse backed out of the room and into the hall again and whirled and saw Eck and the little boy just entering the front door. . . ." The horse, confronting Ratliff again, still carrying the sock, now gallops "to the end of the veranda and took the railing and soared outward, hobgoblin and floating, in the moon."

The narrative of the spotted horses, though based on swindle, one more instance of Flem's shrewd rapacity, is more concerned with the appeal of wildness and beauty to the minds of inert men. They are not, except Henry Armstid, drawn to buy the horses by greed, but instead by a phantom and useless beauty inextricable from violence: the horses "like partridges flushing, each wearing a necklace of barbed wire," whipping and whirling "about the lot like dizzy fish in a bowl," or in "the treacherous and silver receptivity" of the moonlight, "huddled in mazy camouflage, or singly or in pairs rushed, fluid, phantom, and unceasing, to huddle again in mirage-like clumps from which came high abrupt squeals and the vicious thudding of hooves." There may well be a sexual component to the taming of the beautiful and wild. The horses, in any event, appeal to something untamed in the hearts of quiet men, and to a not entirely unconscious sense of beauty. The men of this mean dusty village are close to surrounding nature, and can discuss when a mockbird appears, or whether gum or willow flowers first.

The juxtaposition of beauty and violence, embodied in the phantom horses, has its quiet counterpart in rhetoric: meanness and depravity distanced by the beauty of natural objects, and distanced too by beauty of phrasing and the intervention, through fanciful simile and metaphor, of an authorial consciousness. One man holds "a spray of peach bloom between his teeth. It bore four blossoms like miniature ballet skirts of pink tulle." And the twigs and branches of a pear tree stand "motionless and perpendicular above the horizontal boughs like the separate and upstreaming hair of a drowned woman sleeping upon the uttermost floor of the windless and tideless sea." The audacity of analogies so remote from Frenchman's Bend may be disturbing at a first reading. But they are, meanwhile, controlling responses that might otherwise have been too dark. The depressing moment of Mrs. Armstid's defeat is made tolerable by quiet loveliness of phrasing, and the loveliness of a timeless scene evocative both of teeming life and of death: peach and pear trees resembling "a hive swarmed about by a cloud of pink-and-white bees," a graveyard and mourning doves.

The ensuing trial scene, though touching again the pathetic cord of Mrs. Armstid's poverty—"I would know them five dollars. I earned them myself, weaving at night after Henry and the chaps was asleep"—is largely comic, told for the most part through baffled, outraged dialogue. It is followed by two expository pages devoted to the trial of Mink, who watches the back of the courtroom for Flem to appear, and who scarcely seems to pay attention even when sentenced to life imprisonment. The final chapter, as Ratliff, Bookright and Armstid dig for treasure at the Frenchman's Place they have gullibly bought from Flem, is a further removal from the poetic intensities and passions of "The Long Summer." The house they have bought is a decayed relic of a glamorous past; the coins they find were seeded by Flem. But even the sardonic last lines, as Flem watches the maddened Armstid dig, have their place in a controlled and serene *composition. The Hamlet,* though less eccentric than a number of other Faulkner novels, and though certainly lacking the tragic magnitude of *Absalom, Absalom!,* deserves to be read far more than it has been, and read as an essentially poetic achievement.

The relationship of Faulkner's temperament to his fictional techniques and imagined world—his discovery of his true voice—could well occupy a long book, the more so because his practice was far more varied than Conrad's. The problem of assessing fictional energy is, with Faulkner, more elusive. Conrad's imagination noticeably dulled, and his prose faltered, whenever the creative situation was in some way false. But Faulkner, notoriously, could develop intellectual and imaginative excitement and continue to write vigorously (though not "well") even when, for a few sentences or paragraphs, he scarcely knew what he was talking about. He could also write well (and this was rarely true with Conrad) in a manner that was not noticeably his own: even, as in *Sanctuary,* in the manner of Flaubert. There are, moreover, wide variants within a recognizable Faulknerian voice, as there are wide variants in the voice of Dickens.

There is very little that is recognizably Faulknerian in the language of the *New Orleans Sketches,* and much imitative or decadent writing in *Soldiers' Pay.* Yet a Faulknerian voice and play of irony are present in the novel's second sentence, as Conrad's voice in the first sentence of *Almayer's Folly:*

> He suffered the same jaundice that many a more booted one than he did, from Flight Commanders through Generals to the ambrosial single-barred (not to mention that inexplicable beast of the field which the French so beautifully call an aspiring aviator); they had stopped the war on him.

Mosquitoes too is a relatively imitative book. But a characteristic playfulness (a visual absurdity, amusingly inflated rhetoric) appears abruptly early in the novel: "She had a brief and dreadful vision of having to put back short one guest, of inquest and reporters and headlines, and of floating inert buttocks in some lonely reach of the lake, that would later wash ashore with that mute inopportune implacability of the drowned." The classic instance of full self-discovery is, surely, that apostrophe to the mule in *Sartoris* (and *Flags in the Dust*). The first sentence is precise, controlled, beautifully modulated traditional writing. But with the third sentence, as Faulkner suddenly recognizes what he is free to do—e.g. anything—we find the running rhythm and analogical extravagance of much later fiction. The third sentence is certainly not as good as the first, but it takes a necessary step toward the great prose of *Absalom, Absalom!*.

> Round and round the mule went, setting its narrow, deer-like feet delicately down in the hissing cane-pith, its neck bobbing limber as a section of rubber hose in the collar, with its trace-galled flanks and flopping, lifeless ears and its half-closed eyes drowsing venomously behind pale lids, apparently asleep with the monotony of its own motion. Some Homer of the cotton fields should sing the saga of the mule and of his place in the South. He it was, more than any other one creature or thing, who, steadfast to the land when all else faltered before the hopeless juggernaut of circumstance, impervious to conditions that broke men's hearts because of his venomous and patient preoccupation with the immediate present, won the prone South from beneath the iron heel of Reconstruction and taught it pride again through humility, and courage through adversity overcome; who accomplished the well-nigh impossible despite hopeless odds, by sheer and vindictive patience. Father and mother he does not resemble, sons and daughters he will never have. . . .[12]

To move thus from book to book, to the genial extravagances of *The Reivers,* would be tempting. Instead I will merely suggest, in highly schematic brevity, what appear to be the most congenial and uncongenial materials for Faulkner, and the most congenial and uncongenial techniques.

Uncongenial Materials. The early Faulkner here too shows affinities with the early Conrad of *The Sisters* and "The Return": a lack of dynamic interest in sophisticates, bohemians, artists. The liberated authorial consciousness of the later fiction delights in the play of logic and, especially in *A Fable,* in a flow of erudition. But "intellectuals" are as a rule unenergizing, and, luckily, few. So too ministers, unless they are black. Faulkner loves legal nonsense. But the well-meaning, often sentimental lawyers with whom he sometimes identifies, even while satirizing them—notably Horace Benbow and Gavin Stevens— rarely evoke dynamic writing; the moral intelligence of Ratliff, with his country humor and colloquialism, is more congenial. Faulkner's imagination, like Conrad's, is ill at ease in coping with normal love and normal sexuality, as we have seen, or with young white women generally. It is of course axiomatic that imagination flagged on the rare occasions that it abandoned Yoknapatawpha County, though a few very isolated places are rendered vividly: the mine and the lakeside cabin in *The Wild Palms,* the desert outpost in *A Fable.* An exception to the general urban failure is Memphis. The familiar axiom is that the novelist is at his best with what he "really knows": Conrad's sailing ships or, for Hemingway, the minute rituals of fishing. But Faulkner was far from his best in writing about flyers and flying. The romantic Levine of *A Fable* may have evoked the wrong kind of authorial identification in Faulkner, who wove devious myths about his period with the Canadian Air Force.

Congenial Materials. The great energizing subjects and zones of interest are too familiar, even too unmistakable, to require illustration: the history, sociology, geography of Yoknapatawpha County and Mississippi, the Snopeses and Sartorises and Compsons and McCaslins and Beauchamps, the shadowy impinging of the romantic and cursed past, the sense of historical fatality; negroes and black-white relations generally; family tension, love and conflict, with incest and fratricide tragic potentiality; individual and collective self-destructive drives; obsessive ambition and obsessive desire for revenge; hunting, and the masculine society of hunters; even drinking, which may overcome barriers of neurosis, race, caste—the jug of whiskey and toddies lovingly made; the ideal Quest and fulfillment of an obligation, which may be absurd (*As I Lay Dying*) or noble (*The Bear*) or both noble and absurd. The "old man" looking down from a hilltop on Jefferson and the county, in *The Town,* is surely not Gavin Stevens, not yet forty, but Faulkner himself:

> And you stand suzerain and solitary above the whole sum of your life beneath that incessant ephemeral spangling. . . . you to preside unanguished and immune above this miniature of man's passions and hopes and disasters—ambition and fear and lust and courage and abnegation and pity and honor and sin and pride—all bound, precarious and ramshackle, held together by the web, the iron-thin warp and woof of his rapacity but withal yet dedicated to his dreams.[13]

The Faulknerian imagination, surely more than most great writers', is both compassionate and ironic. We have already seen, as particularly energizing, the irony of paradoxical sympathies. Walter Slatoff has exhaustively defined Faulkner's polar imagination, and its love of antithesis and paradox, a world of pairs of entities in opposition or tension. These may also be said to belong to a general vision of *the absurd* (or, in Faulkner's word, *outrage*): the sudden shifts in circumstance, the backfiring of reasonable plan, the thwarting of obsessive expectation. This pessimistic vision is essentially comic, as it is not in Camus. Particular absurdities of every kind are energizing. The absurd predicament may be macabre: Mink compelled to wrestle with a disintegrating corpse or Gowrie, in *Intruder in the Dust,* to watch the corpse of his son emerge from quicksand. The dissolution of Eck Snopes, with only the neck-brace left for ceremonial burial, has the more genial tonality of black humor. Faulkner delights, as did Dickens, in mad logic and forensic nonsense, in legal absurdities and complicated swindles, in petty chicanery, in barter so involved as to invite, from Cleanth Brooks, scholarly footnote and diagram.

Above all, and repetitively, at last tiresomely, Faulkner is drawn to the comedy (which was sometimes tragic) of locked mental process. Dostoevsky had, of course, a greater and far subtler psychological understanding of the unconscious. But no writer has emphasized more insistently than Faulkner the discrepancy between conscious awareness and preconscious or unconscious drive, or dramatized more frequently less than conscious "knowledge": *he did not even know that he knew that he did not know that he knew,* etc. ("thinking" and "believing," at a crucial moment in *Light in August,* specifically refer to unconscious mental processes). A character may be unaware of his motives, of his unformulated "thoughts," even of his present physical actions, and so experience the delayed reaction of a figure in a film cartoon who falls to earth only when he discovers he is flying. Faulkner is fascinated by the obsessive who, like McEachern, moves as in a trance, by the group that acts without volition. Irresolution and neurotic immobilization are the converse of obsessive-compulsive drives that occupy the better part of a lifetime, Thomas Sutpen's most notably. Some characters are released from tension only in dying; some, Slatoff remarks, "presumably go on seething forever." [14]

Uncongenial Techniques. Here too Faulkner exhibits Conradian tendencies and difficulties. He is least at his ease, or least interesting, with impersonal third-person narration through one character's relatively normal consciousness: with, that is, the standard point-of-view of run-of-the-mill realistic fiction. "If George had just stuck to farming the land which Edmonds had allotted him he would just as soon Nat married George as anyone else, sooner than most of the nigger bucks he knew." He is also, even more than Dickens, uncomfortable with realistic dialogue in standard middle-class English. His imagination—though there are notable exceptions (*Sanctuary,* some of the short stories)—is thwarted by an unmediated fictional *presentness.* There are great dramatic scenes that appear to take place before our eyes in a present place and time. But we may discover, on close scrutiny, that some form of distance usually exists for the author's imagination. Strict chronology as well as chronological presentness, the attempt to convey an even flow of time, can also have a stultifying influence.

In one area my own reaction is, I suspect, not widely shared: that Faulkner did not find the truncated interior monologue, the monologue in which we have a shorthand reduction of the flow of consciousness, congenial: Benjy's monologue and some of the monologues in *As I Lay Dying.* These monologues are ingenious, intelligently conceived, perhaps plausible in their content. But they are not, I think, the work of an *energized* imagination.

Congenial Techniques. Even more than Conrad, Faulkner delighted in the "prolonged hovering flight of the subjective," the meditative freedoms, leaps and surprises of the impressionist narrator. He flourished on a total authorial freedom (sometimes with no narrator) to sweep back and forth in time and place and from the abstract to the particular, from concrete event to extended commentary. His great pleasure was to surprise with a fine excess: a rich play of simile and metaphor and extended fanciful analogue, with the referents as wildly mixed as in *Paradise Lost*. The temperamental delight in evasiveness and irresolution led him to erect many screens between himself and the fiction, the fiction and the reader. But imaginative freedom as well as deliberate obfuscation could profit by specific techniques: notably the technique of narration by conjecture learned from Conrad. A further freedom was to dramatize vividly and at length what did not happen but might have: a modified play of conjecture.

It may be appropriate at this point to comment on an interesting and ambitious failure which receives little critical attention, but which illustrates starkly some of these assumptions concerning the congenial and the uncongenial: *Pylon*. The treatment of flying is conventionally dramatic but generally more convincing than in *A Fable*. Faulkner did not fly overseas, but did have a small aerial circus, with his brother Dean killed in a crash shortly after *Pylon* was completed, life strangely imitating art. Faulkner's indirect responsibility—he had encouraged his brother's flying—was distantly comparable to that of the novel's newspaper reporter. Faulkner was also writing for the first time extensively about something else he knew well: drunkenness. The craving for alcohol in *Pylon* is authentic, and the stumbling confusion of the drunk; what is lacking is the powerfully analogical, at times demonic consciousness of Malcolm Lowry's Consul, and its consistently rich language. *Pylon* and *Absalom, Absalom!* are contemporary. But an aerial circus amid the confusion of Mardi Gras, and the reporter's dismayed venture into the alien lives of the barnstorming sexual triad, could not challenge the imagination as did the mythical grandeur of Thomas Sutpen's story in its nineteenth-century simplicities and, even, Old Testament timelessness. The intruding yet passive reporter has his affinities with both Byron Bunch and Gavin Stevens. The insistence on his cadaverous appearance, vaguely reminiscent of *Death in Venice,* even gives him a certain interest they lack.

The greatest difficulty was that of uncongenial technique, very evident in the odd mixture of styles. The action takes place in an ongoing present time and fixed present place, with the flyers' actions and their tough unstylized colloquialisms for the most part rendered naturalistically: a *presentness,* for the imagination, that Faulkner regularly found uncongenial. The novel lacks *Sanc-*

tuary's protective obfuscations and taut selectivity, and lacks the compelling unity of "Wild Palms," where the solitude of the lovers was protective. *Pylon*'s fairly standard realist method had to struggle, moreover, against both a macabre conception and a strong impulse to liberate language: to use the running rhythms and ironic elaborations of *Absalom, Absalom!*. The rhetorical situation was even more complicated than this. For Faulkner was also experimenting with two other styles. One involved distinctly Joycean rhythms and word play; the other an altogether mechanical production of doublets made from very common words (*windowbase, lightpoised, greasestained* in the novel's first short sentence). The novel's second paragraph, to befuddle further an unprepared reader, attempts the dry geometric notation of trivia exploited in the 1950's by Robbe-Grillet: "rubber soles falling in quick hissing thuds on pavement and iron sill and then upon the tile floor of that museum of glass cases lighted by an unearthly daycolored substance in which the hats and ties and shirts. . . ."

The two more consciously new styles—the doublets made of common words and the richer Joycean coinages—may be combined in a single sentence, and combined too with flat standard English. The "subject" is, simply, the confusion of downtown traffic:

> Now they could cross Grandlieu Street. There was traffic in it now; to clash and clang of light and bell trolley and automobile crashed and glared across the intersection, rushing in a light curbchanneled spindrift of tortured and draggled serpentine and trodden confetti pending the dawn's whitewings—spent tinseldung of Momus' Nilebarge clatterfalque.[15]

Joyce, confronting the distantly comparable confusions of Nighttown, succeeded by assuring the dominance of a distancing and distorting consciousness: the "mind" and "voice" of the italicized stage-directions. So too, in *Absalom, Absalom!* an overriding Faulknerian "voice" dominates and permeates the voices of the several narrators and even the letter-writing of Charles Bon.

There is, then, an initial tension between a realistically noted urban and professional world and a macabre vision of doomed flyers, observed by a sometimes symbolic reporter; and a conflict in method between the realistic notation and several experimental styles. What Faulkner needed, since *imaginative presentness* was at the root of his troubles, was a focus of narration that would permit him to distance the material, that would achieve the congenial "prolonged hovering flight of the subjective." There are isolated moments where the attempt to convey drunkenness so liberates: "All he heard now was that thunderous silence and solitude in which a man's spirit crosses the eternal repetitive rubicon of his vice in the instant after the terror and before the triumph becomes dismay—the moral and spiritual waif shrieking his feeble I-am-I into the desert of chance and disaster.'' But Faulkner's most desperate (and most obvious) stratagem for achieving needed distance was to have the reporter, telephoning or talking to his editor, recapitulate the action in the manner of an impressionist narrator. The exasperated editor—who says he wants no Lewises or Hemingways or even Tchekovs on his staff—simply becomes the generally silent listener of *Lord Jim* or *Absalom, Absalom!*.

The reporter, with his instant commitment to the flyers and his faintly occult overtones, is one of Faulkner's more interesting fictional "ideas." But his role is doubly uncertain: rhetorically awkward, as we have seen, but psychologically too, since his sentimental attraction to Laverne must also serve as a vehicle for the author's misogyny. In any event he is not present, as actor or direct observer, in the novel's two finest scenes—the flashback account of Laverne's absurd sexual assault on the pilot, on the occasion of her first parachute jump, and the very moving straightforward narrative of her leaving her son with Schumann's father. In this second scene, at least, imaginative presentness was not crippling.

Albert Camus's high praise of *Pylon* can hardly be explained except in terms of an inadequate knowledge of English. But the novel is one of those strange, courageous, ambitious failures by which Faulkner thought a writer should be judged.

The authorial voice, at its most liberated, is (for better and worse) what I call "Faulknerese." The allusion is to Conrad's reference, protectively ironic, to his own luxuriant early style as "Conradese." It may be useful, finally, to look at some of the variants of "Faulknerese," and note under what conditions the liberations occur.

The extreme examples of liberated prose, in *Requiem for a Nun* and especially *A Fable,* combine mental gymnastics with racing rhythms that can become obsessive: a broken record spinning out of control. The elaborate language of "Old Man," to return to it once more, shows masterful control of distance. It conveys the essentials of the convict's experience, yet remains savingly outside the moment-by-moment flow of his limited consciousness. The stylistic elevation permits the narrative to generalize that experience, make it as symbolic of fundamental human plight as *The Nigger of the Narcissus* or "Amy Foster," where a simple well-meaning peasant is cast up from the waters and born into a hostile incomprehensible environment. It is doubtless excessive to say that the convict's prison is the secure place from which we are unwillingly drawn and to which we long to return. But the river in flood is unmistakably symbolic, and the convict's "absolutely gratuitous predicament." His simple longing for order *and meaning* is incessantly flouted by nature and circumstance. The narrative is dominated by imagery of birth. The actual birth of the child is coincident with the skiff reaching "that quarter-acre mound, that earthen Ark out of Genesis, that dim wet cypress-choked life-teeming constricted desolation" (with the first life encountered a snake) where darkness had "crept forth again to spread upon the waters."

The language of philosophical discourse, of mythical and archetypal experience, even of Biblical overtone, has much the effect it has at a crucial moment in *The Nigger of the Narcissus*. Thus Conrad, in the transitional paragraph that follows the storm and old Singleton heroically at the wheel: the men reprieved by the sea's disdainful mercy "must without pause justify their life to the eternal pity that commands toil to be hard and unceasing, from sunrise to sunset, from sunset to sunrise. . . ." The passage is echoed by Faulkner, with the convict about to fight his first alligator before the eyes of the astonished Cajan, in a place

> set in that teeming and myriad desolation, enclosed and lost within the furious embrace of flowing mare earth and stallion sun, divining through pure rapport of kind for kind, hill-billy and bayou rat, the two one and identical because of the same grudged dispensation and niggard fate of hard and unceasing travail not to gain future security, a balance in the bank or even in a buried soda can for slothful and easy old age, but just permission to endure. . . .[16]

The historical essays of *Requiem for a Nun* contain some of the most liberated examples of "Faulknerese": non-stop sentences seemingly as effortless as Wordsworth's blank verse paragraphs. The three long essays exploit the freedoms of Conradian impressionism, and many more. The "hovering flight of the subjective" is not limited to named narrators, as in much of *Absalom, Absalom!,* nor is there a dominating fictive intelligence (Ike's blending with the author's) as in Part Four of *The Bear*. The freedom is, simply and totally, the author's in his congenial *persona* as historian of Yoknapatawpha County. The stranger of the third essay, "The Jail," taken to see the name of Cecilia Farmer etched in glass, 1861, and to hear her story, finds himself in the position of the helpless listener of Captain Mitchell, the historian of Costaguana, stunned and annihilated by obscure allusion. Even this stranger can become a vehicle or pretext for intensely visualized conjecture, as he is drawn

> from ninety years away by that incredible and terrifying passivity, watching in your turn through and beyond that old milk-dim disfigured glass that shape, that delicate frail and useless bone and flesh departing pillion on a mule without one backward look, to the reclaiming of an abandoned and doubtless even ravaged (perhaps even usurped) Alabama hill farm. . . .[17]

The merit of the method is also, of course, its defect: the freedom to admit "anything"—even, with the uncongenial return to modern times, Mistinguette: "possessed of a half-century more of years than the mere three score or so she bragged and boasted. . . ." There is a more pleasing freedom to remanipulate old legend, a new version of Sutpen's French architect, a nightly captive now, "tied wrist to wrist with one of his captor's Carib slaves," and imagined by day (a reminiscence of *Benito Cereno?*)

> in his mudstained brier-slashed brocade and lace standing in a trackless wilderness dreaming colonnades and porticoes and fountains and promenades in the style of David, with just behind each elbow an identical giant helf-naked Negro not even watching him, only breathing, moving each time he took a step or shifted like his shadow repeated in two and blown to gigantic size. . . .[18]

A baffled glance at *Requiem for a Nun* (the unheard-of interlocking of essays and play, the first marathon sentences) has probably deterred many readers who might enjoy the book. The prose is on the whole distinctly less irresponsible than *A Fable*'s, and the impressionist history is by no means as difficult as *Absalom, Absalom!*'s, since essential information is rarely withheld. It is perhaps best to read the essays as mythologized history, distorted to render a more poetic if not truer meaning, history as metaphor. The fanciful story of the "ancient monstrous padlock" is the vehicle for a fine detailed evocation of very early Jefferson. "The Courthouse" essay concludes with a beautiful image of the continuity of the South's history and its survival of periodic shocks: the pigeons and sparrows that for over a century have clustered in the courthouse belfry and still burst "out of the cupola at each stroke of the hour in frantic clouds," but after each stroke return.

There is much that is worth quoting in these essays, though the rhetoric of any one passage is almost too complicated for analysis. This is not the prose of a tired writer. The greatest passages combine, at times with highly allusive brevity, two of Faulkner's most congenial subjects—the geography of Yoknapatawpha County and Mississippi and their history. The beginning of the "Golden Dome" essay is amusing Shakespearean parody. From earliest prehistory the dome of the Jackson, Mississippi, capitol "was already decreed this rounded knob, this gilded pustule," "this knob, this pimple-dome, this buried half-ball hemisphere," "this miniscule foetus-glint," etc. The most beautiful writing interweaves glittering particular moments and large historical generalization to give a poignant sense of passing time. First the

> rich deep black alluvial soil which would grow cotton taller than the head of a man on a horse, already one jungle one brake one impassable density of brier and cane and vine interlocking the soar of gum and cypress and hickory and pinoak and ash,

printed now by the tracks of unalien shapes—bear and deer and panthers and bison and wolves and alligators and the myriad smaller beasts, and unalien men to name them too,[19]

the predecessors, recorded in Miltonic bead-roll, "the wild Algonquin, Chickasaw and Choctaw and Natchez and Pascagoula, peering in virgin astonishment down from the tall bluffs at a Chippeway canoe bearing three Frenchmen," and at last "the Anglo-Saxon, the pioneer . . . a married invincible bachelor, dragging his gravid wife and most of the rest of his mother-in-law's family behind him into the trackless infested forest,"

and at the same time scattering his ebullient seed in a hundred dusky bellies through a thousand miles of wilderness; innocent and gullible, without bowels for avarice or compassion or forethought either, changing the face of the earth: felling a tree which took two hundred years to grow, in order to extract from it a bear or a capful of wild honey. . . .[20]

A Fable, for all its obvious weaknesses, deserves more critical attention than it has received. It is a culminating work not merely in the appalling ambitiousness and formal freedom and playfulness a great writer may eventually allow himself: *Finnegans Wake, Joseph and His Brothers,* and the genial *Felix Krull* and *Ada.* It is a culminating work too in that Faulkner's temperamental ambivalence is here given its fullest play: the temperament on the one hand irresolute, evasive, ironic, infinitely devious in its protective or screening rhetoric, holding the emotion-charged material at a distance; and on the other romantic, eloquent, unashamedly poetic, at times frankly sentimental, and finding a release from tension in the rich running rhythms and in large affirmations. *A Fable* is the most generally pessimistic of Faulkner's novels but also the one with the largest number of statements about Man enduring and prevailing. The pessimism is in some respects like that of Conrad, which Conrad in turn ascribed to Anatole France:

He knows that our best hopes are irrealisable; that it is the almost incredible misfortune of mankind, but also its highest privilege, to aspire towards the impossible; that men have never failed to defeat their highest aims by the very strength of their humanity which can conceive the most gigantic tasks but leaves them disarmed before their irremediable littleness.[21]

Highly schematic and apparently written with much difficulty, *A Fable* is nevertheless more obviously charged with personal emotion than most of the earlier books: emotion not recollected in tranquility, yet immediately distanced through structural and rhetorical complication. The ideas and affirmations are from the heart; the obliquities and sudden transitions are of the nerves. Some of the most emotion-laden incidents are scarcely distanced at all; their simplicity is the more striking in a work of such baroque complication. The Christ-corporal's two earlier deaths and implied resurrections and the wedding-feast at Montfaucon reach us fairly directly through dialogue, and the last supper of the corporal and his squad is given largely scenic treatment. The final resurrection brings a chapter to a close with three simple sentences: "That was Sunday. When the girl returned with the shovel, still running, they took turns with it, all that day until it was too dark to see. They found a few more shards and fragments of the coffin, but the body itself was gone." So too there is little screening distance between the reader and the macabre ironies of the final chapter, "Tomorrow": the army detail sent to select a body for the tomb of the unknown soldier, selling the body for liquor; buying another body (the Christ-corporal's) with the proceeds of a stolen watch for which a soldier had murdered a paralyzed German colonel; and Zsettlani-Judas returning to the farm of Marthe and Marya, hoping to rid himself of the thirty coins, "the only money in my life I ever earned by honest sweat." Here Marya is both an ordinary woman on a French farm and one who knows her place (and Zsettlani's) in the Christian myth:

> "That's right," Marya said in her serene and unpitying voice. "Go now. It is not much further. You dont have much longer to despair": at which he turned, framed for a moment in the door, his face livid and intolerable, with nothing left now but the insolence, the tall feather in the hat which he had never removed breaking into the line of the lintel as if he actually were hanging on a cord from it against the vacant shape of spring darkness. Then he was gone too.
> "Have you shut up the fowls yet?" the tall sister said.
> "Of course, Sister," Marya said.[22]

This scenic simplicity is far less characteristic than distance and obliquity, and the two movements of playful or eloquent "Faulknerese": the Jamesian extremes of qualification, logic-chopping, involution, nuance; the Miltonic lyrical extravagance and running rhythms, with much delight in extended simile and esoteric allusion: a generally broken, self-denying movement on the one hand, a highly liberated one on the other. There are, of course, a number of long passages in which one mode gives way to the other, and this may occur even within a fragment of a long sentence. Thus the heroic turnkey, who had promised "to be as brave and honest and loyal as anyone could or should expect . . . turning to meet his one high moment as the male mayfly concentrates his whole one day of life in the one evening act of procreation and then relinquishes it." One of the most eloquent Miltonic surveys of civilization and its accomplishments (since rapacity does not fail) ends in dizzying involution and logic. The division into balanced pairs and triads, and the periodic inversions of syntax and, of course, the allusions to different cultures, are altogether Miltonic:

> civilization itself is its password and Christianity its masterpiece, Chartres and the Sistine Chapel, the pyramids and the rock-wombed powder-magazines under the Gates of Hercules its altars and monuments, Michelangelo and Phidias and Newton and Ericsson and Archimedes and Krupp its priests and popes and bishops; the long deathless roster of its glory—Caesar and the Barcas and the two Macedonians, our own Bonaparte and the great Russian and the giants who strode nimbused in red hair like fire across the Aurora Borealis,

on to

> Not rapacity: it does not fail; suppose Mithridates' and Heliogabalus' heir had used his heritage in order to escape his inheritees: Mithridates and Heliogabalus were Heliogabalus and Mithridates still and that scurry from Oran was still only a mouse's, since one of Grimalkin's parents was patience too and that whole St. Cyr-Toulon-Africa business merely flight, as when the maiden flees the ravisher not toward sanctuary but privacy, and just enough of it to make the victory memorable and its trophy a prize.[23]

There are times when the digressive play of mind is willfully perverse, the manipulation of distance almost compulsive, the erection of screen behind screen of allusion rather closer to Ezra Pound than to Conrad or Milton or James. This is strikingly true of the courthouse scene in the stolen horse narrative, a moment of intense drama for the participants, even of some violent physical action, but with only four hundred words of about three thousand directly recording that scene, all the rest vivid digression and delay. Some twelve hundred words convey the lapse of time, presumably less than a minute, between the lawyer's recognition that he must be a leader, one of those who control men, and his beginning to speak. There are a number of brief digressive and vivid particulars, within the three thousand words, and (if we include the beginning of the lawyer's rabble-rousing speech, which takes us very far from the courthouse) five major digressions:

1. The lawyer is not alone, since he has behind him the "long heroic roster who were the milestones of the rise of man": "Caesar and Christ, Bonaparte and Peter and Mazarin and Alexander, Genghis and Talleyrand and Warwick," etc. 175 words. (The Faulknerian lists of worthies are, to be sure, generally shorter than those of Joyce.)

2. The lawyer's driver, a mulatto murderer, is compared to d'Artagnan, to a disobedient hunting dog wired to a dead game bird, to a surgeon (in the backhanded slash of the razor), to a bullfighter. The murder, as the lawyer imagined it, had the quality of ballet. 275 words.

3. The lawyer, also compared to a bullfighter at the outset, as well as to the old pagan splashing the hearth ritually, "in recognition of them who had matched him with his hour upon the earth," decides to speak. There is a long disquisition on a painting which he claims "to have bought for the sole purpose of not having to pretend that he liked it." The passage seems to say that heroic opportunity, like aesthetic experience, is gratuitous. But I would not bet on this meaning. 385 words.

4. The rabble-rousing speech, which warns of capitalists and New England factory owners willing "to divert to the farthest corners of the earth the just profits of your sweat and labor," etc. 300 words.

5. The crowd, with "the remorseless unhurried flow of spilled ink across a table cloth," evokes a commentary on man's "ability to move *en masse*" (which will presently be exploited in Detroit), and a Miltonic wild congeries of examples. 500 words.

It may be of interest, finally, to enumerate some of the conditions under which unironic or sentimental Faulknerese appears in *A Fable:* elevated diction and highly emotive abstraction, running rhythms that move toward incantation, euphoniously and logically balanced syntax. The prose can be a reliable index to the fictional and historical materials that particularly moved Faulkner in this novel. This could also be put in a less friendly way by lovers of the plain style. What areas of sentimental affirmation evoke such relaxed and often self-imitative writing? Either way we discern a close correspondence of temperament and prose style. The one thing we cannot say (as we have to say of the later Conrad) is that words failed him.

A few of the conditions of liberated "Faulknerese" in *A Fable:*

Echoes, possibly unconscious, of his own work. The forms of Faulknerian self-imitation are legion, and can be unconsciously amusing. The rescue of the fabulous horse in Cajan country echoes directly the rescue of the pregnant woman in "Old Man": (the hummock and small island in the swamp, the pirogue and gobble talk, the groom's setting of the horse's hip corresponding to the tall convict's assistance at the birth). The most interesting form of reminiscence would seem to involve "objective correlative." A strong emotion, in the contemplation of a "new" situation or character, appears to evoke certain verbal formulas and even physical movements associated with deeply moving moments in earlier work. Virtually ritual phrases and gestures, perhaps coming automatically to mind, determine the emotional response to the "new" material. The division commander under arrest—"solitary, kinless, alone, pariah and orphan"—evokes not merely some of *The Bear*'s larger affirmations but even the very language of Ike's confrontation with the bear, and the bear's backward look. An anthology could be made of significant backward looks in Faulkner's work.

The improbable heroism of the "little man." The condemned man who suddenly elects life over salvation, on hearing the bird, is an obvious instance. The groom-sentry evokes a rich rhetoric even in the listing of his negative qualities:

> fatherless, wifeless, sterile and perhaps even impotent too, misshapen, savage and foul: the world's portionless and intractable and inconsolable orphan, who brought without warning into that drowsing vacuum an aggregation bizarre, mobile and amazing as a hippodrome built around a comet. . . .[24]

The grand movement of history, which may connect the present with both a remote past and the earth's last days. The garrison town with its Place de Ville, as the general looks out on it, is effaced "back into man's enduring anguish and his invincible dust," and evokes a Miltonic evocation of hierarchy, a long enumeration of civilians and their professions of even Roman times (with characteristically Miltonic absurd analogy), at last a reveling in language evoked by "the dark Gothic dream." The long flight, some thirteen hundred words, undergoes a number of changes in tone.

Generalizations on "Truth," which is suddenly recognized and accepted. The presumably nebulous and elevated emotion involved in such passages calls forth rhetorical devices which have a sentimental effect: the *not even . . . but, not only . . . but* sequences and their balancings of paradox. The "then in the next instant dismissed it forever" formula has been used more than once before in highly emotive contexts and moments of recognition:

> and then in the next second dismissed it forever because what remained had not only to be the answer but the truth too; or not even *the* truth, but *truth,* because truth was truth: it didn't have to be anything; it didn't even care whether it was so or not even, looking (the deputy) at it not even in triumph but in humility, because an old Negro minister etc.[25]

Legend. The very concept of legend and man's response to it evokes a rich and emotional prose. The General is told he "will lie weightless across the face of France from Mozambique to Miquelon, and Devil's Island to the Treaty Ports like a barely remembered odor, a fading word, a habit, a legend—an effigy cut by a jigsaw for souvenirs, becoming whole only over a café or mess table in Brazzaville or Saigon or Cayenne or Tananarive. . . ." Like Milton, Faulkner reserves his richest eloquence for the extreme situations in which his Satan (who is also God the Father and at times even Christ) finds himself. His desert post, as imagined by his admirers, evokes a decidedly Miltonic rhetoric and play of mind: "would slumber hierarchate and superposed benignant and inscrutable, irascible and hieroglyph like an American Indian totem pole in ebon Eden innocence. . . .''

It is easy to ridicule the more mechanical moments of the Christ-corporal allegory. But it is obvious that the author, for all his time-charts and schematic structurings, was deeply moved by it. It would appear to be most successful where the participants exhibit both the bewilderment of a simple peasant mentality in the presence of events moving beyond their volition and a dim sense that they are playing a part in a myth. The return to the farm, after the execution of the corporal, leads to a curious suspension of disbelief in the Christian story itself; one finds himself thinking, *Yes, it might have been like that!* The voice of Marthe-Magda combines simplicity and richness of language in describing the corporal's birth, becomes suave and philosophical as it evokes the westward journey to rescue the son from his father: "A curse and doom which in time was to corrupt the very kindly circumambience which harbored us because already you are trying to ask how we managed to pass through Asia Minor in order to reach Western Europe, and I will tell you."

Ceremony. An elaborately sacramental prose is prompted, not surprisingly, by the ossuary where the men go to select the Unknown Soldier. But a final irony is that Faulkner was so deeply moved by his account of the old General's (now Marshal's) funeral that he momentarily subverted his own repudiation of war. The emotion may have been generated by the "aged batman who had outlived him," carrying "the sheathed sabre, his head bowed a little over it like an aged acolyte with a fragment of the Cross or the ashes of a saint." The old General was born in the same year as Marshal Pétain, who put down the French army mutiny of 1916. But in the novel's final pages he would appear to be Marshal Foch:

> But still there was only the dirge of day, the dirge of victorious and grieving France, the dirge of Europe and from beyond the seas too where men had doffed the uniforms in which they had been led through suffering to peace by him who lay now beneath the draped flag on the caisson, and even further than that where people who had never heard his name did not even know that they were still free because of him. . . .[26]

It is the mark of the great writer that he can make readers believe anything: the sun standing still over Gibeon, and the moon over Ajalon. Less frequent (but with Milton the great historic example) is the writer whose rhetoric is sufficiently powerful as to make himself believe anything; or, even, for a brief time, subvert his own strongest beliefs.

9
MARTIN CHUZZLEWIT: THE NOVEL AS COMIC ENTERTAINMENT

No single novel is as representative of Dickens as *The Possessed* is of Dostoevsky or *Absalom, Absalom!* of Faulkner. For the idiosyncratic *Old Curiosity Shop* and the quietly personal *David Copperfield* are quintessential Dickens; so too the masterfully controlled *Bleak House,* with its dark vision of an England menaced by inefficiency and waste, and by criminal neglect of the poor. But *Martin Chuzzlewit* is a superb model of the novel as comic entertainment, one that shows Dickens at the height of his inventive (not programmatic) powers, and with possibly the greatest triumphs in the area where he excelled all other novelists: the creation of life through absurd mannerism and speech. It transcends, moreover, most of the limitations its early Victorian public would have liked to impose. We can enjoy its dark sardonic side and anti-realist distortions far more than the 1840's (or even 1940's) could, and tolerate better its looseness of structure.

A number of reasons have been adduced for the relatively poor sale (20,000 at the outset, rising to 23,000) of the monthly parts. Forster stresses the change back to monthly publication after the public had become accustomed to the weekly installments of *The Old Curiosity Shop* and *Barnaby Rudge*. Harsh criticism of *American Notes* may have had some effect. But it is also true that the novel begins very uninterestingly, and achieves sustained life only in the third monthly part, with the movement to London in chapter 8. There are further *longueurs* in chapters 10 and 12; and it is only with the desperate stratagem of the move to America that the novel discovers energies that carry through to the end.

In the eighth monthly part, the gloomy but interesting household of Anthony Chuzzlewit, Chuffey and Jonas awaits the reader, and most of all Sairey Gamp, who lodges at a bird fancier's. Such is the energy that radiates from her that even the birds are brought instantly to life:

> in every pane of glass there was at least one tiny bird in a tiny bird-cage, twittering and hopping his little ballet of despair and knocking his head against the roof: while one unhappy goldfinch who lived outside a red villa with his name on the door, drew the water for his own drinking, and mutely appealed to some good man to drop a farthing's worth of poison in it.[1]

We see this bird again some five hundred pages later, alarmed by the uproar of Sairey Gamp and Betsy Prig that follows upon the latter's denial of Mrs. Harris's existence, and "drawing more water than he could drink in a twelve-month." (Dickens himself bought a goldfinch that drew its own water in a little bucket, but refused to do so when taken away from the shop. The merchant, appealed to, came with his evil eye. "Instantly a raging thirst beset that bird; when it was appeased, he still drew several unnecessary buckets of water; and finally, leaped about his perch and sharpened his bill, as if he had been to the nearest wine vaults and got drunk."[2])

Martin Chuzzlewit was by no means as heart-warming as its early readers would have liked. Jeffrey found it an "unpleasant" book; some reviews complained of its lack of idealism. Even the somber *Barnaby Rudge* had its blooming *soubrette* Dolly Varden (who has since lost her charm for readers) and its happy reconciliations and escapes. For nine of its nineteen months *Martin Chuzzlewit* offered little happiness and little moral goodness, and few glimpses of feminine purity and innocence. It lacked too the heart-rending (and therefore heart-warming) death scenes which, as with Little Nell or Smike, evoked religious feelings. The seventh, eighth and ninth parts ended with the apparent triumph of the wicked or the frustration of good intentions: the emigrants ruined in Eden, and Martin ill, not to be seen again for four months (chapter 23); Merry married to the vengeful Jonas (26); the cynical exchanges of Sairey and undertaker Mould (29). The superb chapter of the death watch over Anthony Chuzzlewit and the black humor of the funeral arrangements (19) might well have been repulsive to many Victorian readers. Two scoundrels dominate the novel, Pecksniff and Jonas, along with Sairey wrapped in her creature comforts and her fantasies. Pecksniff, moreover, like Monsieur Homais if not Tartuffe, could seem the very image of normal respectability in whom it was only too easy to recognize, disagreeably, oneself.

Dickens apparently could not escape this prevailing pessimism (in which he took, of course, great creative pleasure, as did Hardy with his gloomiest poems). But he was intensely aware of his readers, and at times mindful of the half-literate and the explanations they might need: "Martin's nature was a frank and generous one, but he had been bred up in his grandfather's house," etc. He was determined to provide a varied entertainment. Within a few pages, in chapter 5, there is a playful address to Tom Pinch that blends Carlyle and Sterne; and an evocation of merry England on a frosty morning, the friendly tollman and his family; and a picture of Salisbury on market-day, bursting with life. Later there is the poetry of walks in the country, edging on blank verse, and the genial Pickwick warmth of a good dinner in a well-kept inn (12). The occasion of Tom Pinch's dismissal leads to one of the novel's longest set-pieces, an exhilarating coach ride to London (36). The poetry of the Covent Garden market, an area whose disorder terrified Dostoevsky, richly anticipates Joyce's great catalogue of the Dublin market (40): pleasure in the things themselves, and in the literary act of inventory. More traditionally literary is an altogether Shakespearean flight on "braggart duty" (31).

Martin Chuzzlewit possesses its obvious themes, as is to be expected in classical comedy, and first that of isolating Self, of natural inborn egoism compounded by greed, with a rich man testing his would-be heirs. Old Martin collects his relatives at the outset, the seedy and the squabbling and the rebellious, and collects the just and the unjust near the end, for the distribution of punishments and rewards. Young Martin has escaped the prison of self, thanks to suffering and Mark Tapley's good example, but his ultimate humility toward his grandfather is hardly disinterested. All this is, on the whole, uninteresting; the theme of Selfishness seems no more central to the novel's power than Prudence to *Tom Jones*'s. Those who seek no material reward get comparatively little. Tom Pinch has his organ playing to look forward to, and his bystander's place in two *ménages-à-trois;* Mark Tapley has Mrs. Lupin and the inn. But it is noteworthy that Mark is still a servant at the celebration dinner, happily keeping his place. The real problems of education and class barriers, so prominent in *Our Mutual Friend,* are scarcely touched upon.

The more complex problems of self, of the creation and dissolution of identities, of factitious and authentic being, are raised with Pecksniff and Sairey Gamp, and subtly with Montague Tigg, for whom the money obtained by swindling seems less compelling than the pleasure of playing a role. Victorian and post-Victorian criticism emphasized moralizing theme; modern criticism discovers hidden structure and unintended "visions of things." The isolation stressed by Hillis Miller—the prison of self seen in terms of spatial enclosure, and the crisis of meaninglessness described by him and by Dorothy van Ghent, with the self lost in dizzying things—illumines certain scenes. But this may tempt us to take the novel too somberly, and to minimize its comic vivacity. Is the London labyrinth really as threatening as in other novels of Dickens? Or is it not rather exciting (the disorderly London Dickens loved) or even, as for Steven Marcus, benign?

The most isolated figures in the book, literally speaking, are Tom Pinch, while working alone for an unknown employer, and the detective-spy Nadgett, who is a solitary by profession. It might even be possible to argue an overall vision of community and connection, however intense the separative egoisms. For nearly everyone has at least a single companion. Sairey Gamp, for all her monstrous attention to her creature comforts, is physically in touch with others. The solipsistic Mrs. Harris may suggest a fundamental isolation. But isn't she, just as plausibly, the creation of an active, playful, even novelistic mind that enjoys seeing life dramatically? The novel's vision would seem less one of general isolation and confusion than of chicanery, greed, falsehood. It is the abuse of language that destroys. Pecksniff apparently believes much of what he says, and can see himself, in moments of almost unconscious hypocrisy, as a moral force. At the public level the swindle of the Anglo-Bengalee Disinterested Loan and Life Assurance Company balances, in its urban capitalist setting, the frontier swindle of Eden. Abuse of language is the strongest impression left by the American journey.

Martin Chuzzlewit offers an exceptional opportunity to examine the dynamics of fictional creation, and the flowing and fading of creative energy in a relatively simple novel. We can watch Dickens try various stratagems in an effort to bring his novel to life. The signs of fictional energy, often easy to discern, are by no means easy to define. One is *momentum:* a chapter, a scene, even a page suddenly seems to be moving under its own power. In Dickens even material things, chairs and chimneys and umbrellas, are animated, become watchful or malevolent. The pace of the novel quickens, but without apparent prodding. A second sign of fictional energy is that of *inert people suddenly taking on new life,* either because they face a new challenge or because they come into vitalizing contact with others. Confrontation and shock ("outrage" in Faulknerian terms) may touch hidden traits or longings, and bring them to the surface; authentic feeling breaks through hypocrisy, restraint, role. The encounter may be that of author and an unexpectedly strange new character; Dickens was exceptionally capable of the depersonalization to which Gide laid claim in vain. "Assumption has charms for me so delightful—I hardly know for how many wild reasons—that I feel a loss of Oh I can't say what exquisite foolery, when I lose a chance of being someone not in the remotest degree like myself." [3] A third sign of energy, in a writer of great stylistic gifts, is simply *quality of prose*. The writing of *Martin Chuzzlewit* is very uneven. We can be sure something in the creative situation is amiss when we come on such prose as this:

> Mr. Pinch had listened to all this with looks of bewilderment, which seemed to be in part occasioned by the matter of his companion's speech and in part by his rapid and vehement manner. Now that he had come to a close, he drew a very long breath; and gazing wistfully in his face as if he were unable to settle in his own mind what expressions it wore, and were desirous to draw from it as good a clue to his real meaning as it was possible to obtain in the dark, was about to answer. . . .[4]

It would appear Tom Pinch's sluggish consciousness invited Dickens to parcel it out in a sluggish way; elsewhere Tom and Ruth seem responsible for unenergized or sentimental writing, perhaps because Dickens found their attachment embarrassing. With Tom, as with young Martin and John Westlock, Dickens faces his usual hazard of the good rational man condemned to use shapely standard English. Surrounding them, and always more alive, are the eccentrics, the compulsive and the obsessed, and those who speak in some occupational cant, or who delight in forensic nonsense.

Martin Chuzzlewit begins as badly as any important English novel, with a chapter of random and juvenile garrulity on the forbears of the Chuzzlewits. The second chapter brings pretentious literary flights: on autumn leaves, on a sunset, an evening wind, a merry forge. The oily essentials of Pecksniff and the simplicities of Tom Pinch are presented blatantly from the start. So too for old Martin in chapter 3, who expresses his distrust and cynicism in long abstract monologues. Even the first exchange with Pecksniff is unenergized: a collision less of living persons than of thematic *données*. But the substantial fourth chapter, which opens the second monthly part, is far more alive. The vivifying confrontation of Pecksniff and Montague Tigg begins with a literal collision in the dark, as their two heads meet at old Martin's keyhole. The shabby-genteel Tigg of the fierce and scornful moustache—"very dirty and very jaunty, very bold and very mean, very swaggering and very slinking"—controls their interview from the first, and cuts through Pecksniff's hypocrisies. Tigg's cynical realism is balanced by wit and seedy charm. He has created a personality for himself (as he will create a different, gaudier one for the Anglo-Bengalee Company), and would seem to have created Chevy Slyme as well. The creative paradox is that Tigg—all but silencing Pecksniff with his flood of talk—brings him to life by the very act of piercing his defenses. It is he, moreover, who organizes the meeting of relatives that Pecksniff will unsuccessfully chair: a scene of comic disorder not unlike the political meeting maliciously organized by

Pyotr Verkhovensky in *The Possessed*. The scene explodes with life, far more life than the unfolding plot demanded. In this Dickens again seems close to the more abundant comedies of Molière as well as to Dostoevsky and to the picaresque novel. *Tartuffe* is appropriately among the books that tumble about Pecksniff in Phiz's illustration of the final exposure.

But the fifth and sixth chapters are a falling off. Much of the fifth is devoted to a tedious introduction of character traits—young Martin's inconsiderateness that conceals a fundamental good nature; Mark Tapley's "humor," his desire for such adversity as will make his optimism more estimable; Tom Pinch's modesty, generosity, goodness. The sixth chapter further develops, in simplistic dialogue, the novel's thematic preoccupations, and young Martin's plight. The seventh is given some energy by Tigg and by the disintegrating Chevy Slyme. But it is with chapter 8 (the coach ride to London) that the novel at last shows an almost uninterrupted flow of fictional energy. The confrontation at close quarters of Anthony and Jonas Chuzzlewit and Pecksniff and his daughters (with whom Jonas wants to have his tousling fun) brings personality dramatically into play. The Chuzzlewit brutal openness quickly pierces Pecksniff's hypocrisies. But even Pecksniff, enlivened by brandy, is in a holiday mood.

The entry into London, where the travelers separate, is into a dense fog as of a city in the clouds "which they had been travelling to all night up a magic beanstalk." The ninth chapter, "Town and Todgers's," is beyond praise. The labyrinth that makes Todgers's inaccessible to all but the initiated, the staircase window unopened for a hundred years and "begrimed and coated with a century's mud"; the grand mystery of the cellarage, the revolving and whispering chimney-pots seen from the roof, and those other chimney-pots "maliciously holding themselves askew"—all this is seen as by a child, in its aura of enchanted gloom, but with an exciting befuddlement rather than terror. Todgers's is hidden from the light, damaged oranges fester in boxes or molder away in cellars, mansions converted to storehouses are grim. But in all this the author takes unmistakable pleasure. The undermined ground and the stables troubled by rats may have echoes of the blacking house. Yet there is here little of the fear and disgust sometimes evoked by the river and riverside tenements, or by the pauper's burial ground of *Bleak House*. The gloom of Todgers's surroundings is congenial.

For the dark boarding house is full of life: an enchanted place where a newspaper can shove itself through the grating, and a clock is a gruff old giant, and where Mrs. Todgers, the presiding deity, has curls "shaped like little barrels of beer and a head-net like a black cobweb." Todgers's is a place of communion and good-nature, where every commercial gentleman has a "decided turn for pleasure.'' It might have appeared in *Pickwick Papers;* it would perhaps reappear, almost a century later and distantly disguised, in *Sanctuary* (with the anomalous Charity and Mercy, in an exclusively male establishment, replaced by Virgil and Fonzo, and the good-natured Mrs. Todgers by Miss Reba).[5] Mrs. Todgers—who fondly remembers Pecksniff's particular attentions, but now gently eludes his embraces—is one of the hundreds of Dickensian minor figures whose dialogue brings scenes to life. She hardly resembles the face in the oval miniature once made for Pecksniff. For presiding ''over an establishment like this, makes sad havoc with the features, my dear Miss Pecksniffs. . . . The gravy alone, is enough to add twenty years to one's age.'' Such is her anxiety that any commercial gentleman may say of a Saturday evening, '' 'Mrs. Todgers, this day week we part, in consequence of the cheese.' '' She, like the irrepressible and playful servant Bailey, is not a freak or caricatured ''original,'' but simply a normal Londoner of her time and social position, seen affectionately but without patronizing hauteur. So too for the good-humored commercial gentlemen. Inevitably they prefer Mercy. But there is still a ''small cluster of admirers around Charity'' of those who cannot get near her sister. Neither they nor Mrs. Todgers bear ill will to Pecksniff, when he is ''took very poorly'' and must be put to bed several times. The great comic scene of his drunkenness, after the long Sunday dinner, endows him with humanity; he ceases to be a mere abstraction of hypocrisy, egoism, self-deception. In the tearful phase he speaks to Mrs. Todgers of his widower's feelings (''She was beautiful, Mrs. Todgers. . . . She had a small property''), then alarms her with a ''ghastly smile.'' She must fend off embraces prompted by her resemblance to the dead.

> ''Has a voice from the grave no influence?'' said Mr. Pecksniff, with dismal tenderness. ''This is irreligious! My dear creature.''
> ''Hush!'' urged Mrs. Todgers. ''Really you mustn't.''
> ''It's not me,'' said Mr. Pecksniff. ''Don't suppose it's me; it's the voice; it's her voice.'' [6]

The alarmed Mrs. Todgers diverts Pecksniff's attentions by a shrewd appeal to his egotism; she changes the subject to his general excellence. But by now he is very drunk. '' 'Bless my life, Miss Pecksniffs!' cried Mrs. Todgers, aloud, 'your dear pa's took very poorly!' '' Moments later he has fallen into the fireplace. Carried up to bed by several lodgers, Pecksniff reappears, ''seen to flutter on the top landing. He desired to collect their sentiments, it seemed, upon the nature of human life.'' ''In a word, as often as he was shut up in his own room, he darted out afresh, charged with some new moral sentiment, which he continually repeated over the banisters, with extraordinary relish, and an irrepressible desire for the improvement of his fellow-creatures that nothing could subdue.''

An inevitable slackening of energy occurs in the tenth chapter, with Pecksniff restored to his right mind. With chapter 11 the novel moves to a new and challenging scene—the "dim, dirty, smoky, tumble-down, rotten" house and bachelor household of Anthony Chuzzlewit and Son. Jonas's exasperation with the ancient Anthony, who refuses to die, and with the half-idiot Chuffey, may at times seem, like Jason Compson's, understandable. It is possible a dim or unconscious memory of *Martin Chuzzlewit* contributed to the configuration and names of *The Sound and the Fury;* and pleasing, at least, to find a Faulknerian household in early Victorian London and early Victorian fiction: Jonas/Jason; Mercy (Merry)/Candace (Caddy); Chuffey/Benjy; even perhaps, since she too will know how to handle the dim-witted: Sairey/Dilsey. (Sairey headed Faulkner's 1955 list of favorite characters, followed by Mrs. Harris, Falstaff, Prince Hal, Don Quixote, Sancho: "a cruel, ruthless woman, a drunkard, opportunist, unreliable, most of her character was bad, but at least it was character"; [7] Chuffey (whom Jonas will eventually think of putting away, as Jonas puts away Benjy) at table distinctly anticipates Benjy, and must be helped to eat: "breathing on his shrivelled hands to warm them, remained with his poor blue nose immovable about his plate, looking at nothing, with eyes that saw nothing, and a face that meant nothing." The relationship of old Anthony and his clerk of many years provides one of the great somber sequences in Dickens's fiction: an altogether persuasive picture of two senile men who "learnt tare and tret together at school." Even after sixty years or more Chuffey remembers with something like contrition that he once "took down" Anthony in an arithmetic class. The theoretical conception is one of dehumanization by the grim business world; Chuffey might have been as symbolic as Bartleby. What dynamically emerges is, rather, an impressive rendering of death-in-life. Anthony takes pleasure in Jason's jibes at the old clerk; he has educated his son in hardness. But Chuffey understands only Anthony, and emerges from his stupor only at his words. The tensions and hostilities are doubtless those of many old people who have lived long together, but there is love as well as dependency on Chuffey's side, even some affection on Anthony's. The two have become extensions of each other's personalities, but in an everyday rather than occult psychological sense.

The ensuing chapters (12, 13, 14) reveal in sharp contrast to those preceding the deadening effect of oversimplified conceptions and of characters who are by nature passive and inert. For over twenty thousand words the novel remains close to the benumbing consciousness of young Martin, with matters made worse by the priggishness of Tom Pinch. Mary Graham is hardly more helpful in what is, fortunately, virtually the only exchange between nominal hero and heroine. She too elicits a debased prose: "Unspoiled, unpampered in her joys or griefs; with frank and full, and deep affection for the object of her early love; she saw in him one who for her sake was an outcast from his home and fortune," etc. The failure of young Martin is beyond debate. As the good man who must be reformed and freed from egoism, who must discover his own true qualities, he is less interesting than Pip, less interesting even than Eugene Wrayburn, who has at least a languid sense of humor and a few flickerings of sexual life. Humorless, and as sluggish of mind as Tom Pinch, altogether conventional in his reactions to American vulgarity, theatrical in his scathing denunciation of Pecksniff, and condemned to stilted standard English—young Martin is an extreme example of conceptual as well as dramatic failure. A major difficulty lies in the fact that nothing exists, nothing at all, between the two *données* of his temperament: a virtually total egoism blinding him to reality and a fundamental good nature that will be brought out by Mark's good example and by adversity and a near brush with death. At the level of comic or sardonic consciousness where his best work would be generated, Dickens simply did not believe, one suspects, in such an automatic emergence of hidden goodness, nor in the spoiled good young man.

Martin Chuzzlewit wholly lacks the tidiness of structure so much admired in the second half of the nineteenth century and in the first three or four decades of the twentieth. Its free and wandering movement encouraged invention and permitted anything. The great beneficiary of this structural freedom is the American journey. By chapter 15, after six months and some 125,000 words, the time had come for a major change.

Dickens's American journey of January–May 1842 appears to have been one of the central experiences of his life. He was not quite thirty when he received, in Boston, both the warm welcome of Boston and Cambridge intellectuals, and a frenzied public adulation, with women pleading not only for autographs but locks of hair. Even in those first days Dickens writes with odd detachment, in a letter to Forster, of the way his fictions and fantasies, his "fancies," had won such a triumph. "I feel, in the best aspects of this welcome, something of the presence and influence of that spirit which directs my life, and through a heavy sorrow has pointed upward with unchanging finger for more than four years past." [8] It is significant that Mary Hogarth should be summoned, a saving *anima,* in these first hours of turbulent and dazing apotheosis. Dickens was, in the months to follow, an unusually obliging celebrity, and his early impressions were largely favorable. But fatigue was inevitable. One feels, in the brief interview with President Tyler, the presence of two men too exhausted for real communication. Dickens's exasperation increased as his pleas for protection of British authors (who received nothing from American editions) fell on deaf ears. His horror of slavery, like his horror of spitting, became more intense with time, and he resented increasingly the gross invasions of privacy. Strangers even stared in their Lake Erie stateroom window while he washed and his wife lay in bed. The journey west, by canal and steamboat, culminated in the Conradian horror of the Cairo settlement and the filthy, choked Mississippi, and the disappointing impression of the prairie as a blankness, "oppressive in its barren monotony." John S. Whitely and Arnold Goldman suggest that Dickens "underwent a form of psychic collapse in America—though to the public eye he fulfilled his outward obligations. A sense of spiritual strain and chaotic feeling, of an upheaval of personality, is difficult to suppress. He strove for a kind of balance, even in the act of crystallizing this discontent, through his letters home during the trip. . . ." [9]

Two experiences, in the last month of the trip, reflect significant rhythms of the Dickensian personality, though the first may be an altogether natural response to fatigue. This was the ten days spent beside Niagara Falls, which is remembered in tones of Wordsworthian apocalypse: "the tremendous ghost of spray and mist which is never laid: which has haunted this place with the same dread solemnity since Darkness brooded on the deep. . . ." The ten-day respite (during which he remained on the Canadian side "to shun strange company") must have restored Dickens to his normal condition of excess energy. For in Montreal there is another ten-day experience of which *American Notes* says nothing: stage-managing and acting in a theatrical performance for a local charity. He warned everyone "they would have to submit to the most iron despotism. . . . The pains I have taken with them, and the perspiration I have expended, during the last ten days, exceed in amount anything you can imagine." [10] A normal pleasure in this activity must not be discounted; Dickens wondered again whether he was not a born stage manager. But it is also pertinent to see him, at the end of the unsettling four-month journey, need both to reassert his administrative bent and to feverishly expend energy.

The journey resulted in two much underrated works of art: *American Notes* and the American chapters of *Martin Chuzzlewit*. The intentions of the two are entirely different. *American Notes* is an extremely vivid and entertaining travel book, warmly personal in tone, written in the lovely conversational style of the best parts of *David Copperfield*. It shows a genuine effort to be fair to a country Dickens looked forward to seeing, the "republic of my imagination," but that he finally did not like. He was much taken by Boston and New England, and by the kindness and good nature of many individual Americans, but dismayed by the discrepancies between American rhetoric of freedom and the higher moral sense and the materialistic, cynical or defensive reality.

The two books intersect relatively little, though there are obvious places in which *American Notes* drained off material that might have been used in the novel. So for the earlier book's great visionary account of the wild westward passage. There are many good Americans in the travel book, but only Mr. Bevan in *Martin Chuzzlewit,* and the novel contains a far higher proportion of freakish eccentrics. Some of the extreme cases of barbarism and violence in the late chapter (17) on slavery in *American Notes* are reflected in Martin's early experiences. The levee forced upon Dickens, to his intense outrage, is echoed in Martin's levee prior to his leaving for Eden. The vivid picture of Cairo, Illinois (the Eden of the novel) reaches us in less than three hundred words: "a breeding-place of fever, ague, and death"; "a hotbed of disease, an ugly sepulchre, a grave uncheered by any gleam of promise." One is reminded of the way in which an unpleasant luncheon in the same room as a fanged mestizo and a casual reference to a futile whiskey-priest (in *Another Mexico*) soon led to two great fictional beings in *The Power and the Glory.* The "hateful Mississippi" of *American Notes* evokes a long sentence of startlingly Faulknerian power, detail and even ("from the interstices of which") syntax:

> An enormous ditch, sometimes two or three miles wide, running liquid mud, six miles an hour: its strong and frothy current choked and obstructed everywhere by huge logs and whole forest trees: now twining themselves together in great rafts, from the interstices of which a sedgy, lazy foam works up, to float upon the water's top; now rolling past like monstrous bodies, their tangled roots showing like matted hair; now glancing singly by like giant leeches; and now writhing round and round in the vortex of some small whirlpool, like wounded snakes.[11]

The American chapters, about one seventh of the novel, doubtless occupy a larger place in most readers' memory of *Martin Chuzzlewit,* as they have had a larger place in the strictures of criticism. The first essential is to insist that the question of their balanced "fairness" to the American scene is, for modern readers at least, totally irrelevant. The chapters are profoundly *true* in their insistence on the propensity of Americans to deceive themselves with rhetoric, and to believe that the constant reiteration of "freedom" and "equality" and higher "moral sense" constitute or create realities. But these chapters are not documentary and do not pretend to be. Dickens was concerned about the fairness of *American Notes,* his "perplexingly divided and subdivided duty there," but in the next sentence defines just such a selective impulse as would be realized in the novel: "Oh! the sublimated essence of comicality that I *could* distil, from the materials I have." [12] The novel's American chapters are indeed distilled, exaggerated, willfully distorted, "symbolic" and "anti-realistic," comic. They exist firmly within the fictional world of *Roughing It* and Kafka's *Amerika,* of West's *Day of the Locust* and Hawkes's *The Beetle Leg,* of Charyn's *The Tar-Baby* and *Eisenhower, My Eisenhower,* of various chapters in Pynchon and Barth, of, at an anti-realist extreme, Mirsky's *Proceedings of the Rabble.* One thing *Martin Chuzzlewit's* picture of America shares with all these is a pure creative joy in grotesque invention.

The American chapters are an act of the imagination rather than a disguised report of personal experience. For Dickens (inevitably the most honored ship-board passenger, lionized in New York as few or none had ever been, safely watching Cairo appear and recede) set himself no less a task than to imagine what it would be like to cross the Atlantic in steerage, arrive in New York unknown and virtually penniless, and settle in the pestilential Eden; and to imagine, also, what the New World would look like to such a vain consciousness as Martin's. The American chapters occasionally break into direct and unfortunate editorializing. But this programmatic side exists apart from the comic and the dark vision. Only the genteel, courteous, cultivated Norris family—egalitarian yet name-dropping snobs, abolitionists who find negroes funny and essentially alien—asks for the kind of serious moral judgment which Dickens brings to bear on the Veneerings and the Dedlocks. The most villainous of the American freaks, in terms of real reality, would no doubt be Hannibal Chollop. But to criticize him for his violence would seem as misplaced as to criticize Sairey Gamp for her drinking. Dickens makes a half-hearted effort to editorialize on Chollop, but is ultimately bemused by the pure comic creation.

The highly inventive section divides into two parts. The first consists of the freaks and their verbal nonsense. The second, compressed but unforgettable, involves the visionary journey into solitude, up a river more forlorn than Conrad's Congo, to the pestilential dying Eden community. The introductions of the freaks are brief, incisive, unfailingly brilliant. As a rule they appear unannounced, shamelessly intrusive, like the assistants in *The Castle.* They are simply and suddenly there. The landlord Captain Kedick sits on the bed before speaking, then moves to the pillow for greater comfort; Chollop comes into the cabin uninvited and sits down on the chest with his hat on. Mrs. Hominy, the philosophizing authoress and "Mother of the Modern Gracchi," consigned to the care of the travelers, at once makes herself at home in the room to which they have retired, and helps herself to their milk. Mr. La Fayette Kettle, seated behind Martin and Mark on the train, thrusts his head between them, the better to enjoy their conversation. A few sharp strokes bring these *fantoches* to life with Stendhalian economy. Kettle's cheeks "were so hollow that he seemed to be always sucking them in." The first impression may be followed by a leisurely itemizing of old or shabby clothing, or a characterizing childish act: as Kettle's proud display of his old tobacco plug (previously stuck to the back of Martin's seat) to show that it was "used up considerable." Mrs. Hominy's speech is as delightfully close to parody as Faulkner's Lena Grove's:

> "A'most used-up I am, I do declare!" she observed. "The jolting in the cars is pretty nigh as bad as if the rail was full of snags and sawyers."
> "Snags and sawyers, ma'am?" said Martin.
> "Well, then, I do suppose you'll hardly realise my meaning, sir," said Mrs. Hominy. "My! Only think! *Do* tell!" [13]

The first view of the freaks may be as languid or inert men functioning as machines. Zepheniah Scadder the Eden agent sits in a rocking chair with his legs planted high against the doorpost: "a gaunt man in a huge straw hat, and a coat of green stuff." Every "time he spoke something was seen to twitch and jerk up in his throat, like the little hammers in a harpsichord when the notes are struck." He is blind in one eye, and the blind side of his face seems to listen to what the other side is doing, and is in the "coldest state of watchfulness." This contemplative self can enjoy, aesthetically, the swindler's successes. The forensic nonsense, the chauvinistic or anglophobe railings, emerge as from puppets. The freaks, however idiosyncratic, have no other inner life than the words they utter, and exist in an immediate fictional present. They have no past or future fictional life. The Eden agent is hardly felt as an evil force, but rather as an actor playing the sharper's role: doing his bit part. Even one of those he has ruined—"a pestilence-stricken, broken, miserable shadow of a man"— derives pleasure from Scadder's sharpness.

Dickens insists in both books on the absence of individuality in Americans. Yet each freak seems a fresh creation with his own capacity to surprise. The first impression—of eccentricity immobilized and sunk in languor—scarcely prepares us for the flood of speech that will emerge. Martin's first American, Colonel Diver, is a "sallow gentleman" with "a mixed expression of vulgar cunning and conceit." Significantly his "discoloured shirt-frill struggled to force itself into notice; as asserting an equality of civil rights with the other portions of his dress. . . ." His thick cane anticipates his role as editor of a scandal sheet, ready either for moralizing chastisement or brutal destruction. The introduction of his staff member is even more vivid: "a figure with a stump of pen in its mouth," "a small young gentleman of very juvenile appearance and unwholesomely pale in the face. . . ." He seems to be in early adolescence.

His lank hair is a "fragile crop"; his "loftiest developments" are "somewhat pimply"; on his upper lip are "tokens of a sandy down." The vignette, continuing for nearly four hundred words, and suggesting a child playing at editor, cutting clippings and snapping scissors for fun, is suddenly interrupted by Colonel Diver's proud introduction: "My War Correspondent, sir. Mr. Jefferson Brick." (Compare "My critic" of *Pickwick Papers,* chapter 33.) Brick at once utters patriotic sentiments when his employer pulls the right string. Mrs. Jefferson Brick, "a sickly little girl," is in the Colonel's eyes a "matron in blue." Another youthful eccentric, "a pallid lad," can issue patriotic nonsense the moment he is called on, and excites the Watertoast Sympathizers with his taunts of the British lion. Responses are as automatic as those of the parrot that shrieks, in the hubbub of a political meeting in *Nostromo,* "Viva Costaguana!"

These are American voices, though the two Transcendental Literary Ladies are intoxicated by language in the way some of the British originals are. In general Dickens's British originals defend themselves, through sarcasm or verbal fun or eccentricity of dress, against the aristocratic world and its tendency to deny identity to the poor. The British originals rebel against stereotype; the American freaks fall into it. Dickens had a superb ear for American rhythms and locutions, as he had a fine eye for postures characteristic of the time. The great brief portrait of Congressman Elijah Pogram (for all the portraits are brief, the American chapters always keep moving) shows Dickens's method at its most efficient, surprise following upon surprise. We first see him "with his legs on a high barrel of flour, as if he were looking at the prospect with his ankles." His linen is soiled, his face insufficiently washed. Another passenger on the steamboat informs Martin he is fortunate to have this opportunity to behold Pogram, one of the country's master minds. "Yes, sir. Our own immortal Chiggle, sir, is said to have observed, when he made the celebrated Pogram statter in marble, which rose so much con-test and preju-dice in Europe, that the brow was more than mortal." The passengers gather around to hear the famous orator put down Martin, who failed to speak admiringly of Eden, which nearly killed him, and of the murderous Chollop. For Pogram, Chollop is a splendid example of native raw material: "He is a true-born child of this free hemisphere! Verdant as the mountains of our country; bright and flowing as our mineral Licks; unspiled by withering conventionalities as air our broad and boundless Perearers! Rough he may be. So air our Barrs. Wild he may be. So air our Buffalers."

This then is the great and precarious achievement: to create out of remembered absurdities and irritations, and out of serious perceptions of American faults, a number of comic personages who underline those weaknesses yet remain uncontaminated by a documentary "real life" and so also remain exempt from ordinary moral judgment. They are pure fictional creations who exist only, but marvelously there, in the closed world of a book. They arouse a uniquely objective comic pleasure; exist, in Nabokovian phrase, in a world of "aesthetic bliss."

The journey to Eden, though the harmless villain Chollop intrudes upon it, exists in a different kind of non-realistic world, and derives from intense felt experience and genuine horrror. John S. Whitley and Arnold Goldman see the American West of *American Notes,* including of course Cairo, "as symbolic of his sense of the inner meaning of the more settled areas." Dickens's imagery of decay and dissolution "takes on a life of its own, as a symbol of the inner reality of America, a nightmarish and horrific vision." [14] This language may suggest, not irrelevantly, *Heart of Darkness* and its highly personal and charged landscape of a largely interior journey. "Amateurs in the physiognomical and phrenological sciences" rove about Martin, for the same reason the doctor in Brussels measures Marlow's head—curiosity concerning those who go "there"; and, at least by him, are never seen again. This is the secret of the interest in Martin and Mark: that "nobody as goes to Eden ever comes back a-live!" There are resemblances in the two voyages that would exist in any deep penetration of strange country. The last proprietor of their hut in Eden had been buried there, which might suggest a source for Marlow's dead predecessor on the *Roi des Belges,* were there not the historic *Freiesleben* to account for him. But the two voyages are into deepening solitudes, with fewer and fewer people on board the American steamboat until at last it suggests "old Charon's boat, conveying melancholy shades to judgment." The Congo is a place of inertia, apathy, demoralization, but there is violence behind the screen of trees, an incomprehensible frenzy. The Ohio suggests only inertia, decay, a vacancy, with nothing behind what one sees. Both voyages are as it were backward in time, to Dickens's Eden, the natural habitat of serpents, to Conrad's "earliest beginnings of the world." The experience of disorientation is dazing; in time one's past life, and the possibility of return, have the quality of dream. The resemblance is of tone, and of a landscape that threatens engulfment. The two destinations are places of pestilential fever in which the sick men lose all sense of time.

> On they toiled through great solitudes, where the trees upon the banks grew thick and close; and floated in the stream; and held up shrivelled arms from out the river's depths; and slid from the margin of the land, half growing, half decaying in

the miry water. On through the weary day and melancholy night: beneath the burning sun and in the mist and vapour of the evening: on until return appeared impossible, and restoration to their home a miserable dream.

Martin Chuzzlewit, Chapter 23

"Going up that river was like travelling back to the earliest beginnings of the world, when vegetation rioted on the earth and the big trees were kings. An empty stream, a great silence, an impenetrable forest. The air was warm, thick, heavy, sluggish. There was no joy in the brilliance of sunshine. The long stretches of the waterway ran on, deserted, into the gloom of overshadowed distances. . . . There were moments when one's past came back to one, as it will sometimes when you have not a moment to spare to yourself; but it came in the shape of an unrestful and noisy dream, remembered with wonder amongst the overwhelming realities of this strange world of plants, and water, and silence.

. . . The steamer toiled along slowly on the edge of a black and incomprehensible frenzy."

Heart of Darkness, Chapter 2

The first company station in *Heart of Darkness* is a vision of demoralization, with a boiler wallowing in the grass, and a railway-truck lying on its back with its wheels in the air; at the Central Station white men "with long staves in their hands appeared languidly from amongst the buildings." So in Eden they will see signs of an effort to clear the land. "In some quarters, a snake or zigzag fence had been begun, but in no instance had it been completed; and the fallen logs, half hidden in the soil, lay mouldering away." The culminating experience, for Martin as for Marlow, is a disorienting and nearly fatal sickness, and the two emerge from their journeys changed men. A case might be made for *Martin Chuzzlewit* as a parodic redreaming of *Heart of Darkness,* were their dates of publication reversed. For the megalomaniac Kurtz, who has reverted in some sense to a state of nature, in the practice of terrorism and unspeakable rites, is taken with intense seriousness by the author. But Hannibal Chollop the unspoiled natural man (the terrorist who had gouged the eye of a man surprised in the act of knocking at his own street-door) is not.

My intent is not to suggest that *Martin Chuzzlewit* necessarily influenced *Heart of Darkness,* nor that Dickens's vision approaches the subtle sustained power of Conrad's, but only to remark that the western journey has some of the same qualities of dream. The American chapters of *Martin Chuzzlewit,* so far from disrupting or weakening a coherent comedy of British society, charge the novel with an energy that holds to the very end. They are, in this very important sense, a turning point.

Martin Chuzzlewit, like Todgers's boarding house and the National Hotel in America, teems with life; its rich creativity is universally recognized. More difficult to define is the pervasive sense of connection between people, of life energy circulating among two or more characters. This is a quality Dickens shares with Dostoevsky (most notably the Dostoevsky of the first part of *The Idiot*) and that is often missing from Faulkner's major scenes, where the obsessed personages are rigidly locked within themselves, or wear masks that prevent real human connection. The sense of vibrant community, of characters setting off sparks from each other, of constantly renewed energy, accounts in part for the wide appeal of *Pickwick Papers*. Dickens may invest with life a scene involving a number of persons and several levels, as in cinema montage, and lend to the whole a sense of mysterious connection. Such is the scene (40) of Jonas Chuzzlewit's attempted flight with Mercy on the Antwerp packet. We approach the river through the calm consciousness of Tom and Ruth Pinch, out for a stroll on a bright morning. The steamboats and their funnels create an animated confusion. Also animate is a large umbrella that attacks Tom, catching him around the throat, its hook entangling his ankles, flapping at his hat like a bird. The umbrella is charged with the life of its owner, Sairey Gamp, looking for the ''Anksworks package,'' and worried about someone on board. Her commentary gives life to the mysterious couple seen on the ship, and to the woman (Mercy) who goes ''like a lamb to the sacrifige!'' Another person suddenly appears, the Pinch landlord, not yet known to them as a detective or spy. He asks Tom to carry a message to the man wrapped in a cloak. The astonishment of Tom and Jonas, when they come face to face, is succeeded by Jonas's violent reaction to the message and abrupt decision to leave the ship. On shore he is confronted by Tigg, now known as ''Mr. Montague,'' who has intercepted the flight abroad and by so doing prepared his own murder. As the two men walk away, the intimate connection has become that of doubles. For Jonas felt ''as if he were bound and in the other's power, but had a sullen and suppressed devil within him, which he could not quite resist.'' The chapter ends with mysterious authorial speculation on the landlord Nadgett, ''who must have had some business there.'' The business in the past has been to watch Jonas. But from now on Jonas will also be watching himself, eventually with fear.

The characters, even more than is usual in Dickens, go in pairs. The Anthony Chuzzlewit–Chuffey relationship is the work of a masterful and compassionate understanding. The young Martin–Mark Tapley connection, nominally at the book's center, is one of the least interesting; Martin's education by his good servant is arbitrary, repetitious, tiresome. The two pairs of lovers who come forward near the end are of even less interest. The love of Martin and Mary Graham is scarcely dramatized at all, and the coyly unfolding love of John Westlock and Ruth Pinch evokes some of Dickens's most lubricated prose. "Oh, foolish, panting timid little heart, why did she feign to be unconscious of his coming?" The only interesting erotic relationship is that of Tom and Ruth Pinch and their mock marriage. The protective brother seems, as we near the end, a rather glib lover: "For you women . . . know so well how to be affectionate and full of solicitude without appearing to be; your gentleness of feeling is like your touch; so light and easy, that the one enables you to deal with wounds of the mind as tenderly as the other enables you to deal with wounds of the body." Ruth's erotic attraction for Tom is as strong as any in Dickens's fiction, so much so that in her presence Tom's attention wanders from his writing every moment. "Oh, heaven, what a wicked little stomacher! and to be gathered up into little plaits by the strings before it could be tied, and to be tapped, rebuked, and wheedled, at the pockets before it would set right. . . ." This *ménage-à-trois* is completed in the next to last chapter when Tom goes up to his room, thinking husband and wife would want to be by themselves, but first John, then Ruth comes to protest his isolation. "As to Tom, he was perfectly delighted. He could have sat and looked at them, just as they were, for hours."

The interest in this will be for the psychiatrist, or for the historian of Victorian taste and mores.[15] The relationship of Montague and Nadgett, nominally that of employer and company spy, long carries an aura of strangeness, and leaves Nadgett in dehumanized solitude. Earlier we have seen the seedy actor Montague (then Tigg) in a double relationship with Chevy Slyme—initially creating for Slyme a vivid fictitious personality, but later seeming to usurp and annihilate it. Slyme has his drunken existence only through Tigg until he reappears in the sinister and degraded role of a policeman accepting the desperate bribe of his relative Jonas. One cannot emphasize too strongly that if Tigg/Montague takes life from these doubles or extensions of his own personality, he also gives fictional life to every scene in which he appears. Without him Jonas Chuzzlewit would not have been the same, nor the intensely dramatic movement toward the murder.

The portrait of Jonas is richer, in a number of ways, than the pendant one of Bradley Headstone in *Our Mutual Friend,* whose destructive will derives from fierce sexual and other repression and from humorless resentment of the fortunate and well-born. Headstone, seen in retrospect, appears to be the same from beginning to end; his true self breaks through. But Jonas's personality undergoes real change. The earlier Jonas, we have seen, had the sympathetic attraction of a rough humor as well as great vitality, and a cynical honesty that broke through the hypocrisies of Pecksniff. As we look back there is little to forewarn us of his ultimate cruelty and determination to revenge himself for Merry's childish teasing, or to prepare us for the revelation that he did buy poison with the intent of killing his father. On a first reading Jonas's anxiety when Anthony suffers his attack of fits, and his insistence that Pecksniff remain with him as a witness of his innocence, suggest the Dostoevskyan or Freudian equation of crime and criminal wish.

A different Jonas, wholly unredeemed in his cruelty to Merry, with all humor gone from their relationship, is coincident with his association with Montague (27), to whom he goes for an insurance policy on her life. Montague—very much in the role of a Dostoevskyan double, both instigator and agent of criminal impulses—has a diabolic insight into Jonas's character and invites him to join the company. He is one worthy to be taking in premiums for the Anglo-Bengalee rather than to be paying them. The cynical Montague knows that Jonas has or will have something to hide, by which he can be blackmailed, and at once sends Nadgett to spy on him. The report (whose secret is kept from the reader until near the end) shows a "deeper impression of somebody's hoof" than even Montague had expected; he awaits Jonas's coming with some trepidation. The remarkable and prolonged drama is of a murder which both the criminal and his victim increasingly forsee. Montague is the first to show some awareness, as his eye falls on razors.

The preparations for the murder—as Jonas struggles toward his crime, and works to release rather than subdue criminal impulse, and with Montague in growing knowledge of his danger—result in some of Dickens's most powerful pages. There are real resemblances with *Crime and Punishment,* though Jonas lacks Raskolnikov's moral and intellectual subtlety, and the later novel's selective detail keeps us far closer to his consciousness. Dickens is working in cruder yet grandly theatrical terms. The faintest suggestion (38)—"one red glimmer in a sky of blackness"—becomes more explicit (41): "a dawning and increasing purpose in his face," "one strong purpose wrestling with every emotion of his mind, and casting the whole series down as they arose." Feeling more and more vulnerable, Jonas fixes his eyes on Montague, not on his face, but "on his breast, or thereabouts," and he shows manic excitement after hearing from Doctor Jobling of a murder that, after a stab to the heart, left only one drop of blood. He is unusually boisterous after getting Montague to agree to go with him on the expedition to Pecksniff.

The coach-ride in the dark, through portentous weather, a hot silent night threatening storm (42), meets its difficult challenge: to convey both Montague's fear and Jonas's murderous excitement. A certain obviousness is perhaps necessary if we are to experience both. Jonas, with the sense that watchful faces they pass are looking at them, rather than at the threatening night, draws the blind up on his side. A first threat or symbolic enactment of the murder—Jonas "with his hand lifted and the bottle clenched in it like a hammer"—is left ambiguous. Had it been only a dream? The next morning Montague's dream of a splintered door gives way to waking terror, as he sees Jonas standing at his bedside, and the locked door now wide open. But the great murderous scene is that of the carriage accident, which has left Montague senseless on the road within a few feet of the horses. Jonas, "like a man possessed," and making the horses "wilder by his cries," tries to get them to trample Montague to death. The horses function as violent force under the guidance of murderous will. We must wait thirty thousand words for the actual murder, which occurs between lines.

The aftermath of the crime, which takes Jonas back to the room where he has supposedly been all the time, is told in little more than two thousand words. But these pages have a Dostoevskyan power and even insight. With Montague dead, his body "oozing down into the boggy ground," Jonas creates another double: projects his murdering self into the locked room at home. He has to return to it, and the room seems "beyond comparison more dismal and more dreadful than the wood." He experiences not penitence or remorse or even regret, only dread of that "infernal" room:

> This made him, in a gloomy, murderous, mad way not only fearful *for* himself, but *of* himself; for being, as it were, a part of the room: a something supposed to be there, yet missing from it: he invested himself with its mysterious terrors; and when he pictured in his mind the ugly chamber, false and quiet, false and quiet, through the dark hours of two nights; and the tumbled bed, and he not in it, though believed to be; he became in a manner his own ghost and phantom, and was at once the haunting spirit and the haunted man.[16]

Some sympathy is created for Jonas, as he awaits detection, then is lost through his "base triumph" when Chuffey reveals that he had not in fact poisoned his father, but had fully intended to. But the great dramatic moment and final deep stroke of sympathy—which Dostoevsky re-imagined still more powerfully in *The Possessed*—comes with his attempted suicide in a solitary room, while an attendant impatiently waits. The attendant is Chevy Slyme, disgraced kinsman and now a police officer. Jonas offers Slyme a hundred pounds to be allowed five minutes alone in the next room. He has the means, he suggests, of destroying himself. The greedy Slyme reasons rapidly, though he wishes he had not been told so much. Suicide might be more creditable to the family than execution. Will Jonas engage to say a prayer, "or something of the sort"? With this question, and its implied assent, Jonas breaks from him and goes into the room, closes the door. Slyme listens at the keyhole, talks with men waiting below, gives Jonas his allotted five minutes and more:

> He withdrew from the window accordingly, and walked on tiptoe to the door in the partition. He listened. There was not a sound within. He set the candles near it, that they might shine through the glass.
>
> It was not easy, he found, to make up his mind to the opening of the door. But he flung it wide open suddenly, and with a noise; then retreated. After peeping in and listening again, he entered.
>
> He started back as his eyes met those of Jonas, standing in an angle of the wall, and staring at him. His neckerchief was off; his face was ashy pale.
>
> "You're too soon," said Jonas, with an abject whimper. "I've not had time. I have not been able to do it. I—five minutes more—two minutes more!—Only one!"
>
> Slyme gave him no reply, but thrusting the purse upon him and forcing it back into his pocket, called up his men.[17]

There are a number of reasons why Dostoevsky's pages on Kirillov's suicide are more moving and more intense: the deeper cynicism of Pyotr Verkhovensky, who has skillfully played on Kirillov's fatal reasoning; and the nobility of Kirillov's mad self-sacrificial gesture, his illusion that his philosophical suicide will liberate mankind and give his own life eternal meaning; but also, most poignantly, his inexpungeable love of life here and now. In the background is metaphysical tragedy; in the foreground is Pyotr's cynicism and unmitigated evil intruding on Kirillov's failing quasi-sacred will. The first time Pyotr enters the room, "something uttered a roar and rushed at him"; "he had caught a glimpse of Kirillov standing at the other end of the room by the window" before that savage rush. Will he have to kill Kirillov himself? He enters the room again, at first sees nothing. Then:

> Against the wall facing the windows on the right of the door stood a cupboard. On the right side of this cupboard, in the corner formed by the cupboard and the wall, stood Kirillov, and he was standing in a very strange way; motionless, perfectly erect, with his arms held stiffly at his sides, his head raised and pressed tightly back against the wall in the very corner, he seemed to be trying to conceal and efface himself.[18]

The fixity of Kirillov is that of trance, or of the epileptic's priceless few seconds' experience of eternity; the eyes stare in the distance. Or is he watching? Pyotr decides to scorch Kirillov's face with the candle. And now the condemned man does move, knocks the candlestick to the ground, bites the little finger of Pyotr's left hand. It is an act of ultimate exasperation and incorrigible will to live. Pyotr, terrified, rushes out of the dark room, but hears Kirillov shout "directly" ten times, then hears the shot that at last ends his life.

Martin Chuzzlewit's two most famous creations, Pecksniff and Sairey Gamp, belong to different comic modes. Pecksniff could cause discomfort, as model Victorian father and mouther of unexceptionable platitudes, but also because his oily tenderness could resemble the author's at its worst. " 'Ah naughty hand!' said Mr. Pecksniff, apostrophizing the reluctant prize, 'why did you take me prisoner. Go, go!' " is not very different from Dickens on Ruth Pinch. "Oh! foolish, panting, frightened little heart, why did she run away?" Pecksniff, we have seen, has his saving moments of humanity: the holiday mood of the stay at Todgers's, with the landlady to fondle, and the glorious Sunday intoxication. Self-deceived in much else, he may genuinely love his daughters, and especially the less acerbic Merry, who is "constructed on the best models." His is, nevertheless, essentially a stage presence, all brilliant speech and glittering surface and role, but with little sense of an inner life that goes on separately from the outer. In this he differs from Falstaff, even from Tartuffe, certainly from Sairey Gamp.

But to say that Pecksniff is a stage presence, that he *is* his words and fawning gestures and postures, is not to deny the success of the creation. It is merely to define the traditional character of the comedy, and to say that we enjoy him as we would enjoy a person who remains irrepressibly faithful to his "humour." Pecksniff is all calculating mind, but mind freed from the humane burden of introspection. He can adjust rapidly to situations that threaten to entrap him. The portentous knock on the door of old Martin at the worst possible moment—with Jonas in the house to be hidden or not, and the jilted Charity in a rage—can instantly convert Pecksniff into a gardener, "warbling a rustic stave." His vanity for the moment cannot take in anything so preposterous as Mary's rejection: " 'Release me, Mr. Pecksniff. Your touch is disagreeable to me.' " But when she threatens to tell old Martin of his advances, and has expressed her "deepest abhorrence," he can shift his role instantly from that of confident lover to cool blackmailer, or with only such pause as to raise "his heavy eyelids languidly and let them fall again." He is splendidly in character in the exposure scene, with long and brilliant speeches before the assembled dependents (52), not knowing yet that his game is up; even more in character when, briefly silenced by old Martin's stick and by his castigations, he bounces back to deliver reproachful and forgiving moral declarations before leaving the room. His invulnerability is such that his two instances of normal suffering and defeat seem implausible. Left alone after Mary Graham's rebuff, he "seemed to be shrunk and reduced; to be trying to hide himself within himself. . . . For a minute or two, in fact, he was hot, and pale, and mean, and shy, and slinking, and consequently not at all Pecksniffian. But after that, he recovered himself. . . ." And at the very end Tom is haunted by a "drunken, squalid, begging-letter-writing man called Pecksniff" who in the alehouse "shows his elbows worn in holes, and puts his soleless shoes up on a bench, and begs his auditors look there. . . ."

Impeccable as stage creation, Pecksniff thus lacks (and was probably not intended to have) the richer humanity of Stepan Verkhovensky, or Don Quixote, or Pickwick; or Sairey Gamp. "What do you think of Gamp?" Dickens asked John Forster, as Joyce asked his friends how they liked Bloom. "I mean to make my name with her." Sairey Gamp is one of the triumphs of English literature (and language), and to try to account for her success may seem as vain as to propose a final analysis of Falstaff. She has her gross physical presence: the whites of the eyes, the gown worse for snuff, the faded and patched umbrella as a living extension of her being, and the peculiar fragrance "borne upon the breeze, as if a passing fairy had hiccoughed, and had previously been to a wine-vaults." She is fat and old, but her carnality and her language are unsubduable. Like Falstaff, she has a realistic knowledge of life, of birth and death, human weakness and the failure of marriages. She may seem a hard nurse, agreeing with Betsy Prig to take the patient's pillow, yet shows compassion for Merry and even for Chuffey, whom she pacifies with her talk.

Flesh and fantasy, the pursuit of creature comfort and delight in dreaming aloud: her existence is divided between the two. She has, as Faulkner remarked, character. But we are given very little of what normally creates character (as opposed to vivid personality) in fiction: the debating of alternatives, the pondering of gradual adjustments, the fabricating of roles. Instead her accommodation to life, and her ability to make life accommodate itself to her, are instantaneous. She has a "face for all occasions." Told that a gentleman was dead, when she expected to be called for a birth, she looks out the window with her "mourning countenance." But this is not hypocrisy. She simply responds professionally to the occasion.

A unique literary creation, yet of a fundamental humanity. For she is like innumerable people in dividing her life between comfort and survival on the one hand, and a "real life" of fantasy on the other. Sairey Gamp may pass within a sentence from the creature comforts to the spiritual. The essential instructions for tea give way without pause to a story of missing teeth, with both of her favorite inhabitants of fantasy, Mrs. Harris and the late Gamp, involved. Vivacity comes from the rapid movement of her mind, and the preposterous circumstantial detail:

> "And quite a family it is to make tea for," said Mrs. Gamp; "and wot a happiness to do it! My good young 'ooman"—to the servant girl—"p'raps somebody would like to try a new-laid egg or two, not biled too hard. Likeways, a few rounds o' buttered toast, first cuttin' off the crust, in consequence of tender teeth, and not too many of 'em; which Gamp himself, Mrs. Chuzzlewit, at one blow, being in liquor, struck out four, two single and two double, as was took by Mrs. Harris for a keepsake, and is carried in her pocket at this present hour, along with two cramp-bones, a bit o' ginger, and a grater like a blessed infant's shoe, in tin, with a little heel to put the nutmeg in: as many times I've seen and said, and used for caudle when required, within the month." [19]

Her concern for food and comfort, as serious a preoccupation as Falstaff's, is part of British folklore: the reminder to "leave the bottle on the chimley-piece and let me put my lips to it when I am so dispoged," and the half a pint of porter that "fully satisfies, perwisin' Mrs. Harris, that it is brought reg'lar and draw'd mild." To settle for the night with a new patient involves observing a "parapidge in case of fire, and lots of roofs and chimley-pots to walk upon," and an "extemporaneous bed," and, of course supper: the order that begins with a little bit of pickled salmon and ends with Brighton Old Tipper ale.

Sairey Gamp's mind is never at rest; her monologues, as compressed as Falstaff's, with never an inert word, yet give the impression of natural free-association. Her quick mind can move over the present scene, as when she pins the arms of the feverishly ill Lewsome to his sides, and notes he would make a "lovely corpse." But her true fantasy life involves recapitulation of the dramatic past. Revery, compensating for life's tribulations, is instantly translated into words and images. We have no way of knowing how much Sairey herself debated Mrs. Harris's "reality": a personage indispensable as a companion, one aware of her virtues, a thoughtful double ungrudging in her praise. There is a dazed moment of recognition, as when a child puts away an imaginary companion, when Mrs. Prig doubts her existence: "Have I stood her friend in all her troubles, great and small, for it to come at last to sech a end as this. . . ." But her confusion is short-lived. Minutes later, talking to John Westlock, she brings Mrs. Harris back to life through the incontrovertible reality of Mrs. Harris's son Tommy, whom she saved: "ever since I found him, Mr. Westlock, with his small red worsted shoe a-gurglin' in his throat. . . ."

The novel pauses to remind us that Mrs. Harris was an invention of Sairey's active brain, one of those Dickensian redundancies the reader itches to cut. The late Gamp, whatever the historical reality of that distant marriage and its offspring, seems to have as little or as much substance. As Mrs. Harris can remind her of her veracity and sobriety, so husband Gamp can illustrate by contrast what a serious drinker is like. His fictional reality is also incontrovertible, thanks to the wooden leg. For the leg, first seen "vividly" when Gamp is summoned to his long home—"a-lying in Guy's Hospital with a penny-piece on each eye and his wooden leg under his arm"—can be turned into matches when sold, yet return home in the form of liquor. The brief flight of fantasy leads to the sudden and total creation of a truant son:

> "and so do I, although the blessing of a daughter was denigod me; which if we had had one, Gamp would certainly have drunk its little shoes right off its feet, as with our precious boy he did, and arterwards send the child a errand to sell his wooden leg for any money it would fetch as matches in the rough, and bring it home in liquor; which was truly done beyond his years, for ev'ry individgle penny that child lost at toss or buy for kidney ones; and come home arterwards quite bold, to break the news, and offering to drown himself if that it would be a satisfaction to his parents." [20]

The wooden leg (distant ancestor of Eck Snopes's neck-brace?) is animated again when Sairey, in response to Ruth Pinch, evokes with equanimity her dead:

> "Mine," said Mrs. Gamp, "mine is all gone, my dear young chick. And as to husbands, there's a wooden leg gone likeways home to its account, which in its constancy of walkin' into wine vaults, and never comin' out again 'till fetched by force, was quite as weak as flesh, if not weaker." [21]

Marvin Murdick, referring to Sairey's claim that Mrs. Harris is actually upstairs, alternating with her in caring for Chuffey, speaks of "the ultimate nightmare of alienation, as the ego begins to crack like an ice floe. Mrs. Gamp, for the sake of the plot's last surprise, has ventured to the farthest outstation of consciousness, where at last there is only self and no other." [22] One might argue, instead, that this is simply the strategy of a nurse adept at moonlighting and who also loves to invent. But Mudrick is correct in taking her seriously. Sairey Gamp saves herself through fantasy, but her fantasies come out of the world of poverty: a world in which, as in Flannery O'Connor's "Parker's Back," identity and love may try to become articulate through tattoos. One drama is the struggle to get ten and six back when a tattoo's color runs; another concerns disputes over the cost of having a child. For Mrs. Harris's husband's brother was

> marked with a mad bull in Wellington boots upon his left arm, on account of his precious mother havin' been worrited by one into a shoemaker's shop, when in a sitivation which blessed is the man as has his quiver full of sech, as many times I've said to Gamp when words has roge between us on account of the expense. . . ." [23]

These are the real depths of ordinary existence. They anchor the flights of fantasy in the poignant everyday. For her poverty is as real as her umbrella or as the ale she drinks:

> "I am but a poor woman, but I've been sought arter, sir, though you may not think it. I've been knocked up at all hours of the night, and warned out by a many landlords, in consequence of being mistook for Fire. I goes out workin' for my bread, 'tis true, but I maintains my indepency, with your kind leave, and which I will till death. . . . My earnings is not great, sir, but I will not be impoged upon. Bless the babe, and save the mother, is my mortar, sir; but I makes so free as add to that, Don't try no impogician with the Nuss, for she will not abear it!" 24

Her words are indeed mortar, a great triumph of language, drawing the novel together in memory after many years. She endured.

10 THE POSSESSED: THE NOVEL AS TRAGEDY

The European novel achieves, with *The Possessed,* an unprecedented seriousness and richness and complexity. It is a central moment in the history of modern consciousness, and casts a dark spidery shadow over a genre once expected to lightly entertain. But the novel also here achieves, it may seem, an ultimate confusion of aim. "A terrible mess," Dostoevsky observes, at a despairing hour in the Notebooks, as he strikes out in several thematic directions. To read *The Possessed* is a baffling, exasperating, overwhelming experience, and an inexhaustible one: given half a chance, the novel becomes part of one's life.

We are thrust, at a first reading of the first two hundred pages (Part One), into an existential confusion: the unordered life of an unidentified provincial town. We attend, if to one thing more than any other, to the comic discomfiture of a has-been and vain *littérateur,* Stepan Trofimovitch Verkhovensky. But confusion is intensified here, and even after the first part, because the narrator (sometimes a real person with fleshly desires, sometimes only a ghostly voice) is himself often in the dark, and gives us few clues as to what will be important. We are drawn into his bewilderment; and into worse, since he refers familiarly and casually to persons and events of which we know nothing. But the chief source of confusion is Dostoevsky himself, who was so long uncertain as to what his book was about. Was it to be a story of political folly and political crime and nihilist menace (which he referred to as "the pamphlet")? A moral Life of a Great Sinner ("the poem") and psychological study of Nikolay

Stavrogin? A picture of a community in a time of disquiet and transition, and by implication of Russia generally, dreading revolutionary disorder ten years after the liberation of the serfs, and menaced by the ideas of westernizing socialists and unbelievers?

The novel repeatedly threatens to split into two (one plot centering in Pyotr, the other in Stavrogin), but first reading of the first part would hardly reveal this, since the protagonist of one plot appears only on page 180, of the other on page 182. The author gropes, the narrator gropes, inevitably the reader. *The Possessed* is, even in its latest conscious intentions, heterogeneous and polyphonic—a symphony of voices and ideas, a cathedral of many chapels and bays. Interest swings back and forth, after the first part, between the individual destinies and the community threatened by hysteria and disorder. The greatest menace to a minimal necessary coherence would seem to lie, structurally, in Stavrogin's absence from so many pages, a menace aggravated by the suppression of his Confession. But in fact we do not forget him. He remains a shadowy presence, in the consciousness of his disciples and friends, and also in ours. The confusions are slighter than those of *The Idiot* but far greater than those of *The Brothers Karamazov*. Mochulsky's extravagant claim for a unified masterpiece would seem to demoralize criticism and falsify matters from the start: "Every episode is justified, every detail calculated; the disposition and sequence of the scenes are determined by the unity of the design. This world is possessed by a single impulse, animated by a single idea; *it is dynamic, and rushes towards its goal.*" [1]

On a second or later reading we are no longer so concerned with mysteries of plot. But we continue to ponder issues and motives that have been left enigmatic. Incorrigibly the reader expects to locate the author at last, and pin down his sympathies and judgments. In his polyphonic novels, Bakhtin argues, surely going too far, Dostoevsky's voice is merely one of those joined in debate, equal among equals. It is obviously tempting to identify the author with the Slavophil Shatov, who summarizes succinctly what he had learned from Stavrogin: an organic conservative view of church and state that is in some respects recognizably Dostoevsky's. But we may feel identification too with Kirillov and his epileptic's vision of eternity; with Stepan in his eloquent defense of beauty and art; even with Stavrogin and his crimes, moving implacably toward confession and suicide. Dostoevsky projects his feelings and distributes his ideas among these and several others, and aspects of his unstable temperament among all. As a chain-smoking author may scatter his pages with cigarettes, so the harassed Dostoevsky, dreading the recurrence of disabling fits, metes out a more than normal incidence of irritability, *folie circulaire,* epilepsy. It is in the creative splitting of self that Dostoevsky most nearly approaches Shakespeare. But there is a difference, which makes Dostoevsky more "modern": the origins of ideological commitments are repeatedly left uncertain. Is a character's ideological choice rational and unequivocal or neurotic, compulsive, double-edged? The possibility of "brain fever" and insanity is raised with Stavrogin, with Pyotr, of course with Kirillov, even with Liza. Is Kirillov madman or fool or saint? Dostoevsky would insist that an idea may be valid, however neurotic its origin. This great ideological novel—philosophical, religious, political—is also, inescapably, psychological. But definitive dissection of motives is avoided. Dostoevsky is very modern in his deliberate refusal to explain.

The result of so much ambiguity of motive, and of so many ideas left half-developed, is that a second or third reading may occur in some sense *outside the novel*. Kirillov becomes a "problem" to be meditated, for us as for Gide and Camus. Stavrogin's Confession, like the pages of the Grand Inquisitor, can be read apart from its intended novelistic context: a great self-contained psychological document, a novel in miniature. As we ponder motives, and the conscious and unconscious in conflict, so too we come to think, outside the novel, about the problem of ends and means. There is, moreover, another great dramatic book to induce speculation outside the novel: the Notebooks. Political theory and speculation are there much richer and more explicit than in the novel; Dostoevsky struggled with certain formulations in the Notebooks, and got some of them out of his system. The entries devoted to Nechaev's political principles (341–58) are as ruthlessly schematic as the famous "Catechism of a Revolutionist" of history, perhaps jointly authored by Bakunin and Nechaev. Some recent interpretations of *The Possessed* appear to be based on the explicit doctrines of the Notebooks, rather than on the scantier ones of the novel. This would seem a first critical obligation: to keep notebook and novel characters separate: not confuse the theorizing Nechaev with the Mephistophelian Pyotr, nor the influential Granovsky with the vain and long-futile Stepan.

There is a further reason why a rereading of *The Possessed* may be a largely meditative experience, one that invites many pauses for speculation "outside the book." This is the fact that some of the essential and most dramatic events occur off-stage or are scarcely dramatized at all (the murder of the Lebyadkins and Liza's surrender to Stavrogin); or have occurred in the past (Stavrogin's crime against the little girl). This crime, which would seem to explain so much, reaches us through a Confession not published in Dostoevsky's lifetime, and now sometimes published in appendix, if at all, rather than in its intended place after Part Two, chapter 8. The dramatic present time of *The Possessed* reveals completed states of the soul and will (or absence of will) and the ruthlessly completed, inescapable logic of Kirillov and Shigalov. The time for spiritual change is, with one notable exception, past. The passions of the characters, moreover, themselves determined by past events, are for the most part kept under severe, even neurotic control. Central figures—Stavrogin, Shatov, Kirillov, even Liza, even Dasha—are thus doubly unfree. They are prisoners of the past and, in the present, often suppress or disguise their deepest feelings. Only Stepan, the slave of slovenly habits and of his vanity, breaks free at last—both to achieve a genuine change in life, and to say eloquently what he feels and believes. In *The Brothers Karamazov,* by contrast, the passions are directly, openly, violently expressed—rage, envy, lust, self-lacerating spite, contrition and shame and guilt. Even where the material is speculative and problematic, as at the trial, the voices of the prosecutor and the lawyer for the defense keep the reader in a dramatic present. The spiritual crises are here and now.

The Possessed has, to be sure, its great scenes of comic and tragic drama in a true fictional present. The end of the first part, culminating in Liza's ominous fall to the floor, is splendidly theatrical, with little meditative interruption; so too the extended comic disorder of the governesses' benefit. There are carnivalesque scenes, in Bakhtin's term, where confrontations occur in a public place, with social barriers breaking down and pretenders overthrown. And no dramatic literature is more enthralling than the sections leading to the deaths of Shatov and Kirillov. But Dostoevsky knew that not everything on that terrible night could be shown. We have only glimpses of Kirillov on the brink of suicide. We are not brought inside the anguish of Marya Shatov, as she comes upon Kirillov's body but fails to read the letter announcing her husband's death. "The terrible effect on her of what she saw may well be imagined." That is all. Dostoevsky invites us to pause or return to this moment, fill in subjective details, imagine it for ourselves.

The history of *The Possessed*'s composition shows a fascinated and speculative response to contemporary events. *The Idiot,* coldly received in 1868, by no means exhausted the creative impulses which pointed to the never-written *Atheism* and to the also unwritten fictional "poem," *The Life of a Great Sinner*—a swarm of ideas in orbit on which Stavrogin and both Ivan and Alyosha Karamazov would draw. Dostoevsky interrupted his plans for *The Life of a Great Sinner* early in 1870 to compose a political "pamphlet." But this pamphlet became *The Possessed,* finished late in 1872. The pamphlet was inspired by the assassination, in November 1869, of the student Ivanov on the grounds of the Petrovsk Agricultural Academy, because he challenged the authority of Nechaev, the leader and organizer of a cell or committee of five and of a pretended network of such secret committees. Other members of the cell were involved in the murder, possibly to cement the leader's hold over them. The crime would have the more readily caught Dostoevsky's attention because he had already concluded that political troubles were likely to occur at the Petrovsk Academy, where his young brother-in-law was a student. Anna wrote in her memoirs:

> Fearing that my brother, through lack of years and weakness of character, might take an active part in them, my husband persuaded my mother to send him to stay with us in Dresden. . . . My brother enthusiastically told him everything in detail. It was from this that Fedor Mikhaylovich conceived the idea of depicting the political movement of the time in one of his novels, and of taking, as one of the chief heroes, the student Ivanov (under the name of Shatov) who was later to be killed by Nechayev. My brother spoke of this student as an intelligent person, remarkable for his firmness of character, who had radically changed his former convictions. How deeply shaken my husband was when he learned later from the papers of the murder of Ivanov.[2]

Nechaev, who at twenty-two had become the intimate of Bakunin and had appeared in Moscow as the famous exile's official representative (thanks to a series of audacious pretenses), returned to Switzerland. The other conspirators were captured and tried in July–September, 1871. Among papers uncovered were a copy of "The Catechism of a Revolutionist," and data calling for a revolution on February 19, 1870. But there had been predictions well before the Ivanov murder that 1870 would be a critical year, since it would complete a nine-year period for full implementation of the liberation of the serfs, and would bring decisions on the peasants' tenure of the land. There were other anxieties in 1870 and 1871: the Franco-Prussian War, the siege of Paris, and the Paris commune (March 18 to the end of May, 1871), so briefly flourishing and so violently overthrown. Nechaev himself was not arrested and extradited until October 1872.[3] The novel was written, that is—and it would be hard to overstress the importance of this to the creative imagination—while Nechaev was still at large. He was tried in January and condemned to twenty years' hard labor, to be followed by exile for life in Siberia. But he was taken instead to an impregnable part of the Peter Paul Fortress, where he died the year after Dostoevsky, but not before organizing his jailers with some success into revolutionary groups, and even attempting to plan an assassination of the Czar. He is, among Max Nomad's "Apostles of Revolution," the prototype of the fanatic; for Albert Camus, the logical extreme of the immoral terrorist.[4] Not impossibly he was, in addition to the fantastically successful double agent Azeff, an inspirer of Conrad's great Dostoevskyan novel, *Under Western Eyes*.[5]

The year 1867 also was important for the author of *The Possessed:* a dark difficult year, with disabling fits, the usual financial troubles, compulsive gambling losses in Baden. In 1867 he married Anna, and they went to Geneva to prepare for the birth of her child, who died in May 1868, to the father's great grief. At Baden too occurred the famous confrontation with Turgenev, mercilessly satirized in *The Possessed* as the effeminate Karmazinov. Declaring himself an atheist, and in spirit a German not a Russian (for Russia had no future), and eager for a rapprochement with the younger generation of revolutionaries . . . Turgenev seemed the very type of the hazy liberal corrupted by western influences and the spirit of 1848. In Geneva, significantly, Dostoevsky associated with the Russian political emigrés, including Herzen and Bakunin, great names of that earlier generation. He met them at the lodgings of his old friend Ogarev, who in time would write a poem (ostensibly by Herzen) in honor of the infamous Nechaev.[6] Dostoevsky, moving perhaps unwittingly toward a political novel, was intensely interested to see the new socialist militants and revolutionaries in the flesh.

His great opportunity came with the congress of the League for Peace and Freedom of September 1867, in Geneva. It was planned as a meeting of essentially democratic pacifists alarmed by the prospects of war, with pure liberals or heroes of the "old abstract revolutions" (Conrad) in attendance—Victor Hugo, John Stuart Mill, Louis Blanc, Littré and many more—Ogarev as a vice-president and Garibaldi in the president's chair. The meeting was infiltrated by members of the Internationale, who had been meeting nearby, and who constituted some two-fifths of the audience. The great dramatic moment was the appearance on a political platform of Bakunin for the first time in twenty years, in his historic gray cape: a standing ovation as Garibaldi threw himself into his arms. Bakunin's speech, which outraged Dostoevsky, was a stunning success. It began with a protest against the very existence of the Russian Empire, based as it was on a denial of human liberty. The ideas bruited at the Geneva congress—the abolition of Christianity, the destruction of national states in favor of a United States of Europe, the apocalyptic destruction of the Old World and the achievement of peace through violence—seemed to Dostoevsky stale and sinister follies. So too the anarchist strategy of revolution through association with the outlaws of society, even murderers and wandering brigands.

The meetings with Bakunin, his speech at the congress and the enthusiasm it aroused in suddenly radicalized old-fashioned liberals, no doubt contributed to the early dreaming of *The Possessed*. But surely Leonid Grossman is mistaken in assuming that the fictional Stavrogin is a portrait of Bakunin. There is too wide a gulf between Bakunin's volubility and undiminished anarchist faith and the silences of the aristocratic Stavrogin, who believes in nothing at all. The important political manipulator of *The Possessed* is not Stavrogin but Pyotr Verkhovensky.

THE POLITICAL NOVEL: PYOTR AND THE QUINTET

Within the rich but often confused ideological complex of *The Possessed,* one theme has been overstressed by critics: the influence of the liberal idealists of the 1840's (Belinsky, Granovsky, Stepan the father) on the nihilists and even anarchists of the 1860's (Nechaev, Pyotr the son). We have a clear example of critics seizing on statements made outside a novel—declared intentions, autobiographical musings—for the purpose of interpreting the novel itself. An early Notebook entry has Granovsky (later Stepan) debate the effect of his "uprooted generation." [7] Dostoevsky, member of the vaguely subversive "Petrashevsky Circle" from 1847 to 1849, raises the question in the *Diary of a Writer* for 1873: "How do you know that the Petrashevists could not have become the Nechayevists . . . ?" Probably, he writes, "I could never have become a *Nechayev,* but a *Nechayevist,* this I do not vouch; it is possible, I too could have become one . . . in the days of my youth." [8] Even here, as the last clause suggests, we are not dealing with two generations but with two forms of radicalism. Elsewhere he writes more succinctly that the "Belinskys and Granovskys would not believe it if you told them that they were the direct fathers of the Nechaevs. It is precisely the close development of this thought, going from fathers to children that I want to express in my work." [9]

These statements, especially when so extracted, sound persuasive, and suggest a calculated response to Turgenev's *Fathers and Sons.* But the Stepan of the novel is in no sense the intellectual father of Pyotr, whom he has hardly known, and there is little ideological debate between the two. His responsibility is moral not intellectual. He had shipped Pyotr off as a child and gradually sold most of his son's inherited woods, as he had sold his serf Fedka to pay a gambling debt. The victims return to haunt him. Sentimentality not radicalism made him a bad tutor for Liza and Stavrogin. Stepan is no more a true representative of the forties than Pyotr (socialist or scoundrel or madman?) is a "new man" of the sixties. They are both, in their way, pretenders.

The novel, Dostoevsky wrote Alexander II, was to be a study of Russian radicalism. How many high officials of the 1870's reached Lenin's succinct judgment of it: "repulsive but great"? *The Possessed*'s brilliant story of political influence concerns less generational change than the manipulation of fools and the ·radicalizing of liberal enthusiasts. The manipulator is Pyotr, though Stavrogin could have been the original corruptor. Pyotr is the only *active* force of evil in the novel, disrupting and contaminating a weak and passive society. Remove him from the novel, leaving Stavrogin in his chronic immobility, and nothing would happen. Edward Wasiolek's interesting formula—that Stepan's circle *"is both ideologically and structurally the source of the public events that follow"* [10]—needs qualifying. For *ideas* bruited in the circle have little to do with what happens. The circle, though rumored to be a hotbed of nihilism, merely indulges "in the most harmless, agreeable, typically Russian light-hearted chatter," and "fell into generalizing about humanity." Only the Fourierist Liputin and Virginsky, at this early stage, seem to have genuinely radical ideas, and the conservative Shatov is a member. The shifting membership and the movement to the salon of the governor's wife, Yulia von Lembke, takes place unobtrusively, but with Pyotr controlling all. He trades on her foolish dream of keeping young people from the brink of the political abyss, and on her longing—shared with Karmazinov/Turgenev—to keep in touch with the radical younger generation.

The structure and relationship of the various groups is very complex, and my own sorting out (based strictly on the novel's text) may well be more orderly than any Dostoevsky had time to make. No doubt he saw ambiguity and mystification as essential to his picture of this murky world; moreover he deliberately leaves the narrator (who does not at first see Shigalov's role) in the dark. But, also, it may be, Dostoevsky did not realize how little of his conception of the secret groups was transferred from the politically richer Notebooks to the novel.

There appear to be six interlocking associations, listed here from more to less secret, with a seventh (the *Internationale* of history) alluded to:

1. *The Original Disciples of Stavrogin, the Lost Leader:* Pyotr, Shatov, Kirillov. Pyotr has had and perhaps still clings at times to his mad dream of revolution, from which Stavrogin is to emerge as leader of the nation (Part Two, chapter 8: "Ivan the Tsarevitch"): a Pretender. Shatov and presumably Kirillov had looked up to him as a potential leader. Two years before Stavrogin had (according to Shatov) preached a Slavophil nationalist Christianity to him and, simultaneously, atheistic materialism to Kirillov. The friendship of the four in the past, although it is, in a hypothetical undramatized "real life," the ideological core of the novel, reaches the reader through hints, allusions and enigmatic dialogue, and is likely to be overlooked by many.

2. *"The Society":* Pyotr, Shigalov, Liputin (?), Tolkatchenko (?), and marginally Stavrogin, Shatov, Kirillov, Lebyadkin. Based abroad, and possibly

connected with the socialist *Internationale,* it has succeeded (according to Stavrogin) in establishing agents in Russia. Shatov joined the Society, just after listening to Stavrogin's conservative teachings, partly because it "is difficult to change Gods," and so "plunged for the last time into that sewer" of atheist materialism. Now he wants to resign and is told he will be permitted to do so if he surrenders a hidden printing press. But he is assassinated by the Quintet. There had been an "old organization" and Stavrogin "took some part in reorganising the society on the new plan," Yet strictly speaking he does not belong to it. Here too we see the lost leader who acts, if he acts at all, without belief. The convict Fedka (in keeping with Nechaevan principles of using the only true revolutionaries) is also a marginal member and, the narrator believes, has joined in agitating among the factory workers. It is not clear whether the members of the Quintet, which is largely a private operation of Pyotr's, automatically becomes members of the Society. In Lyamshin's confession, the two groups are seen to be interlocked, with the aim of "systematically destroying society and all principles. . . ."

3. *The Quintet:* the secret activist cell, modeled on the quintet of the historical Nechaev, and the murder of the student Ivanov. It still is not known whether Nechaev's Quintet was the only one in existence or whether, as he claimed, there was a network of quintets controlled by a central committee. It is to be assumed, in *The Possessed,* that Pyotr's is the only one. The Quintet is originally composed of Liputin, Virginsky and Lyamshin (recruits from Stepan's circle), Shigalov and Tolkatchenko, who knows the world of thieves. The quintet was apparently formed by Tolkatchenko and Shigalov, as emissaries of Pyotr; he, when he arrives, makes a sixth. And the Quintet becomes a group of seven when joined by Erkel, the cold emissary of death.

4. *The Ad Hoc Committee* and association of liberals and radicals, meeting on the occasion of Virginsky's name-day. About fifteen, including the Quintet, are present. This is a potential "front organization," still secret but distinctly less secret than any of the preceding. Some have no idea why they have been invited. One is reminded of the categories of persons to be radicalized, as outlined in sections 19 and 20 of the Nechaev-Bakunin Catechism: ambitious officeholders and liberals of various shades, doctrinaires, conspirators, revolutionaries talking idly in groups and on paper. The confusion of the meeting (even the uncertainty as to whether it really is a "meeting") will be familiar to readers of *The Sentimental Education* and to all who attended comparable meetings in 1968 and 1970 in the United States. The confusion is intensified when Shigalov rises to read from his immense manuscript that perplexes even him, since it starts with unlimited freedom and ends in unlimited despotism. Pyotr

manipulates the group brilliantly, and guides it to the crucial question: would the members, if they knew of a projected political murder, inform and give warning? Shatov (whom Pyotr has brought to the meeting for this purpose) gets up in disgust and leaves . . . an act which seals his doom.

5. *Yulia von Lembke's Circle:* Pyotr, Liputin, Lyamshin, Karmazinov, the Narrator, others. A wholly unsecret group of friends, firmly and at times secretly controlled by Pyotr, with Liputin and Lyamshin active members and minor devils, and with the great writer Karmazinov in bungling association. Yulia, with her dream of saving young radicals, is totally unaware of Pyotr's skillful plans to disrupt the governesses' fete she has organized and thus, by exasperating everybody, release latent forces of violence and anarchy.

6. *Stepan's Circle,* which virtually dissolves after Pyotr's arrival: the Narrator, Stepan, Shatov, Liputin, Virginsky, with Lyamshin coming as a guest and Shigalov (not yet known as an emissary of genuine radicalism) coming from abroad. Another guest is mentioned, one Captain Kartuzov, who immediately disappears from the book. Very important in the Notebooks, he gives many of his traits to Captain Lebyadkin. This too is an unsecret, largely social group of friends. Its reputation as a hotbed of radicalism is undeserved, and the raid on Stepan's lodgings a bureaucratic blunder.

The picture of interlocking associations, though perhaps more confusing than Dostoevsky intended, corresponds with the bewildering reality of most times of crisis and transition: the France of 1944 and 1945 as well as 1848, for instance.

Pyotr dominates all. The critic Mikhailovsky, while applauding Dostoevsky's "brilliant psychiatric talent," asked whether he had any "basis . . . for grouping around the Nechaev affair people soaked through with mysticism. I think not, and even less does he have the right to present them as types of contemporary Russian youth in general." [11] But Dostoevsky's famous letter to Katkov of October 8, 1870, is remarkably succinct and persuasive. Though Pyotr may not be like the real Nechaev, "in my astonished mind imagination has created that character, that type, which corresponds to this crime. . . . To my personal amazement, this character developed in my hands into a half-comic character. . . ." [12]

At one point in the Notebooks, fascinated with Stavrogin as a potential leader and as his "successor," Pyotr intends to bind him though crime: the murder of Marya Lebyadkin.[13] The motivations in the novel are by no means so clear, and no little of the ambiguity is deliberate, as a crucial Notebook entry indicates. Pyotr is to be a shadowed character, his true self revealed only gradually.[14] Is it ever definitively revealed? There would seem to be, in the novel, three distinct personalities: the real or pretended *revolutionary;* the trickster or Mephistophelian *imp;* the true *devil* and cold cynical lover of evil, who seeks out and trades on human weakness. The personalities alternate within a single chapter or even momentarily blend. There is in addition Pyotr's psychological, internalized role as a double for Stavrogin: the instigator of a crime that another double, Fedka, will commit.

The revolutionary who dreams of absolute power for Stavrogin, in the aftermath of a general upheaval, may be sincere at times. But he is also almost in delirium, behaving as though drunk, a madman, in Stavrogin's frightened whisper, staring with wild eyes. The novel confirms the Notebooks' picture of a man with little sense of political reality. At times he seems motivated only by malice and scorn, and acts without political aim. The murder of Shatov is problematic. The great dark picture of almost gratuitous political crime, of motiveless malignity, is attenuated by the narrator's remark that Pyotr really was convinced Shatov would betray the group, as by the revelation that he had been insulted by Shatov in the past. But there is nothing equivocal or inauthentic in the picture of the terrorist who keeps his men under full control at moments of crisis. At the gloomy scene of the murder (with one of Dostoevsky's very rare evocations of landscape) Liputin and Virginsky and even the mad Shigalov want to back off from the crime, now that Shatov's wife has returned. But Pyotr easily holds the first two in line and, as Shigalov walks away, seems to be condemning him too to death.

The trickster or Mephistophelian imp, the half-comic character who emerged in spite of Dostoevsky's intentions, is present on many more pages: the subtle serpent of the last pages of Part One, who exposes secrets and dethrones the complacent. An abandoned plan had him introduce counterfeit money as a way to foment disorder: precisely what Gide had in mind for the devil who was to circulate incognito in *The Counterfeiters.* Once Pyotr even lays claim to a Mephistophelian occult power to peer in every corner and behind closed doors: he overheard a whispered conversation and knew Liputin had pinched his wife black and blue at midnight, three days before. The Hardyish suggestion of dark mystery is unfortunately destroyed by the explanation that he had paid Liputin's servant to spy. The Mephistophelian Pyotr seems driven by a malicious but real sense of fun. He likes to pierce the bubble of vanity, create chaos among those overly concerned with order. The governesses' benefit fete admirably serves a symbolic function: both conveys the latent hysteria and violence of a society in transition and suggests that schemes for social leveling may be snares, defrauding the lower classes of promised benefits. Yet one feels that for Pyotr, as certainly for the reader, disruption of the fete, and the outraging of the foolish

Yulia, is above all good fun. Pyotr's merciless treatment of his father springs less from a sense of injustice than from a desire to prick the windbag. Stepan's pretense of paternal feeling for a son abandoned many years before is cut away by Pyotr's very first lines.

The impish Pyotr is always extraordinarily alive, as he puzzles and bedevils the governor, taunts his father and teases Karmazinov. Pyotr's bad manners shock Karmazinov, wrapped in his mantle of the great writer's vanity and aristocratic breeding, and bring him to outraged attention. He has been awaiting Pyotr eagerly, because he wants to be in contact with the younger generation, and because he has given him the manuscript of his farewell address, *Merci,* to read. Pyotr is irritated (as was Dostoevsky at the famous meeting in Baden) by the great man's proffered cheek. He rudely demands a cutlet, coffee, wine, and calmly scrutinizes Karmazinov's effeminate attire and the plaid robe over his knees. Pyotr's every line, as in a Molière comedy, is a stab at the writer's vanity. Dostoevsky returned Turgenev's *Spectres* unread. Pyotr cannot remember the title of the manuscript he has been given and, to the writer's consternation, is not even sure where it is. The trickster's game, which is to speak rapidly and as though free from guile, at last drives the writer to an enraged and hissing response: "You don't read very much, it seems?"

The great fictional success of this half-comic Pyotr derives from his incessant activity, and incessant talking, in a society of the apathetic, the restrained or conventional, the fearful. His introduction to the novel, in Varvara's drawing-room near the end of Part One, is highly dramatic. He moves into a situation where everyone is tense, suppressing either questions or answers. Within a few pages, guilelessly talking and talking, he has repudiated his father and (by revealing an indiscreet letter) jeopardized Stepan's relationship with Varvara, foreclosed any possibility of the marriage with Dasha; has terrified Captain Lebyadkin by threatening to reveal Stavrogin's secret; has talked freely of Stavrogin's "life of mockery" in Petersburg; has humiliated Liza, Dasha and Varvara before her old rival; has precipitated the emotional crisis which leads to Shatov's blow, and Stavrogin's astonishing acceptance of it, and thus to Liza's fainting which brings the great scene to a close.

Pyotr has his playful bustling moments with Stavrogin, though his ultimate role is to implant criminal impulses or awaken dormant ones. The coldly diabolic Pyotr, absolutely in control of himself and others, is revealed in his manipulation of Shatov and above all Kirillov. His is the cynic's pleasure in trading expertly on weaknesses. But, also, he simply wants to see Shatov and Kirillov die. The ostensible political motives—to preclude informing by Shatov, to cover the crime with Kirillov's false confession—seem almost irrelevant, given the forceful sense of pure "motiveless malignity" and ruthless exertion of power. Of the many scenes in which Pyotr controls others, to their discomfiture or ruin, his last interview with Kirillov is probably the greatest. The time has come for Kirillov, though he is not yet aware of Shatov's death, to commit suicide after signing a dictated confession, a last service to the party ostensibly, in reality an assertion of philosophical indifference. But Pyotr, as though to intensify the pleasure of the game, refuses to make things easy for himself. He outrages Kirillov by sitting down to eat the boiled chicken and rice that his victim will not, after all, need. Moments later, bluntly, he reveals Shatov has been killed: the crime to which Kirillov must confess. He knows how to overcome Kirillov's refusal to sign the document, and go through with his suicide: by putting the philosopher back on his fatal track of reasoning. Pyotr is even willing to admit to this strategy, which Kirillov recognizes, yet quickly leads him through a chain of seemingly neutral concepts and words—*scoundrels, words, comfort*—to the traumatic premise that God does not exist. Five pages later, after Pyotr has skillfully led him to his old conclusion that he must kill himself to prove his independence and freedom, Kirillov is in a "positive frenzy" and ready to sign anything, and, after poignant hesitation, to shoot himself. There is no more intensely visualized figure in Dostoevsky's fiction than Kirillov standing in the dark room, in the immobility of death, still clinging to life. And no more brutal act than Pyotr's response: to scorch the unmoving man's face with his candle. The playfully malicious and half-comic Pyotr has given way to a figure of cold and absolute evil.

THE IDEOLOGICAL NOVEL: STAVROGIN AS LOST LEADER

The ideological core of *The Possessed* (as distinct from Pyotr's political plot) is to be found in the long night of Stavrogin's several confrontations, in the first two chapters of Part Two: with Pyotr, with Kirillov, with Shatov, with the convict Fedka, with his wife Marya Timofyevna. By the end of this night of intense dialogues, with Stavrogin sometimes listening to ideas he no longer believes in, the drama of belief has modulated to a psychological scrutiny of will and motive. The night really begins, after two expository scenes with Pyotr, with Stavrogin in trance-like sleep, sitting quite erect and with the look of a lifeless wax figure. This is followed by ten minutes in which he sits with his eyes open, as immovable as before: a striking foreshadowing of Kirillov's trance-like immobility in the minutes before his death. There is a hint of demonic possession; his mother, terrified, makes the sign of the cross over him. We are thus prepared for a night of spiritual crisis, as Stavrogin is let out through a door always kept locked, enters Filipov's house through a gate that is also kept locked. The ostensible reasons for his visits—to arrange for Kirillov to second him in a duel with Gaganov, to warn Shatov that the revolutionaries may murder him—are subordinated to the ideological, even metaphysical dialogues that follow. The crucial issue underlying both scenes, and tormenting both Kirillov and Shatov, is whether they can believe in God. Kirillov had already echoed one of Dostoevsky's recorded sayings: "God has tormented me all my life." And Shatov echoes another famous one: "But didn't you tell me that if it were mathematically proved to you that the truth excludes Christ, you'd prefer to stick to Christ rather than to the truth?"

Kirillov, who came very late in the conception of the novel (the Engineer of the Notebooks) is its most enigmatic figure: the lover of life who can have moments of innocent happiness as the time for his suicide approaches; the man who believes "everything is good," but must repudiate the cosmic scheme; the Christ-like sacrificer of self for an Idea and for the future freedom of mankind who takes pride in his revolvers, is willing to serve as second in a duel, and even condone in a sense the murder of Shatov and falsely confess to it. His happiness (in the hours he clings to it) is in part that of a man who has achieved indifference and denied value, given the certainty of death. The man who kills himself for philosophical reasons will explode the myths of God and an after-life, kill the fear of death, and thereby himself become God. The happy indifference to be won is close to that of Meursault at the end of *The Stranger,* Claude Vannec's at the end of Malraux's *The Royal Way,* Julien Sorel's at the end of *The Red and the Black:* the skeptic's pride in a lucidity that has triumphed over illusion and myth, and dispelled the shadow cast by concern for an after-life.[15] But if there is no God, with everything therefore "my will," the implicit nightmare is that everything is permitted. Kirillov cannot tolerate the absurd, though he preaches it, and he longs for God too much to endure the non-existence he is trying to prove.

In the first major confrontation with Stavrogin we feel the divided human being and saintly mystic, rather than the relentless logician. He is delighted by Stavrogin's late-evening visit and says significantly, at the end of the scene, "Remember what you have meant in my life, Stavrogin" . . . words that will be echoed by Shatov on the next page, and by Lebyadkin later in the evening. Stavrogin has found him playing ball with a baby, and seemingly in a happy mood. Kirillov is happy because he is fond of life and because everything is good; he who teaches that all are good will become the man-god. "I pray to everything. You see the spider crawling on the wall, I look at it and thank it for crawling"—a benign spider in contrast to the one that will haunt Stavrogin. Kirillov's vision of universal goodness leads to his idea of eternal life, not a future eternal life, but one experienced here and now, during moments when time stands still. Idea (a conception of the eternal that particularly attracted Gide) and neurosis are again intertwined. For such moments, we are reminded, are like the ecstatic ones immediately preceding an epileptic fit.

Much in addition to absurd reasoning remains enigmatic. What precisely was Kirillov's relationship with Stavrogin in the past, and what did he learn from him? Atheistic materialism, according to Shatov. Or are we to believe that Stavrogin encouraged fatal theories of self-mastery and independence of the will? In the present time of the novel we see in Kirillov no philosophical repudiation of Stavrogin comparable to Shatov's violent one. The most likely explanation, once again, is that Dostoevsky (granted his belief in shadowed characterization) was unaware of how little of his own conception of the Kirillov discipleship was getting onto the printed page. And was he aware of how vestigial and unexplained is Kirillov's other role as activist and member of the Society?

The final contradiction, which leaves Kirillov intellectually exciting but fictionally implausible, lies in the collision between his kindly personality, deeply moved by the reconciliation with Shatov and by the return of Shatov's wife, and the theorist who (thanks to philosophical indifference) harbors a murderer and accepts the murder of his friend. For many western readers the false confession of Shatov's murder will remain a stumbling-block, whatever rationalization is brought to it. The harboring of the convict is more easily explained: he shelters Fedka because, given the denial of value, the murderer too is good; shelters him out of Christian compassion for a fugitive brother too, and also because Fedka was an outlaw and "true revolutionary" in the archaic political plot; and, finally (as we go back to the mysteries of composition) because Fedka and Kirillov had split off from the Kulikov of the Notebooks. Kirillov, one of Dostoevsky's most fascinating creations, entirely discredits Mochulsky's conception of a unified novel in which everything falls into place.

The personality, beliefs and behavior of Shatov (whom Stavrogin visits next) are far more of a piece, though the attraction Stavrogin held for him in the past and still at times holds has to be taken on faith. Even in the disillusioned present Shatov can momentarily think of Stavrogin as a potential leader: "You, only you can raise that flag!" The intensity of their connection, deeply felt by Shatov and resisted by Stavrogin, brings them together as "for the last time in the world." Shatov's irritability and irascible bad manners are highly plausible. He has the pride of the former serf as educated as the aristocrats with whom he was brought up, though he had been expelled from the university, and has too the familiar morose seriousness of the ideologue for whom the socialist God has failed. At the end of Part One he had broken deliberately through intense restraint to deliver the smashing blow that Stavrogin did not return, to the astonishment of all. Stavrogin had lived with Shatov's wife and was rumored to have seduced his sister Dasha. There was the other rumor, now confirmed, that he had married Marya Lebyadkin . . . out of aristocratic boredom? Moral sensuality? Pleasure in laceration of the nerves? There had been rumors too of his practicing beastly sensuality in Petersburg and decoying, corrupting children. Shatov implies he struck Stavrogin because of his lie, and because of his "fall," the generalized betrayal by the lost leader and idol. "I did it because you meant so much to me in my life."

Shatov is an intensely real, entirely coherent personage, and a very poignant one as he responds joyfully—again to look far ahead—to his tired wife's return and to the fact that she is about to give birth. His presence is also very moving in the long night of spiritual crisis that opens Part Two. But his deepest function is to articulate Dostoevsky's own convictions, i.e. those that Stavrogin himself had preached. There are, Shatov explains, two great western menaces to the nationalist idea and the Russian God: worldly and internationalist Roman Catholicism and atheist socialism, with its assumption that society should be founded on principles of science and reason. Nations are built up and moved, instead, by a different force, "the origin of which is unknown and inexplicable," and every national movement must seek its own God. Becoming more and more eloquent, Shatov defines Russia's Messianic destiny, to bring the word of "renewal and resurrection." For only one nation, the Russian, is "God-bearing." Stavrogin is momentarily moved by this eloquent restatement of ideas he once preached, but remarks that "to cook your hare you must first catch it." Does Shatov himself believe in God?

> "I believe in Russia . . . I believe in her orthodoxy . . . I believe in the body of Christ . . . I believe that the new advent will take place in Russia . . . I believe . . . ." Shatov muttered frantically.
> "And in God? In God?"
> "I . . . I will believe in God." [16]

Such dialogues are confrontations as of beings "come together in infinity," inward debates in a sense, or debates with the suppressed thoughts of one's spiritual brother. The ideological, which for some pages has been presented in fairly abstract terms, though always passionately, shifts to psychological terms. Why, Shatov asks, is Stavrogin incapacitated? What is his motive for such a base and shameful marriage? What (picking up Pyotr's words, repeated by

Stavrogin himself) is his "extraordinary aptitude for crime"? Shatov's final succinct explanation of his moral sensuality is that Stavrogin is an atheist because a snob. "You've lost the distinction between good and evil because you've lost touch with your own people."

Stavrogin next visits his wife, Marya Timofyevna. On the way there he encounters Fedka, and repudiates his suspect offer of unspecified services. Stavrogin says to Captain Lebyadkin, the Falstaff of his Petersburg debauches, that he intends to make the marriage public: an alarming prospect, since it would mean an end to subsidy or blackmail. Marya herself, talking incoherently, and oscillating between terror and gaiety, is not sure what to make of a public announcement, or whether she can fulfill the social role of a wife living in a palace. Stavrogin proposes instead that they live together in the mountains in Switzerland. Marya responds that such a gloomy prospect is not worthy of her "falcon," her "prince." The man before her must be an impostor. She possesses the intuitive power of the holy fool. Now she claims she saw, though apparently asleep, a knife in Stavrogin's hand when he first came into the room. But "I'm the wife of my prince; I'm not afraid of your knife!" She shouts after him as he rushes off into the darkness: "A curse on you, Grishka Otrepyev!" He is a pretender like Otrepyev, cursed in seven cathedrals. In fact there had been no knife in Stavrogin's hand, but Marya was intuitively aware of the one in his mind. (Richard Peace takes Marya at her word: she was not really asleep when Stavrogin came in; she did see a knife.[17] Such an interpretation radically alters, and diminishes, the force of the scene.) Now Stavrogin finds Fedka lying in wait for him. And a real knife appears, gleaming in Fedka's hand. Stavrogin no longer resists. As though to accept Fedka's offer of murderous services, he flings bundles of rubles in the air. We will return to Fedka, and to the brilliantly executed psychological pattern.

The relationship with Marya Timofyevna, and certain aspects of Stavrogin himself, have religious overtones. Was his marriage with the crippled idiot a compulsive guilt-ridden response to his violation of the little girl; or the bored aristocrat's search for new sensations; or an act of true Christian humility? Stavrogin's name points in two ways: *Nikolay* (conqueror of nations) and *Vsevolodvitch* (master of all), but also to the Greek word *stavros* or cross. He is, as Kirillov observes, a man seeking a burden. George Steiner's interesting discussion in *Tolstoy or Dostoevsky* [18] points to various allusions to Christ, as well as to marks of a false Messiah, the bright guise of the antichrist. Soloviev, who claimed to know Dostoevsky's intentions, felt Stavrogin was the Judas or antichrist, with devils at his command.

The moving figure of the insulted and injured Marya Timofyevna is less ambiguously religious, though the psychological connections of child/idiot/cripple are important. Her language, Steiner notes, is saturated with Biblical phrases and allusions and her very name alludes to the theme of the pure white swan in the folklore of Russian heretical sects. She is presumably a virgin but has a baby in her dreams or fantasies, and is a movingly humble figure as we see her at the cathedral, in Varvara's drawing-room, and now in her poor room with her ikon, her pack of cards, her little looking glass, her song books and books with colored pictures. The meek and the half-witted shall inherit the earth. In the convent she had learned the heresy of the Mother of God as *magna mater,* the damp earth. She moves from half-witted inconsequence to beautiful eloquence, as she speaks of her tears of joy, and of going up a mountain near the convent: "I would turn to the east again, and the shadow, the shadow of our mountain was flying like an arrow over our lake, long, long and narrow, stretching a mile beyond, right up to the island on the lake and cutting that rocky island right in two, and as it cut it in two, the sun would set altogether and suddenly all would be darkness." She is the Marya Anonyma of Captain Lebyadkin's unconsciously profound saying: a potential savior, like Dasha waiting in the wings for Stavrogin to exhaust himself and come to her. His complicity in her murder is thus, in still another sense, a self-destructive act.

The enigmatic personality of Stavrogin broods over the novel, though he appears on comparatively few of its pages. Do not, Dostoevsky admonished himself, "explain the Prince." The psychological portrait, if we exclude the Confession at Tihon's, is as darkly shadowed as Dostoevsky could have wanted. Stavrogin is a figure of Byronic inscrutability: proud, isolated and possibly damned, harboring some dark secret. He has qualities, Peace notes, of the Byronic nobleman of the twenties and thirties; Shatov sees him as the "last of the noblemen's sons." We hear of riotous living in Petersburg in the past, a savage recklessness, with one man killed in a duel and another maimed, and gratuitously insulting behavior. He had lived there, Pyotr says, a "life of mockery," pursued (according to Stepan) by a demon of irony, with (Varvara) an "insatiable thirst for contrast." He had been listless and rather morose on his previous visit to the town, but suddenly the "wild beast showed his claws": leading the dignified older Gaganov by the nose, kissing Liputin's wife on the lips, biting the governor's ear. He is diagnosed as suffering from acute brain fever.

One other analysis of Stavrogin is of interest: his own, in the letter to Dasha, written shortly before his suicide—Dasha, the one person for whom he always shows some respect, and to whom he seems bound to tell the truth. He describes his present state, after his various experiments in testing his strength, as virtually one of *accìdie,* an absence of will or even strong desire. Was her brother right in saying that the man who loses his country loses his Gods? His weariness is that of Michel at the end of his inward journey in *The Immoralist,* and like Michel he has long failed to reveal a force lying behind his self-destructive drives. Within the novel proper (omitting, that is, the Confession) there are two crucial acts: the unexplained marriage to Marya Timofyevna and the criminal wishing for her death. The great difference from *The Brothers Karamazov* is that there is here no powerful, depraved, usurping father to be wished dead, and that Stavrogin lacks Ivan's intelligence and Dmitri's aggressive energy. He wholly lacks the Karamazov love of life. But Fedka as the agent of criminal will and projection of aggressive self is a worthy counterpart to Smerdyakov.

The confrontation with Fedka, on the long night of Part Two, is an extremely compact dramatization of traffic with such a double. The compactness is the more remarkable because Fedka (in the guise of the roaming convict Kulikov) was crucially important in very early plans for the book, and was associated from the start with Stavrogin's two great crimes: the murder of a lame woman, the violation of a child. Dostoevsky, who elsewhere allowed so much rich irrelevant life to enter his novel, wisely keeps Fedka's rare appearances very brief. His few speeches—claiming intimacy at once; rich in folk sayings and religious overtone, in the wisdom of the poor—preclude the quotidian banality that would have destroyed belief in his psychological role. Stavrogin's first encounter with him occurs on a floating bridge. He wakes from a profound revery to find himself alone there, then hears a deferential voice asking to share his umbrella. "There actually was a figure that crept under his umbrella, or tried to appear to do so." The tramp looming in such a sudden occult fashion gives an immediate impression of primitive, even savage energy, with his shaggy, curly hair and black eyes with a hard glitter and yellow tinge. He knows Stavrogin's name, has been waiting for him on the bridge for four nights. Stavrogin knows who the convict is, though he is seeing him for the first time. Psychologically, he is a criminal wish or impulse that has lain in wait where the night-walking Stavrogin was bound to come. He has in a sense risen from within. At this first meeting, walking toward the Lebyadkins, Stavrogin repudiates him. "Don't meet me in the future on the bridge or anywhere."

There follows the baffling scene with his wife, which concludes with her declaration that she is not afraid of his knife. The strangeness of her dialogue continues to keep Stavrogin's experience on a level of intimate communion, transcending everyday banality. Thus we are prepared for the second meeting with Fedka, which occurs almost at once, at the same place on the bridge.

There is a very precise statement of repression. "A knife, a knife," Stavrogin mutters angrily, thinking of Marya's words, and at first paying no attention to Fedka's greeting. "He was suddenly struck by the thought that he had entirely forgotten him, and had forgotten him at the very moment when he himself was repeating, 'A knife, a knife.' He seized the tramp by the collar and gave vent to his pent up rage by flinging him violently against the bridge." Stavrogin takes off his scarf to tie the convict's arms, then suddenly, "for some reason," desists. At once Fedka is on his feet, a short broad boot-knife in his hand. Stavrogin is almost ready to acknowledge the disowned wish.

He is encouraged, in the dialogue that follows, by the frankness with which Fedka, in the humble tones of a believing sinner, confesses his murder of the night watchman; such already is their intimacy. Fedka subtly suggests giving fifteen hundred rubles to Captain Lebyadkin (who drunkenly leaves his door open) and so creating a motive for murder. For the moment he asks only for three rubles, as to seal a bargain. And now, laughing aloud, Stavrogin no longer repudiates the outlaw thought, and flings bundles of rubles in the air for the convict to catch or pick up. Stavrogin clearly understands what he is doing, as he admits to Dasha shortly thereafter. On one more occasion Fedka will suddenly appear out of darkness, upon hearing the price of fifteen hundred rubles mentioned by Pyotr. He was brought there by Pyotr, original instigator of the criminal thought, but once again seems to rise from within Stavrogin. The doom of the Lebyadkins is sealed. With the announcement of their death—a bungled crime, since the bodies were not burned—Stavrogin makes his succinct, not entirely accurate statement to Liza: "I did not kill them, and I was against it, but I knew they were going to be killed and I did not stop the murders."

STAVROGIN'S CONFESSION

Such is the psychological pattern as it was published in Dostoevsky's lifetime, with so many of Stavrogin's neurotic responses and eccentric acts left unexplained. When we turn to the Confession "At Tihon's," first published in 1922, and consult also the early pages of the Notebooks, we discover that both the ideological and the psychological centers of the "intended" novel were omitted from it. For *The Life of the Great Sinner* was to have its climax in a confrontation with Bishop Tikhon Zadonsky, a debate on God between the nihilist and the saint rooted in the soil. In the Confession itself we learn that Stavrogin's whimsical behavior (biting the governor's ear, etc.) followed immediately upon his marriage to Marya Timofyevna, and that he was indeed tempted to bigamy, presumably with Liza, out of a need to commit a new crime, and though he was incapable of love and experienced only lust. (The *donnée* of sensual lust is nowhere made convincing, in novel or Confession or Notebooks; even the crucial note which assumes it gives more attention to psychological complications.[19]) This part of the Confession follows upon the report of his terrifying hallucinations of Matryosha. Above all the Confession evokes the two crimes quite sufficient to justify Stavrogin's gloomy self-destructiveness—the violation of the child and the passive attendance at her suicide. These explain the marriage "for no reason at all" to Marya Timofyevna: "I conceived the idea of somehow crippling my life in the most repulsive manner. . . . The thought of Stavrogin's marriage to a creature like that, the lowest of the low, tickled my nerves." Whether regarded as such an act of masochistic moral sensuality, as suggested here, or a lofty act of contrition (Mochulsky) or as compulsive self-degradation, the marriage is a direct response to Matryosha's hanging herself. As elsewhere in Dostoevsky, there is a close association of cripple, half-wit, child. (The ensuing discussion assumes without hesitation that a sexual violation did occur. Richard Peace, arguing from Stavrogin's disclaimer to Shatov and to Tihon, believes this is problematic.[20] One of Dostoevsky's notes says the Prince must drop a hint "that he actually did commit the sin, and that he did not lie to Tikhon". It is clear from the Confession itself that Tihon himself has no doubt.)

Dostoevsky made some effort to modify the Confession for *The Russian Literary Messenger,* to meet the objections of Katkov, but in the end abandoned the attempt. (There occurred, after this contretemps, a fourteen-month interruption in publication.) The Confession exists, in any event, as one of Dostoevsky's most powerful narratives and as a great psychological document. The self-analysis, with its crucial moments of repression and deliberate censorship, is absolutely authentic. But so too is Tihon's role, which is precisely that of the psychiatrist or analyst: listening sympathetically and asking the few right questions, wanting to help Stavrogin forgive himself and so circumvent merely neurotic self-punishment. Tihon's objective of true Christian penitence and the psychiatric aim of freedom to choose rationally are thus essentially the same: to obviate compulsive action. Above all Tihon sees Stavrogin is in danger of committing a new crime in order to avoid the publication of this Confession: not very far from the psychiatric view that a crime may be committed to justify an intolerable existing burden of guilt.

The written confession is framed by a leisurely introduction that takes us far from the ordinary world of the novel, where Shpigulin workers are encountered, to the Monastery, to Tihon's cell; and into the darkness of interior discourse. Stavrogin is irritable and evasive, and is surprised to hear from Tihon that he is regularly visited by his mother,[21] and speaks of hallucinations, of feeling an evil being close beside him. The experience is not unlike that recorded by Henry James Sr. at a time when he was refusing to admit to himself that his basic religious and life views had changed, the sense of "some damned shape squatting invisible to me within the precincts of the room, and raying out from his fetid personality influences fatal to life."[22] Is Stavrogin's an earthly double, himself in various forms, or perhaps the devil? Can one believe in the devil without believing in God? Tihon recognizes that Stavrogin is struggling with a "fearful intention" and implores him to tell everything. As a final preparation for the document itself, the Narrator intervenes to remark that its fundamental idea seems to be "a terrible, undisguised need of punishment, the need of the cross, of public chastisement."

The written confession is a model of the intense self-analytic *récit*. Though appearing to be the informal statement of one who is not a man of letters, it is really an intensely controlled presentation, written in full knowledge of the things that have to be said. Tihon objects to the kind of detail which in fact makes the document so masterful, "as to amaze the reader by a callousness and shamelessness which isn't really in you." The Yarmolinsky translation of Stavrogin's narrative results in a prose far superior to that of the body of the novel as translated, long before, by Constance Garnett. But Mochulsky speaks of the original's "verbal slovenliness."[23] The selectivity is in any event, that of very modern understatement. Stavrogin knows what must be left unsaid. And he withholds from Tihon, "for the present," the crucial second page on which the violation of the little girl is presumably evoked or stated.

The written confession describes, with great brevity, the Petersburg life of a bored aristocrat performing experiments—as to have assignations with both a maid and her mistress, and look forward to the fun of one day bringing them together. The first mention of the child Matryosha, who is eleven, and first recollection of her behind a screen, are followed by a singularly apt symbolic instance of repression. Stavrogin has forgotten the house-number and the child's family name. "On inquiry I found out that the old house had been torn down and where two or three buildings used to stand, there is now one large new one." Dostoevsky has imagined a physical event that would precisely correspond to a successful effort to cancel or forget.

After this hesitant start Stavrogin plunges directly into his account of a first major incident. He has lost a penknife and the child Matryosha, who has already been beaten unjustly by her mother, is beaten again in consequence.

Stavrogin finds his knife, but instead of revealing this he throws it away far from the house. Like Rousseau, who sees the servant girl punished for a theft he committed, he feels he has done something vile; like Michel in *The Immoralist,* watching Moktir steal his wife's scissors, he does not analyze his reasons for keeping silent. But he "experienced a pleasurable sensation because suddenly a certain desire pierced me like a blade, and I began to busy myself with it." In the next days he asks himself whether he could "give up my intention"; and feels that he still could. But he returns to the house, finds Matryosha alone, and steals toward her, his heart beating fast, takes her hand and kisses it, presently seats her on his knees. (A chaotic early Notebook entry—which includes references to the child Katia, to a Lame Girl, to a period of disbelief in God, to Kulikov (Fedka), to a house on fire—has an unexplained scrap of dialogue: "Theater. 'Sit on my lap.' " [24]) The child, disturbed, wavers between terror and laughter, but suddenly throws her arms around him and begins to kiss him violently of her own accord. He feels a repulsion born of pity . . . At this point the narrative breaks off, since the second page was withheld. (A variant, in which no confiscation of the page occurs, begins "When everything was over she showed embarrassment." He believes "all that had happened must certainly have seemed to her infinitely abominable, she must have thought of it with deadly horror." It "must surely have seemed to her that she had committed an unspeakable crime, that there was deadly guilt upon her, that she had 'killed God.' " Stavrogin's first thought on waking the next morning was: "did she tell, or not?" [25]

In the definitive version Tihon, reassured by Stavrogin that nothing happened, resumes his reading with the third page. But the narrative must have soon disabused him. Several days later Stavrogin returns to the house, with the intention of giving up his room, and learns that Matryosha has been ill and delirious, and keeps saying "I killed God." Presently he is once again alone with her. She jumps from behind her screen and stands on the threshold of the room, raises a little fist and begins to threaten him. Her face betrays intolerable despair; she shakes her head in reproach, then turns away from him to stand by the window. Perhaps he "would have sat a while and then would have gotten up and killed her." But she moves away and steps into "a tiny cubicle, something like a hen-coop, adjacent to a privy." The "fearful thought" that flashes through his mind is, presumably, his recognition that she is about to commit suicide, and so put him once for all out of danger. The hen-coop may be linked in the imagination with the garret where Stavrogin hangs himself, as Richard Peace suggests. He sits down to wait. He waits twenty minutes, then decides to wait exactly another quarter of an hour.

The period of his waiting is recorded with a kind of detail rare in Dostoevsky, the dead silence intensified by the buzzing of every fly and the rumbling of a cart in the courtyard, where ordinary life goes on. Stavrogin looks at a tiny red spider on a geranium leaf at the very moment that he thinks of how he will stand on tiptoe so as to be able to look into Matryosha's cubicle through a crack. Then deliberately, careful to see that he has left no trace of being there, Stavrogin goes to the cubicle. "I stood peering through the crack for a long time, because it was dark inside, yet not altogether, so that at length I saw what I had to see."

Later that day, a "coward rejoicing in his deliverance," chatting with friends, he decides for the first time not only that he has lost the sense of good and evil, but that good and evil really do not exist, and are but a prejudice. "I can be free of all prejudice, but at the very moment when I achieve that freedom I shall perish." For some time Stavrogin believes he has mastered his memories. But one night, after a beautiful dream of Greece in the golden age, he wakes with a piercing feeling of happiness, his eyes wet with tears. He sees a dot that becomes a tiny red spider, and remembers the spider on the geranium leaf on the day of the suicide. And now he sees Matryosha, haggard and feverish, threatening him with her little fist. "Pity for her stabbed me, a maddening pity, and I would have given my body to be torn to pieces if that would have erased what had happened. What I regret is not the crime, not her death. I'm not sorry for her, what I cannot bear is just that one instant, I can't, I can't, because I see her that way everyday, and I know for a certainty that I am doomed."

The ensuing dialogue is one of Dostoevsky's greatest scenes of spiritual confrontation. Tihon observes that Stavrogin's decision to publish the confession would be an admirable act of self-chastisement, if only it were really one of Christian repentance. But he suspects Stavrogin hates and despises in advance those who will read the document, and that he takes pride in his own psychologizing. Stavrogin in his pride will feel more comfortable if hated rather than pitied, but Tihon (anticipating Camus's *The Fall*) wonders whether he will be able to endure, in addition to hatred, men's laughter. Even in the very intention of Stavrogin's great "penitence" there is something ridiculous and false, since the humility is not sincere. Tihon is horrified by "so much idle power spent on abominations. Apparently one does not become a foreigner in one's own country with impunity. There is one punishment that falls upon those who divorce themselves from their native soil: boredom and a tendency toward idleness even where there is a desire for work." As for his crime:

"Christ too will forgive you if you reach the point where you can forgive yourself. . . ." But Tihon, his face contorted with an overwhelming fear, knows that the debate has been lost: " 'I see . . . I see clearly,' exclaimed Tihon in a penetrating voice and with an expression of most intense grief, 'that never, poor lost youth, have you stood nearer to a new and more terrible crime than at this moment.' " [26]

This is the Stavrogin of the Confession. The immobilized Stavrogin of the novel as originally published, though darkly memorable, rarely has the kind of life we find in other great tormented fictional creations, Dmitri Karamazov or Raskolnikov or Myshkin. We see them involved, at times, in the give and take of normal human relationships, talking, responding as social beings; we are, moreover, often privy to their thoughts and feelings. They are vibrantly *present*.

Stavrogin's stated physical appearance and personality—his beauty, elegance, charm—are overwhelmed by a towering impression of brooding gloom. He would seem much older than his years: a man with a dark past of known social crimes and possibly fatal secrets, old enough to be a lost leader who has outlived the doctrines he preached. We come to know him through stories of whimsical behavior, and see him either act in odd ways or in a strange stillness: irritable yet listless, his face like a mask, the light dying from his eyes. At times he seems merely bereft of will, at others to be holding aggression under control, as when, after Shatov's slap, he holds his hands clasped behind his back. The hollow man, on a few occasions, seems boiling with criminal energy. But either way he does not as a rule seem to be present . . . in the present time of the novel. Psychologically he would seem to be, and turns out to be, like Conrad's Razumov, the "puppet of the past." Ideologically too he is scarcely present, as he listens passively or ironically and with irritation to his doctrines of two years before.

We rarely see him, then, in the active relationships and extended scenes that normally constitute a novel's world. His few scenes are moments of crisis. He makes his brief genuine effort to communicate with Marya Timofyevna; his irritation is normal enough, and his effort to get her attention. The Stavrogin of the duel, firing in the air, as well as the aristocrat of the gratuitous insults, is a recognizable social and literary type. He has, that is, such a presence here as we are accustomed to from reading nineteenth-century fiction, and this is true of his brief exchange with Maurice over Liza, and of his early-morning dialogue with Liza, though it is she who gives that gloomy scene its life. The dynamic relationships with Fedka and occasionally Pyotr, the sense of occult connection and of a flow of criminal energy between them, are highly interesting. But they exist in an interior not social world.

All in all Stavrogin thus exhibits little ordinary novelistic life in the ongoing present time. Yet he is unmistakably at the center of *The Possessed,* and all revolves about him. Without Pyotr nothing would have happened, politically. But without Stavrogin there would be no ideological or personal tragedy. Remove the two, and we would be left with "Scenes of Provincial Life" and the comic exchanges of Stepan and Varvara. Instead, and more perhaps than any other great novel, *The Possessed* is built on *a structure of relationships to its central figure,* largely but not entirely conceptual, which may exist all the more firmly, *as structure,* because there are so few normally dramatized scenes involving him. The structure is one that may become more and more abstract in the reader's mind, after a first or second reading, and even seem separable from the novel's existential reality (the reality, for instance, of Stepan). Yet the structure is built on real and powerful feelings and on ideas and attitudes that have changed the lives of the other characters; none of them, without Stavrogin at the center of his world, would be the same. Each of a number of characters "represents" an aspect of Stavrogin or a force in his life, and Stavrogin is in all of them. A number of critics have recognized this movement toward abstract pattern, while applauding the novel's overall vividness and moments of dramatic immediacy, and have seen it as a source of originality and strength. Bakhtin's polyphonic and carnivalesque novel is largely ideological, with each character's ideas related to Stavrogin's inner debate. René Girard discerns a pattern of mediated desire, with Stavrogin as mediator between Pyotr, Kirillov, Shatov and the ideals they seek. "Everyone needs him," Wasiolek observes, and "Stavrogin needs no one. He is detached, quiet, calm. He is like a dead sun about which the planets continue to move with borrowed light and heat. We learn of him by these fragments of himself, which he has thrown off and which continue to live in the persons of others. Of these, Kirilov and Shatov are the most important." [27] Richard Peace speaks of the Dostoevskian "law of the endless division of idea cells." [28]

The relationships, in their puzzling complexity, invite the further abstraction of a chart. A student, when I made some such remark, produced a complicated mobile, a useful reminder that even conceptual relationships are subject to change. A very full chart would record doublings of incident: Matryosha's suicide as prefiguring Stavrogin's. A still more elaborate chart, shadowily behind the present one, might reflect the process of creation: how "Golubov" split into Stavrogin, Shatov, Kirillov, Tihon; how "Kulikov" split into Kirillov and Fedka; how family relationships kept changing (with Stavrogin at one point longing to marry the person who would become his mother) . . . and who, this repeatedly changing, slapped whom. In the present very simple chart Stavrogin's only erotic relationship in the present (Liza) and only close family tie (Varvara) seem to have no dynamic place. Liza and Varvara are dismayed helpless onlookers at Stavrogin's ruin.

STAVROGIN'S RELATIONSHIPS

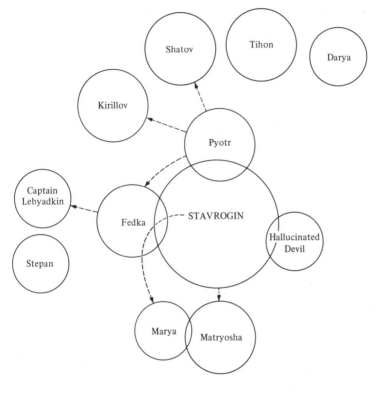

◄-------(kills)

Stavrogin's circle overlaps those of Pyotr, Fedka and the hallucinated devil-double of the Confession, since they are in some sense real and continuing extensions of his personality, and not (like Kirillov and Shatov) ideological projections or aspects of the self some time since "thrown off." The broken line of killing runs from him through Fedka to Marya, but extends only from Fedka to Captain Lebyadkin, since Stavrogin no more wished Lebyadkin's death than he wished Shatov's or Kirillov's. Pyotr is a counter-force separating Stavrogin from three potential saviors: Shatov, Tihon and Darya, and perhaps even Kirillov should be regarded as a potential savior. Captain Lebyadkin and Stepan stand far from the center as bad but not strong influences in the past: the Falstaff of the Petersburg days, the tutor who was bad for the child's nerves. To be sure the chart underrepresents Pyotr's role as instigator. If the chart were properly set in motion, a moving constellation, Pyotr would circle that "dead sun" in rapid if erratic orbit. Pyotr had, on the other hand, nothing to do with Matryosha's violation and death, presumably the central incident of Stavrogin's life. The chart intends, of course, to show that Little Girl and Lame Woman are linked in Stavrogin's mind as well as Dostoevsky's.

STAVROGIN'S CRIMES: A NOTE ON CREATIVE PROCESS

We have already observed that Dostoevsky had to work his way through to the painful discovery that Stavrogin could not be saved, and must end in despair and suicide. A brief note asks why he must die: *"There is no reason to kill the Prince."* [29] But the final novel gives reason enough. In the long struggle with the "terrible mess" of his novel plans Dostoevsky repeatedly evaded the two central and related crimes.

The notes for *The Life of a Great Sinner* suggest this would have been Dostoevsky's most autobiographical novel. In the first sustained outline Alfonsky has taken Osip's sister as a mistress and, for this reason, flogged Osip's brother to death. He has taken the lackey Osip (later Kulishov, later Kulikov, later still Fedka) to a recruiting station, but Osip makes his escape. The possibility is raised "that Alfonsky was killed by his peasants when he started fooling around, and the boy may have been a witness. . . ." [30] The prospective hero's life was divided, like Dostoevsky's, between the city (where he is exposed to the depravity of Lambert, who makes a corrupt appearance in *A Raw Youth*) and the country, where he has as companions both a Lame Girl and a Katia, though sometimes they seem to be the same person, and an Umnov, the real name of a childhood friend. At one point the hero is said to be eleven, the lame girl ten; he evidently shifts from the tutelage of Souchard to Cermak's school, a change Dostoevsky himself made at twelve or thirteen. At one point Umnov peeps at nudes and has designs on the Lame Girl. The hero has evidently told her his fantasies of someday being king: the future falcon-Pretender of Marya Timofyevna's musings? He has forced Katia to bow before him in worship: "I myself am God." There are several references to beating the Lame Girl, once to trying to force her to fight with the boys, and thrashing her when she tries to leave. But there are also times when they are close companions. Recurringly in the background is Kulishov, in some sense an outlaw. This character will split, mainly into the aggressive Fedka, but also into the Kirillov who substitutes himself for God.

A not uncommon experience for novelists is to discover their real subject almost at once, then evade it; put it aside during months of futile groping. In an early note the hero (now "The Atheist") keeps a wife locked up; there is a Lame Girl across the courtyard, "the daughter of a drunken beggar of a lieutenant." Kulishov rapes and kills her. On the one hand we see Kulishov bargaining, presumably with The Atheist; on the other, a total outsider has incited Kulishov to murder: "a Tartar princeling who owed some money to the murdered captain. . . ." [31] Kulishov thus anticipates with a single act Stavrogin's two crimes: violation of a helpless girl, incitement to murder of his wife. To achieve the final plot, which might not seem very far off, Dostoevsky must split the two crimes, with only the second committed by proxy. The crime, with its instigator-actor association, must involve the hero, not a casual "Tartar princeling." And he must be married to the Lame Girl.

Important progress is made soon thereafter, in notes for *The Life of a Great Sinner*. There are enigmatic notes with references to a cornfield, and to Kulikov and a murder. A number of extremely compressed and challenging entries take us far toward *The Possessed:*

> N.B. Flight with the little girl and encounter with the bandit Kulikov immediately after changing from Souchard to Cermak.
> . . . After the experience with Kulikov he *seems* to have turned more quiet both at home and at school (to think things over and FIND HIMSELF, to get settled).
> Yet he is unsociable and uncommunicative. His silence is broken a year and a half later, when he makes a confession about Kulikov. And, of course, it couldn't have been any other way, for he remembers, and has guilty knowledge of so horrible a thing that he must, for instance, look at all the other children as though they were completely alien to him, as though they were something from which he has been carried away as if on wings to entirely different parts, for better or for worse. Sometimes he is tormented by the blood. But also,
> *what is most important:*
> It isn't this alone which isolates him from everybody else, but even more so his dreams of power and of reaching exorbitant heights so as to be above everything. [32]

Shortly thereafter a note refers to Katia's disgrace, to a hellish orgy with *"Albert"* (Lambert?), to confession of a murder committed with Kulikov, to a monastery. The encounter with Kulikov would seem to have been a chance one, on the occasion of flight "with the little girl"; he and Kulikov kill "a deserter'' together. Kulikov at one point is seen to have a strong influence on his omnipotence fantasy of ''dethroning God and putting himself in His stead.'' It is not clear what part the hero had in the implied crime against a child. But ''Kulikov'' would appear to be an experience that must be lived through, as it were incorporated and expelled or survived.

These altogether essential dreams of crime and punishment—packed into long notes of December and January 1869–70—are soon put aside, as other characters and issues are explored: Granovsky (later Stepan), the murder of Shaposhnikov (later Shatov), numerous romantic complications. There are one-line references to a girl drowning herself, as in recollection of plans for *The Idiot,* and a sudden one-sentence discovery, ''THE PRINCE SHOOTS HIM-SELF.'' [33] Then (July 9, 1870), after a quick allusion to raping the Ward (Darya), there is the renewed possibility that he has committed two major crimes:

> ?N.B. He has killed somebody. (Most doubtful.)
> The Prince confesses his villainy involving the child (he raped her) to Shatov. He has written a confession, wants to have it printed, shows it to Shatov, asking him for advice. But after that, he begins to hate Shatov and is glad that he gets killed. He says that he would like people to spit in his face.

And in the same note, with ''Uri'' presumably meaning suicide rather than mere retreat to the Swiss canton:

> The Prince has been visiting with the Bishop. He has actually come to Russia in order to have his confession printed. But if he *can not make up his mind, then Uri.* [34]

By August (Dostoevsky is beginning again, has crossed out 250 pages) the two women, lame wife and raped child, are certainly one, and both ''The Beauty'' (Liza) and ''The Ward'' (Darya) suspect him. In successive lines we have an oblique reference to rape and confession, but also an evasive suggestion that Kulishov is wholly responsible for the murder. He has done opportunely, by a ''trick of fate,'' what the hero had perhaps wished. Then, on a single page of the translated text, come references to his suicide and to the fact that he is free from pursuit or suspicion of either crime, and, at last, acknowledgment that he was himself really guilty of the murder:

> Or: It is he who has killed the Lame Woman, through Kulishov, and a day later Kulishov is himself killed accidentally.

And

> (Only Tikhon knows about the little girl.)

And

> N.B. Couldn't he incite Kulishov to kill [the Lame Woman], not telling him directly, but merely mentioning casually that he has given 4,000.[35]

The essential configuration has been found, though repeatedly in notes to follow it seems lost. The notes for November 1, 1870, go, in terms of murder by proxy, straight to the point:

> It was necessary that the Prince knew for sure that Fedka would commit murder, *but did not say a word,* even though he did not personally participate in the killing.
> He had the intention to hire a killer, but he merely let him see that he was taking 1,000 rubles there.[36]

The allusions to the rape of the little girl are regularly extremely brief, as are most of those to the visit to Tikhon, possibly because Dostoevsky did not want to dwell on a fantasy that had become unpleasantly vivid, or because he still hoped half-consciously to keep the incident out of the book, but more probably because the crime against the child had long since been clearly imagined, and there was no need to rehearse it in the notes. There are, for instance, few notes on Kirillov, who came late to the planning. One of the greatest moments in all fiction (as Pyotr goes into the room where Kirillov has not yet killed himself) gets only three short sentences: "He takes another look. He's hidden himself. He bites his finger." [37]

VIS COMICA

The tragic ideologist is also a great comic writer, peopling an exceptionally active fictional world counterpoised against the psychic immobilities. The creative power which conceives likeable or interesting people *in extremis*—Shatov welcoming Marie's child, on the last day of his own life; or Kirillov summoning courage to go on with his suicide; or Stavrogin attempting full confession—carries over to the lives of secondary personages trapped in their everyday (but not banal) vanities and contradictions. The very great comic creation is Stepan Verkhovensky, as even Dostoevsky's first critics recognized. But there are a number of minor characters who give substantiating life to the major ones. Dostoevsky catches with Stendhalian brevity and bite the anxiety and eagerness of the fool or egotist waiting to speak in public. The mad professor at the governesses' fete walks up and down flourishing his fist while Stepan tries on different smiles before a mirror, as the young Bishop of Agde his gestures of blessing. Virginsky's sister, come to protest the sufferings of the poor students, rosy-cheeked and plump and round as a little ball, is instantly alive, as is Shigalov, rising "with a gloomy and sullen air" to expound his system. Stendhalian too is the rapid presentation of Praskovya Ivanovna, the more addlebrained when her legs swell, and whose dog creeps under the sofa when she calls.

Characters come to life in the act of breaking through embarrassment, fear, restraint, to reveal what they are or what they deeply feel. Virginsky has appeared to accept his wife's affair with Lebyadkin; she is a liberated woman. "But suddenly, without any preliminary quarrel, he seized the giant Lebyadkin with both hands, by the hair, just as the latter was dancing a *can-can* solo, pushed him down, and began dragging him along with shrieks, shouts, and tears." This swift stroke is completed by several more: the panic and honorable man's resentment felt by Lebyadkin, and the whole night Virginsky spent on his knees begging his wife's forgiveness, a forgiveness that was not granted. Liza's "peculiar unconscious hatred" for Maurice, which underlies her respect and esteem and even love, breaks through in the presence of the saintly fool Semyon Yakovlevitch, as she compels her suitor to kneel, then screams at him in rage to get up. An essential self breaks through, after the murder of Shatov, as Lyamshin seizes and squeezes Virginsky convulsively, and gives vent "to a scream more animal than human."

But it is most of all through talk, and the dramatic collision of personalities in dialogue, that the characters are brought to life. Fedka the murderer is given depth, like Graham Greene's *mestizo,* by his Christian belief. He had stripped the ikons, yes, "but I only took out the pearls; and how do you know? Perhaps my own tear was transformed into a pearl in the furnace of the Most High to make up for my sufferings, seeing I am just that very orphan, having no daily refuge." Captain Lebyadkin, the most Dickensian personage in the novel, is comically alienated from self when drunk, and likes to speak of himself in the third person. He too, with his babble and literary clichés, can rise to eloquence. "Oh, madam, wealthy are your mansions, but poor is the dwelling of Marya Anonyma, my sister, whose maiden name was Lebyadkin, but whom we'll call Anonyma for the time, only for *the time,* madam, for God himself will not suffer it for ever." His ravings are allowed to interrupt the long night of Stavrogin's confrontations, perhaps to help modulate from one crisis to the next, but perhaps only because meaning gave way to unsubduable comic life. He speaks of conquering drunkenness; of having a new skin, like a snake; of making his will. He will leave all to the fatherland, to humanity, to the students. But the metaphor of *skin* recalls an American who left his "skeleton to the students, and his skin to be made into a drum, so that the American national hymn might be beaten upon it day and night.'' He would like to leave his own skin to his regiment, but is afraid it would be taken for liberalism, and his skin prohibited.

There are other great talkers: the lisping monumentally vain Karmazinov, and the governor von Lembke on the verge of mental collapse, and Praskovya Ivanovna still nourishing schooltime hostilities. But the finest talkers are Stepan and, especially when she is with him or describing him, Varvara Petrovna. She cannot forbear insisting on his weaknesses, even as she urges Darya to marry him. It is a great Molièresque scene, in which Varvara's irritated love keeps breaking through. ''He's frivolous, shilly-shally, cruel, egoistic, he has low habits. But mind you think highly of him, in the first place because there are many worse.'' She will, moreover, be there to watch: a wonderfully revealing refrain. Her irritation is evident even as he takes the last sacraments. Stepan, reviving, thanks the priest in French, the Westerner's bad habit persisting to the end:

> ''*Mon père, je vous remercie et vous êtes bon, mais . . .*''
> ''*No mais* about it, no *mais* at all!'' exclaimed Varvara Petrovna, bounding up from her chair. ''Father,'' she said, addressing the priest, ''he is a man who . . . he is a man who . . . You will have to confess him again in another hour! That's the sort of man he is.'' [38]

One of the secrets of interesting fictional life, as of real life, lies in the way people energize each other. A in the presence of B is dull, apathetic, half-asleep, but face to face with C begins to talk vivaciously. Stepan's dignity, following on the raid on his lodgings, reduces Lembke to babbling rage in a splendid comic scene. And Stepan pierces with extraordinary rapidity the gospel woman Sofya Matveyevna's reserve to evoke a gentle warmth and charm. The exchanges of Stepan and Varvara are energizing from first to last. This is the great ''normal'' relationship of the novel. There are, the narrator remarks, friends ''always ready to fly at one another, and go on like that all their lives, and yet they cannot separate.'' A comic essential is for each to express with unusual openness the terms of their surface relationship, its vanities and exasperations and shames; but also to betray at times, unwittingly, another relationship that lies half-concealed. The surface relationship, of rich patronness and faded littérateur, is also one of mother and middle-aged son. With a mother's solicitude Varvara sends Stepan abroad and takes him to Petersburg to advance his career, designs his clothes, tries to arrange a marriage that will provide him with a lifetime nurse (*but she too will be there*), tries to break him of his bad habits and rouse him from his long stagnation. She rearranges his rooms, wants him to hold his own with the great visiting writer.

But beneath the surface relationship, and playing subtly against it, is another, which itself causes a collision of personalities: the widow's real erotic feeling, so that the mother would also want to be a wife, and on Stepan's part a chivalric fantasy of love for her which is nine-tenths literary sentiment. This underlying relationship is exposed at the beginning, on a springtime evening. But Stepan, holding an unlit cigar, does not act when, after they have said good-night, she unexpectedly comes to his lodge. "I shall never forgive you for this," she whispers to the petrified man. The chivalric side of Stepan can hardly believe her, when she insists he leave the house at the end of Part One or, later, as she proposes terms for the separation yet wants him to perform creditably at the governesses' fete.

The next to last chapter, "Stepan Trofimovich's Last Wandering," brings his Christian redemption, and his redemption too as a comic character long ridiculed for his many weaknesses, but now achieving a kind of mad heroism and magnitude. This chapter, taking us at last inside his consciousness for an extended period, achieves a remarkable blend of comedy and compassion. We have seen from the outside his sentimentality, vanity, indolence and shameless dependence, and his lifetime of lip service to beauty and honor. But we have seen too his good humor and gregariousness and a few moments of blundering courage, as when he defies his hecklers at the governesses' fete. His quixotic fidelity has been to a romantic conception of self as one who has been "of service," who has been brave, who has held aloft a high ideal (though he is not sure what it is) . . . and who will once again achieve distinction. And he has talked. The sprightliness of a mind that can never keep to the subject, or keep to one language, and whose speech at every moment reveals his weaknesses and vanities, is appealing throughout. The inconsequent babble continues in the chapter of his wanderings. But in the end Stepan achieves a crucial recognition: he has been telling lies all his life. "The worst of it is that I believe myself when I am lying. The hardest thing in life is to live without telling lies . . . and without believing in one's lies." And he achieves sufficient eloquence to interpret succinctly one of the book's two epigraphs, the parable of the swine.

The fictional vitality comes in part from the mobility of his mind and from the comedy of outraged consciousness. But it is now his turn to astonish. He has set out in the early morning, with stick and bag and umbrella, to encounter Russian reality on the open road; instead he encounters Liza and Maurice in the mist, hurrying toward the fire. His high adventure begins (but only ninety pages later, after we have seen the deaths of Shatov and Kirillov) with him sitting at the side of the road in the rain, and the passing of a peasant cart. He fears a band of robbers, but is reassured to see a woman in the cart, and even a cow:

"c'est rassurant au plus haut degré." He walks behind the cart and, when offered a lift, thinks of the event as "real life." Now in touch with Russian reality, he learns why peasants have cows, and observes that their language has changed a little since the emancipation in 1861. But he is totally unaware, as he enters a cottage in Hatovo where travelers stop, of the outlandish impression he makes, with more and more people coming into the room to watch him. A double vision is maintained throughout: we see the peasants through Stepan's dazed consciousness, and see him through theirs. His own eye falls almost at once, since he cannot live without a woman, on the gospel woman Sofya Matveyevna. "There was something very kindly in her face which attracted Stepan Trofimovitch immediately." He is distressed, presently, to see her drink tea from a saucer and nibble at a lump of sugar. But she is a woman and *très comme il faut . . . "Ce petit morceau de sucre, ce n'est rien . . .* There is something noble and independent about her, and at the same time—gentle. *Le comme il faut tout pur,* but rather in a different style." In no time at all he has arranged for a carriage to take him to Ustyevo, and swept the gospel woman into it, and announced that he will join her in the gospel-selling enterprise. He will treat that remarkable book "with the utmost respect," while explaining its mistakes to the peasants. Sofya Matveyevna can hardly get in a word as he babbles on:

> "Will you allow me to remain with you? I feel that the look in your eyes and . . .
> I am surprised in fact at your manners. You are simple-hearted, you call me 'sir,'
> and turn your cup upside down on your saucer . . . and that horrid lump of sugar;
> but there's something charming about you, and I see from your features . . . Oh,
> don't blush and don't be afraid of me as a man. *Chère et incomparable, pour moi
> une femme c'est tout.* I can't live without a woman, but only at her side, only at her
> side . . ." [39]

Arrived at Ustyevo, and another peasant cottage, he insists on a private room, since he must tell her everything. "He saw before him the woman whom he had already elected to share his new life, and was in haste to consecrate her, so to speak. His genius must not be hidden from her."

The autobiography, which the poor woman finds obscure and "so very intellectual," is a shameless romantic recasting of his life, and of his relations with Varvara and Darya. But an important turn comes with his sickness from summer cholera, his delirium which keeps Sofya up all night, and his admission that it was all lies—"to glorify myself, to make it splendid, from pure wantonness—all, all, every word, oh, I am a wretch, I am a wretch." In the two days that follow, the most terrible of Sofya Matveyevna's life, her compassion throws a changing light on Stepan. She reads the Sermon on the Mount to him, and he hears for the first time of the Laodiceans who were neither hot nor cold. And presently (by now the people of the house are tremendously uneasy) he asks to hear about "the pigs" . . . *ces cochons,* the story of the devils entering the swine. Now at last he understands this passage which has been a stumbling-block all his life, and with compact eloquence begins to speak for the author:

> "You see, that's exactly like our Russia, those devils that come out of the sick man and enter into the swine. They are all the sores, all the foul contagions, all the impurities, all the devils great and small that have multiplied in that great invalid, our beloved Russia, in the course of ages and ages. *Oui, cette Russie que j'aimais toujours.* But a great idea and a great Will will encompass it from on high, as with that lunatic possessed of devils . . . and all those devils will come forth, all the impurity, all the rottenness that was putrefying on the surface . . . and they will beg of themselves to enter into swine; and indeed maybe they have entered into them already! They are we, we and those . . . and Petrusha and *les autres avec lui* . . . and I perhaps at the head of them, and we shall cast ourselves down, possessed and raving, from the rocks into the sea, and we shall all be drowned—and a good thing too, for that is all we are fit for. But the sick man will be healed and 'will sit at the feet of Jesus,' and all will look upon him with astonishment. . . ." [40]

Stepan now sinks into delirium and loses consciousness. But he is not yet dead; the chapter must move to another statement and climax of redemption. He, who has paid lip service to beauty all his life, turns out to have been, however unconsciously, sincere. "And what is more precious than love? . . . If I have once loved Him and rejoiced in my love, is it possible that He should extinguish me and my joy and bring me to nothingness again? If there is a God, then I am immortal. *Voilà ma profession de foi."* The modulation from one high moment to the last one is accomplished by the brilliant stroke of bringing the outraged Varvara onto the scene—furious with Stepan as a shameless reprobate, ready to turn Sofya outdoors, then ordering her back when she realizes how sick Stepan is; and listening in exasperation, she who even at this moment remembers the cigar, to his final declaration of love.

The characterization of Stepan Trofimovitch is a humane triumph of comic realism, based on a delicate interplay of ridicule and sympathy. Two other sections of *The Possessed* display exceptional mastery within traditional modes: the social realism of the governesses' fete, and the tragic irony of the last days of Shatov's and Kirillov's lives.

The governesses' benefit and its violent aftermath, some twenty-five thousand words, are largely free of ambiguity or metaphysical speculation. These are among the easiest pages of the novel, with the author and his well-placed narrator (one of the stewards at the afternoon fete) telling us nearly everything they know. The section openly creates expectations—of comic entertainment, of hysteria and disorder—which it straightforwardly proceeds to satisfy. Here at least Dostoevsky is in full control of his book, and of his readers, timing his scenes with great tact. The chapters (1 and 2 of Part III) also constitute a uniquely successful symbolic picture of an historical moment, and a plausible picture of any society in "turbulent times of upheaval or transition," with restlessness and boredom and cynicism become hysterical, and turning at last to violence. Events spring from the hearts of men, but the hearts of men are affected by their times. It is a time of restless indolence and fitful apathy, of *ennui,* when young aristocrats pause to gaze at a suicide on their way to an entertaining session with Semyon Yakovlevitch, the sugar-dispensing holy fool. No one appears to be working in the town except Mrs. Virginsky the midwife and the Shpigulin factory hands in a distant background, corrupted by Pyotr but with real grievances too.

The chapters are admittedly the work of a political conservative, scornful of the Yulia von Lembkes who would temporize with nihilists and who conceive schemes for social leveling and promise entertainments they cannot provide. Riff-raff always rise to the surface in times of transition, the narrator observes, but this rabble is controlled by an elite: Pyotr, Liputin and Lyamshin. Dostoevsky perhaps satirizes the extremists who attribute everything disruptive to the *Internationale.* (There is even a distinguished councilor who confesses he has been under the influence of the *Internationale* for three months, though his only evidence is that he had "felt it in all his feelings.") But the narrator certainly speaks for the author in his editorial statement on the poets and intellectuals and public servants who betray their trust. The disruptions of Yulia's fete are directly traceable to the three subversives who pretend to be helping her plan its success. But it is her fault that the expensive entertainment is by its very nature a swindle. The poor, who have been made welcome thanks to Yulia's democratic sentiments, ruin themselves to pay for tickets and for their daughters' dresses, and have been led to expect a free luncheon and champagne, a Belshazzar's feast. Instead they are to receive, in addition to lemonade, Karmazinov's farewell speech *Merci* and, in the evening, an incomprehensible "literary quadrille."

There is a continuing uncertainty: are Pyotr, Liputin and Lyamshin disrupting the public entertainment out of an impish sense of fun and love of disorder for its own sake, or because they are at least semi-serious revolutionaries? The first meaning may be closer to Dostoevsky's heart: capriciousness, irresponsibility, a whimsical playing with ideas as sources of social collapse. The transitions are absolutely convincing, from the exasperations of the beginning of the fete to panic over the fires. The scene of the ball, by morning, is one to rival the disorders of revolution. The aristocratic stall for the buffet has been pulled to pieces, the rooms left a shocking mess, and the few remaining, having drunk themselves senseless, dance the Kamarinsky in its unexpurgated form. Such is Dostoevsky's warning, never stated as explicitly as it would have been by Dickens, in the aftermath of the Paris commune.

The rhythm of events, excellently expressive of theme, the movement from capriciousness and boredom to hysteria and violence, is also high entertainment. It is part of the carnivalesque success to keep us aware of the restless exasperated audience. Karmazinov's speech (a parody of at least three of Turgenev's writings, according to Peace [41]) reaches us largely through the narrator's continuously ironic summary. Aware that he has lost his audience and must stop, the great man cannot forbear skipping ahead to his last monstrously egotistical lines. Stepan's speech reaches us more directly. In a sense it is a turning point for him, since from the first, courageously or foolishly, he attacks the stupidity of the revolutionary leaflets, and presently launches into the comparisons that outraged his Petersburg audience ten years before. *Agent provocateur!* a member of the audience calls. Stepan proceeds with shrill excitement, at last is shrieking incoherently, and brings the audience to a "perfect panic." The mad professor who succeeds Stepan on the stage appears delighted at the disorder, and shouts of the degradation of Russia until dragged away by six officials. But even that is not the end. For the narrator stays long enough to hear the first words of the girl student, Virginsky's sister, who leaps onto the platform: "Ladies and gentlemen, I've come to call attention to the sufferings of poor students and to rouse them to a general protest . . ."

The preparation for the evening holocaust is complete.

The arrangements for the murder of Shatov, the return of Shatov's wife, and the deaths of Shatov and Kirillov, a connected narrative of some forty thousand words (Part III, chapters 4–6), constitute one of the great tragic sequences in literature. In a sense *The Possessed* has to begin again at this point, since the narrative of the fete and the scenes ending in Liza's death were so brilliantly self-contained. And it will have to begin a third time with the story of Stepan's last wandering, since the death of Kirillov and departure of Pyotr conclude what would seem an altogether definitive commentary on suffering, confusion, evil. This splitting apart of the novel—a splitting James and Flaubert would not have tolerated—may be attributed to Dostoevsky's scorn for the *petit-point* of modulation and harmony, but also to the richness and intensity of each of the narratives. One result of the splitting is that it may be hard to realize that these events occur simultaneously or follow each other very closely in time. In the last third of the novel these great happenings seem to escape or transcend chronological time. And if the governesses' fete and the wanderings of Stepan are in some ways of their historical time and place (though with a moving universality too), the night of Shatov's wife's return would seem to achieve an altogether timeless humanity.

The scenes succeed each other with great rapidity while seeming unhurried and unselective. Only a cold enumeration of pages can convey this extreme compression: Marie Shatov's unexpected arrival (576); the moving and immediate reconciliation with Kirillov, to whom Shatov goes for tea and a samovar (580); the arrival of Erkel and his reptilian touch, to make the fatal appointment for the next day (582–83); the great scene of Marie's unexplained irritability, and the revelation that she is in labor (591); Shatov's desperate visits to two of those planning his murder—to Virginsky's in search of a midwife, to Lyamshin's to sell back a revolver (593–97); the dialogue of Marie and Mrs. Virginsky, two liberated women threatening to regress to a simpler humanity (597–600); Kirillov's discourse on the five or six seconds of eternal harmony (601); the birth of the child, whom Marie wishes to name after Shatov (601–5), and the arrival of Erkel (606) to conduct him to the scene of the murder.

There are a number of narratives as dramatic or melodramatic in plot, and that thus juxtapose within a few pages birth and death, reconciliation and ruin. The particular power of Chapter 5 derives from its picture of normal human feeling in conflict with the ideological or the compulsive or the habitual; and at least momentarily triumphing over them. We have known Shatov as an almost exclusively ideological being, tormented by the delinquency of Stavrogin and passionately expounding his abstract view of Russian destiny. More recently we have seen him try to extricate himself from political entanglement, and debate whether to inform on his former associates. For a few moments only in the whole novel (when he considers Liza's proposal that he edit a yearly almanac) he seems to escape the encompassing prison of ideology and politics. We have known him as surly, irritable, enraged; his most human act has been to strike Stavrogin. But now, waking from a dream in which he is tied to his bed by cords, he hears his wife's voice and welcomes her. He has a "look of new life" as he returns her "long, harassed and weary gaze." "Three years of separation, three years of the broken marriage had effaced nothing from his heart." He rushes to Kirillov for help, though they have been completely estranged: "Kirillov, we lay side by side in America . . . My wife has come to me . . . I . . . give me the tea. . . . I shall want the samovar." The terrible irony, as he learns Marie is in childbirth, is that of a reawakened warm humanity appealing for help—in the visits to Virginsky and Lyamshin—to the world of political evil he has left. And the deep humanity appears in his delight over the birth of the child, though it is not his own. A basic feeling ("so great a mystery, the coming of a new creature") prevails, rather than a conventional one, jealousy of Stavrogin. When Erkel, Pyotr's emissary, takes his hand, Shatov shudders, "as though he had touched some terrible reptile." It is as though the new man had some occult knowledge of Erkel's real role. In fact, Erkel has given him the handshake of the secret society. But this too is terrible, since Shatov has left the political behind and reentered the purely human.

The juxtaposition of the ideological and the human, or the compulsive and the human, is dramatized in Kirillov's simple and immediate response to Shatov's need. It occurs again, shortly after the child is born. For we see Kirillov once more locked in his fatal speculations, as he walks up and down all night, and now speaks of the vision of eternal harmony which lasts for only five seconds . . . but for which he would give up his whole life. A fundamental humanity triumphs over Mrs. Virginsky's cold scientific rationalism; she chatters gaily and feels an amused sympathy for Shatov and his incorrigible love. Even the two conspirators Virginsky and Lyamshin, terrified by Shatov's appearance in the middle of the night, seem to recover a non-political humanity.

Perhaps the most surprising creation, one that might have collapsed into sentimentality, is Marie Shatov. We see her arrive weary and sick, her eyes glittering with fever, with little more to show for her life than a cheap canvas bag. It is a very great portrait of a woman at the end of her tether, beaten and harassed, brutally direct in her tired speech, rendered cynical by "scoundrels," locked too in a cluster of liberated woman's attitudes. We hear her abuse the carriage driver and belabor Shatov and ridicule his kindness. But she is even here deeply human, in the distracted movement of her mind, as she momentarily recalls that Shatov had shown some sign of intelligence during their marriage of two weeks and a few days. The scene, as she collapses on his bed and Shatov hovers over her, is one that might have evoked pages of Dickensian *attendrissement*. So too the moment when she breaks through her cynicism to signal, behind the midwife's back, that she wants to hold the baby and, shortly afterward, when she kisses Shatov. She too seems now to look forward to a new life.

But on the next page Erkel arrives. It is time for Shatov to go to meet the conspirators in the park at Skvoreshniki, and die.

The almost universally acknowledged greatness of *The Possessed* reminds us, even more than *Martin Chuzzlewit,* that the novel form (which justly prides itself on the perfections of Flaubert and James, on the subtler complications and labyrinthine artistries of Conrad and Faulkner, on the civilized precision of Jane Austen and more daring precision of Stendhal) is indeed inexhaustible, and can even survive an apparent failure of harmonious form: survive a disorder that at times seemed bent on destroying both author and reader. There are moments of great artistry in *The Possessed*. But its ultimate strength would seem to lie rather in the amount of life it has penetrated, encompassed, evoked, understood. Only rigid preconceptions concerning "what the novel should be" will lead a lover of this one to affirm unity, harmony and unflagging control. *The Possessed* would appear to be, to speak more generally, the very type of a modern tragedy, as true for the twentieth century as for the late nineteenth. As against the simpler classic tragedy of conflicting loyalties, or of conflict with destiny and the Gods (whether these be truly external or enemies within) this modern tragedy juxtaposes, under extreme pressures, natural human feeling and not a few of the forces that try to destroy it: psychic damage and repression; logic and abstraction; the disruption of traditional faiths and bonds; political and religious ideology generally. *The Possessed,* the greatest of all political novels, is more unpolitical than its author knew.

11
ABSALOM, ABSALOM!:
THE
NOVEL
AS
IMPRESSIONIST
ART

The great human drama of the Notebooks for *The Possessed*—the mind's effort to understand the enigmatic personages and brutal events it has imagined (as well as certain *données* of tragic social history)—becomes in *Absalom, Absalom!* a central preoccupation of the novel itself. The search for the appropriate analogy, the blocked flow of reasoning, the renewed assault on the ambiguous—Quentin and Shreve take us closer to Hawthorne's interpolations in *Dr. Grimshawe's Secret* or to James's and Dostoevsky's speculations on their characters than to *The Counterfeiters* or other novels about novel-writing; but with the difference that *Absalom, Absalom!* is a finished work of art. It is the culminating novel of Conradian impressionism. But it is also, in this far beyond Conrad, a major moment in the novel form's freeing of itself from mimesis: from an obligation to be or even seem an authentic report on reality. *Absalom, Absalom!* dramatizes (and makes us believe) a number of things that presumably could not have happened, builds on knowledge that has no cognitive source, and records voices, both interior and speaking, as remote from everyday speech as those in Shakespeare's verse plays. It asserted in 1936, in the heyday of a denuded, artless social realism:

The primacy of fiction, and of the creative and speculative mind, over verifiable reality; the right to invent over the obligation to represent;

The primacy of the artifact, the novel as an intricately constructed and mobile thing of beauty, over the novel as essentially a vehicle—for entertainment, persuasion, easy vicarious living, etc.;

The primacy of language as joyful play over language as mere communication: "All my writing life I have been a poet without education, who possessed only instinct and a fierce conviction and belief in the worth and truth of what he was doing, and an illimitable courage for rhetoric (personal pleasure in it too: I admit it) and who knew and cared for little else." [1]

Absalom, Absalom! was a very "new" book, but in some ways looked like a standard novel, as even *Ulysses* did not. As a result most critics have discussed it chiefly in terms of the old: sociology, ethics, psychology; character, theme, plot. Much energy has gone into puzzle-solving, and to summarizing clearly and chronologically events that the author scrambled. A number of critics have talked of intensity of feeling and intensity of language, but rarely for more than a paragraph. Concern with genre, and purity of genre, has as usual been an obfuscating force. James Guetti, a young critic with many interesting things to say, is finally driven to write that the "failure to compose a story is the failure to compose a novel" and that *Absalom, Absalom!* "is possibly no novel at all." [2] The reaction of John Paterson is even more controlled by a consciousness of genre and by a need for authority from the past. By combining a classicist's theoretical demands of tragedy as a mode with the common reader's expectations of the novel as a genre, Paterson manages to repudiate Faulkner on two counts. "Eventually more formidable as a work of art and certainly more complete as a novel" than *The Mayor of Casterbridge, Absalom, Absalom!* is "conspicuously inferior as tragedy" [3] because of "rhetorical complexity and richness," the little immediacy(!), Sutpen's lack of Henchard's objective reality, the absence of "the ultimate peace of traditional tragedy." Paterson notes that Faulkner's characters' freedom from realistic psychology may "suggest the abstract creatures of classical tragedy" and that the distance he creates between the reader and the "principals of the action" has "an effect presumably justified by the authority of Greek tragedy." [4] But distance and generality are for the drama not the novel. Paterson writes as though Melville, Hawthorne, Joyce, Conrad, Proust, Mann did not exist:

> the problem of the novelist as tragic artist is less to create distance between the reader and his images than to remove it. The generalized character makes, moreover, a poor and unconvincing showing in a form that thrives on particularity. It offends against the sense of lifelikeness which is among the novelist's chief resources at the same time that it weakens the reader's identification with the protagonist which is among the tragedian's chief resources. [5]

Absalom, Absalom! is, of course, immeasurably enriched by literary allusion and a consciousness of ancient tradition; my protest is simply against judgment by genre. Ilse Dusoir Lind's 1955 essay, "The Design and Meaning of *Absa-*

lom, Absalom!'' (still one of the best), emphasizes the enlarging and deepening effect of wide literary and mythological reference: Sutpen as the "ancient, stiff-jointed Pyramus" and "ancient varicose and despairing Faustus," but also the King David implicit in the book's title, "to whom it was promised that God would build him a house and establish his kingdom forever." [6] Henry and Charles "are the Biblical Absalom and Amnon in mortal conflict over a sister; they are Polyneices and Eteocles, sons of the cursed family of Oedipus"; Judith, like Antigone, "dignifies the rejected brother with the appropriate rites of burial"; she is, also, "the righteous Judith of the Old Testament." Ilse Lind comments on the "formalized, almost choreographic" gestures of Sutpen's brood, and their freedom from psychological analysis. Clytie, especially, remains unknown as an individual; "she exists as the pure, abstract embodiment of the theme." A number of critics have attributed the panoply of classical allusion to Mr. Compson's weary and ironic scholarship. But the other narrators offer their share. The novel as a whole, Ilse Lind writes, invokes the Greek sense of fate, with slavery going against nature and "the will of the gods." Structurally Miss Rosa, Mr. Compson and Quentin might be compared "to a display of the talents of three Greek dramatists composing tragedies about the same mythical figure, each poet having access to his predecessor's interpretation and adding insights and flourishes of his own." [7]

The Old Testament, Greek drama and myth, presumably too the rhetorical conventions of Shakespearean blank verse: these were deliberate enrichments. But *Absalom, Absalom!* is also illumined by the reflected light of other great novels: the Dickensian mysteries of fallen houses, fatal obsessions, secret misalliances—*Little Dorrit* and *Bleak House;* the ambiguities of *The Possessed* and the impressionist method of its first part; the essential information so long withheld in *The Brothers Karamazov.* The brilliant but crucially misinformed conjectures of prosecuting and defending lawyers there, the subtle play of mind that achieves a kind of truth in despite of fact, offer important adumbrations of Faulkner's method; so too the speculations of Melville's Ishmael and Proust's Marcel, faced by cosmic and urban mysteries. The full technique of narration by conjecture appears momentarily in *The Blithedale Romance.* But the choreographic aspect of *The Scarlet Letter,* and the Biblical simplicity of its confrontations, Dimmesdale and those watching him in Faulknerian frieze, suggest an even closer affinity. And, surely, *The Great Gatsby:* the puzzled narrative stance of Carraway, his stern judgment and growing sympathy; the large generality of Gatsby himself, his design and schedule and great failure of a house, his American optimism and incurable innocence that assumes one can always "start over." Michael Millgate has called attention to striking similarities with the plot of *Jane Eyre* and with the technique of *Wuthering Heights,* which Faulkner admired.[8] The "demonizing" of Nelly, like that of Miss Rosa, ends by increasing the reader's sympathy for its victim. *Wuthering Heights* anticipates more fully than any other novel the techniques of Conrad's impressionism, and hence of Faulkner's: the play of narrative voices and chronological dislocation, the massing of evidence through imagery as well as event, the continuing conflict of sympathy and judgment, our greatly changed experience on a second or subsequent reading. We will return to Conrad and narration by conjecture. One of the most strikingly analogous works appeared after *Absalom, Absalom!: Joseph and His Brothers.* Mann's narrator (with the difference that he debates only with himself) also struggles to understand and bring to life personages of stark simplicity and magnitude, fulfilling their obsessive designs and fatalities. It is his task, as it was Quentin's and Shreve's, to try to make sense of sparse, contradictory legends. What "really happened" at the well? Why did the brothers throw Joseph in? How provoked were they? *Genesis* doesn't "make sense"; some essential information is lacking. Hence Mann's narrator conjectures that there were two caravans not one, and "invents" an angel by the well, just as Shreve "invents" Eulalia Bon's lawyer.

Joseph W. Reed, Jr.'s *Faulkner's Narrative,* by far the most valuable discussion of *Absalom, Absalom!*'s narrative technique, simply takes for granted the larger issues that have bemused most critics; he confines himself admirably to his by no means limited subject. But a general assessment must at least touch on these larger issues, overly familiar though they be: sociology, ethics, psychology. For *Absalom, Absalom!* rests, like *Lord Jim,* on the bedrock of a deep humanity: great human situation ("true," whether conjectured or not), important moral issues and such conflicts as wear out the most stubborn spirit. Mature readers have become understandably impatient with glib reasonings on "the curse of the South"; one is reminded of Faulkner's wry comment, on trying to sell the novel to the films, that it's "about miscegenation." But the institution of slavery was as central to Thomas Sutpen's story as to Carothers McCaslin's, and fratricide at the gate came at the conclusion of a fratricidal war. The question of degrees of racism is of genuine interest: the difference between Sutpen's attitude toward Clytie and that of Miss Rosa, who cannot bear her touch. But the behavior of Henry, who can put up with incest but not miscegenation, is a *donnée* that one must simply accept (or not) in obedience to the novel's rhythms; the racist feeling is not really examined. Richard Poirier argues that Henry "acts not in obedience to his father, but to an inherent sense of a moral code which is stronger than his love for Bon." [9] Code, yes, and its enactment following upon a long period of inward debate. But the murder itself would appear as doomed and irrational, as emblematic, as Old Testament slaughterings. Henry and Charles at the gate would seem, paradoxically, to have transcended their roles as Southerners.

It is difficult to imagine Thomas Sutpen speaking with a southern accent, or to see him as representative of a slave-owning planter aristocracy. The wild negroes who help him build his house and meet him in "raree show" combat are never seen as domesticated field hands, nor the completed Sutpen's Hundred as a working cotton plantation. The patriotic colonel who replaces John Sartoris at the head of the regiment is undramatized; the reality is the obsessed giant of myth, traveling with the enormous gravestones. For Miss Rosa he is altogether an anomaly in an established community of gentlemen. By 1909, if not long before, she has come to believe in an old Deep South of enduring grace and tradition. In fact less than thirty years intervened between the founding of Jefferson and the war. Melvin Backman makes a plausible case for Sutpen as a representative "new man" of the southwestern frontier, and notes that McCaslin and Compson as well as Sutpen "got their land by hook or by crook." The Tidewater and Carolina plantation aristocracy could indeed serve as "symbol and goal" for men from the backwoods, who would themselves become aristocrats in one generation. But they had first, like Lord Jim in Patusan, to get a foothold. "The getting of the land, the hacking of a plantation out of the wilderness, and the establishment of a family dynasty would naturally promote violence, ruthlessness, and strength of character, and not 'vital morality and humanism.' " [10] *Absalom, Absalom!* would thus appear to have a double historical reality. Such men as Thomas Sutpen did exist. And so too did the post-war fantasy of a Mississippi plantation aristocracy.

Cleanth Brooks, as always informative, suggests a number of ways in which Sutpen remains outside the community, and sees him as "secularized Puritan," [11] even as a Yankee and representative American, a "planner." Given southern mores, and the Puritan abstractness of the "design" (which demanded even "virginity" of the man founding a dukedom or royal line), given too that the purity of the design must first of all satisfy himself, Sutpen is after all correct in believing Eulalia and her son could not be "incremental" to his plan. But the compromise that would have saved the dukedom (to give Charles his nod of recognition) is shunned with a rigidity as implacable as any conceived by Hawthorne. Sutpen is doubtless more representative of his time, and of the American character generally, in seeing material possessions as a source of honor and visible reward of virtue, courage, will; and, of course, in his "innocence" that simplifies all moral and psychological issues, and that rests its faith on the discovery and correction of an initial mistake. Innocence means an unawareness of the complexities of life and of social gradations. Cleanth Brooks dislikes Ilse Lind's characterization of Sutpen's original home as a "mountain paradise," given eye-gouging and other brutalities. But Sutpen does remember it as an archetypal classless America, a primitive society in which no one owns the land, and none has "authority or warrant to look down at others, any others." Sutpen "fell into it" (echoing Stein's famous image of man born falling into a dream and falling into the sea): fell into a different world that violated his ideal of equality. Turned away from the front door of the plantation, he retreated to his cave and there carved his resolve and design.

Thus Sutpen, who decidedly possesses a "certain magnitude," is both a figure of mythical grandeur and Old Testament simplicity ("brave" for Wash Jones, a demon for Miss Rosa, an "innocent" for General Compson) and a symbolic presence of some historic validity: a representative "new man" hacking an estate out of the southwestern wilderness, a Yankee secularized Puritan, a nineteenth-century rugged individualist, an American. It took Sutpen to make all of us. But he is almost never dramatized as an "ordinary" human being who can be subjected to psychological analysis; his childhood trauma lasts a lifetime. The suggestions of an ordinary humanity—the Sutpen who kisses Henry in the tent, or who drinks with Wash under the scuppernong arbor—are kept brief. To have given more attention to this ordinary humanity, as most novelists would, might have destroyed the larger image. Faulkner's Sutpen is a selective distortion of any conceivable "full reality"; and it is better so.

How much of ordinary humanity remains in the portrait of Judith—who, if we are to believe Miss Rosa, looked down unmoved on her father fighting a slave, and who, on the death of her fiancé, her face *"absolutely calm,"* said *"I will have to speak to Mr Jones about some planks and nails"*? The *"tearless and stone-faced daughter"* (still Miss Rosa) who held the door open for the body of her murdered father? Shreve, whose authority would appear to be General Compson through Quentin, evokes Charles Etienne cared for by Judith, "whose every touch of the capable hands seemed at the moment of touching his body to lose all warmth and become imbued with cold implacable antipathy. . . ." The novel's dominant picture is of iron will, an undeviating acceptance of what must be done and what must be borne, a masculine ruthless strength (and the ability to plough like a man). She evidently did not know, Brooks reminds us, "why her marriage was forbidden nor did she know why her brother killed Charles Bon." [12] How much, within the novel, is there to correct this picture of mythical strength and rigidity? Brooks (whose own humanity informs every chapter of his book) goes beyond any of the narrators to discern a humane as well as heroic Judith, who is to be known by her actions not her tranquil countenance: the Judith who invites the octoroon to visit Bon's grave, who tries to rear the son and ultimately "tries to free him (as Quentin conjectures) by promising to take care of his Negro wife and child if he will go to the North to pass as white. . . ." [13] My own feeling is that Faulkner saw, even in the generosities, a marble coldness.

The portraits of Sutpen and Judith are not, then, "psychological" in a Dostoevskyan or even Dickensian sense; inflexible character and resolve, once established, almost never waver, and are never fully analyzed. Father and daughter occupy, immovably, their given tragic roles, and this is eventually true of Charles Bon. This is a fictional world of obsessive-compulsive personalities, chronically self-destructive, but without the involutions of Dostoevsky's underground men and self-lacerating women, or, even, of Dickens's Miss Wade and Tattycoram. Faulkner's view of his characters may well be the same as Mr. Compson's:

> people too as we are, and victims too as we are, but victims of a different circumstance, simpler and therefore, integer for integer, larger, more heroic and the figures therefore more heroic too, not dwarfed and involved but distinct, uncomplex who had the gift of loving once or dying once instead of being diffused and scattered creatures drawn blindly limb from limb from a grab bag and assembled. . . .[14]

The characters, like the actors in Greek tragedy, wear masks larger than life; they are the helpless victims and avatars of the obsessions and passions. Rosa, though locked in her trauma and forty-three years' rage, is far more individualized than Judith or Clytie or Ellen, since we do hear her talk and talk. (Her abrupt and violent reaction to Sutpen's proposal, to be sure, would not be anomalous in the South of her time.) Mr. Compson's picture of her preparing garments "for her own vicarious bridal" with an unseen Charles Bon is not discredited by her highly erotic rhetoric and spinsterly memories. The touch of Clytie's "black arresting and untimorous hand" on her white woman's flesh evokes immediately the fleshly touch of lovers: *"the liquorish and ungirdled mind is anyone's to take in any darkened hallway of this earthly tenement. But let flesh touch with flesh, and watch the fall of all the eggshell shibboleth of caste and color too."* We are to assume, I think, that the long italicized discourse of chapter V is of an interior voice, a stream flowing beneath full consciousness even, what the innermost spirit would say if it could. And this revealed essential self (*"all polymath love's androgynous advocate"*) is highly sexualized:

But it was no summer of a virgin's itching discontent; no summer's caesarean lack
which should have torn me, dead flesh or even embryo, from the living: or else, by
friction's ravishing of the male-furrowed meat, also weaponed and panoplied as a
man instead of hollow woman.[15]

The brief portrait of Charles Etienne de Saint Velery Bon is the novel's only
approach to a controlled psychological "case"; and the case is, in miniature,
Joe Christmas's, but with important differences. He is translated not from an
orphanage to the iron rigidities of the McEachern farm (where feminine pity
also threatens) but from a "cloyed and scented maze of shuttered silk" and a
mother Beardsley might have dressed to a world of "harsh and shapeless
denim" and the frightening attentions of Judith and Clytie: "picked suddenly
up out of whatever debacle the only life he knew had disintegrated into, by a
creature whom he had seen once and learned to dread and fear yet could not
flee. . . ." Sleeping between Judith on the bed and Clytie on the floor, forbidden to play with negroes but told at last he is one, scrutinizing his features in
the shard of broken mirror he keeps hidden under the mattress, his very existence long concealed—the narrative moves without pause from the formative
childhood and adolescence to the completed self-destructive drive and compulsive reenactments. Like Joe Christmas he must, though he could pass for a
white man, flaunt his unendurable negro identity, start fights and compel situations in which he will experience "blows and slashes" he "did not even seem
to feel." His ultimate revenge, on the world and on self, is to marry a "coal
black and ape-like woman," drag her through a "maelstrom of faces and bodies" and places where he will receive the necessary maulings, at last bring her
home to "kennel" her in a nearby ruined cabin; and show Judith the license.
The conflict between sympathy and judgment that intensifies the portrait of Joe
Christmas here scarcely exists, since there is no ground for moral judgment of a
person who has never been free. No character in fiction is more firmly locked
in compulsion, or more poignantly does what he must.

But if there is no fully developed psychological portrait in *Absalom, Absalom!* there is an exceedingly interesting triangular pattern, one that fascinates
the speculative Mr. Compson and significantly disturbs Quentin. The pattern is
close to René Girard's "triangular desire," in which a mediating or surrogate
figure stands between the lover and the loved person or ideal. It would be described by most psychiatrists (as it is by Mr. Compson) in psycho-sexual terms.
It is tempting to dismiss the complications as to some extent Mr. Compson's
sophisticated fantasy, who lovingly projects his image of Bon's Scythian glitter, indolence, passivity, satiety, "the effluvium of knowledge, surfeit." But

not all is fantasy. Henry did give up his birthright out of loyalty to Bon, and did, to prevent the marriage, kill Bon at the gate. The triad, however conjectural, is worthy of *The Idiot*'s configurations. The supposition is that Bon effortlessly "seduced the country brother and sister," though we know little of Judith's response. Henry is attracted ("with the knowledge of the insurmountable barrier which the similarity of gender hopelessly intervened") to a figure of idealized (and feminized) urbanity. In time he gives him that "complete and abnegant devotion which only a youth, never a woman, gives to another youth or man." But as Henry may share his sister through his devoted identification with Bon, so at least wishfully he could share the brother-in-law through that fancied union with her. Bisexual incest (which would later be seen as doubly incestuous, with Bon known as blood brother) thus combines with a familiar homosexual or homoerotic maneuver. "In fact," Mr. Compson says,

> perhaps this is the pure and perfect incest: the brother realizing that the sister's virginity must be destroyed in order to have existed at all, taking that virginity in the person of the brother-in-law, the man whom he would be if he could become, metamorphose into, the lover, the husband; by whom he would be despoiled, choose for despoiler, if he could become, metamorphose into the sister, the mistress, the bride. Perhaps that is what went on, not in Henry's mind but in his soul.[16]

Henry could seduce Judith (into loving Bon, whom she had not yet seen), Mr. Compson opines, thanks to a telepathic rapport as of two people who "had been marooned at birth on a desert island: the island here Sutpen's Hundred." The reader bent on remembering *The Sound and the Fury* may well believe that Mr. Compson's fantasies are based on observation of his own son and daughter. But Caddy, it must be emphasized, it nowhere mentioned in the later novel. Mr. Compson evokes Henry reading the letters "without jealousy, with that complete abnegant transference, metamorphosis into the body which was to become his sister's lover." Charles Bon in turn can be subject as well as object in this pattern of triangular desire, with Judith again the mediator:

> Perhaps in his fatalism he loved Henry the better of the two, seeing perhaps in the sister merely the shadow, the woman vessel with which to consummate the love whose actual object was the youth—this cerebral Don Juan who, reversing the order, had learned to love what he had injured; perhaps it was even more than Judith or Henry either: perhaps the life, the existence, which they represented.[17]

A large body of critical opinion has come to see Quentin as the novel's central "subject," with the emphasis given Sutpen in the first half shifting to him in the second. His refusal to respond to Shreve's suggestion that an incestuous love, being sinful, might permit no escape, no uncoupling—Quentin's "shoulders hugged inward and hunched, his face lowered"—recalls the appeal of damnation reasoned in *The Sound and the Fury;* and therefore recalls too our very moving experience of his last day, the flatirons that will rise or not and the door that separates life from death. There is, moreover, the authority of Faulkner's "genealogy" (in spite of its errors) to connect the two novels, and the lesser authority of his statements outside the novel. His undated but obviously early letter to Harrison Smith has the ring of an author hoping to trade on a past achievement:

Quentin Compson, of the Sound & Fury, tells it, or ties it together; he is the protagonist so that it is not complete apocrypha. I use him because it is just before he is to commit suicide because of his sister, and I use his bitterness which he has projected on the South in the form of hatred of it and its people to get more out of the story itself than a historical novel would be. To keep the hoop skirts and plug hats out, you might say.[18]

At Virginia Faulkner argued that the two Quentins were consistent. Quentin could face neither the reality of his sister's sexual life, nor the reality of the South, and

approached the Sutpen family with the same opthalamia that he approached his own troubles, that he probably never saw anything clearly, that his was just one of the thirteen ways to look at Sutpen, and his may have been the—one of the most erroneous.[19]

The internal evidence for connecting the Quentin Compsons of the two novels is singularly slight. The Sutpen story (though he had been hearing fragments of it most of his life) never enters his consciousness in the earlier novel; Caddy and her troubles never enter his consciousness in the later one. His speaking voice in *Absalom, Absalom!* is described as flat and dull, as might befit a disturbed man not far from suicide. But his "inner" and narrative voice—the one we as readers hear—is disturbed, yes, but vivacious, often humorous and sardonic, interested. Where, a literalist might ask, are Dilsey and Jason and Benjy in the physical environment of *Absalom, Absalom!*, or even momentarily in Quentin's stream-of-consciousness? I think Faulkner was wise to omit them, as one Marlow to omit Patusan from his recollections and the other to omit the Congo; there are enough vivid particulars and digressions as things stand. The actual connections come down, very nearly, to a home town, a father, a freshman year at Harvard; and, briefly, Luster. *The Sound and the Fury* and *Absalom, Absalom!* are (like *Heart of Darkness* and *Lord Jim*) great autonomous novels, not two fragments of a *roman-fleuve* or Balzacian series, and our feelings for one Quentin should not control our feelings for the other.

A more legitimate approach locates the novel's central interest in this other

Quentin's desperate attempt to cope with the southern heritage he has explored: with Thomas Sutpen and what he has done and meant, with the traumatic excursion to Sutpen's Hundred and the wasted form of Henry still alive. Good readers have been deeply moved by the reality of the two young men talking in the iron New England cold, and their growing identification with Henry and Charles . . . though one could argue the probable identifications would have been between Quentin and the complex Charles Bon (who, if anyone, will sleep with the sister) and between the burly curious outsider Shreve and the uninitiated Henry. Those who center the novel's interest in Quentin have at least seen the primary importance of contemplative mind and its exploratory, interpretative acts. But it may be they have been unduly controlled—in seeing Quentin as subject not narrator, contemplator—by the vividness of the short last chapter: the intense particulars of the trip to Sutpen's Hundred (Clytie striking the match, the circular dialogue with Henry) but also the particulars of the Cambridge room, as Quentin began "to jerk all over," claiming to feel all right, but "lying there and waiting in peaceful curiosity for the next violent unharbingered jerk to come." The novel's last lines are memorable, the more so because Shreve's question itself comes as a dramatic surprise: *"I dont hate it he thought, panting in the cold air, the iron New England dark; I dont. I dont! I dont hate it! I dont hate it!"* But I suspect these lines have, for many readers, dominated or minimized what went before. For those who read the novel only once, this is a telling last impression. But *Absalom, Absalom!* is generically— like *Benito Cereno, Lord Jim* and other great novels of explored ambiguity—a novel to be reread, with those last lines given less weight on a subsequent reading.

For me, after a good number of readings, the great human and dramatic subjects are Thomas Sutpen, and the poignant curve of his life; the relationship of Henry and Charles Bon, with Judith as "vessel" or catalyst in a distant background; the *novel's* (not any one narrator's) contemplation of the people, the events, the ambiguities. The fraternal relationship of Henry and Bon moves from Mr. Compson's intellectual comedy of corrupting sophisticate and aghast country bumpkin to the wartime dawn confrontation of Shakespearean magnitude, after Henry reveals what he has just learned from his father. The trip to New Orleans as Mr. Compson conceives it (pp. 106–18), and with some of Faulkner's most brilliant writing, is less concerned with a warm human relationship than with the catlike effeminate Bon, taking an active pleasure in exposing "the innocent and negative plate of Henry's provincial soul and intellect," and "corrupting Henry gradually into the purlieus of elegance." There is the fascination, for Mr. Compson and certainly for Faulkner too, in the purlieus themselves and the revealed institutions: the "row of faces like a bazaar of flowers, the supreme apotheosis of chattelry, of human flesh bred of the two races for that sale" and the female principle inherited from the "hot equatorial groin of the world," evocative of "strange and ancient curious pleasures of the flesh," pleasures as indeterminate as the unspeakable rites of *Heart of Darkness.*

But the start of the journey, as we see it over two hundred pages later, after Henry has given his father the lie, and given up his birthright, evokes two men, certainly equals now, who can communicate without words: the two riding over the frozen ruts of that Christmas Eve, and on Christmas morning past the decorated plantation houses "in something very like pariah-hood," and on the steamboat, not attending the Christmas supper and ball but instead "in the dark and the cold standing at the guard rail above the dark water and still not talking since there was nothing to say. . . ." The picture of conflicting loyalties intensifies a few pages (and years) later, in Shreve's plausible conjecture: Henry's effort to make himself accept incest, as the two men walk toward Shiloh; Bon's bitter suggestion that Henry will have, in battle, a chance to shoot him with impunity; Henry not Bon wounded in battle, picked up by his brother, and struggling, asking to be allowed to die. "Let me die! I won't have to know it then. . . ." On the next page, with italics, we move into an omniscience which, though still at times using the language of conjecture, is presumably as close to historical truth as we will ever come; and Henry gives Charles permission to write the letter to Judith that says "We have waited long enough." There follows (after Henry's interview with his father in the tent, and the revelation that Bon's mother was part negro) the dawn scene, as Bon puts his cloak about Henry's shoulders. The first crucial words are not reported, only the comment that the "voices are not much louder than the silent dawn itself," then Bon's *"—So it's the miscegenation, not the incest, which you can't bear."* There is nothing now of the world-weary corrupter, only the man ready to die on principle and to assert the identity his father will not grant him. *"He did not ask you to send me to him? No word to me, no word at all?"*

It is the destiny of intellectually or psychologically complex novels, and novels of moral ambiguity—*Moby Dick, Lord Jim, The Brothers Karamazov, Absalom, Absalom!*—to draw the attention of critics to their ideas and labyrinthine methods, to the neglect of the great dramatic moments of colliding purpose or suddenly revealed destiny. But none of these novels would be the same without these moments of intensely revealed humanity (or inhumanity), nor would we care so much about those ideas, insights, complexities. The great moment may be compressed to a phrase, a few spoken words that bring a character at once to life. Or the few spoken words may seem to touch on limits of human endurance because they emerge from so much conflict, anguish, resolution. It is conceivable that Wash Jones has the greatest lines in the novel: " 'I'm going to tech you, Kernel' " (as he approaches, with the scythe, his overthrown God wielding the whip), and when, commanded to come out by Major De Spain, and in the moments before cutting Milly's neckbones, " 'In just a minute. Soon as I see about my granddaughter' "; and, in response to the girl's " 'Light the lamp, Grandpaw' " his " 'Hit wont need no light, honey. Hit wont take but a minute.' " Or the few words may, by picking up and exploiting a previously playful metaphor, movingly sum up a situation, a life. Thus "Ellen the butterfly, from beneath whom without warning the very sunbuoyed air had been withdrawn, leaving her now with the plump hands folded on the coverlet in the darkened room" has, five pages later, been dead two years: "the butterfly, the moth caught in a gale and blown against a wall and clinging there beating feebly. . . ." Few novels, if any, are richer in metaphorical surprises, but surprises that prove to be meaningful and appropriate.

The critic's difficulty with the larger dramatic moments, the connected scenes or carefully constructeed tableaux, is that they require either to be quoted at length or fully paraphrased. And even this, with a writer who likes to end paragraphs and chapters very dramatically, must omit the contexts which could do them justice. The least or perhaps most one can do is (as I did with *Lord Jim* long ago) to cite what seem to me some of these great moments. A number of the scenes, as a rule dramatically placed, bring a sudden revelation of character or situation: *multum in parvo*. The suspect newcomer Sutpen's silent pride, and his relationship to the community, is revealed in the paragraph of the vigilance committee's following him to the Coldfields' house, where he will propose to Ellen, the committee outraged by a "final gratuitous insult," his "newspaper cornucopia of flowers." The paragraph is representative of a number of scenes that have the quality of choreographic movement or of silent tableau: the very silence itself dramatic, and lending force to the few words spoken at last. Most of the memorable scenes appear, like this one, to have a strongly compassionate component, though the compassion may be disguised by irony or verbal play.

But here is a brief list:

—Rosa's *tableau* (rephrased by the novel's original narrator) of Sutpen abrupting out of "quiet thunderclap": "faint sulphur-reek still in hair clothes and beard, with grouped behind him his band of wild niggers like beasts half tamed to walk upright like men, in attitudes wild and reposed, and manacled among them the French architect with his air grim, haggard, and tatter-ran.'' The Miltonic rhythms and syntax (the splitting and post-positioning of adjectives) and the humorous paradox hold in suspension a highly visual frieze. Mr. Compson, twenty-seven pages later, offers his own vivid, corrected *tableau* of the arrival. Not manacled, and ''come all the way from Martinique on Sutpen's bare promise,'' the architect is now seated beside the negro driver, ''a small, alertly resigned man with a grim, harried Latin face, in a frock coat and a flowered waistcoat and a hat which would have created no furore on a Paris boulevard. . . .'' The negroes are still there, not grouped behind Sutpen, but under the wagon hood for someone to peer at: ''a black tunnel filled with still eyeballs and smelling like a wolfden.''

—The *tableau* (Mr. Compson's) of Sutpen at work on his house: ''the bearded white man and the twenty black ones and all stark naked beneath the croaching and pervading mud.'' The coon-hunter Akers, on the previous page, ''claimed to have walked one of them out of the absolute mud like a sleeping alligator and screamed just in time.'' Sutpen here naked with his negroes, as when half-naked fighting with one of them, may leave a virtually indelible impression, though a subordinate clause reminds us of a prosaic reason for being plastered over with mud: protection against mosquitoes.

—Rosa's expertly suspenseful *tableau* of Sutpen fighting with one of the negroes, ''naked to the waist and gouging at one another's eyes,'' and the beaten negro lying bloody at Sutpen's feet, which gives way to *scene* and *dialogue* as Ellen breaks in on the gathering, looking for the children, two of whom (Judith and presumably Clytie) had been watching from the loft while the weaker Henry vomited.

—Mr. Compson's *tableau* of Sutpen and Ellen emerging from the wedding, to be pelted with clods of dirt and vegetable refuse—Sutpen holding the wild negroes back with the one unquoted word in an unknown tongue, the bride shrinking but Sutpen motionless, his teeth showing through the beard, ''while about the wedding party the circle of faces with open mouths and torch-reflecting eyes seemed to advance and waver and shift and vanish in the smoky glare of the burning pine.'' The scene, intensified by the prolonged silence, is resolved by Mr. Compson's cool compassionate commentary: '' 'Yes, she was weeping again now; it did, indeed, rain on that marriage.' ''

—Mr. Compson's *tableau* of Wash Jones at Miss Rosa's gate, ''a gaunt gangling man malaria-ridden with pale eyes,'' shouting '' 'Air you Rosie Coldfield' '' at the end of Chapter III, a shout to be completed only forty-six pages later at the end of Chapter IV: '' 'Henry has done shot that durn French feller. Kilt him dead as a beef.' '' The announcement is immediately preceded by the *tableau* (as it seemed to Quentin he could actually see them, after listening to his father) of Henry and Bon at the gate, "with unkempt hair and faces gaunt and weathered as if cast by some spartan and even niggard hand from bronze. . . ." The calm diction and classical analogy intensify the moment of confrontation and Bon's saying *I am going to pass it, Henry . . .* which gives way without transition to Jones's brutal announcement.

—Rosa's highly rhetorical and digressive evocation, both *tableau* and *scene,* of Judith's calm acceptance of Bon's murder: blocking the way to the closed door, saying she will have to see Mr. Jones about planks and nails, giving directions for the making of the coffin (and *"the slow, maddening rasp, rasp, rasp, of the saw"*), and presently *"in the barnlot in a cloud of chickens, her apron cradled about the gathered eggs."*

—Rosa's *actualizing digression* (one of many in the novel) that in a few lines gives earthly reality to a murder as from ancient myth: *"a shot heard only by its echo, a strange gaunt half-wild horse, bridled and with empty saddle, the saddle bags containing a pistol, a worn clean shirt, a lump of iron-like bread, captured by a man four miles away and two days later while trying to force the crib door in his stable."*

—Rosa's *tableau,* giving way to *choreographic scene,* of Sutpen's return from the war, on his *"gaunt and jaded horse"* and in his *"leaf-colored and threadbare coat with its tarnished and flapping braid."* Twenty-four words in all are spoken: in greeting, and to inform him that Henry killed Bon and is gone, and to explain Rosa's presence. Only now Judith bursts into tears. Of the twenty-four words the most moving are those of Sutpen, who has learned so much so suddenly and, still with his hands on Judith's shoulders, turns to his negro daughter: " 'Ah, Clytie.' "

—Rosa's ironic and detached *summary* and *picture* (as though an omniscient author's) of herself reaching through the garden fence to steal vegetables, not using a stick to *"draw the vegetables to where she could grasp them, the reach of her unaided arm being the limit of brigandage which she never passed."* Here and on a number of other occasions Rosa's frenzied and neurotic self-scrutinies are redeemed by both verbal and visual humor.

—The *tableau* (as imagined by Quentin after listening to Rosa) of Henry's confrontation with Judith, as he bursts in on her minutes after the murder, and the five sentences as they speak "to one another in short brief staccato sentences like slaps."

—The historian's *omniscient account* (but an omniscience intuited by Quentin) of certain events leading to the murder of Sutpen, and of the murder and its aftermath, with an intricate play of shifting distances that becomes more rather than less moving on second and subsequent readings, and the more *scenic reconstruction* of the events (conjectured by Quentin, but with an unmistakable ring of truth) over a hundred pages later. The story is here carried further to include the death of Milly.

—The *scenic* account, for the most part conventional in method, of the trip to Sutpen's Hundred with Rosa, and the discovery of Clytie and Henry there. Nominally recollected by Quentin lying in bed, after his long colloquy with Shreve, this would appear to be the work of an omniscient narrator or observer who takes us into a fictional present. But at a crucial point the omniscience is limited. We never learn how (if through words at all, rather than intuition) Quentin acquired the knowledge on which the whole novel's plot spins. The twelve-line circular exchange of dialogue with Henry, perhaps not spoken at all, conveys Quentin's shock as well as information to the reader. The excursion to Sutpen's Hundred constitutes the longest instance in the novel of straightforward, relatively unmediated scene. The impact of this unusually direct narrative is all the greater because of the hundreds of circling and evasive pages that precede it. Intensely dramatic at a first reading, certain moments have an added poignancy as we return to them: "the tiny gnomelike creature in headrag and voluminous skirts" and her great lines "Don't let her go up there, young marster" and "Whatever he done, me and Judith and him have paid it out." Or the exchange between the fallen Rosa and "the hulking slack-faced negro," Sutpen's last male descendant:

> "You, nigger! What's your name?"
> "Calls me Jim Bond."
> "Help me up! You aint any Sutpen! You dont have to leave me lying in the dirt." [20]

And, of course, Henry, forty-five years after the event: "the wasted yellow face with closed, almost transparent eyelids on the pillow, the wasted hands crossed on the breast as if he were already a corpse. . . ."

—The compressed *scenic* account of the burning house (nominally as imagined by Quentin), and Clytie's face appearing in the window, "the tragic gnome's face beneath the clean headrag" and the howling of Jim Bond, "the scion, the last of his race," whom they were unable to catch.

It is time to return to my assertion that *Absalom, Absalom!* "dramatizes (and makes us believe) a number of things that presumably could not have happened, posits knowledge that has no cognitive source, and records voices, both interior and speaking, as remote from everyday speech as those in Shakespeare's verse plays." The fire at Sutpen's Hundred, to look at the last of these "probable impossibilities," could hardly have blazed so high or consumed so much in the three minutes Clytie had counted on as enough. The collapse of the house in *Little Dorrit* and of the mine in *Germinal* have a scientific (not fictional) authenticity that Faulkner's fire does not; house and mine have been alike subject to periodic slippages. There is a feeble effort at circumstantial realism—the closet under the stairs kept full of tinder and trash, "the kerosene and all"— before the fire is actually seen. Something is accomplished by a staccato unpunctuated prose of seemingly precise notation, more by diverting the reader's attention to a mysterious bellowing that will turn out to be Jim Bond's:

> the monstrous tinder-dry rotten shell seeping smoke through the warped cracks in the weather-boarding as if it were made of gauze wire and filled with roaring and beyond which somewhere something lurked which bellowed, something human since the bellowing was in human speech. . . .[21]

The entire staircase is at once on fire; the whole lower hall vanishes. But our attention is fixed on the altogether credible figure of Rosa "clawing and scratching and biting at the two men who held her," and moments later on Clytie's face at the window. The fire *must* burn this rapidly so that she cannot be saved and so that we can see her there, "possibly even serene above the melting clapboards before the smoke swirled across" the window again. The whole novel, moreover, has prepared us to believe that Sutpen's Hundred is a place where strange, emblematic, mythical, "impossible" things can happen.

The incidence of literal impossibilities in serious fiction (say death by spontaneous combustion) is small prior to the 1960s. (Hawkes's *The Cannibal* of 1949 asked for a kind of belief in its impossibilities that surrealist fantasy, say *The Dream Life of Balso Snell,* did not; in this it was unique.) The coincidences of Dickens and Hardy are not literally impossible. The unhinged Kirillov might well have been willing to take responsibility for Shatov's death; the also unhinged Mathilde have wanted to hold her lover's severed head on her lap. But to assert impossibilities, to say that a novel's report on life is in places "inauthentic," is not in the least to question its "truth"—whether *Ada*'s or *One Hundred Years of Solitude*'s or *The Cannibal*'s; or *Absalom, Absalom!*'s. Even historical truth. The good reader's fourteenth way of looking at a blackbird, Faulkner held, would be right. History is the carefully weighed, imagined sum of available fact, opinion and distortion, conjecture, legend. Clytie's death in the fire, like Jim Bond's survival (with further debasements of the dukedom thus possible), is a necessary and "higher truth."

Credibility and literal authenticity are, of course, altogether different affairs. The puzzled dialogue of Wash and Sutpen, under the scuppernong vine afforded them in after-life—'' '' *'What was it, Wash? Something happened. What was it?'* ''—is very nearly the most moving moment in the novel, with its reminder of the tragic bewilderment that may follow upon accident, blunder, separation. The scene, because it so moves us, suspends disbelief. (The dialogue of Flem and Satan in *The Hamlet,* on the other hand, does not achieve or attempt credibility.) The question of ''impossibility'' should also be kept separate from the question of conjecture true or false. Most of the events fantasied or distorted by Rosa and Mr. Compson could have happened.

The comic ''tall tale'' may be based on impossibilities, yet induce a kind of belief. The virtual enslavement of the French architect could well have occurred on the southwestern frontier in 1833; any abuse was possible. Mr. Compson's version of the man lured by bare promise is perhaps more likely than Rosa's view of him manacled, or *Requiem for a Nun*'s version of him shadowed by a negro guard. But I think we have to assume that his Tarzan mode of escape, discovered when they found the ''sapling pole with his suspenders still knotted about one end of it,'' was impossible, would not and could not have happened—though luckily for the fiction it did.

These minor examples merely underline the obvious: the strength and playfulness of Faulkner's anti-realist impulse. What is not so obvious is that three crucial events or assumptions of *Absalom, Absalom!* may also be regarded as virtual ''impossibilities.'' That we believe them is a measure of Faulkner's fictive power. The first is perhaps debatable. Would Sutpen in real life—and since to grant it would have saved Judith, Henry, the dukedom, as well as Bon— have refused the mere nod of recognition, the word, even the command that Charles asked? In psychological terms one could argue that Sutpen was disarmed and paralyzed by such an unexpected fillip of fate, as Macbeth dismayed by the movement of Birnam Wood, or Lord Jim paralyzed by Gentleman Brown and his reminders of the *Patna* and his suggestions of a common guilt. Once committed to silence, Sutpen had to hold inflexibly to it, as he held inflexibly to everything else. And yet (to become still another narrator of the novel): It wouldn't have happened, though happen it must if we are to have our story. Within the novel we believe it, I assume, because it is offered as an astonishing but unquestioned historical event, because it fits in so well with our general picture of Sutpen's stubborn blindness and rock-like determination, and most of all because so much that is unquestionably true is woven about it by the novel's impressionist method.

The second impossibility: Neither Henry nor Clytie (if we assume one of them did) would have given Quentin (or Miss Rosa) the information on which the whole plot depends: Charles Bon's brotherhood and his negro taint. Clytie, who wants only to get them out of the house? Henry, moving his wasted hands, and seeing Quentin for the first time in his life? "I didn't expect you tonight but I might as well tell you why I killed my brother (he was my brother) forty-five years ago. . . ." Cleanth Brooks reasons, in his book, that there would have been at least ten minutes for a talk with Henry.[22] In a recent article he notes that the italicized thirty-six-word exchange with Henry (which I believe may have taken place only in Quentin's mind) would have required no more than twenty seconds, with "all the proper pauses." He suggests that another brief exchange would have been enough: "If Quentin had merely formed the words 'Charles Bon was your friend—?', it is easy to imagine Henry replying: 'More than my friend. My brother.' "[23] Quentin and Mr. Compson, in this new version, would have inferred the negro blood in their discussions the next day. But the novel, as Brooks notes, leaves these matters to the imagination of the reader. And surely this was necessary. Logically we know, at least on a second reading, that the crucial information had to be obtained at this time if at all. And there is the logical possibility too, in a novel that elsewhere assumes the possibility of wordless communication, that Quentin, staring at Henry, reached the truth intuitively. But we believe whatever we do believe without or in spite of time-schemes and logic. Faulkner simply had to omit what could not be presented plausibly. Certainly all credibility would have been lost had he given us an actual scene, had he dramatized either illuminating dialogue or a Proustian moment of intuitive discovery. Beyond this we can only helplessly remark that whatever happened on such a long-prepared and harrowingly real excursion must indeed have happened . . . but fictionally not literally.

The third impossibility—though this too is perhaps debatable—is the murder at the gate to Sutpen's Hundred. Too many better opportunities would have offered themselves, in "real reality," to test or deny a principle and moral code, draw a line; and, if necessary, kill. The "showdown" is classic frontier Americana. But these particular brothers, given what we have seen of them, would presumably have found some other way. *Absalom, Absalom!* is not, fortunately, working within such "real reality." The emblematic act and drawing of a line must occur at the gate, if not at the door to the house or door to Judith's room; experience must be starkly symbolic. How, then, does the novel induce us to believe? The act, for one thing, is a crucial event in a story of Old Testament simplicity (for all the complexities of narration); the emblematic is in a sense the normal. People are "uncomplex": rectilinear in their obsessions and pertinacities and loyalties; even the sophisticated Bon is at last single-minded. It is a Shakespearean world, too, in which virtually impossible choices are posed in extreme terms: Hamlet and Macbeth as well as Oedipus and Abraham.

The "impossible" emblematic event is, perhaps more than one realizes after a first reading, almost completely free of realistic detail, movement, dialogue: little more than the gaunt horses and the "unkempt hair and faces gaunt and weathered," and the two short scraps of dialogue, as Quentin imagines it: " *'Don't you pass the shadow of this post, this branch, Charles;* and *I am going to pass it, Henry.'* " We have tableau, not scene. When we return to the murder, 225 pages later, it is for less than fifty words: "only then that one of them ever rode ahead or dropped behind and that only then Henry spurred ahead and turned his horse to face Bon and took out the pistol; and Judith and Clytie heard the shot. . . ." The narrative has avoided, for its grand event, what James called "weak specification."

Absalom, Absalom! departs even more obviously from the realism of the 1930's, or from any authentic report on actual life, in its elaboration of dialogue, with all the narrators partaking of a familiar Faulknerian "voice": both the nervous evasive involuted movement of mind and the formal components of style that convey it: highly abstract and often recondite diction, startling metaphor and simile, complication of syntax, unpunctuated running rhythms tending at times to high-pitched monotone. The literary convention and the relationship to everyday speech appear to be nearly identical with those of Shakespearean blank verse. In diction, syntax and rhythm we have, simply, a "literary language" formally elevated above ordinary prose discourse. The characters may at times, as in Shakespeare's plays, begin speaking colloquially or, at dramatic moments, fall back into colloquialism (even "prose"). Quentin and Rosa speak with the normal accents of Jefferson during the essentially realistic, straightforward excursion to Sutpen's Hundred; unmediated dramatic presentness is essential. So too we hear real voices as Sutpen questions the negro midwife and in his brief final exchange with Wash. But the narrators, and those who silently meditate and conjecture, generally use variants of the overriding Faulknerian voice.

This arbitrarily elevated language preserves the pleasing values of human speech; we hear voices speaking rather than watch a machine writing, and are conscious always of active minds. All the narrators share Faulkner's ironic love of hyperbole and paradox, of absurd oxymoron and analogy drawn from an alien area of discourse. All are repetitive in their allusions, and frequently tautological; all are evasive and oblique; all indulge in sudden transitions; all enjoy ending scenes, paragraphs, even sentences dramatically. All the narrators, in brief, have the right to enlist the author's highest imaginative and stylistic powers, though Miss Rosa is at times invited to abuse them.

And there are, of course—again as in Shakespearean blank verse dialogue—individual variants on this second language and Faulknerian voice, differentiations between characters at least as great as in standard realistic dialogue. The unnamed narrator or alleged author who opens the novel, and who appears to blend with Mr. Compson's consciousness in the first twelve pages of the second chapter (before surrendering to his actual voice) is perhaps cooler and more formally in control of his presentation than the others; he is not personally involved. This voice is to be distinguished from that of the deeply moved ghostly spectator of the italicized wartime scene (351–58), reporting Henry's conversations with his father and with Charles in the present tense. Mr. Compson's voice is quieter, moves more circumstantially and often more self-consciously than the others', and enjoys composing literary effects. But this is not to say that he writes or "speaks" badly. Shreve, who "sounds just like father," has in fact a far more forceful voice. His sardonic parodies and flights of irony (which cover a sympathy that grows more and more intense) create and control effectively the distance between the reader and the events: "That this Faustus, this demon, this Beelzebub fled hiding from some momentary flashy glare of his Creditor's outraged face exasperated beyond endurance, hiding, scuttling into respectability like a jackal into a rockpile, as she thought at first. . . ." What would have been Faulkner's despair had he known that some critics have seen Shreve as sadistic, obtuse, lacking in sympathy! The interplay of Shreve's and Quentin's voices (and their protesting or ironic corrections) raises the question of the degree to which they seem complementary doubles, two sides of a shared consciousness. In an earlier conception of the novel there were two Quentins in inward debate, as there are now on the third page. They sound, of course, exactly like Quentin-Shreve: *"and built a plantation—(Tore violently a plantation, Miss Rosa Coldfield says)—tore violently."*

The most audacious flouting of mimetic convention occurs with Charles Bon's letter to Judith (pp. 129–32): an actual non-conjectural letter written during the war—"the dead tongue speaking after the four years and then after almost fifty more, gentle sardonic whimsical and incurably pessimistic"; and speaking, of course, in an unmistakably Faulknerian manner: the digressions and playful evasions and the long withheld "point"; the parentheses; the abstractions and metaphors (*"it is only the mind, the gross omnivorous carrion-heavy soul which becomes inured"*); and the reiterated injunction to imagine the scene about to be evoked. But here too there are individualizing traits, a certain sophisticated languor that seems closer to the sybarite of Mr. Compson's conjectures than to the man willing to die to assert principle and identity.

Miss Rosa's is an interesting "special case," prompting very different responses from readers. Her ornate, often sexualized rhetoric and rhythms of almost insane intensity, running off more than once into blank verse, admirably convey a particular disturbed personality. We have seen, moreover, that she is responsible for more than her share of the novel's great tableaux. (She is the only living narrator to have witnessed some of the events. But how many witnesses could have evoked that runaway gaunt half-wild horse, and thus brought the myth down to earth?) Her long chapter, unquestionably too long, contains some of the most inventive writing in the novel and perhaps its most consistently dramatic syntax: the ranting controlled by exquisitely timed periodic sentences, and sudden shifts from mad abstraction to the intensely visual: *"and then the two of them, the two accursed children on whom the first blow of their devil's heritage had but that moment fallen, looking at one another across the up-raised and unfinished wedding dress."* The highly literary play of mind— Cerberus, sphinx, Moloch within ten lines—is amusing, and certainly characterizes the town poetess out of touch with mundane reality. But the turgid involutions of the next paragraph—four completed parenthetical asides within twelve lines—are exasperating. There is no doubt far too much of this sort of thing. Some of the most Shakespearean passages also border on logorrhea (of which, after all, Shakespeare was not entirely free):

> *the prime foundation of this factual scheme from which the prisoner soul, miasmal-distillant, wroils ever upward sunward, tugs its tenuous prisoner arteries and veins and prisoning in its turn that spark, that dream which, as the globy and complete instant of its freedom mirrors and repeats (repeats? creates, reduces to a fragile evanescent iridescent sphere) all of space and time and massy earth, relicts the seething and anonymous miasmal mass which in all the years of time has taught it-self no boon of death but only how to recreate, renew. . . .*[24]

I think it important to repeat, since misconceptions exist, that Miss Rosa presumably does not say this aloud, though I would be not unhappy if she did. It would be pleasing to think that Faulkner could carry his defiance of realistic dialogue so far. But generally in Faulkner, and I think here, extensive italics indicate a state different from that of normal consciousness or speech. The "notlanguage" conveys, to borrow Mr. Compson's distinction, not what was in Miss Rosa's mind but in her soul: what the whole personality (conscious, preconscious, unconscious) would say if it could speak. The information in the chapter was indeed conveyed to Quentin, but presumably not in these words. The opening pages modulate very carefully, and swiftly, from what was or could have been said (*"So they will have told you doubtless already how I told that Jones to take that mule,"* etc.) to more extravagant language: *"traverse"* (line 11), *"brute progenitor of brutes"* (line 14), *"incept in the individual"* (line 18) and so on. The moment of transition from presumed real speech to what-Rosa-would-have-liked-to-say may well be the beginning of the third paragraph, which is also the top of the third page.

The rationale for Faulkner's arbitrary literary dialogue would seem self-evident; and it is exactly the same as for Shakespeare's. On the one hand, it allows the writer to use, whenever he pleases, his full rhetorical inventiveness and skill. The convention frees the writer from that obligation to imitate imperfect speech which, according to Winters, inevitably debased the genre. But, more important for the reader, the high language helps "carry" (or lend necessary distance to) events of tragic, mythical grandeur. Or, to change the figure slightly, the language helps carry the reader out of his everyday rational world of disbelief in major tragic confrontation and plight. In a world where such language is "common," both Thomas Sutpen and Charles Bon can sacrifice everything for a principle or design, and Henry can kill his brother at the gate.

To speak of *Absalom, Absalom!* as the culminating novel of Conradian impressionism may suggest, incorrectly, that no further developments and audacities of the kind would occur. Nabokov, Durrell, Pynchon, Hawkes, García Márquez, to name the most obvious, have continued in the impressionist tradition, in some of their work, and experimented with conjectural narration. But *Absalom, Absalom!*, more than any work by these writers, has close affinities with the rhythms and incremental repetitions of *Heart of Darkness,* with the vivid moments of conjecture in *Chance,* and with *Lord Jim* generally. In both *Absalom, Absalom!* and *Lord Jim* we have complex and multiple responses to relatively simple men who have made initial "mistakes" (but "mistakes" that were inherent in their characters) and who doggedly refuse to give in to seemingly unfair fatality. Both are magnified by local legend, by deifying or demonizing myth, by imagery, by historical situation and physical surroundings; and both are destroyed by paralyzing returns of the past. The two novels, like much of *The Brothers Karamazov,* are dramas of conflicting evidence and conflicting character witnesses. The original narrator, the "privileged man" who appears briefly and sternly near the end of *Lord Jim,* Stein, and Marlow have their subtly differing views of Jim (all very different from his view of himself); Gentleman Brown and Cornelius scorn or repudiate him as violently as Miss Rosa does Sutpen. The central task of Marlow and of Quentin-Shreve is also that of the novels generally: to penetrate ambiguity and attempt to see things as they are, and so arrive at a fair balance of sympathy and judgment. These explorations are intensely personal, though Sutpen can hardly become an unfortunate

younger brother. Marlow and Quentin are alike concerned with the moral violation of traditions they want to honor.

The second objective of both novels is to create, through structure and minu-
tiae of technique, a more interesting and more active relationship between the
reader and the events than is normally possible in standard realist fiction. Both
novels, almost more than any classics (though not more than *Benito Cereno*),
become radically different works on a second reading, with the most obvious
ambiguities now resolved. Suspense, befuddlement, and exploratory excitement
give way, on a second reading, to tragic irony, as we contemplate the blunder-
ings and distortions, and see the foreknown casualties approach. But there is
also, now, a new contemplative pleasure in the artifact itself: the rhythms of
plot, the foreshadowings and reflexive references. We examine with a new interest what the writers have, with technique and language, done to us. Both
novels, commercially unsuccessful in their time, could be dismissed as "intellectual." Certainly both were, again for their time, "art novels."

Sympathy and judgment are controlled in both *Lord Jim* and *Absalom, Absalom!* by the close juxtaposition of favorable and unfavorable evidence, fair and
unfair witnesses. We have seen, in discussing paradoxical sympathies, how
Faulkner presented the strongest appeal for sympathy for Sutpen (his childhood
trauma, the forming of his design) in the context of an inhuman enterprise, the
hunting down of the French architect. Both novels, without sacrificing moral
judgment, are finally sympathetic with their dogged protagonists . . . neither
of whom would make very good company in "real life." The most interesting
problem of sympathy and judgment involves Charles Bon, of whom we have so
little direct knowledge: a letter written in Faulknerese, the facts of his death and
his negro strain. For Mr. Compson's picture of the sophisticated corrupter, exposing the sensitive plate of Henry's soul to New Orleans, is perhaps the
strongest and most coherent personality impression of any in the novel: the
"Scythian glitter," "the sardonic and indolent detachment" like that of a
youthful Roman consul "among the barbarian hordes," the "flowered, almost
feminized gown"; the "tangible effluvium of knowledge surfeit: of actions
done and satiations plumbed," the "sybaritic privacy," the "elegant and indolent esoteric hothouse bloom," the "cold and catlike inscrutable calculation"
. . . exposing Henry to an "atmosphere at once fatal and languorous." The
dismissal of the ceremony with the octoroon as meaningless, and an apparent
willingness to commit bigamy, make much sense in the light of this adjectival
insistence. The involutions of the three-page letter do not entirely contradict, at
our first innocent reading, this personality impression, though we also discern a

more humane side. There remain, on that first reading, other dubieties: the problematic locket, the willingness to commit incest. On a second reading, to be sure, we take the measure of Mr. Compson's distortions, and read between the lines of the letter. Nothing could be more moving than that wartime dawn colloquy between brothers, as Charles must face the fact of his negro strain, and that his father has even now not sent for him, and must face too Henry's new resolve. Charles Bon's death, though logical connections could be made, is less ambiguous than Lord Jim's. His desperate but still prideful assertion of his identity is different in kind from Jim's response to the shadowy call of his exalted egoism, if only for historic reasons. For Jim had his clear second opportunity, which his temperament made him miss, whereas Charles was the victim of a known historical injustice. But this is a moral judgment. How much still denigratively remains, in the fringes of the reader's consciousness, of Mr. Compson's sybarite?

The impressionist circlings of *Absalom, Absalom!* are in many ways comparable to those of *Lord Jim*. One source of difficulty (and pleasure) is chronological dislocation: the free wandering flow of mind, back and forth in time, over names and events at least dimly known to the narrators, but not to us on a first reading. We learn on the third page that Sutpen built a plantation, married Ellen, begot a son and daughter, died. But this is followed by nearly twenty pages of angry conjecture concerning events of which we know nothing. We must wait until page 32 to get a clearer picture of Sutpen arriving in Jefferson. But now we're largely limited to what the villagers knew or thought in 1833, and they thought Sutpen was a criminal who held up steamboats. We must wait until page 220 for the chronological beginning of the story: Sutpen's birth in 1808 in what would later be West Virginia. The events that occurred in time exist for us spatially, but in cluttered disorderly space, as in a dark room illumined here and there by a randomly moving flashlight. But it would be hard to improve on Mr. Compson's description of the narrative problem, which a number of critics have quoted:

> We have a few old mouth-to-mouth tales; we exhume from old trunks and boxes and drawers letters without salutation or signature, in which men and women who once lived and breathed are now merely initials or nicknames out of some now incomprehensible affection which sound to us like Sanskrit or Chocktaw: . . . Yes, Judith, Bon, Henry, Sutpen: all of them. They are there, yet something is missing; they are like a chemical formula exhumed along with the letters from that forgotten chest, carefully, the paper old and faded and falling to pieces, the writing faded, almost indecipherable, yet meaningful, familiar in shape and sense, the name and presence of volatile and sentient forces; you bring them together in the proportions called for, but nothing happens; you re-read, tedious and intent, poring, making

sure that you have forgotten nothing, made no miscalculation; you bring them together again and again nothing happens: just the words, the symbols, the shapes themselves, shadowy inscrutable and serene, against that turgid background of a horrible and bloody mischancing of human affairs.[25]

The crucial revelations of what the narrators know but the reader does not come as casually as in *Lord Jim:* and still the *Patna* floated, its sleeping pilgrims destined to some other end; "Even if Charles Bon had not died. . . ." Hasty readers of *Absalom, Absalom!* have blundered as grossly as the reviewer of *Lord Jim* who spoke of the rotten craft shooting to the bottom. But also the novel must hint to the reader on his first reading (and intensely, dramatically remind him on a second) what a narrator himself does not know. Mr. Compson (p. 62) remarks that Sutpen named Clytie (perhaps intending "Cassandra") "as he named them all, the one before Clytie and Henry and Judith even, with that same robust and sardonic temerity, naming with his own mouth his own ironic fecundity of dragon's teeth." (The allusion, which functions usefully, may in fact be due to an authorial lapse: failure to make the logical change from an earlier draft.[26]) The alert reader is in any event here put on the *qui vive*. Who was "the one before"? And he must watch carefully for suggestions originally made by General Compson, who did not know what he was suggesting: what the flashlight reveals, or, in the book's image, the flash of a musket:

> the girl just emerging for a second of the telling, in a single word almost, so that Grandfather said it was like he had just seen her too for a second by the flash of one of the muskets—a bent face, a single cheek, a chin for an instant beyond a curtain of fallen hair, a white slender arm raised, a delicate hand clutching a ramrod, and that was all.[27]

The briefness of Sutpen's allusion is portentous, but the "white slender arm" deceives. Three pages later, and following a vivid picture of the island's violent black heritage, we learn that on the first night of the siege Sutpen did not even know the girl's name:

> He also told Grandfather, dropped this into the telling as you might flick the joker out of a pack of fresh cards without being able to remember later whether you had removed the joker or not, that the old man's wife had been a Spaniard, and so it was Grandfather and not Sutpen who realized that until that first night of the attack he had possibly not seen the girl as much as a dozen times.[28]

Ten pages further there is reference (which General Compson would not have understood) to "misrepresentation of such a crass nature as to have not only voided and frustrated without his knowing it the central motivation of his entire design. . . ." Ninety-two pages later Sutpen tells Henry that the girl's mother had been misrepresented as a Spanish woman: " *'it was not until after he was born that I found out that his mother was part negro.' "* But meanwhile, even more subtly, the novel may drop a preparatory hint into the fringes of the reader's consciousness. It makes connections, verbal juxtapositions, that a narrator could not. Thus the remark that Sutpen's fellow citizens "believed even yet that there was a nigger in the woodpile somewhere. . . ." To see Bon as a "blackguard" may be of little significance itself. But why is Mr. Compson's hand dark as a negro's immediately before the crucial reference to Bon?

> the letter in his hand and the hand looking almost as dark as a negro's against his linen leg.
> "Because Henry loved Bon. He repudiated blood birthright and material security for his sake, for the sake of this man who was at least an intending bigamist even if not an out and out blackguard. . . ." [29]

Just so, in *Lord Jim,* a seemingly "literary" image of its passengers streaming onto the *Patna,* "like water filling a cistern," opens, to the fringes of consciousness, the possibility of drowning.

One of the great beauties of impressionist structure lies in controlled movement, both musical and cinematic, toward revelation: the rhythms of changing, presently diminishing distance; of approach and withdrawal and reapproach; of shifts in lighting, with the verbal screens suddenly less opaque; of oblique and incremental allusion—the allusions understood by the novel's listener/thinker (Quentin, for instance) but not at first by the reader. The approach to the deaths of Sutpen and Jones (177–87) is as minutely controlled as any sinuously rhythmed sequence in *Lord Jim.* This narrative has its tantalizing, mysterious moments at a first reading: words, phrases that touch the fringes of consciousness. But it appears to center in compassionate recapitulation of what is already known. We are not led to expect major new revelations. The experience at a subsequent reading is both that of tragic irony, as we approach obliquely the known events, and of aesthetic contemplation of Faulkner's consummate art: an art of transition especially, and of subtly misplaced emphasis.

There has been, we may see at a second reading, some preparation at the end of Rosa's hysterical narrative in chapter V: almost parenthetical allusion to Jones's granddaughter and her place in a *"descending (do you mark the gradation?) ellipsis"* from Ellen and herself, and to the demon finding *"severence"* in *"the stroke of a rusty scythe."* This time, she notes, it is not Jones who informs her of the event. But Quentin was not listening, nor perhaps the reader, after so many pages of wild rhetoric. Our attention is focused instead, through Quentin's imagining, on the confrontation of Judith and Henry and their brief terrible exchange, and, at the very end of the chapter, on Rosa's announcement that "something" has been living hidden in Sutpen's Hundred for four years. The following chapter also takes us far, in its first pages, from a granddaughter or a rusty scythe, with the letter announcing Rosa Coldfield's death and the vividly remembered September excursion with her.

The impressionist movement toward the deaths of Sutpen and Jones begins with Shreve's sardonic allusion to the ancient stiff-jointed Pyramus and the untried Thisbe, and to a brutal unevasive statement of the outrage: to "suggest that they breed together for test and sample and if it was a boy they would marry." This is followed by unexplained allusions to Rosa's "successor," to the demon's death ("since she doubtless foresaw the scythe"), and to the scythe as garlanded with gaudy ribbon or cheap bead. The ribbon and bead may seem mere rhetorical adornment or deceptive digression from the casually referred-to death:

> he would be dead too since she doubtless foresaw the scythe if for no other reason than that it would be the final outrage and affront like the hammer and nails in her father's business—that scythe, symbolic laurel of a caesar's triumph—that rusty scythe loaned by the demon himself to Jones more than two years ago to cut the weeds away from the shanty doorway to smooth the path for rutting—that rusty blade garlanded with each successive day's gaudy ribbon or cheap bead for the (how did she put it? slut wasn't all, was it?) to walk in. . . .[30]

The hammer and nails of her father's business may remind us of Bon's coffin as well as of Mr. Coldfield's suicidal "business," nailing himself up in the attic. And the final outrage is any death. Rutting, moreover, has its sexual connotation. But as yet there is no lethal connection between Jones and scythe, or any clear connection between Jones, gaudy ribbon and bead, slut.

At this point, after one more abrupt allusion to Sutpen's death (the Creditor overtaking him "for good and all"), Shreve offers an intensely sympathetic retelling, in ironic metaphor and with ironic brevity, of the whole story, beginning with the Faustus arrival one Sunday with "twenty subsidiary demons." Two more references to the Creditor occur in the first long paragraph, however: one a mere allusion, seemingly, to fatality or death, but the second oddly extending the trite metaphor: "the Creditor's bailiff hand." Only on a second reading is the reader likely to think of Wash Jones as in a sense Sutpen's bailiff.

Shreve's ironic recapitulation of the career, and of the outrage of Rosa, is vividly resumed at some length. But the vain dream of restoring Sutpen's

Hundred suddenly leads to the old man running a little crossroads store, Jones as clerk, with "cheap beads and ribbons" among its other stock, for the nigger and white trash clientele. The outrage to Rosa had seemingly set Sutpen free "from threat or meddling from anyone." The paragraph concludes with a most oblique reference to his buying his way back into being "unfree" with beads and calico and striped candy. There is a shift here (181), after Quentin notes that Shreve sounds exactly like father, to narration in italics: to the flow of Quentin's thought, which has an omniscient power to evoke the past dramatically. The rhetoric has its connection with Shreve's, but is calmer, more distant, less ironic. In this recreation of the story Sutpen must have seen himself as a *"wornout cannon which realizes that it can deliver just one more fierce shot."* The emphasis is on the general ruin of Sutpen's dream, the loss of Henry as potential heir and the daughter doomed to spinsterhood. But a parenthetical reference to help given the women by Jones, during the war, takes a crucial step forward, a very dramatic one on second reading:

> (*excusing what help they had from Jones who lived with his granddaughter in the abandoned fishing camp with its collapsing roof and rotting porch against which the rusty scythe which Sutpen was to lend him, make him borrow to cut away the weeds from the door—and at last forced him to use though not to cut weeds, at least not vegetable weeds—would lean for two years*). . . .[31]

At least not vegetable weeds? The Creditor's hand is already on the shoulder of *"the ancient varicose and despairing Faustus."* And now we hear that ribbons and beads and candy *"can seduce a fifteen-year-old country girl . . . ruin the granddaughter of his partner, this Jones. . . ."* There is a parenthetical suggestion of Jones's connivance in the courtship-seduction, and an allusion to the girl's "increasing belly." But the emphasis is on Sutpen and Jones drinking together beneath the scuppernong arbor, and on Jones's hero-worship, who *"apparently saw still in that furious lecherous wreck the old fine figure of the man who once galloped on the black thoroughbred. . . ."*

The allusion to the black thoroughbred evokes the "son" the stallion had of his wife Penelope, then the negro midwife (who had to be *"caught"*) beside the pallet on which the granddaughter Milly and her baby lie; Sutpen's brutal words overheard by Wash; the midwife's hearing of the last exchange between the two: " *'Stand back. Don't you touch me, Wash.'—'I'm going to tech you, Kernel'* and she heard the whip too though not the scythe, no whistling air, no blow, nothing since always that which merely consummates punishment evokes a cry while that which evokes the last silence occurs in silence." We hear nothing further at this point of Jones, or of Milly and her baby, but instead of the *"tearless and stone-faced daughter"* Judith receiving Sutpen, *"quiet and bloody and with his teeth still showing in his parted beard."* We hear too in some detail of Judith's appearance as a woman of thirty and of her capacity for work, then of Sutpen's ride to church in the coffin (with the wagon turning over and tumbling him, *"sabre plumes and all,"* into a ditch), and of the fact that Judith and Clytie now did all the plowing. For at last we learn of Jones's death. We will have in time a fuller and more dramatic version of it: his confrontation with Major de Spain and the posse, and the quiet murder of Milly. But this first brief allusion to Jones's death, followed by the puzzled colloquy with Sutpen in after-life, all passion not only spent but forgotten, is surely one of the compassionate summits of Faulkner's fiction. Is there, in an after-life, as some conjecture, at least shadowy recollection of earthly passions? The passage mirrors in miniature or metaphor the novel's overall vision of the remoteness of the past, and its tragic events attenuated, reduced to dim legend. For Judith and Clytie

> *did all the plowing which was done, now that Jones was gone too. He had followed the demon within twelve hours on that same Sunday (and maybe to the same place; maybe They would even have a scuppernong vine for them there and no compulsions now of bread or ambition or fornication or vengeance, and maybe they wouldn't even have to drink, only they would miss this now and then without knowing what it was that they missed but not often; serene, pleasant, unmarked by time or change of weather, only just now and then something, a wind, a shadow, and the demon would stop talking and Jones would stop guffawing and they would look at one another, groping, grave, intent, and the demon would say, 'What was it, Wash? Something happened. What was it?' and Jones looking at the demon, groping too, sober too, saying, 'I don't know, Kernel. Whut?' each watching the other.* [32]

This sequence is followed immediately by one nearly as moving in its modulations and time shifts, and rhythms of poignant revelation. Quentin's memory of the quail hunt with his father, slightly distanced by Shreve's recapitulation, moves into unmediated narration of the gray afternoon, and their coming upon the heavy marble slabs of Sutpen's and Ellen's gravestones, and the three others. How could they have had money to buy marble? Mr. Compson tells the story, which Quentin soon visualizes, one more Sutpen instance of obsessed pertinacity and dream of grandeur: having gravestones brought from Italy, dragged behind the regiment in a wagon, left at home during his twenty-four-hour return from the war. Two further stones, we learn, are Charles Bon's and one Charles Etienne Saint-Valery Bon's (1859–84); there is a third, also with 1884 as the date of death. Nineteen pages later we learn that this is Judith's, who died from yellow fever contracted from Charles Etienne while nursing him. This mention of Charles Etienne will lead, after digression, to the octoroon's visit to Charles Bon's grave, with his eleven-year-old son, and this in turn to the son's very moving life story (197–209), "treading the thorny and flint-paved path toward the Gethsemane which he had decreed and created for himself, where he had crucified himself and come down from his cross for a moment and now returned to it." As obliquely, five pages later, we are introduced to the son's son Jim Bond, *"the hulking slack-mouthed saddle-colored boy a few years older and bigger than you were. . . ."* The beauty of the impressionist method, in these pages, lies less in the irony of misplaced emphasis (though that once more makes its skillful appeal to our sympathy) than in the swift movements in time, and movements among lives tragically connected, as the contemplating minds play over them: so much suffering and confusion become "history," myth, epitaph.

Of the traveling gravestones, and Sutpen's brief return home with them, Quentin thinks: *"If I had been there I could not have seen it this plain."* It is time, finally, to comment more theoretically on the technique of *narration by conjecture* by which Faulkner most notably extends and intensifies Conrad's impressionist method. It is essential to emphasize the word *narration*. Fiction (like life) is full of people engaged in conjecture, trying to make sense of each other and of what happens—James's novels as well as notebooks, certainly Dickens's and Dostoevsky's. "Faulkner's method," Richard Poirier remarks in his fine early essay, "is really the method of historical research and re-creation." [33] The historian bent on both clarifying and vivifying the past must reason from often sparse, distorted, conflicting evidence, and commit himself to the plausible. Sometimes he will scrupulously refuse to decide between alternatives, and even describe his process of inconclusive reasoning. The historical novelist is also engaged in conjecture. But traditionally he hides this fact and pretends to omniscience or, at least, to the authority of an eyewitness. Scott and Hawthorne, among others, may talk about the problems of penetrating the past before proceeding to a nominal omniscience.

Narration by conjecture (in Conrad, and much more in Faulkner) brings the act of conjecturing to the forefront, and makes the struggling speculative mind (as Marlow's or Quentin's) a major interest. Conjecture, after all, is among the most humane of our mental activities—more humane than blind belief, or than flawless reasoning on unassailable evidence. We care not only about what Marlow will discover, but also about the way his subtle mind suavely moves and about his initially reluctant, at last intense involvement in the mysteries he explores. But the major difference from Jamesian studies in ambiguity, the great technical step forward, is to dramatize the events conjectured as though they were true; the accents of speculation shift to those of direct narration or observation. *Conjecture thus becomes a point-of-view and basic vehicle for real story-telling and for the plausible creation of time, place, atmosphere, emotions, events.* The story-telling in *Absalom, Absalom!* was so vivid for many early readers that the various clues to conjecture—*maybe, perhaps, I imagine*—simply passed over their heads. And even today the Cleanth Brooks chart [34] separating fact or event from conjecture may come as a considerable shock—a shock to be reminded that General Compson did not know that Bon was Henry's part-negro half-brother, and that neither "did Miss Rosa know this, unless she learned it at the same time that Quentin did, in Sept. 1909." A further audacity is the implicit claim that the suppositious acts dramatized as true often *are* true in some higher or metaphysical sense. "History" (say the irrecoverable history of Mississippi 1833–1909, or of Sutpen's arrival in Jefferson) is what, after truly scrupulous effort, we discern it to be. Myth and legend, which inhabit individual and collective consciousness (and the unconscious too), are also components of "history." Conjecture, we are told at one point, can be collaborative fantasy, Shreve and Quentin "creating between them, out of the rag-tag and bob-ends of old tales and talking, people who perhaps had never existed at all anywhere": we are here about to get much inventive speculation concerning the lawyer. But we are closer to Faulkner's faith in fiction when he speaks of that New Orleans "drawing room of baroque and fusty magnificence which Shreve had invented and which was probably true enough" and the vivid presence of Eulalia Bon ("untidy gray-streaked raven hair coarse as a horse's tail," etc.) "whom Shreve and Quentin had likewise invented and which was likewise probably true enough." Over all is the classic idea that poetry has a higher truth than history/fact: "What was it the old dame, the Aunt Rosa, told you about how there are some things that just have to be whether they are or not, have to be a damn sight more than some other things maybe are and it don't matter a damn whether they are or not?"

The basic method, then, is to summon up events, scenes, persons through conjecture, then vivify them (with the most efficient verisimilar techniques) as true: *make the reader see*. A difference from Conrad lies in Faulkner's ultimate refusal, on occasion, to define his cognitive authority or lack of it. All conjecture, even the most biased, can be made credible, since Faulkner is a skilled novelist—through the authoritative or passionate ring of a narrator's voice, and the scrupulous quality of his mind; through vivid detail and surrounding circumstance; through skillful, virtually unseen modulation from the indisputably known to the speculative. But not all conjectures, in *Absalom, Absalom!*, have the same degree of truth, nor does Faulkner want us to think they do. Only the novel in its entirety is indisputably true.

1. *There are conjectures which are presumably, even demonstrably false,* though they may continue to affect our feelings. We come to recognize Rosa's general demonizing of Sutpen as distorted; it creates sympathy in us as in Shreve. Her vision of the manacled architect is presumably less true than General Compson's picture of the architect, an employee who has come on Sutpen's bare promise, seated beside the driver. Mr. Compson's account of the trip to New Orleans is a magnificent, fictively real and largely distorted picture of life, if the original narrator is to be trusted. Shreve and Quentin were "probably right" in supposing "the octoroon and the child would have been to Henry only something else about Bon to be, not envied but aped if that had been possible. . . ." Yet Mr. Compson's picture of subtle corrupting and of the country boy's resistance makes its small "true" addition to our *connaissance du cœur humain*.

2. *There are conjectures that are presumably true:* some because they correlate with known fact; some because there is no sign that risky conjecture has been involved (no *maybe*'s or *I imagine*'s); some because they come to us from the original narrator or "alleged author"; some because he says the inventions are "probably true enough." But I must urge again that *italics* generally indicate access to real knowledge (whether knowledge of the unconscious mind and its tribulations, the personality and its mysteries, or an omniscient knowledge of historical event) which a narrator may intuit, or which may come directly to the reader. Here I differ from Brooks's description of the crucial events or exchanges of the wartime climax (346–56)—Sutpen telling Henry that Bon's mother was part negro, for instance—as conjectural, with the source of the conjecture, Shreve or Quentin, uncertain. The italicized consciousness of 346–50 uses some of the language of conjecture: "So that it must have seemed to him now that he knew at last," etc. But this passage begins with presumed fact ("—*the winter of '64 now, the army retreated . . .*") and ends in presumed fact, speech: " '*Sutpen, the colonel wants you in his tent.*' " The italicized consciousness of 351–58 moves, after a dozen lines, into a position and authority comparable to that of the roving conductors and ghostly watchers of *Bleak House* and *The Counterfeiters,* reporting action in the present tense, speculating not on fact (which is going on before his eyes) but rather on the implications of what he sees. Thus he observes that Henry "*is not as tall by two inches as he gave promise of being, and not as heavy by thirty pounds as he probably will be a few years after he has outlived the four years, if he do outlive them.*" This ghostly watcher is, indubitably, there; he is inside the tent with Henry and his father, reporting exactly what they say. As we look back to the beginning of these italicized pages we see the "alleged author," or simply

Faulkner, modulate to this assumption of true knowledge. Mediating or conjec-turing consciousness has, with the word *bivouac,* been left behind. Now neither Shreve nor Quentin is talking:

> Because now neither of them were there. They were both in Carolina and the time was forty-six years ago, and it was not even four now but compounded still further, since now both of them were Henry Sutpen and both of them were Bon, com-pounded each of both yet either neither, smelling the very smoke which had blown and faded away forty-six years ago from the *bivouac fires burning in a pine grove.* . . .[35]

The past has been recaptured.

Cleanth Brooks's 1975 article, "The Narrative Structure of *Absalom, Absa-lom!,"* sees the italics as the mark of joint visualization: "the author is here reproducing the thoughts of Quentin and Shreve, thoughts about Henry and Bon—in fact, this third-person account is a kind of joint re-creation of what Quentin and Shreve evidently believed must have been experienced by the young Confederate soldiers."[36] However, the "imagined events (pp. 351–358) are given something like the authority of objective events." I would say they simply have that authority. Brooks suggests the technique in both italicized passages is "cinematic," with a "fade-out-dissolve" into a sequence that *presents* the experience. He might have learned the method "from going to the movies at the local Oxford moving picture theater."[37] The analogy is an il-luminating one for that moment of transition to what I consider objective real-ity. But the other essential—action going on before a watcher's eyes (and so our eyes) in an unrolling present he cannot control—Faulkner could have learned from a reading of *Bleak House.*

3. *There are conjectures whose factual truth or falsity remains variable or altogether uncertain.* In places we do not know and cannot. This would seem to be the case with a number of Mr. Compson's psychologically plausible con-jectures, but conjectures frankly acknowledged to be such, and where his plea-sure in fantasy is whimsically indulged. At times we must simply fall back on intuitive response: does the conjecture (where there is little supporting and little discrediting evidence surrounding it) have the ring of truth? Is its truth essential to the novel as a whole? The novel firmly intends, in any event, that a number of conjectures should have no definable cognitive source. I do not believe Falkner wanted the reader to do what Brooks attempts: make all the pieces fit and so achieve, at last, a clarified story. I think Brooks wrong in "refuting the notion that Faulkner has deliberately tried to baffle the reader" or in denying the planting of "clues that are bound to mislead the reader."[38] Not only *Absalom, Absalom!* but *The Brothers Karamazov* and *The Possessed, Wuther-*

ing Heights, Benito Cereno, Lord Jim (not to mention *Pale Fire, V,* etc.) intend to baffle the reader and leave him, even at their exhausting conclusions, in at least some moral uncertainty. Ambiguity (and the effort to survive it) is central and continuing, not peripheral or provisional, in *Absalom, Absalom!*, as it is in much of our lives. (A technique permitting free play of conjecture, and that regards most fact as problematic or irrecoverable—that could justify invention as an avenue to "truth"—would seem particularly congenial to two writers who showed remarkable indifference to the literal truth in the accounts of their own lives. We still do not know, after almost a century and much scholarship, how much truth lies behind Conrad's romantic picture of his youth—the smuggling of arms, the affair with a mistress of Don Carlos, the wound near the heart that he attributed to a duel, but that may have come from a suicide attempt. With Conrad the wound at least existed. But Faulkner's fictitious wartime wound appears to have become more serious with the years. By 1925, for *Double Dealer* "Notes on Contributors," he had been "severely wounded." [39] Both Conrad and Faulkner were, altogether sincerely, concerned with achieving moral truth with their fictions. And I continue to hold to my 1958 insistence on shyness and "temperamental evasiveness" as largely explaining their love of formal involution, of screens and distances. But writers who could create and stubbornly maintain personal myths [and—who knows?—perhaps come to half-believe them] would find particularly congenial a method so little bound to fact.)

Narration by conjecture, and impressionist complications generally, must not then be regarded as primarily techniques for elaborating conventional suspense. Nor should they be regarded as academic exercises in the problematics of cognition and perception, though Claude Simon's modifications of Faulkner's methods take us far in that direction. The essential question is whether the methods work, for the reader and for the novelist, and whether they bring to the novel form new resources and opportunities. Beyond this, in the larger area of aesthetic theory, we may deplore or rejoice in the new primacy of fiction (and the act of making fictions) over verifiable reality, of the speculative mind over the impersonally recording one.

It is again important to distinguish between first and second readings; *Absalom, Absalom!*, reread, becomes a different book. No doubt the serious reader today, as not in 1936, would open the book with some knowledge that he is facing a difficult masterpiece, not a story to be casually enjoyed. Yet the first reading is still likely to be a vertiginous experience of struggle with the ambiguous, with many pauses for the rereading of sentences or paragraphs, and with a continuous, at times oppressive awareness of language. The clues to conjectural narration will of course invite the reader to speculate; some readers will enjoy Quentin and Shreve as surrogates, others will be irritated by them. But the amount of conjecture involves, above all, an exceptionally intense exposure to the real complexity of experience, and to the ambiguity inherent in even starkly simple or obsessive lives. Much of what happens to the reader, at this first reading, will happen on the fringes of consciousness: words, images, juxtapositions, stated hesitancies saying more than they seem to. And the reader, guided or misguided by conjecture, will develop sympathies or repugnances he may later have to modify.

At a second reading, with much important information in hand, pleasure becomes more contemplative, but by no means less emotional. We experience the tragic irony of seeing the known fatalities and revelations approach; the comic irony of recognizing the narrators' mistakes, their false moves and distortions. And we have, now, a much enriched delight in the artifact, the thing that has been (with whatever small lapses and inconsistencies) beautifully and intricately made—the hints so casually introduced (some by the novelist rather than a narrator), the repetitions and reflexive references (some from one speaker to another), the digressions and analogies, the now significant chronological dislocations, the carefully placed screens. The play of shifting distances—between conjecturing narrators and hypothetical action, between ourselves and both—becomes a source of active pleasure. So much contemplative aesthetic pleasure may suggest that, at a second reading, human interest has been lost. But this is not true for *Absalom, Absalom!,* as it is not true for *Wuthering Heights* or *Lord Jim . . .* or *Hamlet.*

The values of narration by conjecture for the highly imaginative novelist are obvious. For the technique, without sacrificing many of the resources of Flaubertian or other realism (for *anything,* however conjectural, can be intensely visualized), frees the writer from mimesis narrowly conceived, from documentary inhibition, from the need to pretend to be giving an authentic report. The boring obligation to demonstrate authority has been largely removed. For the authority is now that of the speculative mind free to wander in space and time, and always alert to potentiality as well as hard evidence. The method invites the use at every moment of a real speaking voice and (as after all in Sterne) a convincingly wandering mind. And the initial audacity—the right to present the conjectural as true—naturally encourages others. The conjecturing mind is freer than any other to hazard restless, even fantastic metaphor, and engage in verbal play. Joseph Reed, Jr., speaks of metaphor as the basic mode of *Absalom, Absalom!* I would regard conjecture as the basic mode, with the play of metaphor its consequence.

The advantages of conjecture to the novelist with a philosophical mind are obvious, though there are dangers of diffuseness and abstraction. But the new freedom would appear to be valuable most of all to the temperamentally evasive novelist, the novelist whose imagination is fructified not crippled by irresolution, and who is reluctant to report experience photographically: e.g., Conrad and Faulkner. For them especially the impressionist method meant freedom from *presentness,* from the obligation to report things happening in a time flowing onward at an even pace, and happening (for the imagination) here and now. More generally they could enjoy—yes, even enjoy perversely—the intricacies we have been describing, and the manipulation of their readers' minds. The impressionist method more than any other controls the reader's responses and sympathies.

The freedom of narration by conjecture has its dangers; it can substitute casual fantasy or whim for significant imagination. The method seems most vulnerable with the lawyer of Chapter VIII (300–338, but especially 300–311), largely conjectured by Shreve. The symptoms of imaginative lapse are evident: circular ratiocinations and madly involuted asides, the Jamesian Faulkner at his most exasperating; the virtually incomprehensible quasi-financial speculations (*"Emotion val. plus 100% times nil. plus val. crop."*); elaborate analogies that illumine nothing (the sherbet vs. whiskey debate, a rare revelation, in the writing, of the author's alcoholism). The conjectured lawyer follows, moreover, some of the most dramatic pages of the novel (Wash's killing of his granddaughter) and precedes the moving pages of Bon's first visit to Sutpen's Hundred. The mean sinuous mentality of the lawyer further detracts from fictive truth; his conniving subtlety is too small, seen against the grand simplicities of the major characters. But there is one more very important reason for the lawyer's pallidness: he exists nowhere except in the conjectures. He has no previously felt material presence on which the speculative mind can play. The great conjectural creations of the novel have, by contrast, a foothold in historical reality. It is not an act of fantasying alone, of creating out of whole cloth, that moves us. It is, instead, the movement of minds embroidering, playfully or perhaps desperately, on real events and real people who suffered and died.

The last pages of this essay, with their emphasis on technical niceties and strategies, on screens and distances, will doubtless seem implacably cold to some lovers of this novel, as of course to those who believe the novel form generically naive, with, ideally, a simple relationship both to story and to reader. And it is certainly true that the structural innovations of *Absalom, Absalom!* would interest us only casually, an evening or two of higher mathematics, if they existed independently of powerful and meaningful human story. But this novel is—like *The Brothers Karamazov* and *The Possessed,* like *Lord Jim,* like *Moby Dick*—one of the great exhaustive visions of man's capacity to aspire, suffer and endure, at times in the face of seemingly malicious fatality, and of his humane longing to understand the mysteries of suffering and endurance. It could not otherwise be, as I think it is, perhaps the greatest American novel. The intricate and labyrinthine form, as most sympathetic readers have seen, is precisely suited to a full rendering of exploratory subject; and also becomes subject. But the form is more than vehicle, as the language more than meaning. The richness and intensity of language (by which *Absalom, Absalom!* differs in kind from any other novel we have examined) can be enjoyed unanalytically, though not passively. But this is not true of form, which we may also enjoy *in itself. Absalom, Absalom!* demands, if we are to experience it fully, the kind of intense and more than once renewed attention to form—to the curves and rhythms of structure—that we give to the greatest painting, representational or not, and to the most complex classical or modern music. Form and imagination, that is, both illumine "real life" and triumph over it. In *Absalom, Absalom!* the novel takes another long step toward becoming an autonomous fine art.

NOTES

Unless otherwise indicated page references are to the texts of the New Oxford Illustrated Dickens, and the translations from Dostoevsky are those of Constance Garnett. But the major novels of Dostoevsky exist in so many editions that only book and chapter references are normally given. The texts for Faulkner are, except as noted, those of Random House editions.

INTRODUCTION

1. Donald Fanger's admirable *Dostoevsky and Romantic Realism: A Study of Dostoevsky in Relation to Balzac, Dickens, and Gogol* (Cambridge, Mass., 1967) sees Dostoevsky as "the inheritor of romantic realism in the sense that he knew the work of Balzac, Dickens, and Gogol and gauged the novelty of his own 'new word' in terms of theirs." But Fanger is preoccupied with critical cross-illumination rather than influence, and remarks that influence is a "conception that has always appealed more to the cataloguing than to the critical mind." P. 253. Two recent studies of influence do, nevertheless, have interesting things to say: N. M. Lary's *Dostoevsky and Dickens: A Study of Literary Influence* (London, Boston, 1973) and Jean Weisgerber's heavily documented *Faulkner and Dostoevsky: Influence and Confluence* (Athens, Ohio, 1974), translated from *Faulkner et Dostoïevski: Confluences et influences* (Paris, 1968).
2. *"Bleak House:* Structure and Style," *The Southern Review,* Vol. 5, New Series, No. 2 (Spring, 1969), 332–49. A fuller version of this essay appears as Afterword to the Rinehart edition of *Bleak House* (New York, 1970).

3. *Problemy tvortchestva Dostoïevskovo,* revised as *Problemy poetiki Dostoïevskovo* (Moscow, 1963), translated by Isabelle Kolitcheff as *La Poétique de Dostoïevski* (Paris, 1970) and by R. W. Rotsel as *Problems of Dostoevsky's Poetics* (Ann Arbor, 1973).

4. *Dostoevsky: The Major Fiction* (Cambridge, Mass., 1964), the introductions and commentaries of his editions of Dostoevsky's Notebooks, and "Raskolnikov's Motives: Love and Murder," *American Imago,* Vol. 31, No. 3 (Fall, 1974).

5. In 1950 Leslie Fiedler, in "William Faulkner: An American Dickens," saw a shared "demonic richness of invention" as well as "an obsession with the grotesque." *Commentary* 10 (1950), 385. Joseph Bold saw Chaucer, Shakespeare, Fielding, Dickens and Faulkner as constituting "an alternative 'great tradition' to that of Leavis," in "Dickens and Faulkner: The Uses of Influence," *Dalhousie Review* 49 (Spring, 1969), 70. Leavis, in reviewing *Light in August* more or less unfavorably for *Scrutiny* ("Dostoevsky or Dickens," 2, June 1933, 91–93), found Faulkner closer to Dickens than to Dostoevsky. In 1974 he felt obliged to write a note to go with the reprinted review in John Bassett, *The Critical Heritage* (London and Boston, 1975), p. 145: "I wrote the review of *Light in August* years ago, and I am horrified to take, from the journalistic heading, the implication that Dickens, regarding whom I am now certain that he is among the very greatest, is less profound than Dostoevsky, who doesn't much matter to me. Nevertheless, the suggestion isn't fair to Dostoevsky either; he certainly exists."

6. *The Rise of the Novel: Studies in Defoe, Richardson and Fielding,* first published in 1957; Pelican Books (London, 1972), p. 35.

7. In this article I use *illuminating distortion* in a more special sense, in referring to "the oddity, the anomaly, the moment of strangeness which (if understood at last) may reveal a scene's or even a book's larger meaning, and the source of its creative energy and dynamic power over us." By distortion I here refer not to tendentious selection or exaggeration but to all that can be embraced by a psychology of significant errors: "Freudian displacements and slips of the tongue; inexplicable or gratuitous events; absurd declarations; misplaced sympathies, perverse reactions; violations of a system of imageries; in brief, everything that seems 'out of place' . . . or, at least, everything that unaccountably stirs us." *Novel: A Forum on Fiction* (Winter, 1972), 101, 102–3.

8. Frank Kermode, "The Structures of Fiction," in Richard Macksey, ed., *Velocities of Change: Critical Essays from MLN* (Baltimore and London, 1974), p. 201.

9. René Girard, "Critical Reflections on Literary Studies," in Macksey, op. cit., p. 78.

10. Edward Wasiolek, "Raskolnikov's Motives: Love and Murder."

11. "Notes on the Rhetoric of Anti-Realism," *TriQuarterly* 30 (Spring, 1974), 3–50.

1. ANTI-MIMESIS

1. John Forster, *The Life of Charles Dickens,* ed. J. W. T. Ley (London, 1928), p. 721.

2. George Gissing, *Charles Dickens* (1898), chapter 5, cited in Stephen Wall, ed., *Charles Dickens* (Penguin Critical Anthologies, Harmondsworth, Eng., 1970), p. 226.

3. *Soliloquies in England* (1922), in Wall, op. cit., pp. 264–65.
4. Cited and translated by Fanger, op. cit., p. 147.
5. Cited by Konstantin Mochulsky, *Dostoevsky: His Life and Work* (Princeton, 1967), p. 28. Michael A. Minihan translated both Mochulsky's text and the passages from Dostoevsky quoted by Mochulsky.
6. Ibid., p. 382.
7. Steven Marcus, *Dickens from Pickwick to Dombey* (New York, 1968), pp. 78–79.
8. *Poor Folk,* last paragraph of Barbara's Narration. Everyman ed., p. 51.
9. Cited in Mochulsky, op. cit., p. 37.
10. Part Five. In Faulkner, *Three Famous Short Novels* (New York, 1961), pp. 314–15. This text was chosen because of its wide classroom use.
11. *Little Dorrit,* Book Second, Chapter 30, p. 776.

2. PARADOXICAL SYMPATHIES

1. Albert J. Guerard, *Conrad the Novelist* (Cambridge, Mass., 1958), p. 1.
2. Mochulsky, op. cit., pp. 608, 610.
3. See Harvey Peter Sucksmith, *The Narrative Art of Charles Dickens: The Rhetoric of Sympathy and Irony in his Novels* (Oxford, 1970) for a very full and richly documented discussion.
4. *Charles Dickens,* chapter 5 in Wall, op. cit., p. 225.
5. *The Hamlet* (New York, 1940), p. 251. Vintage edition (New York, no date), pp. 222–23.
6. Ibid., p. 256. Vintage edition, p. 227.
7. See the conclusion to Irving Howe's fine essay on *The Possessed,* "Dostoevsky: The Politics of Salvation," in *Politics and the Novel* (New York, 1957).
8. *The Notebooks for "The Idiot,"* ed. Edward Wasiolek (Chicago, 1967), p. 173.
9. Ibid.
10. Richard Peace, *Dostoevsky: An Examination of the Major Novels* (Cambridge, Eng., 1971), p. 123.
11. *The Idiot,* Part III, Chapter 6.
12. Ibid.
13. Cited in Mochulsky, op. cit., p. 584.
14. *The Brothers Karamazov,* Part Two, Book V, Chapter iv.
15. Cited in Mochulsky, op. cit., p. 590. Letter of Aug. 24, 1879.
16. *The Brothers Karamazov,* Part Two, Book V, Chapter v.
17. See "The Two Dimensions of Reality in *The Brothers Karamazov,*" from *Creation and Discovery* (New York, 1955), reprinted in René Wellek, ed., *Dostoevsky: A Collection of Critical Essays* (Englewood Cliffs, N.J., 1962), pp. 81, 87. Twentieth Century Views series.
18. Introduction to Signet edition (New York, 1968) of *A Fable,* pp. xix–xx.
19. *A Fable* (New York, 1954), p. 348. Signet edition, p. 308.
20. *The Brothers Karamazov,* Part Two, Book V, Chapter v.

3. FORBIDDEN GAMES (I):
DICKENS AND THE FORBIDDEN MARRIAGE

1. *Joseph Conrad: Achievement and Decline* (Cambridge, Mass., 1957), passim.
2. *Charles Dickens: The Dreamer's Stance* (Ithaca, N.Y., 1965).
3. Edmund Wilson, *The Wound and the Bow* (Boston, 1941); Marcus, op. cit.
4. Angus Wilson, "The Heroes and Heroines of Dickens," in J. Gross and G. Pearson, eds., *Dickens and the Twentieth Century* (1963), and Wall, op. cit., p. 435.
5. Ernest Jones, *Life and Works of Sigmund Freud* (New York, 1953), I, 174, quoted in Mark Spilka's interesting "Little Nell Revisited," *Papers of the Michigan Academy of Science, Art, and Letters,* Vol. 45 (1960), 432.
6. See Edgar Johnson, *Charles Dickens: His Tragedy and Triumph* (New York, 1952) I, 518.
7. Ibid., I, 200–201.
8. Ibid., I, 201.
9. Ibid., I, 438.
10. Jack Lindsay, *Charles Dickens: A Biographical and Critical Study* (London, 1950), pp. 134–35. "The sister-relationship which had made her the perfect foil for the child-bearing wife was what made her so terribly potent in death." "Alive, with Kate acquiescent, Mary was the magic restorer of the dream Eden—the sister re-created as an other-half of the wife. But when she died, the whole machinery of taboo-fear was set in motion. Her relationship with Charles became the utterly forbidden thing, and she was snatched away by omnipotent authority." Guilt was owing to his death-wish, which "wanting her irredeemably his and all his, had killed her off." Fanny was a mother-substitute. Dickens's "background of infantile memories and desires for mother-union . . . lay behind his frustrated loves and . . . found simplest expression in his emotion for Mary" (p. 255). See also Harry Stone, "The Love Pattern in Dickens' Novels," in Robert B. Partlow, Jr., ed., *Dickens the Craftsman: Strategies of Presentation* (Carbondale and Edwardsville, Ill., 1970), pp. 1–20.
11. Spilka, op. cit., pp. 431–32.
12. Ibid., p. 432.
13. Marcus, op. cit., pp. 289–92.
14. Arthur Washburn Brown, *Sexual Analysis of Dickens' Props* (New York, 1971), p. 127.
15. Quoted by Lionel Trilling in Introduction to New Oxford Illustrated Dickens edition, reprinted in *The Opposing Self* (New York, 1955) and in Wall, op. cit., p. 372.
16. *David Copperfield,* chapter 64, p. 877.
17. Wall, op. cit., p. 372.
18. For a fuller discussion see my "The Illuminating Distortion."
19. The wedding is for Brown (op. cit.) the culminating and most overtly sexualized scene in Dickens's work.
20. *The Old Curiosity Shop,* chapter 1, p. 2.
21. Quoted by Malcolm Andrews, Introduction to Penguin edition of *The Old Curiosity Shop* (Harmondsworth, Eng., 1972), p. 14.

22. Letter to John Forster, 8? Jan., 1841, in Wall, op. cit., pp. 53–54.
23. Andrews, op. cit., p. 29.
24. Spilka, op. cit., p. 429.
25. *The Southern Review,* Vol. 3, New Series, No. 3 (July, 1967), 653–720.
26. Marcus, op. cit., p. 142.
27. *The Old Curiosity Shop,* chapter 32, p. 242.
28. Ibid., chapter 42, p. 311.
29. The first chapter ("Why Cribbage Represents Sexual Intercourse") of Arthur Washburn Brown's *Sexual Analysis of Dickens' Props,* especially pp. 26–40, offers an ingenious account of the novel's disguises. (Brown contrasts cribbage and its holes—always played in the presence of paired or potential sexual partners in *The Old Curiosity Shop* and later—with asexual backgammon.) Building on the assumption that Sally and Quilp are the Marchioness's real parents, and that Swiveller, who names her, is a father in role and function, Brown sees the novel's psychical intensities displaced from grandfather (really a father) and Nell, and from Dickens and Mary Hogarth, onto the relatively minor Swiveller and Marchioness, and further concealed by being displaced onto the innocent game of cribbage they play (p. 27). Less convincingly, Brown sees Swiveller as in a sense representing Quilp, but Quilp also functioning as Swiveller's father (p. 35) and as Little Nell's (p. 36). He is an alter-ego for the grandfather when the mania is upon him (p. 36). Dickens is, not for the first time, identified with *Dick* Swiveller. (It might as well be added that *to swive* means "to copulate with.")

4. FORBIDDEN GAMES (II): DOSTOEVSKY'S PAEDOPHILIA

1. Edward Wasiolek, ed., *The Notebooks for "The Possessed"* (Chicago, 1968), p. 40.
2. "He sells his sister to a dandy from K—— Boulevard." Wasiolek, ed., *The Notebooks for "Crime and Punishment"* (Chicago, 1967), p. 176.
3. Mochulsky, op. cit., p. 45.
4. Ibid., p. 158.
5. Marc Slonim, *Three Loves of Dostoevsky* (New York, 1955), p. 188.
6. "Night-Walks," *The Uncommercial Traveller,* p. 133.
7. William Woodin Rowe, *Dostoevsky: Child and Man in His Works* (New York, 1968), p. xi.
8. *The Diary of a Writer,* Feb. 1876, Chapter II.
9. "Some Recollections of Mortality."
10. *The Diary of a Writer,* Oct. 1876; Dec. 1876; April 1877; Dec. 1877.
11. Mochulsky, op. cit., p. 486.
12. Avrahm Yarmolinsky, *Dostoevsky: Works and Days* (New York, 1971), p. 311.
13. Ibid., pp. 311–12.
14. Ibid., p. 309.
15. Ibid.
16. Rowe, op. cit., p. 27.
17. Ibid., pp. 208–13.

18. Ibid., p. 208.
19. Ibid., p. 209.
20. Wasiolek, ed., *The Notebooks for "A Raw Youth"* (Chicago, 1969), p. 24.
21. *The Notebooks for "The Idiot,"* pp. 31, 126–27, 130.
22. *The Notebooks for "A Raw Youth,"* p. 27.
23. *The Notebooks for "Crime and Punishment,"* p. 197.
24. Ibid., p. 198.
25. Ibid., p. 197.
26. *Crime and Punishment,* Part Four, Chapter I.
27. *The Notebooks for "The Idiot,"* pp. 31, 34.
28. Ibid., p. 103.
29. Ibid., p. 126.
30. George Ford shrewdly notes that "Dostoevsky's Nellie combines the role of Little Nell with that of the Marchioness, which makes her a more interesting figure." *Dickens and His Readers* (New York, 1965), p. 193n.

5. FORBIDDEN GAMES (III): FAULKNER'S MISOGYNY

1. See Cleanth Brooks, *William Faulkner: The Yoknapatawpha Country* (New Haven, 1963), pp. 196–204. On Faulkner's misogyny generally Leslie Fiedler is amusing: *Love and Death in the American Novel,* revised edition (New York, 1966), pp. 320–25.
2. Joseph Blotner and Frederick L. Gwynn, *Faulkner at the University* (New York, 1965), p. 6.
3. Epilogue, section 6.
4. *Intruder in the Dust* (New York, 1948), p. 177.
5. *The Sound and the Fury* in Modern Library edition of *The Sound and the Fury* and *As I Lay Dying* (New York, 1946), p. 147.
6. Joseph Blotner, *Faulkner: A Biography,* 2 vols. (New York, 1974), p. 675. Pagination is continuous through the two volumes.
7. Ibid., p. 614. Blotner quotes from Chapter II of the typescript.
8. *The Sound and the Fury,* p. 9.
9. Ibid., p. 135.
10. *Absalom, Absalom!,* Modern Library edition (New York, 1951), p. 96. Same paging as original edition (New York, 1936).
11. *Mensonge romantique et vérité romanesque* (Paris, 1961), translated as *Deceit, Desire, and the Novel: Self and Other in Literary Structure* (Baltimore and London, 1965).
12. *Absalom, Absalom!,* pp. 107–08.
13. *Pylon,* Modern Library edition (New York, 1967), pp. 193–94. Same paging as original edition (New York, 1935).
14. Ibid., p. 195.
15. Blotner, op. cit., p. 613.

16. *Sanctuary* (New York, 1967), chapter XVIII, p. 141.
17. Ibid., chapter XI, p. 91.
18. Ibid., chapter XVIII, p. 146.
19. Ibid., chapter XVIII, pp. 150, 151.
20. Ibid., chapter XXIV, pp. 231–32.
21. Ibid., chapter XI, pp. 88–89.
22. Ibid., chapter VII, p. 60.
23. Ibid., chapter XVI, p. 112.
24. Ibid., chapter XV, p. 107.
25. Ibid., chapter XXV, p. 241.

6. THE DICKENSIAN VOICES

1. John Holloway, Introduction to Penguin edition *Little Dorrit* (Harmondsworth, Eng., 1967), p. 13.
2. Forster, op. cit., p. 35.
3. *David Copperfield,* chapter 52, pp. 742–43.
4. *Great Expectations,* chapter 54, p. 412.
5. Ibid., chapter 5, p. 31.
6. *Dombey and Son,* chapter 23, p. 325.
7. *David Copperfield,* chapter 47, p. 680.
8. *The Uncommercial Traveller,* p. 264.
9.. Sylvère Monod, *Dickens the Novelist* (Norman, Okla., 1968), p. 353. Translation of *Dickens romancier* (Paris, 1953).
10. *David Copperfield,* chapter 18, p. 265.
11. Ibid., chapter 2, p. 15.
12. *The Old Curiosity Shop,* chapter 51, p. 374.
13. *Bleak House,* chapter 55, p. 758.
14. *Dombey and Son,* chapter 59, p. 828.
15. Ibid., chapter 23, p. 318; chapter 18, p. 249.
16. *Barnaby Rudge,* chapter 64, p. 492.
17. *Oliver Twist,* chapter 12, p. 82.
18. Marcus, op. cit., p. 293.
19. *Dombey and Son,* chapter 23, p. 319.
20. *Our Mutual Friend,* Book II, Chapter 13, p. 378.
21. Ibid., Book I, Chapter 10, p. 119.
22. Arthur Washburn Brown, op. cit., pp. 204–14, analyzes at some length the "intense sexual imagery on the occasion of Bella's wedding." He finds much displaced sexuality in Gruff and Glum and his wooden leg. The passages involve extremes of rhetorical evasion and play; sentimental or fanciful rhetoric could function as a protective screen. Obvious displacements are often comic in Dickens as they are, more consciously, in the novels of John Hawkes.
23. *The Mystery of Edwin Drood,* chapter 14, p. 154.

7. THE PSYCHOLOGY OF DOSTOEVSKY

1. "Dostoevsky and Parricide," in Wellek, ed., op. cit., p. 98.
2. Wasiolek, "Raskolnikov's Motives: Love and Murder," p. 268.
3. Simon Lesser, "The Role of Unconscious Understanding in Flaubert and Dostoevsky," *Dædalus* (Spring, 1963), pp. 363–82.
4. Lawrence Kohlberg, "Psychological Analysis and Literary Form: A Study of the Doubles in Dostoevsky," *Dædalus* (Spring, 1963), p. 346.
5. Ibid., p. 349.
6. "Wanted: A New Contextualism," *Critical Inquiry*, Vol. I, No. 3 (March, 1975), 631. Robert Rogers's humane discussion recognizes the value of the story's ambiguity, with "no single nosological label of psychiatry" applicable to Golyadkin. See *A Psychoanalytic Study of the Double in Literature* (Detroit, 1970), pp. 34–39.
7. *Der Doppelganger, psychoanalytische Studie* (Leipzig, 1925); *Don Juan: Une étude sur le double* (Paris, 1932), and *The Double: A Psychoanalytic Study* (University of North Carolina Press, 1971).
8. Kohlberg, op. cit., p. 350.
9. Ibid., p. 351.
10. Ibid., pp. 351–52.
11. Ibid., p. 352.
12. "The Phantom Double: Its Psychological Significance," *British Journal of Medical Psychology* 14 (1934), 265–66.
13. Kohlberg particularly recommends N. Lukianowicz, "Autoscopic Phenomena," *Archives of Neurology and Psychiatry* 80 (1958), and J. Todd and K. Dewhurst, "The Double: Its Psychopathology and Psychophysiology," *Journal of Nervous and Mental Diseases* 122 (1955).
14. Andrew MacAndrew, Introduction to *The Adolescent* (New York, 1972), p. xix. This is another title for *A Raw Youth*.
15. Mochulsky, op. cit., p. 243.
16. MacAndrew, op. cit., p. xx.
17. Mochulsky, op. cit., p. 256.
18. *Notes from Underground*, Part One, vii. In *Three Short Novels of Dostoevsky*, translation of Constance Garnett, revised and edited by Avrahm Yarmolinsky (New York, 1960), p. 201.
19. Ibid., p. 220–21.
20. Mochulsky, op. cit., p. 314.
21. *The Gambler*, chapter 15, translated by Victor Terras (Chicago, 1972), p. 160.
22. Lesser, op. cit., pp. 364–66 and *passim*.
23. *Netochka Nezvanova*, chapter 2, translated by Ann Dunnigan (Englewood Cliffs, N.J., 1971), p. 50.
24. Ibid., p. 49.
25. *The Notebooks for "Crime and Punishment,"* p. 64.
26. Wasiolek, "Raskolnikov's Motives: Love and Murder."
27. *The Notebooks for "Crime and Punishment,"* p. 172.
28. Ibid., p. 225.
29. Mochulsky, op. cit., p. 304.

30. Ibid., p. 311.
31. Wasiolek, "Raskolnikov's Motives: Love and Murder," p. 342.
32. *The Notebooks for "Crime and Punishment,"* p. 176.
33. W. D. Snodgrass, "Crime for Punishment: The Tenor of Part One," *Hudson Review* 13 (Summer, 1960), pp. 202–53.
34. Wasiolek, "Raskolnikov's Motives: Love and Murder," p. 254.
35. Ibid., p. 266.
36. Ibid., p. 267.
37. Ibid., p. 259.
38. *Dostoïevski: du double à l'unité* (Paris, 1963), p. 42.
39. Girard's interest in the *structure* of triangular desire leads him to argue that nothing "is gained by reducing triangular desire to a homosexuality which is necessarily opaque to the heterosexual." *Deceit, Desire and the Novel,* p. 47.
40. "Certain Neurotic Mechanisms in Jealousy, Paranoia and Homosexuality," in *Collected Papers,* Vol. 2 (London, 1924), pp. 232–33, cited by Lesser, op. cit., p. 363.
41. Freud, "Dostoevsky and Parricide," op. cit., p. 104. Also cited by Lesser, op. cit., p. 377.
42. For a highly illuminating discussion see Branwen E. B. Pratt, "The Role of the Unconscious in *The Eternal Husband,"* *Literature and Psychology* 21 (Winter, 1971), 29–40. I discuss *The Eternal Husband,* with fuller reference to *Under the Volcano,* and noting marked resemblances in Saul Bellow's *The Victim,* in "The Illuminating Distortion."
43. Mochulsky, op. cit., p. 603.
44. Peace, op. cit., p. 253. On the Oedipal jealousy that demands reenactment, however painful, see my own novels *Night Journey* (New York, 1950) and *The Bystander* (Boston, 1958).
45. Peace, op. cit., p. 253.
46. *The Brothers Karamazov,* Part Four, Book XI, Chapter VIII.
47. Peace, op. cit., p. 262.
48. *The Notebooks for "A Raw Youth,"* p. 337.
49. *A Raw Youth,* Part Three, Chapter 2, v, translated by Andrew MacAndrew as *The Adolescent* (New York, 1972), p. 379.
50. Mochulsky, op. cit., p. 345.
51. *The Notebooks for "The Idiot,"* p. 74.
52. Ibid., p. 131.
53. Ibid., p. 132.
54. Ibid., p. 122.
55. Mochulsky, op. cit., p. 379.
56. See Murray Krieger, "Dostoevsky's 'Idiot': The Curse of Saintliness," from *The Tragic Vision* (New York, 1960), pp. 209–27, reprinted in Wellek, op. cit., pp. 39–52.
57. Mochulsky, op. cit., p. 378. Dots are Mochulsky's.
58. *The Notebooks for "The Idiot,"* p. 242.
59. Peace, op. cit., p. 85.
60. *The Notebooks for "The Idiot,"* p. 149.

61. Ibid., p. 101.
62. The essentials of this discussion of *The Idiot* appeared in my article "On the Com-
    position of Dostoevsky's *The Idiot*," in *Mosaic* 8, 1 (Fall, 1974), 201–15. This is
    the *Mosaic* published by the University of Manitoba Press.

8. FAULKNER: PROBLEMS OF TECHNIQUE

1. Olga Vickery, *The Novels of William Faulkner: A Critical Interpretation* (Baton
   Rouge, 1961), p. 181.
2. *The Town* (New York, 1961), p. 371. Warren Beck notes that "the passage serves
   the aesthetic purpose of closing the novel diminuendo." *Man in Motion: Faulkner's Trilogy* (Madison, Wis., 1961), p. 34.
3. *The Mansion* (New York, 1965), pp. 435–36.
4. *The Hamlet,* p. 213, Vintage edition, p. 189. On page 207 (Vintage edition, p. 184)
   we have "the constant and unslumbering anonymous worm-glut and the inextricable known bones—Troy's Helen and the nymphs and the snoring mitred bishops,
   the saviors and the victims and the kings. . . ." Faulkner is apparently echoing his
   1925 poem "Floyd Collins," quoted by Blotner, op. cit., p. 397:
   > Kings and mitred bishops tired of sin
   > Who dreamed themselves of heaven wearied,
   > And now may sleep, hear rain, and snore again.
5. But see Warren Beck, "William Faulkner's Style" in *Faulkner: A Collection of Critical Essays,* ed. Robert Penn Warren, Twentieth Century Views (Englewood
   Cliffs, N.J., 1966), pp. 55–56. Beck refers there to *The Hamlet* as "a sort of prose
   fantasia." My own *Boston Evening Transcript* review (April 13, 1940) recognized
   Faulkner's genius, but was troubled by a lack of unity.
6. *The Hamlet,* pp. 155–56, Vintage edition, p. 137.
7. Ibid., p. 189, Vintage edition, p. 168.
8. In Faulkner's self-parody read to Maurice Coindreau and others in 1937, "The Afternoon of a Cow" (ostensibly by Ernest V. Trueblood), where the Faulkner cow
   Beulah is rescued from a fire, "Mr. Faulkner underneath received the full discharge
   of the poor creature's afternoon of anguish and despair." But at the end of the story
   she is at peace, "freed now of anguish and shame she ruminated, maiden meditant.
   . . ." See Blotner, op. cit., p. 962.
9. Brooks, op. cit., p. 408.
10. Ibid.
11. *The Hamlet,* pp. 273–74, Vintage edition, p. 243.
12. *Sartoris* (New York, 1956), p. 278; Signet edition (New York, 1964), p. 226.
13. *The Town,* pp. 315–16.
14. Walter Slatoff, *Quest for Failure* (Ithaca, N.Y., 1964), p. 131.
15. *Pylon* (New York, 1935), p. 77.
16. *The Wild Palms* (New York, 1939), pp. 255–56.
17. *Requiem for a Nun* (New York, 1951), p. 258.
18. Ibid., p. 38.

19. Ibid., p. 101.
20. Ibid., p. 102.
21. *Notes on Life and Letters,* (New York, 1928), p. 33.
22. *A Fable,* pp. 432–33, Signet edition, p. 377.
23. Ibid., pp. 259–60, Signet edition pp. 235–36.
24. Ibid., p. 189–90, Signet edition, p. 178.
25. Ibid., p. 159, Signet edition, p. 152.
26. Ibid., p. 435, Signet edition, p. 379.

9. *MARTIN CHUZZLEWIT:* THE NOVEL AS COMIC ENTERTAINMENT

1. *Martin Chuzzlewit,* chapter 19, p. 311.
2. *The Uncommercial Traveller,* p. 96.
3. Forster, op. cit., p. 839.
4. *Martin Chuzzlewit,* chapter 2, p. 24.
5. The resemblances were pointed out by my wife Maclin Bocock.
6. Ibid., chapter 9, p. 150.
7. Interview with Jean Stein vanden Heuvel, *Paris Review* (Spring, 1956), in James B. Meriwether and Michael Millgate, eds., *Lion in the Garden* (New York, 1968), p. 251.
8. Jan. 29, 1842, quoted in Appendix to Penguin edition of *American Notes* (Harmondsworth, Eng., 1972), p. 305. Introduction by John S. Whitley and Arnold Goldman.
9. *American Notes,* Penguin edition Introduction, p. 35.
10. Letter to Forster, May 26, 1842, cited in Johnson, op. cit., I, 423.
11. *American Notes,* Penguin edition, p. 216. Letters refer to "the beastliest river in the world" and to shooting out "of that hideous river, thanks be to God; never to see it again, I hope, but in a nightmare." *The Letters of Charles Dickens,* Vol. III, edited by Madeleine House, Graham Storey, Kathleen Tillotson (Oxford, 1944), pp. 194, 195.
12. Letter to Forster, April 26, 1842. Quoted in Appendix to Penguin *American Notes,* p. 323.
13. *Martin Chuzzlewit,* chapter 22, p. 368.
14. *American Notes,* Penguin edition Introduction, pp. 32, 33.
15. Brown, op. cit., pp. 121–27, suggests a much fuller sexual content behind Ruth Pinch. He would appear to offer a further explanation for Sairey Gamp's energies. She is the castrating mother, whose bedroom is "full of sexually symbolic images and objects" (p. 114). Her vibrant umbrella "is *the* archetypal phallus of the novels" (p. 111).
16. *Martin Chuzzlewit,* chapter 47, p. 706.
17. Ibid., chapter 51, pp. 836–37.
18. *The Possessed,* Part Three, Chapter 6, ii. Modern Library edition (New York, 1936), p. 634. Further page references will be to this edition.

19. *Martin Chuzzlewit,* chapter 46, p. 706.
20. Ibid., chapter 25, p. 405.
21. Ibid., chapter 40, p. 625.
22. Afterword to Signet Classic edition (New York, 1965), p. 888.
23. *Martin Chuzzlewit,* chapter 46, p. 704.
24. Ibid., chapter 40, p. 667.

10. *THE POSSESSED:* THE NOVEL AS TRAGEDY

1. Mochulsky, op. cit., pp. 438–39.
2. Memoirs of Anna Dostoevsky, quoted and translated by Peace, op. cit., p. 140.
3. Mochulsky, op. cit., p. 421.
4. Max Nomad, *Apostles of Revolution;* Albert Camus, *The Rebel.*
5. Nechaev represented himself to Bakunin as an important revolutionist. Was the craggy giant Bakunin a prototype for Conrad's revolutionary feminist and exile leader, Peter Ivanovitch, who also endured well-publicized sufferings? Cynically, to get hold of the money of the dead Alexander Herzen, Bakunin tried to arrange a romantic match between Nechaev and the bereft daughter Nathalia Herzen (cp. Nathalie Haldan). The most remarkable conjunction seems fortuitous, since Conrad could not have read Dostoevsky's Notebooks. "One of the murderers, Uspensky, was in love with Shaposhnikov's (*e.g. Shatov's,* A. G.) sister. After having killed Shaposhnikov, he feels the pangs of conscience and confesses, at first only to Granovsky (can this be true?)." *The Notebooks for "The Possessed,"* p. 87. Perhaps some book or article on Bakunin is a common source for Dostoevsky and Conrad.
6. "The Student," reflected in the poem "A Noble Personality" that Pyotr finds on Lembke's desk. Pyotr claims to have seen it abroad, and says it refers to Shatov.
7. *The Notebooks for "The Possessed,"* p. 97.
8. Cited in Mochulsky, op. cit., p. 423.
9. Letter to A. A. Romanov, February, 1873, cited in Wasiolek, *Dostoevsky: The Major Fiction* p. 112.
10. Ibid., p. 113.
11. Cited in Joseph Frank, "Dostoevsky and Russian Populism," in *The Rarer Action: Essays in Honor of Francis Fergusson,* ed. Alan Cheuse and Richard Koffler (New Brunswick, N.J., 1970), p. 312.
12. Mochulsky, op. cit., p. 409.
13. *The Notebooks for "The Possessed,"* pp. 350–51.
14. Ibid., p. 343.
15. See my "The Illuminating Distortion," especially pp. 106–10.
16. *The Possessed,* Modern Library Edition, Part II, Chapter 1, vii, p. 256. The dots indicating pauses and hesitations are in the text. Further page references are to this edition.

17. Peace, op. cit., p. 196.
18. Steiner, *Tolstoy or Dostoevsky: An Essay in the Old Criticism* (New York, 1959), pp. 313–18.
19. *The Notebooks for "The Possessed,"* p. 371.
20. Peace, op. cit., pp. 211, 213, 325 (note 9). See note 26 below.
21. The psychiatrist Dr. Irvin Yalom found this significant. (Classroom discussion at Stanford University, 1972.)
22. *Society the Redeemed Form of Man* (1879), quoted by F. O. Matthiessen, ed., *The James Family* (New York, 1961), p. 161.
23. Mochulsky, op. cit., p. 461.
24. *The Notebooks for "The Possessed,"* p. 60.
25. *The Possessed,* "Variant Readings," p. 736.
26. *Note on Stavrogin's Confession.* Dostoevsky said, in order to placate Katkov, that "Stavrogin's sin was merely a figment of his disturbed imagination, not an actual fact," according to Leonid Grossman in *Dostoevsky: A Biography* (Indianapolis, 1975), p. 471. The Andrew R. MacAndrew translation (New York, 1962) puts the confession in its intended place as Part II, Chapter 9. In the version translated by S. S. Koteliansky with the aid of Virginia Woolf (London, 1922), Stavrogin does not withhold the crucial page, and the sexual element is more detailed: "I kissed her face and legs" (p. 49). Dostoevsky had struck out an important sentence in the Confession: "Having indulged up to the age of sixteen with extraordinary immoderation in the vice to which J. J. Rousseau confessed, I stopped it at the very moment I had fixed, at the age of seventeen." (p. 45n). The Modern Library edition, seemingly unaware of the Koteliansky-Woolf volume, speaks of the Confession as "Hitherto Suppressed." Robert Lord in turn (*Dostoevsky: Essays and Perspectives,* Berkeley, Los Angeles and London, 1970) was apparently unaware of the Modern Library edition and so, since "it does not appear in any of the translations of *The Devils* (*The Possessed*) with which it is associated," offered his own new translation of the Confession. His translation contains a certain amount of jarring colloquialism, such as "keep her on tenterhooks" (p. 124).
27. Wasiolek, *Dostoevsky: The Major Fiction,* p. 119.
28. Peace, op. cit., p. 231.
29. *The Notebooks for "The Possessed,"* p. 264.
30. Ibid., p. 65.
31. Ibid., p. 40.
32. Ibid., pp. 56, 57.
33. Ibid., p. 178.
34. Ibid., p. 210.
35. Ibid., p. 271. Wasiolek's editorial brackets indicate incomplete words or phrases.
36. Ibid., p. 306.
37. Ibid., p. 393.
38. *The Possessed,* Part III, Chapter 7, iii, p. 673.
39. Ibid., Part III, Chapter 7, ii, p. 655.
40. Ibid., pp. 665–66.
41. Peace, op. cit., p. 159.

11. *ABSALOM, ABSALOM!*: THE NOVEL AS IMPRESSIONIST ART

1. Letter to Bennett Cerf and Robert Haas, in Blotner, op. cit., pp. 1178–79.
2. *"Absalom, Absalom!* The Extended Simile,'' from *The Limits of Metaphor: A Study of Melville, Conrad and Faulkner* (Ithaca, N.Y., 1967); reprinted in *Twentieth Century Interpretations of "Absalom, Absalom!,"* ed. Arnold Goldman (Englewood Cliffs, N.J., 1971), p. 100.
3. "Hardy, Faulkner, and the Prosaics of Tragedy,'' *Centennial Review* 5 (1961); passage reprinted in Goldman, op. cit., p. 35.
4. Ibid., p. 37.
5. Ibid.
6. *PMLA* 70 (December, 1955), 888.
7. Ibid., 896.
8. Millgate, *The Achievement of William Faulkner* (New York, 1966), pp. 162–64, reprinted in Goldman, op. cit., pp. 55–57. See also Guerard, *Conrad the Novelist*, p. 126.
9. " 'Strange Gods' in Jefferson, Mississippi: Analysis of *Absalom, Absalom!"* in Frederick J. Hoffman and Olga W. Vickery, eds., *William Faulkner: Two Decades of Criticism* (East Lansing, Mich., 1951), p. 240; reprinted in Goldman, op. cit., p. 29.
10. Melvin Backman, *Faulkner, The Major Years: A Critical Study* (Bloomington, Ind., 1966), p. 95; reprinted in Goldman, op. cit., p. 64.
11. Brooks, op. cit., p. 302.
12. Ibid., p. 310.
13. Ibid., p. 304.
14. *Absalom, Absalom!*, p. 89.
15. Ibid., p. 145.
16. Ibid., p. 96.
17. Ibid., p. 108.
18. Blotner, op. cit., p. 830.
19. Blotner and Gwynn, op. cit., p. 274.
20. *Absalom, Absalom!*, p. 371.
21. Ibid., p. 375. All but "and filled with roaring" was added in revision. See Brooks, op. cit., p. 439.
22. Brooks, op. cit., p. 441.
23. "The Narrative Structure of *Absalom, Absalom!,"* *The Georgia Review* (Summer, 1975), p. 387.
24. *Absalom, Absalom!* p. 143.
25. Ibid., pp. 100–101.
26. Brooks, for all his awareness of Faulkner's inconsistencies, wants his writer to be, finally, a man of sound sense, not guilty of serious lapses. But in commenting on the passage, which appears on page 62 of the novel, he himself is guilty of one, since he refers "to a child born to Sutpen before Sutpen came to Jefferson." But "before . . . Jefferson" is not in the novel. "The Narrative Structure of *Absalom, Absalom!,"* p. 374.
27. *Absalom, Absalom*, p. 249.

28. Ibid., p. 252.
29. Ibid., pp. 89–90.
30. Ibid., pp. 177–78.
31. Ibid., p. 182.
32. Ibid., p. 186.
33. Poirier, op. cit., in Goldman, op. cit., p. 27.
34. Brooks, *William Faulkner: The Yoknapatawpha Country*, pp. 429–36.
35. *Absalom, Absalom!*, p. 351.
36. "The Narrative Structure of *Absalom, Absalom!*," p. 381.
37. Ibid., p. 382.
38. Ibid., pp. 368, 367.
39. Blotner, op. cit., p. 390. With good reason, and as he saw himself and his myth about to enter "history," Faulkner tried to deter Malcolm Cowley from discussing (in *The Portable Faulkner*) the wartime experiences.

INDEX